THE LAN

CASES IN ABNORMAL BEHAVIOR

Third Edition

KAYLA F. BERNHEIM

is also the author of

Schizophrenia: Symptoms, Causes, and Treatments
(with Richard R. J. Lewine)

The Caring Family: Living with Chronic Mental Illness
(with Richard R. J. Lewine and Caroline T. Beale)

Working with Families of the Mentally Ill
(with Anthony F. Lehman)

The Lanahan Cases in Developmental Psychopathology
SECOND EDITION
(with Leslie Rescorla and Lorraine Rocissano)

A note about the cover

This lone figure was carved from a single apple tree trunk. It was created as a self-portrait by a British mental patient who had a distinctive concave chest from years of tuberculosis. His doctor remembered that he took no interest in making art until he encountered a fallen apple tree during a walk on the hospital grounds and asked for help in dragging it indoors and getting simple carving tools. At that time, there was hospital prohibition for mental patients handling what could be 'lethal' instruments. However, Edward Adamson, a pioneer in using art to treat mental illness persuaded the authorities to relax this rule, and trust the patient. The result, 'Recovery,' was a vindication of Edward's remarkable insight. For a month, the patient whittled the wood down to this figure. The artist, in his thirties, committed suicide about two years after leaving the hospital. This applewood figure is his only known work of art.

—Rebecca Alban Hoffberger
Founder and Director of the
American Visionary Art Museum

THE LANAHAN CASES IN ABNORMAL BEHAVIOR

Third Edition

Kayla F. Bernheim, Ph.D.

LANAHAN PUBLISHERS, INC.

Baltimore

Printed in the United States of America

The text of this book was composed
in Sabon with display type set in Novarese.
Composition by Sheryl Rowe

GRATEFUL ACKNOWLEDGMENT is extended to those who have granted permission to reprint material:
CASE 7: Excerpt from *An Anthropologist on Mars: Seven Paradoxical Tales* by Oliver Sacks, Copyright © 1995 by Oliver Sacks. Used by permission of Alfred A. Knopf, an imprint of the Knopf Doubleday Publishing Group, a division of Penguin Random House LLC. All rights reserved.
CASE 16: From "Dealing with Cross-cultural Issues in Clinical Practice" by Harriet Lefley, in P. A. Keller and S. R. Heyman (Eds.) *Innovations in Clinical Practice: A Source Book* Vol.10 (Sarasota, Fl: Professional Resources Exchange, 1991). Reprinted by permission of Professional Resource Press.
CASE 22: "The Auto Accident that Never Was" from *The Boy Who Couldn't Stop Washing: The Experience and Treatment of Obsessive-Compulsive Disorder* by Dr. Judith Rapoport, copyright © 1989 by Judith L. Rapoport, M.D. Used by permission of Dutton, an imprint of Penguin Publishing Group, a division of Penguin Random House LLC and by Dr. Judith L. Rapoport. All rights reserved.
CASE 29: (1994). "Living and Working with MPD" in *J Psychococ Nurs Ment Health Serv.* 32(8) 17-22. doi 10.3928/0279-3695-19940801-10. Used by permission of Slack, Inc.
CASE 32: From *Eating Disorders: Obesity, Anorexia Nervosa, and the Person Within* by Hilde Bruch, copyright © 1973. Reprinted by permission of Basic Books, an imprint of Perseus Books, LLC, a subsidiary of Hachette Book Group, Inc.
CASE 37: Excerpt from *The Lanahan Cases in Developmental Psychopathology*, Second Edition, by Kayla F. Bernheim, Leslie Rescorla, and Lorraine Rocissano. Copyright © 2010 by LANAHAN PUBLISHERS, INC. Used by permission of the publisher.
CASE 45: From *Ginny: A Love Remembered* by G. Robert Artley, published by Iowa State University Press. Copyright © 1993 by Bob Artley. Reprinted by permission of the author.

ISBN-10 1-930398-21-2
ISBN-13 978-1-930398-21-4

LANAHAN PUBLISHERS, INC.
324 Hawthorne Road
Baltimore, MD 21210-2303
WWW.LANAHANPUBLISHERS.COM

2 3 4 5 6 7 8 9 0

Contents

Preface xiii

CHAPTER ONE **The Scope and Nature of Abnormality**

Approaching Abnormality: Today's Biopsychosocial Model 3

[Biological, psychological, and social factors should all be considered in any comprehensive account of psychological disorder]

Case 1 Abnormality or Eccentricity? The Case of Neil Cargile 10

[This case of a wealthy, prominent cross-dresser raises the question of how we decide whether an abnormal behavior constitutes a disorder]

Case 2 A "Normal" Psychological Disorder: The Case of Martin B. 14

[A man reacts to being rejected and abandoned by his wife of twelve years.]

CHAPTER TWO **Neurodevelopmental Disorders**

Case 3 Severe Autistic Spectrum Disorder: The Case of Amy P. 21

[Parents are mistakenly blamed for the development of autism in their child.]

Case 4 High-functioning Autistic Spectrum Disorder: The Case of Isaac T. 26

[What happens when a young man discovers that he has autism?]

Case 5 Attention Deficit–Hyperactivity Disorder: The Case of Michael C. 32

[Combined biological and environmental factors lead to a poor treatment outcome.]

Case 6 Attention Deficit–Hyperactivity Disorder, Inattentive Type: The Case of Megan D. 39

[Another case of ADHD, with its inattention and disorganization, but without hyperactivity and impulsivity.]

Case 7 Tourette's Disorder: A Surgeon's Life 46

[In his book, *An Anthropologist On Mars*, Oliver Sacks describes a surgeon who functions successfully despite a severe tic disorder.]

Lanahan Notes 53

CHAPTER THREE **Schizophrenia Spectrum and Other Psychotic Disorders**

Case 8 Schizophrenia in a Young Adult: The Case of Steve M. 58

[A typical case of schizophrenia responds moderately well to modern treatment.]

Case 9 Chronic Schizophrenia: The Case of Lenny D. 65

[An individual's almost imperceptible slide into a long-term case of schizophrenia.]

Case 10 Delusional Disorder: The Case of Mr. P. 72

[The father of an adolescent is discovered to be the really disturbed member of the family]

Lanahan Notes 76

CHAPTER FOUR **Bipolar and Related Disorders**

Case 11 Bipolar Disorder Type I: The Case of Noreen W. 80

[The treatment thirty years ago of a young woman illustrates changes in diagnostic thinking and treatment approaches over time.]

Case 12 Bipolar Disorder Type I: The Case of Carla P. 87

[This case offers a more contemporary look at a serious but treatable disorder.]

Case 13 Bipolar Disorder Type II: The Case of Bernie B. 92

[Bipolar Disorder is diagnosed in an adult, many years after the onset of the disorder.]

Lanahan Notes *96*

CHAPTER FIVE **Depressive Disorders**

Case 14 Major Depressive Disorder: The Case of Hannah H. 100

[Genetics and environment combine in the case of this vibrant woman who survived despite the odds.]

Case 15 Persistent Depressive Disorder: The Case of Bonnie D. 107

[A less severe kind of depression, but one that is often very difficult to treat effectively.]

Case 16 Depression in an African-American Teenager: The Case of Takisha Landry 112

[A case reported in the literature highlights the importance of understanding the cultural context in which symptoms occur.]

Case 17 Situational Depression in the Elderly: The Case of Mr. A. 118

[An elderly man and his wife are both depressed and are treated for it. When is depression "normal"? How do we explain differences in treatment outcome?]

Lanahan Notes *123*

CHAPTER SIX **Anxiety Disorders**

Case 18 Simple Phobia: The Case of Philip B. 128

[Extreme fear of enclosed spaces prompts an individual to explore his past and to participate in behavioral treatment.]

Case 19 Panic and Agoraphobia: The Case of Sandy J. 133

[Agoraphobia is successfully treated with cognitive-behavioral interventions in this case, despite lack of therapeutic attention to a childhood history of sexual abuse.]

Case 20 Social Anxiety Disorder: The Case of Timmy R. 139

[A chaotic environment, an overwhelmed mother, and physical disability lead to the development of social anxiety disorder in a six year old boy.]

Case 21 Generalized Anxiety Disorder: The Case of Dawn D. 143

[Constant, diffuse, overwhelming worry preoccupies—incapacitates—an otherwise enviable person.]

Lanahan Notes *149*

CHAPTER SEVEN **Obsessive-Compulsive and Related Disorders**

Case 22 Obsessive-compulsive Disorder: The Case of Dr. S. 153

[In Judith Rapoport's *The Boy Who Couldn't Stop Washing*, a man vividly describes an OCD attack.]

Case 23 Body Dysmorphic Disorder: The Case of Aaron W. 159

[Isolated and lonely at college, a young man comes to believe that his face is "hideous."]

Case 24 Hoarding Disorder: The Case of Susan O. 164

[When objects acquire meaning and emotional attachments form, discarding anything at all can become excruciatingly anxiety-provoking.]

Lanahan Notes *170*

CHAPTER EIGHT **Trauma- and Stressor-Related Disorders**

Case 25 Acute Stress Disorder: The Case of Miss F. 174

[Rape trauma syndrome improves gradually over time without formal treatment. What was curative?]

Case 26 Chronic Post-Traumatic Stress Disorder: The Case of George G. 179

[A case study of a long-term disorder suffered by many veterans of intense military action.]

Case 27 Reactive Attachment Disorder: The Case of Sonja S. 185

[A youngster adopted at an early age is unable to form normal attachments and exhibits behavioral problems.]

Lanahan Notes *189*

CHAPTER NINE **Dissociative Disorders**

Case 28 Depersonalization/Derealization Disorder: The Case of Marie O. 193

[A woman with a history of sexual abuse floats out of her body away from images that are upsetting to her.]

Case 29 Dissociative Identity Disorder: The Case of Anonymous 199

[A psychiatric nurse describes her own struggle with what used to be called multiple personality disorder]

Lanahan Notes *208*

CHAPTER TEN **Somatic Symptom and Related Disorders**

Case 30 Somatic Symptom Disorder: The Case of Lisa L. 211

[A shifting pattern of symptoms presents a confusing and changing diagnostic picture over time.]

Case 31 Illness Anxiety Disorder: The Case of Harry P. 217

[Is an inability to express feelings related to the development of somatic symptoms?]

Lanahan Notes *223*

CHAPTER ELEVEN **Feeding and Eating Disorders**

Case 32 Anorexia Nervosa: The Case of Gail 228

[Hilda Bruch, a pioneer in our understanding of eating disorders, describes the intense power struggle that can develop around food, weight, and eating.]

Case 33 Binge-Eating Disorder: The Case of Sheila A. 235

[Eating can be a comforter, but sometimes it turns into a stressor, as it did for this single, working mother.]

Lanahan Notes *240*

CHAPTER TWELVE **Sleep-Wake Disorders**

Case 34 Insomnia Disorder: The Case of Maisey K. 243

[Chronic insomnia is associated with a host of other mental and physical ailments in a stressed-out woman.]

Lanahan Notes *248*

CHAPTER THIRTEEN **Sexual Dysfunctions**

Case 35 Female Orgasmic Disorder: The Case of Susan C. 251

[A sexual disorder emerges in the course of treating other problems. A biopsychosocial approach is used successfully.]

Case 36 Hypoactive Sexual Desire Disorder: The Case of Sean D. 256

[Women are not the only ones who experience low sexual desire. This case looks at the psychological factors negatively impacting a man's sexual desire.]

Lanahan Notes 262

CHAPTER FOURTEEN **Gender Dysphoria**

Case 37 Gender Dysphoria in a Young Child: The Case of Billy B. 265

[A young boy insists that he wants to be a girl.]

Lanahan Notes 270

CHAPTER FIFTEEN **Disruptive, Impulse-Control and Conduct Disorders**

Case 38 Oppositional-Defiant Disorder: The Case of Timmy G. 273

[Parents' conflicts affect the behavior of their son.]

Case 39 Antisocial Personality Disorder: The Case of William Hardin 279

[A member of a "wilding" gang goes to jail. Does he have a psychological disorder?]

Case 40 Kleptomania: The Case of Donald S. 283

[Kleptomania emerges late in therapy with a man who presents with depression.]

Lanahan Notes 289

CHAPTER SIXTEEN **Substance Related and Addictive Disorders**

Case 41 Emerging Alcoholism: The Case of Simon S. 292

[An attorney arrests his alcohol problem before it destroys his life.]

Case 42 Mixed Substance Abuse: The Case of Miguel S. 299

[Does a "bad trip" indicate that a person was unstable to begin with?]

Case 43 Gambling Disorder: The Case of Veronica A. 306

[An elderly, bereaved woman develops a gambling problem that threatens her very life.]

Lanahan Notes *312*

CHAPTER SEVENTEEN **Neurocognitive Disorders**

Case 44 Major Cognitive Disorder Related to HIV Infection: The Case of Samuel G. 315

[A young sailor is discharged from the service, demented and dying.]

Case 45 Alzheimer's Disorder: The Case of Ginny 320

[A husband chronicles the decline into Alzheimer's Disease of his beloved wife.)

Lanahan Notes *332*

CHAPTER EIGHTEEN **Personality Disorders**

Case 46 Paranoid–Schizotypal Personality Disorder: The Case of Peter N. 336

[This case illustrates the diagnostic uncertainty and overlap that characterize the personality disorders.]

Case 47 Borderline Personality Disorder: The Case of Roberta F. 340

[Is this controversial diagnosis really a pejorative way of describing victims of chronic trauma?]

Case 48 Avoidant Personality Disorder: The Case of Carl S. 348

[A young man makes moderate progress with multiple, brief episodes of treatment over nine years.]

Lanahan Notes *354*

CHAPTER NINETEEN **Paraphilic Disorders**

Case 49 Sexual Masochism Disorder: The Case of The Anonymous Caller 358

[A caller asks a therapist whether wanting to be spanked during sex is abnormal or not.]

Case 50 Pedophilia: The Case of James Q. 363
[The development of pedophilia in an incarcerated prisoner is explored.]

Lanahan Notes 369

Preface

This is the third edition of *The Lanahan Cases in Abnormal Behavior*. It is designed to be used in one of two ways. The first is as an adjunct to basic textbooks in abnormal psychology. Observation of individual cases is the backbone of both research and theory building in the study of psychopathology. But most textbooks have, of necessity, devoted limited space to thorough case material. When they have included case material, there is often little follow-up discussion of the cases. Films and videotapes can offer impressionistic glimpses of abnormality, but only through reading a full case report and its discussion can students capture the richness of a person's experience over time. The book is suitable for courses in abnormal psychology and other courses in psychopathology, as well as courses in related fields like clinical social work and psychiatric nursing.

The second use for *The Lanahan Cases* is as primary source material which a professor or instructor will augment with readings and lecture material about theory and research. In my own teaching of abnormal psychology, I have often felt that textbooks left me nothing to teach—that lectures were too often rehashes of what was included in the text. When cases are used as the primary material, interesting questions flow naturally. What could have caused this problem? How does the person's social context influence the problem? What can be done to ameliorate the problem? *The Lanahan Cases* is the book I would have liked to have available. Perhaps not surprisingly, previous editions have also found their way into high school classrooms since the level of auxiliary material can be chosen by the instructor.

This edition is substantially different from previous editions in a number of ways. First, it conforms to the latest revision of the Diagnostic and Statistical Manual, DSM-5.

Classification and the DSM-5

Diagnosing and categorizing psychological disorders has evolved over time. Unlike some areas of medicine in which physical findings and laboratory tests help define disorders and syndromes, in abnormal psychology it is behavior and behavior only that counts. Since many causes can result in similar behaviors and one cause may also result in different behaviors and since specific behaviors may cluster together in some people but not in others, the problem of definition and classification is a complex one. A classification system must be reliable, meaning, among other things, that clinicians can agree that a particular set of behaviors constitutes a particular disorder. It must also be valid, meaning that syndromes that are grouped together share similar etiologies and/or treatments.

So the diagnostic system is forever being "tweaked" based on new research. Disorders are renamed and reclassified. For example, DSM-IV listed specific autism spectrum disorders, including Asperger's Syndrome, while DSM-5 has only one diagnosis for all these disorders, emphasizing that they are not really different, but rather lie on a spectrum of severity. As another example, childhood disorders were grouped together in DSM-IV, but there is no such grouping in DSM-5.

New schema to simplify or amplify diagnostic acumen are instituted and then, sometimes, discarded. For example, in the previous DSM (IV), an axial system was used in which most clinical disorders were coded on Axis I, while personality disorders (and a few others) were coded on Axis II. Axis III was used for co-occurring medical conditions and Axis IV for relevant environmental stressors. The idea was to emphasize that disorders on one axis could be influenced or modified by disorders on the other axes. DSM-5 has done away with the axial system entirely as it was cumbersome and did not lead to greater clarity.

All of this is to say that this edition of *The Lanahan Cases* is consistent with the new classification system, DSM-5. Since the classification of behavioral disorders is developed by committee and evolves over time, it's safe to say that this DSM will not be the last.

Content and Format

We begin this edition with a chapter that tries to offer a sense of the scope and nature of abnormality. An essay on the biopsychosocial model provides students with different ways of approaching and understanding behavior. This is followed by two cases which explore how we decide which abnormal behaviors constitute a "disorder," and whether some disordered behavior falls within the range of what we could consider normal. The next eighteen chapters take up most of the DSM-5 categories. Here, there are forty-eight cases of which twelve are new to this edition. The cases are chosen to be representative of the major categories, but are not to be considered exhaustive. Rather we have chosen cases that illustrate common disorders, ones that raise important issues related to diagnosis or treatment, and a few that are particularly vivid or distinctive. Each case includes a discussion about the case as well as questions related to the case that encourage the student to go further, either by applying theory to the case or by considering the case within the context of his or her own life.

Each case is "real." They are drawn from my own forty-three year clinical practice, from colleagues, and from such well-known experts as Hilde Bruch, Judith Rapoport, and Oliver Sacks. Identifying information has been changed, of course, and some of the cases have been modified or embellished to illustrate a particular point, but they are otherwise true to life. Because of this, few of the cases are simple and clear-cut or what one might call perfect-fit textbook cases. Some illustrate the fact that many, if not most, patients have symptoms that justify more than one diagnosis. Others show that not all treatment is effective and not all cases have happy endings. In all cases, I have tried to include enough detail to generate a picture of a real person confronting real problems. All, I hope, will hold your attention and generate interesting questions about psychological disorders, their causes and treatments. And all, I hope, will remind you that each "case" is a real person, with hopes, fears, and aspirations like the rest of us.

At the end of each chapter, we have included the "Lanahan Notes." These are meant to be brief study sections for students. They offer, in outline form, a broad overview of the classification, symptomatology, etiology, and treatment of the basic disorders. They are general enough to be compatible with the material in virtually any textbook on abnormal psychology. We envision them as being like the notes that students, themselves, might take of lecture or text material. For that reason, they are very useful as review guides.

A Few Words about the Biopsychosocial Model

It is now clear that few, if any psychological disorders can be fully explained within the rigid boundaries of any one theoretical model. Genetic and biochemical influences on behavior are becoming ever more apparent and the use of psychoactive medications in treatment is becoming ever more widespread. On the other hand, the individuality of human experience, the influences of culture, religion, socioeconomic status, family life, and a host of other factors influence the development, treatment, and outcome of most disorders. In my own abnormal psychology course, I have attempted to teach students to see psychopathology through a wide lens and to keep the individual who is struggling with the disorder always in view. For this purpose, I have adopted a biopsychosocial view in the case discussions of this book. Informed by the research and clinical literature, I have attempted to balance attention to the biological, psychological, and social factors in our examination of the phenomena under study. Discussion questions encourage students to view each case from different perspectives and to blend aspects of different theoretical visions whenever possible.

One final note: I hope that you will find reading and thinking about these cases as stimulating and instructive as I do in working with my patients, teaching the course, and learning more about the changing and challenging field each day.

Acknowledgments

I would like to thank my colleagues, Patricia Fitzpatrick, Ph.D., Lorraine Rocissano, Ph.D., and Stephen Karl, M.S.W., for their contributions of case material. Susannah Bernheim and Caroline Beale made helpful suggestions about both cases and the book's format. Dimitri Papageorgis, Ph.D., of The University of British Columbia and Ann Kaiser Stearns, Ph.D., of Essex Community College both reviewed the manuscript for the first edition, and their thoughts and ideas on it were most helpful. The second edition profited from the insightful comments of Julie Dunsmore of Hamilton College, Mary Lou Frank of North Georgia College and State University, and Robin Hornik Parritz of Hamline University. Among the many who assigned the second edition in their classes, I am indebted to Ryan Blackstock of the Michigan School of Professional Psychology, William Gayton of the University of Southern Maine, and Holly Korta of Caldwell Community College for their critiques which have brought about a greatly improved third edition. Holly Korta was particularly instrumental in bringing the end-of-chapter "Lanahan Notes" up-to-date.To my clients who participated actively in shaping their own case histories, and to those who allowed me into their lives, I owe a great deal. I am particularly grateful to my publisher, editor, and friend of close to forty-five years, Don Fusting. His support, good humor, ability to compromise, and unfailingly useful editorial advice has been invaluable throughout my writing career. He still makes a mean French toast.

—Kayla F. Bernheim, Ph.D.

THE LANAHAN CASES IN ABNORMAL BEHAVIOR

Third Edition

CHAPTER ONE

The Scope and Nature of Abnormality

Behavioral disorders have fascinated humankind from as early as we have written records. References to abnormal behavior and its treatment can be found in the early writings of the Hebrews, Greeks, Egyptians, and Chinese. The Greek physician Hippocrates, writing around 400 B.C., offered a rudimentary classification of mental disorders and suggested that brain pathology, heredity, and environmental factors were all implicated as causal agents.

One might argue that we have not come so very far in the intervening centuries since an exact definition of psychopathology eludes us even today, and precise causes of behavioral disorders have yet to be discovered. How do we know that someone is abnormal? Do we mean by this that his behavior is simply different? Were this all that was necessary, we would find "genius" in abnormal psychology textbooks. Is psychological misery a sufficient criterion for abnormality: It cannot be, because some people who suffer, like recently bereaved people, are clearly "normal" while other people who don't suffer misery, like people who derive sexual stimulation from contact with children, would be considered "abnormal" by most of us. Perhaps an individual who engages in maladaptive behavior can be considered abnormal. Clearly, this criterion is relevant, but not sufficient. Consider, for example, a man who robs people for a living. If he is not very smart, he may get caught and go to jail. This behavior is clearly maladaptive, but he is not necessarily mentally ill. Contrast this with another man who works as a bank teller, all the while believing that he is an alien who is waiting for his spaceship to come and take him back to his native planet. His behavior is not noticeably maladaptive, but most of us would agree that he is clearly "abnormal."

In Part One, we begin by offering a brief piece which will provide a framework for all the discussion to follow. It describes a comprehensive biopsychosocial approach to understanding behavior disorder. This model integrates the various ways by which clinicians and researchers have approached the study of abnormal behavior. It combines elements of medical models, behavioral models, psychological models, and environmental models to create a comprehensive account of the factors that can influence behavior. We will refer back to it often in examining the disorders that comprise the bulk of the book.

In addition, we have provided two cases, one in which a statistically "abnormal" behavior causes no suffering or apparent maladaptiveness and the other in which a statistically "normal" reaction involves substantial emotional pain and dysfunction. In struggling with which, if either of them, reflects mental "disorder" you will sharpen your own definition.

Working with the questions raised in Part One is a huge contemporary endeavor carried out by a large number of scientists whose discoveries are constantly reported in the press. I hope this section will provide a context so that you can make some sense of such reporting and will also perhaps offer some points of departure for your own investigations in this field.

APPROACHING ABNORMALITY: TODAY'S BIOPSYCHOSOCIAL MODEL

Virtually all textbooks in abnormal behavior have a chapter on models of psychological disorder. Major models covered include the biomedical model, psychological models like the psychodynamic, learning, cognitive, or existential models, and environmental models that focus on the role of family and culture. These discussions often give the impression that one must choose between models—that they are mutually exclusive accounts of human behavior. However, this is not true. Instead, they each look at a different aspect or level of organization of behavior.

In what follows, we illustrate how these models can be integrated so that the insights brought by each can be retained. We will call upon this comprehensive approach to understanding behavior, called the "biopsychosocial model," many times in the case discussions that follow. In doing so, we hope that your own ideas about "why" people behave as they do will be infinitely richer and more complex.

CONSIDER A MIDDLE-AGED WOMAN—let's call her Jeanne—who becomes depressed. She neglects her appearance, sleeps twelve to fourteen hours each day and still feels tired. Her sense of humor disappears, as does her interest in intimacy and sex with her husband or lunch with her friends. She spends most of her time staring into the television set, but if you ask her what she's watching, she can't even tell you the plot of the story. But she hasn't always acted this way. What has caused the change in Jeanne's behavior?

Humankind's interest in understanding the causes of behavioral and emotional disorders dates back to earliest times. The ancient Greeks, who approached problems of abnormality from a purely physical or biological perspective, might have explained Jeanne's depression by assuming that she had a dislodged and wandering uterus or an imbalance in the four humors (bodily fluids) that were presumed to be responsible for mood. In the Middle Ages, when explanations relied more on spiritual models, she might have been thought to be possessed by evil spirits or the victim of "hereditary taint." In Freud's day, when the importance of psychological factors in the development of symptoms became apparent, her life history would have been searched for evidence of trauma—repressed and symbolically revisited in the form of her depression. Each society's approach to understanding disturbed behavior reflects the prevailing science of the day.

Today it is clear that developing causal explanations of behavioral disorders is rarely an "either-or" proposition. While the balance of factors may change from disorder to disorder and from individual to individual, a full explanation must include biological, psychological (including spiritual), and social/environmental influences. Therefore, we no longer ask, for example, "is depression a biological disorder?" but rather "what biological factors may influence the onset, course, and prognosis of depression in this woman?" At the same time, we would be asking "what are the psychological and social factors that may have influenced the development of depression in this woman?"

In 1977, George Engel, an eminent professor of psychiatry and medicine, coined the term "biopsychosocial model" to capture the fact that all illnesses (not just psychological ones) must, as he wrote, "take into account the patient, the social context in which he lives, and the complementary system devised by society to deal with the disruptive effects of illness, that is, the physician role and the health care system." He argued eloquently that the road from a biological or behavioral symptom to patienthood is a long one that meanders through the personal and cultural landscape of both the individual and the clinician who "diagnoses" the problem. To understand what "caused" Jeanne's problem, we would need to know much more about her. Let's look at some of the common biological, psychological, and sociocultural influences on behavior and apply them to the changes Jeanne experienced.

Biological Factors

Genetics Depression, like many other disorders, both behavioral and physical, runs in families. Further, adoption and twin studies, which are able to tease out the relative contribution of heredity and common rearing, provide support for the existence of a genetic predisposition for these disorders. We would not be surprised when we find that Jeanne's mother had periods of deep depression that lasted for several months at a time. During these episodes, Jeanne's aunt would come each day to straighten the house and prepare meals for the family. Upon further inquiry, we learn that Jeanne's brother is a problem drinker. This is interesting, too, since alcoholism and depression often run together in families.

Temperament Every mother knows that each child is unique from day one of life. Some are sunny and social while others are fussy and shy. Some can fall asleep anywhere and will eat anything. Others seem to need their own beds, a fairly rigid schedule, and lots of predictability. These and other differences which appear to be innate, and have been shown to be relatively stable throughout life, we describe as traits of temperament. Jeanne, we learn, has a shy and somewhat timid temperament. She never had a lot of friends, although she does have two or three close ones who have been friends for many years. Why would this matter? Well, recently, her very best friend moved away. Her youngest child went off to college last year. We can hypothesize that Jeanne's capacity to fill these gaps in her life may have been hampered by her own particular temperament.

Chemical Use Lots of chemicals have behavioral effects. Among them are lead, nicotine, alcohol, and caffeine, as well as all of the drugs of abuse and many medicines taken for a variety of physical problems. As it turns out, Jeanne is taking a medication prescribed to treat high blood pressure. It is also known to cause depression as a side effect in some patients.

Brain Abnormalities Anything that affects the brain can affect mood and behavior. Brain injury (recent, prenatal, and perinatal) or disturbances in brain biochemistry can contribute to psychological disorders. In fact, the genetic component of depression is almost certainly related to imperfect functioning of the neurotransmitters (chemicals that facilitate nerve function) in the brain, particularly one called serotonin. Since brain imaging techniques, like the C.A.T. scan, which shows the structure of the brain, and the P.E.T. scan, which shows which parts of the brain are functioning at any given time, are so expensive, they are rarely used in cases of depression unless the patient's history is suggestive. Inquiry into Jeanne's history reveals nothing of interest here.

Psychological Factors

Goals, wishes, aspirations, values Each of us wants something different out of life, and we may want different things at different times in our lives. We learn that while Jeanne has spent her adult life raising her children and supporting her husband's career, as a young woman, she had wanted to be a writer. Often nowadays she wonders if she has made any useful contribution to society. Is producing honest and thoughtful children enough, or should she have done more?

She has also begun to revisit spiritual questions that she hasn't thought about in years. What is the purpose of life? How must life be lived so that approaching its end will not bring a flood of regrets? Is there a God? If there is, how can she move closer to him/her?

Psychological Defenses Each of us has acquired some skills in reducing and managing anxiety. Among these are conscious skills, like relaxing or socializing, and unconscious skills, like "discovering" that we really didn't want something that we can't have anyway, or "forgetting" some incident that troubled us. These unconscious skills are called "psychological defenses."

The choice of psychological defenses is an individual matter. Some people rely primarily on denial and repression when they are confronted by anxiety-provoking material, while others are prone to rationalize or intellectualize. Some see themselves at the root of all problems, while others habitually project blame elsewhere for the ills that befall them. Jeanne takes responsibility for things and tends to ruminate a lot. She figures that if she feels lonely or sad, it is her own fault. She feels that she deserves it for being lazy or timid, or just not worthy of more.

Other Psychological Factors There are many more aspects of who the person is that may be relevant to the development of psychological disorder. Among these are pre-existing self-esteem, ego strength (the ability to make reasoned decisions versus behaving impulsively), the level of insight versus denial, and the phase of development—child, adolescent, young adult, middle-aged adult, elderly adult. Each of these may be protective or risk factors, and each may influence how an underlying biological disorder is expressed in a particular person at a particular time in that person's life.

Socialcultural Factors

Cultural Conflicts Jeanne, her husband, and both of their families are of Italian, Catholic heritage. Values of fidelity, self-sacrifice, and family are paramount. Fairly rigid gender role definitions are part of the culture. Jeanne has lived her life according to these values and role definitions. However, Jeanne is also part of early twenty-first century American culture. In this culture, expectations for women are complex and in flux. Involvement in the world beyond family is expected and encouraged. Many women struggle to have both a family and a career. Some forgo having children altogether, a choice that would have been unheard of barely a generation ago. Women are involved in the political and economic life of the community, once areas that were solely men's domain. These values, which may have become more salient to Jeanne once her children began to become more independent, conflict with those of Jeanne's family and church. We can hypothesize that this conflict may play a role in her depression.

Another, more subtle conflict for Jeanne may involve the tension between the materialism and individualism that are espoused in our culture versus the spirituality and communitarianism that characterize her religious and personal values. Perhaps this is at play in her recent re-thinking of the role of religion and spirituality in her life.

The Observer's Perspective Culture also plays a role in how emotional distress is interpreted by both the sufferer and the observer. Were Jeanne to consult her priest about her feelings, he might include prayer as an antidote. Her physician, from a different perspective, would more likely suggest medication, or perhaps, counseling by a psychologist. Her best friend might suggest she take a writing course, no matter what her husband thought about it. Were she living in another place or another time, she might be bled with leeches, psychoanalysed, or exorcised. The lens through which we perceive human behavior can be greatly affected by culture.

Family The family is the carrier of cultural values as well as the inner ring of the concentric circles that make up the person's support network. It is now abundantly clear that what happens within the family can have a powerful impact on an individual's psychological development and on the risk for psychological disorder. We may wonder, for example, what effect Jeanne's mother's depression had on Jeanne's development. We can hypothesize that her mother's emotional unavailability for months at a time might have had a negative impact on Jeanne's developing sense of self worth. We also know that her mother modelled depressed and helpless behavior, which may have affected how Jeanne's own unhappiness is expressed.

Having examined how Jeanne's family of origin might have contributed to her depression, how about the effects of her family of procreation? Jeanne's husband is a hard-working, stolid man. He is reliable and trustworthy, but not very demonstrative. He believes that marriage is a partnership in which the wife's job is to take care of the home. He has, for years, dismissed Jeanne's verbalized longings to take writing courses or to work part-time. We can hypothesize that Jeanne may be harboring buried resentments or wishes to change her situation that her temperament and history have made difficult to express. Perhaps these feelings are relevant to her depression.

Economic Status Poverty breeds psychological and behavioral disorders. For one thing, it can result in biological factors like malnutrition, which, in turn, can have a negative effect on the development of the brain. In addition, poverty can affect the development of self-concept and the availability of environmental support. For example, it has been shown that people from impoverished backgrounds are more likely to view what happens to them as out of their control. Further, it has also been shown that this belief system is associated with clinical depression. However, poverty is not a relevant factor in Jeanne's case.

Other Social Factors Again, there are numerous additional social influences. Media images have a lot to do with what we come to believe about ourselves. The density and quality of our social network is relevant, not only to the development of psychological disorder, but to the likelihood that we will recover successfully. Conflicts or trauma in our social interactions can certainly be precipitants of psychological or behavioral dysfunction. Certainly, major sociopolitical upheavals, like war, can have a major impact on combatants and noncombatants alike.

The above list is only a partial one. No doubt you can think of many more examples of biological, psychological, and social factors in the development of psychological distress and behavioral dysfunction. In Jeanne's case, a combination of genetic predisposition and the possible added physical stressor of a medication, combined with a childhood history of periods of emotional neglect by her mother, an adulthood marked by prolonged repression of personal aspirations, and a couple of important recent losses propelled her into a profound depression.

In order to be successful, treatment would have to take into account who Jeanne is, how she understands her world, the feelings and behavior of those around her, her social context, and her biological makeup. Would Jeanne be a candidate for a biological therapy like antidepressant medication? Possibly, if she were inclined to understand her disorder as a physical "illness," and if her husband saw it the same way. Otherwise, it's unlikely she would take medication for very long or perceive it to be helpful. Might she benefit from individual psychotherapy of some sort? Yes, if the therapist took into account the cultural and interpersonal constraints within which Jeanne functioned. Exhortation to become more assertive and expressive, for example, might not work or might backfire in this case. Perhaps couple counseling would be preferable. Possibly Jeanne's husband could be encouraged to be more supportive of Jeanne's need for some self-fulfilling activity, particularly now that the children need her less. Maybe a support group in which Jeanne could discover that other women who felt much as she did would be of use, although if Jeanne began to change, the homeostasis of the marriage might be undermined. In any case treatment planning would have to be based on a comprehensive biopsychosocial understanding of Jeanne's predicament.

A biopsychosocial model is the basis for genuine understanding of human behavior—both normal and disordered. We will refer to it often in the cases that follow. And the challenge for us is to determine which factors are more influential in each individual case, and which therapies or combinations of therapies will alleviate the suffering and isolation felt by so many individuals.

References

Engel, G. 1977. The need for a new medical model: A challenge for biomedicine. *Science* 196, 129–136.

CASE 1

ABNORMALITY OR ECCENTRICITY? THE CASE OF NEIL CARGILE

NEIL CARGILE IS A SIXTY-FIVE-YEAR-OLD Nashville millionaire. He is a superb pilot, having been trained in Navy jets, who loves to "push the envelope." He has survived so many emergency landings that he carries the nickname, "Crash Cargile." He began flying as a teenager, in a plane he rebuilt out of surplus parts from the Second World War. As an adult, he built a helicopter pad on the grounds of his mansion. He played football at Vanderbilt College, has driven race cars, sailed yachts, and played polo. A daredevil in business as well as pleasure, he has flown crop-dusters and dredged for gold and diamonds in remote parts of the world. Twice married and twice divorced, the father of three grown children, and decidedly heterosexual, Neil Cargile would be the prototypical "man's man" were it not for one thing: he likes to dress up in women's clothing. He doesn't just dress up in private, either. He often appears at parties and even at restaurants dressed entirely in women's clothes. In an article by John Berendt in *The New Yorker* magazine (Jan 16, 1995), Mr. Cargile is interviewed and his behavior described. Is he abnormal? Does he have a psychological disorder? See what you think.

Neil Cargile grew up a privileged member of Nashville society. Mr. Berendt doesn't say much about Cargile's childhood, except that he was a talented youngster, both intellectually and in working with his hands, and that he always loved to be the center of attention. His father was a successful, conservative businessman, and his mother was a high-society, stay-at-home mom.

He has a brother, a born-again Christian, who is appalled by his cross-dressing. His mother is embarrassed but has been unable to convince him to rein in his behavior. His father is dead but when asked what his father would have done if he had seen Cargile in a dress, Cargile replied, "he would have killed me." Cargile's life has been adventurous but not entirely without tragedy: his fourteen-year-old son died of a burst aneurysm in 1970, a few years before the cross-dressing began.

Mr. Cargile first wore women's clothing at an out-of-town Halloween party in the mid-1970s when a few women friends talked him into going to the party as Dolly Parton. He won first prize for his costume. Over the next several years he attended several other costume parties in women's clothes—always out of town. Then, gradually, he began to cross-dress at local private parties, beginning subtly, with a kilt along with a jacket and tie, then adding stockings and high heels to the outfit. Finally, he had a party at his house in which guests were required to come dressed as a member of the opposite sex, and shortly thereafter, he appeared at a local costume party in full drag. After that, to the consternation of his friends and family, he began cross-dressing in public in Nashville itself.

Recently, Cargile has taken to calling himself SheNeil when he goes out in women's clothing. Author Berendt asked him if he felt like a different person when he became SheNeil. He replied "No, I feel like Neil Cargile in a dress."

Cargile seemed to get as much pleasure out of shocking people as in wearing the clothes. He does it, he says, for "fun." Berendt quotes Cargile as saying, "I'm a big showoff. I have a motto: If you aren't doing something different, you aren't doing anything at all. That's the way I've always lived." Still, there were some places Cargile would not go in drag: to church or the local country club. He also attended business meetings dressed in men's clothing, although he sometimes wore pantyhose under his suit and carried a miniskirt and a pair of heels in the car.

At the insistence of his ex-wife, Cargile went to a psychiatrist once about his cross-dressing. After finding out that Cargile was heterosexual, the psychiatrist confided that several of his colleagues cross-dressed too, although in private. Cargile got the impression that the doctor didn't feel there was much wrong with him, and he never returned.

Cargile's current girlfriend affectionately indulges his cross-dressing, helping him select outfits and doing his makeup. His daughter bought him a makeup kit one Christmas. His cross-dressing doesn't seem to have altered his social standing in Nashville, nor his capacity to make business deals.

Thinking About the Case

It is estimated that three to five percent of the male population puts on women's clothes, at least occasionally. It is difficult to access the number of women who cross-dress, since wearing men's clothing is more acceptable and less noticeable for women.

The reasons that men cross-dress vary widely. For some men cross-dressing is a sexual fetish—the clothes themselves cause sexual arousal. For others, the behavior seems to be a relaxation strategy, a way for high-achieving men to get some relief from the demands for aggressive, even ruthless competition to which they perceive themselves subject. In these men, as in Cargile, a female second self emerges in which emotional vulnerability and "softness" can be expressed more freely. Still others were dressed in women's clothing as children by mothers who wanted daughters instead of sons, while others were forced as children to wear clothing of the opposite sex as punishment. For these men, adult cross-dressing is associated with humiliation and poor self-esteem.

While most male cross-dressers are heterosexual and comfortable being men, some are homosexual and a subgroup of these cross-dress as a part of a transsexual syndrome: they wish to be women. Their subjective experience is that they are actually women, mistakenly imprisoned in a male body. (We describe such a person in case 37.)

The meaning of cross-dressing is, at least in part, culturally determined. Anthropologists have found individuals in aboriginal cultures throughout the world (except, curiously, in Europe) who, while masculine in sex, seemed to behave in many ways as women. In these cultures, an institutional role was created for these individuals in which they were neither men nor women. This role varied from culture to culture but could include child-care duties, healing functions, storytelling, or acting as go-betweens in love affairs. The attitude towards these individuals, referred to by anthropologists as "berdache," also varied from society to society. In some they were revered while in others they were reviled. In all these cultures, however, the berdache constituted a third gender, neither male nor female.

Questions to Consider

1. Is Neil Cargile abnormal? Does he have a psychological disorder? Why or why not? Do you think everyone would agree with your assessment? If not, what implications might this disagreement have for the study of abnormal psychology?
2. Would you have a different answer to the first question if
   a. Cargile was poor and homeless rather than wealthy?
   b. Cargile admitted to getting sexual pleasure from the cross-dressing?

c. Cargile only cross-dressed at costume parties?
d. Cargile identified himself as a woman born with the wrong genitalia?
e. Cargile were a woman who dressed in men's clothing?

What do your answers tell you about the role of context in how we evaluate unusual behaviors?

3. Martin Seligman, Elaine Walker, and David Rosenhan, in their classic textbook, *Abnormal Psychology*, Fourth Edition (Norton, 2001), list seven elements that count towards whether we label a person or a behavior abnormal. These are 1) suffering, 2) maladaptiveness, 3) irrationality and incomprehensibility, 4) unpredictability and loss of control, 5) vividness and unconventionality, 6) observer discomfort, and 7) violation of moral and ideal standards. The more of these elements that are present, the more likely we are to call something abnormal. Which are present in Neil Cargile's behavior? Would you delete or add elements to this list?
4. What can you hypothesize about some possible causes for Cargile's behavior? Do you think it's related to his apparent need to be the center of attention? If so, why might Cargile have chosen cross-dressing as opposed to some other flamboyant behavior? Might it be related to the death of his son? How? Might there be relevant factors in his childhood? In his biological makeup? What sorts of data would you need to help you decide whether your ideas were correct?

CASE 2

A "NORMAL" PSYCHOLOGICAL DISORDER: THE CASE OF MARTIN B.

MARTIN B. WAS A WRECK. Sitting in his doctor's office, disheveled, several days growth of stubble on his face, and fourteen pounds thinner than when he was last in, he looked the very picture of misery. Haltingly, and sobbing softly from time to time, he told his physician (and personal friend) that his wife of twelve years had taken their four-year-old son, along with most of the furniture, and left him ten days previously. For the first two days, he had slept almost all of the time, except when he was at work, where he had continued to function as if nothing had happened. But on the third day, he fell apart. He had been sleeping poorly since, often waking in the middle of the night with a pounding heart and feelings of impending doom. During the day, he couldn't sit still, couldn't concentrate, couldn't eat. For the last three days, he hadn't even been able to go to work. He had begun to drink bourbon each evening "to help him sleep," and had occasionally thought that he might be better off dead. His older brother, seeing Martin's despair, not only insisted that he come to the doctor's office, but accompanied him to ensure that he kept the appointment.

Martin was a thirty-nine-year-old engineer when his wife left. He made a good living, though working long hours to do so. His wife had worked as a dental assistant until their child was born, at which time she quit her job to stay home. He had been proud that he was able to support his family without his wife's financial help.

His wife's leaving had come as a complete surprise to Martin. He felt that he had done everything a husband should do—make a living, take care of the yard and auto maintenance, come home directly from work.

He wasn't a heavy drinker nor a womanizer. He didn't abuse his wife in any way; in fact, he loved her devotedly. Her complaints that they didn't communicate, didn't have common interests, didn't have any fun together, he had taken as the sorts of things any wife might say. He had heard them so often that he had learned to tune his wife out when she brought them up. He had been a much more attentive husband and father than his own father had been, and his mother had endured marriage for forty-one years. He felt betrayed and abandoned, humiliated, and enraged . . . and completely defeated.

Martin's physician made three recommendations: first, that Martin stop drinking for at least one month; second, that he take antidepressant medication to help him sleep and to improve his mood; and third, that he get psychotherapy to help him manage the crisis more effectively.

Despite following his doctor's orders, the next several months were rocky ones for Martin. He couldn't stop himself from contacting his wife, despite her repeated request that he do so only if he had some "business" to discuss with her. Her occasional unsolicited calls to him, in which she told him that she really loved him and was sorry about how things had turned out, only fueled the fire and strengthened his resolve to hang on to the hope that they might be reunited. Each time they spoke, he felt anguish as great as he had felt when he first discovered she'd gone. Seeing his son, which he did often, was a mixed blessing. He loved being with him, but it seemed to make the pain of his wife's absence even more intense.

Gradually, however, Martin began to improve. The medication did help him sleep and his appetite improved as well. His lows, while still frequent, weren't as devastating as they had been. Weekly sessions with his therapist were painful but he often felt relieved when he left. In her office he was able to cry without shame. He also began to try to understand what had gone wrong in his marriage and to face the fact that his wife seemed determined to move forward with the divorce. Telling his extended family and his friends at work about the separation, and feeling their support and affection for him, also helped him feel better. His concentration returned, although his zest for his work (or, indeed, for anything) was still missing.

At the end of four months, Martin was still sad, but not despairing. He was still taking the antidepressant although he was uncertain whether it, his therapy, or simply the passage of time, had served to improve his condition. His life consisted of working, visiting with his son, and occasionally seeing his brothers and their families. It was satisfactory, but joyless.

At that point, Martin's therapist suggested that he attend an orientation meeting at a support group for newly single people that existed in his community. For weeks he demurred, saying that he was too busy, that he was satisfied with his life as it was, that his son was his first priority. Finally, though, he acquiesced to his therapist's tenacity and to his own loneliness and attended a meeting. At the orientation, he chatted with a few other anxious newcomers and learned about the organization. Feeling more comfortable than he had expected, he signed up for a six-week introductory "class" in which he and seven other newly separated or widowed people would meet and discuss practical and emotional issues related to being alone. Classes were led by members of the singles' organization who had been in the group awhile, had gone through the orientation themselves, and had received some training in leadership skills. The members of his class quickly became a tight-knit group, carrying on their meetings informally at the local coffee shop, after the class ended each evening. When the class terminated, they kept in touch, forming a sort of extended family for each other.

From this time on, Martin's emotional recovery was fairly rapid. He began to date occasionally and attended social events held by his singles' group. His mood lifted enough so that he was able to discontinue both his medication and psychotherapy over the next six months. At a follow-up session two years later, he was engaged to be remarried and had resumed living a full and happy life.

Thinking About the Case

In the first case in this section, we examined when and under what circumstances behavior that is clearly uncommon should be defined as a "disorder." Neil Cargile's cross-dressing is clearly unconventional and even, for some of us, incomprehensible, but it does not meet the criteria for sexual transvestism since it is not motivated by sexual pleasure, nor, for that matter, any other category in the American Psychiatric Association's *Diagnostic and Statistical Manual*, Fifth Edition (DSM-5). In the case of Martin B., we are faced with behavior and feelings that we all understand and that many of us might experience were we to find ourselves in a similar situation. Yet, Martin's "symptoms" qualify him for two possible DSM diagnoses—major depressive episode and adjustment disorder with depressed mood. It is ironic that were Martin to respond with no distress at all, we might consider that less "normal" and even a bit suspect, but he would not be considered to have a psychological disorder. So perhaps there are situations in which it is "normal" to have a disorder and "abnormal" not to have one!

On a less confusing note, the case raises two noteworthy treatment issues. First, most psychological disorders are often treated as Martin's was—with a combination of approaches. Medication, psychotherapy, group or family treatment, as well as various environmental manipulations, when used together, can produce a more beneficial effect than any one used alone. Second, self-help methods, like reading and attending support groups (in person or on-line), can be a useful adjunct to, or in some cases a substitute for, professional interventions. Today, there are self-help groups for almost any psychological disorder—substance abuse, pathological gambling, overeating, phobias, schizophrenia, and depression among them. There are also self-help groups for people in various isolating situations—singles, vertically over-endowed persons, obese people, and relatives of people with illnesses, among others. These groups have the advantages of being inexpensive (often free), nonstigmatizing, and reducing the sense of isolation that so often accompanies psychological distress. In addition, they afford an opportunity to learn from people who have "been there," and who may have developed coping strategies of which professional helpers are unaware. They are also empowering, since the subtle power differential between "doctor" and "patient" is absent. Many people find interacting with peers less threatening than interacting with authority figures, particularly when self-esteem is already fragile.

Questions to Consider

1. According to Martin Seligman's and David Rosenhan's elements of abnormality listed at the end of the previous case (suffering, maladaptiveness, irrationality and incomprehensibility, unpredictability and loss of control, vividness and unconventionality, observer discomfort, and violation of moral and ideal standards) is Martin B.'s reaction abnormal? Which criteria are met and which are not?
2. Who do you think is "more" abnormal, Neil Cargile or Martin B.? Why? Which of them do you think has a psychological disorder? What does this say about your own criteria for "abnormality" and "disorder?"
3. What are some of the biological, psychological, or environmental elements that might predispose an individual to respond to life events, in this case, marital separation, as strongly as Martin B. did? How might these same elements be relevant in distinguishing between those who will recover well from those who will not?
4. Some might argue (as did Martin, in fact, when he spoke to his physician) that it is not Martin B. who is abnormal but his wife. We use the term "mid-life crisis" to describe the emotional state of people who make abrupt, major life changes between the ages of about 35 and 55 for reasons that are not completely clear to the uninvolved observer. What do you think of this argument?

5. Do you think your answer to question 4 might be different if you and the B.'s had come from a culture in which the expectations for men and women in marriage were markedly different? For example, in some cultures marriage represents an economic partnership—"communication" and common interests are not generally expected. What implications might this have for the cultural relativity of psychological diagnosis?

CHAPTER TWO

Neurodevelopmental Disorders

Neurodevelopmental disorders, presumed to be present either at birth or emerging in early childhood, include intellectual disabilities, communication disorders, autistic spectrum disorders, attention deficit/hyperactivity disorders, learning disorders, and motor disorders. We have chosen to include five cases representing three of the areas of disability. First, we include two cases of autism. Autism has been much discussed in recent years as recognition that mild forms of the disorder might be affecting many more people than had previously been thought. In addition, our understanding of the etiology of autism has changed over time as well. The case of Amy P., describes a severely disabled child whose parents were originally blamed for her disability, while the second tells the story of a less severely impaired young man, treated with newer, one might say more enlightened, understandings of the family's role in habilitation efforts. Together these cases illustrate how wide a range of severity of symptoms a particular disorder might encompass.

Then we include two cases of attention deficit/hyperactivity disorder, one (the case of Michael C.) which presents with primarily hyperactive and impulsive symptoms and the other (the case of Megan D.) with primarily inattentive symptoms. This category of disorders has been somewhat controversial over recent years as some experts feel that it is being overdiagnosed and that many children are being treated with medication inappropriately.

It had once been thought that attention deficit/hyperactivity disorder disappeared in early adulthood. It is now known that many, if not most, individuals with these disorders will underperform at school, at work, and often in social situations throughout their lives. Identification and treatment of adults with ADHD is now more common.

Finally, we include a case of motor disorder, Tourette's Syndrome, described by the late Oliver Sacks, M.D. Dr. Sacks tells us about a physician, a surgeon actually, who has found a way to mount a successful practice despite being plagued by severe tics throughout his life. It is a vivid and compassionate description that reminds us that psychological factors like motivation, self-esteem, and perseverence modify how an illness or syndrome will express itself in a person's life.

CASE 3

SEVERE AUTISTIC SPECTRUM DISORDER: THE CASE OF AMY P.

AT TWO, AMY WAS NOT YET TALKING, and her parents were beginning to worry. She had begun to speak at thirteen months, right on time, but had stopped soon after. Mr. and Mrs. P. had brought their daughter, a beautiful, curly-mopped little girl, to a friend, a psychologist who studied language development, for an informal evaluation.

The family history was unremarkable. Amy's parents were a young married couple who doted on their only child. Mr. P. was a physics professor at a local university who, although deeply engaged in his research and in the struggle to achieve tenure, played with and read to his daughter each evening. His wife, although college-educated, had elected to stay home until Amy reached school age. They seemed a warm and engaging couple. There had been no history of mental illness on either side of their family, nor had there been any complications of pregnancy or birth. Amy had breezed through the early developmental milestones—holding her head up, rolling over, sitting, standing, walking—at an average or quicker than average pace.

The psychologist videotaped a play session with Amy and her mother, and in reviewing it, this is what she saw: Amy was a child who was fascinated with things, but virtually uninterested in people.

Amy's way of playing with toys was decidedly odd. She would pick up a toy, examine it visually and with her hands, then throw it down and pick up another. Her play was manipulative, rather than symbolic. That is, she never used the toys to create a pretend scenario as most children do. In fact, she didn't seem to understand what toys were for; she was interested only in their shapes, colors, and textures.

During the play session, Amy's mom sat or laid on the floor with Amy, talking to her and trying to engage her. Not only did Amy not speak, but she acted as if her mother were not there. She never looked at her, nor did she respond to her mother's questions, comments, or suggestions. It was clear that she could hear, because she noticed noises in the hall, and music coming from a radio in the next room. She simply did not respond to any language input.

The psychologist was struck by one other curious phenomenon. At one point in the session, Amy was drawn to the hallway by a noise. Arriving at the doorway, she stared, rapt, down the hall for four or five long minutes. The hallway was empty of people or objects. All the psychologist could see was the pattern made by the lights on the ceiling—light, dark, light, dark. When she mentioned her observation to Amy's mom, Mrs. P. related that Amy often stood, entranced in the same way, in front of a poster she had in her room at home. Trying to shift her attention would generally result in a tantrum. She herself could never understand Amy's particular fascination with this poster, but, interestingly enough, it too had alternating areas of darkness and light.

Amy's parents had not really thought of her behavior as disturbed. They attributed her lack of interaction to her lack of speech. They assumed that, once she learned to talk, everything would be fine. In the meantime, they treated her like a normal child.

The psychologist suggested to Amy's parents that the problem might be more pervasive than they thought and that a psychiatric consultation might be of use. With some trepidation, they accepted a referral to a child psychiatrist who diagnosed Amy as having childhood schizophrenia. He told the dismayed parents that something traumatic must have happened to Amy to induce her profound emotional separation from others and urged them to search their memories for situations that might qualify. The only thing they could come up with was that Mrs. P. had gone away overnight to visit her parents when Amy was eight months old. The psychiatrist felt that this separation from her major attachment figure might indeed have been so awful for Amy that she developed the isolation as a psychological defense against any future loss of a love object. He further implied that perhaps Mrs. P.'s choice to leave Amy overnight at such a "sensitive" age was an indication of a more general lack of sensitivity to the nurturance needs of her child.

Mrs. P. was devastated by the psychiatrist's pronouncement. She had never meant to hurt her child, but here was an expert saying that she was responsible for inflicting serious, possibly permanent, damage on Amy's psyche. Mr. P. had a host of conflicting feelings. He loved his wife and he felt protective of her. He wanted to support her, but, on the other hand, if she had damaged his daughter, he couldn't help but be furious.

The P.'s continued to see the psychiatrist for several more sessions, but, at the same time, they began to read all that they could find about childhood schizophrenia. In their reading, they stumbled across an article about childhood autism that seemed to describe Amy's behavior perfectly. They were particularly struck by the description of how autistic children require ritualistic sameness in their environment. Amy listened to the same piece of music hundreds and hundreds of times. She would eat only a small number of foods, prepared in only one way. At the moment, she was into bologna sandwiches on white bread with the edges cut off, mayonnaise only on one side, and cut crosswise into quarters. If any of the steps were missing or wrong, she pitched an enormous fit, throwing herself around, and screaming until another sandwich was made, exactly as she wanted it.

They were also struck by the article's description of "autistic aloneness." Amy seemed to fit exactly—she seemed totally walled in. She existed in a world of things where no one else was invited. She didn't dislike people, she simply ignored them. She wouldn't sit on her mother's lap or cuddle. She didn't follow her parents around, even with her eyes.

Mr. and Mrs. P. decided to seek a second opinion regarding Amy's diagnosis and treatment. They took her to a program for autistic children where a multidisciplinary evaluation by a psychiatrist, a psychologist, a speech pathologist, and an occupational therapist confirmed the diagnosis of autism.

Most treatment programs for autistic children follow a strictly behavioral model in which youngsters are rewarded (for example, with candy) for behavior that brings them into contact with others. First eye contact is rewarded, then touching and speaking. The goal is to gradually shape interactional behaviors. At the same time, autistic behaviors, like tantrums or self-mutilative behavior, might be punished. Since autistic children are not innately rewarded by social contact, the use of "time out," which usually works well for normal children, cannot be used with autistic children. In some programs, mild electric shock has been found effective, although its use has been controversial.

The program in which Amy was enrolled was modeled on the principle of "gentle teaching." Instead of a regimented, rewards-and-punishments system, therapists and teachers allowed themselves to be led by the child's own behavior, commenting on the child's choices as the day progressed. While rigorous scientific studies have not yet been done, anecdotal evidence suggests that such an intervention might be a possibly successful alternative to behavioral treatment. Amy's parents are hopeful that she might improve, but they know that they must wait and see. In the meantime, they are learning all they can about autism. They have joined a support group composed of other parents of autistic children. Here they can grieve the loss of the person that Amy might have become and gain strength to accept the person that she is.

Thinking About the Case

Autistic Spectrum Disorders comprise one set of neurodevelopmental disorders. Neurodevelopmental disorders begin in childhood and used to be called "disorders first manifest in childhood and adolescence." The new term communicates the presumption that these disorders have some sort of pre- or perinatal cause or causes. These disorders can include intellectual or learning problems, but autistic disorders are those in which deficits in social development and communication skills are prominent. Another change in classification is the use of the term "spectrum." In the past, severe autism and less severe autism (then called Asperger's Syndrome) were classified as two separate disorders. The change communicates the newer thinking that these disorders are distinct only in severity, not in kind.

Amy's case is fairly typical of severe autism, marked by poor or absent language, almost total lack of relatedness with others, and severely ritualistic and stereotyped behaviors. The next case, that of Isaac T., will consider a person with less severe symptoms. While Amy's prognosis is quite poor—over half of the children who exhibit such severe symptoms are later unable to function as independent adults—those with less severe symptoms as children may do quite a bit better later.

Some individuals with autism, called "autistic savants," display marked intelligence, even brilliance in certain circumscribed areas. For example, some can replicate on the piano any musical piece no matter how complicated having heard it only once. Yet, they are unable to play even the simplest melody from written music or to compose even the most elementary tune. Others are numbers whizzes. They are able to perform instant calculations of very large numbers. Yet, these same people often cannot make change at the grocery store. Some have amassed huge bodies of knowledge about a small area of information. For example, one child could recite all of the bus routes across the country. By now you have guessed the flipside: this same youngster was unable to find his way to the corner store and back home.

The cause or causes of autism are not yet known. The hypothesis put forth by the first psychiatrist who evaluated Amy was common at one time. Parents of autistic children were once thought to be cold, aloof, and unable to create a warm connection with their children. However, the fact that most autistic children have perfectly normal siblings made such a hypothesis unlikely to be true, and in fact, research efforts have been unable to demonstrate any patterns of parental behavior or characteristics that are related to autism. Another idea, that childhood immunizations cause autism, has also been disproved by numerous carefully controlled studies. Since not all mental health professionals are equally conversant with the latest research in every area, parents would be well advised to seek a second opinion as well as to do some research on their own, as Amy's parents did.

Researchers today are looking at possible biological underpinnings and are finding some things. Genetics clearly play a role in autism. Immune dysregulation, inflammation, and environmental toxicant exposure may each play some sort of role in the expression of the genetic predisposition or even in causing the disorder in cases without genetic predisposition.

Treatment for autism is multifaceted. It generally includes some behavioral component in which social and language behaviors are shaped by rewards. In severe cases, many hours a week over many years may be necessary. In addition, speech, occupational, and physical therapy may be employed. While there is no medication for autism itself, associated symptoms that sometimes occur, such as anxiety or depression, may be treated with appropriate medicines. Support and education for parents is a necessary component of treatment as well. Raising an autistic child is challenging, to say the least, and can affect each member of the family as well as the dynamics of the family as a whole.

Questions to Consider

1. What are some reasons why early intervention might be important in the treatment of autism?
2. Assume, for the moment, that some specific brain abnormality will be found in persons with autism. Would you still consider it a psychological disorder? Why or why not?
3. If you were the parent of an autistic child, what information would you want in order to decide which treatment program to place your child in? How would you go about getting this information?
4. What effect might the presence of an autistic child have on the life of a family? How might it affect the parents' relationship? How might it affect the siblings as they face their own developmental tasks? How might it affect the relationship between the parents and the well siblings?

CASE 4

HIGH-FUNCTIONING AUTISTIC SPECTRUM DISORDER: THE CASE OF ISAAC T.

DR. B. WENT TO HIS WAITING ROOM door to welcome his newest client. What he saw was a young man sitting on the floor engaged in building a lego tower from the blocks stored in a box in the corner. In a chair behind him sat a middle-aged woman who smiled up at Dr. B. expectantly. The client had been referred by his physician for help managing panic attacks that had begun following the death of Isaac's father six months prior. No mention had been made of the client's having been intellectually impaired, though this was Dr. B.'s first impression. However, this impression turned out to be decidedly incorrect.

When Dr. B. asked him to enter the consultation room, Isaac hunched his shoulders, frowned, and shook his head rapidly back and forth, so Dr. B. invited Mrs. T. to join them. He also told Isaac he could bring the lego blocks in with him if he wanted—which he clearly did. While Isaac worked on his lego tower, Mrs. T. offered a bit of history.

Isaac was currently twenty years of age. He had always been a shy but bright child. He suffered from many fears—spiders, dark places, large dogs, thunderstorms, getting lost . . . and interacting with people he didn't know. He had also exhibited a number of what his mother called "quirks." He wouldn't eat food that was touching other food on the plate. He wouldn't wear shorts, even on the hottest days, and his clothes had to be made of cotton. He spent a great deal of time drawing and building models of buildings of all sorts—castles, mansions, churches, and modernistic creations. He was generally good natured, but had incomprehensible "meltdowns" from time to time.

Isaac had graduated high school with good grades but he had befriended only one person, another "outsider" youngster like himself. His physician, who had developed a trusting relationship with the family over the years, had suggested that he might want to consider accounting as a career as Isaac was good with math, and the field would not require a great deal of interpersonal contact. He had applied to and gotten accepted at a local college. He had tried living in the dorms, but had been unable to make the transition. Now he commuted from home, and because he had never learned how to drive, his mother drove him there in the morning, and she picked him up in the afternoon after her own work day ended. He spent his free time while at school in the library studying or reading or drawing. In this way, he had managed to complete the first two years. Now, in the middle of his third year he seemed unable to go on.

Isaac had begun having panic attacks within a few weeks after his father had a massive heart attack. The first panic attack occurred in class: he felt that he couldn't breathe, that his heart was pounding out of his chest. He felt as if he, himself, were having a heart attack. He fled the classroom, and called his mother to pick him up. Additional attacks followed, some in class, and some even before the school day began. Because of his social anxiety, Isaac had been unable to get himself to speak with his professors about his difficulties, and so he was now failing almost all of his classes. Finally, with no real options left, his mother withdrew him from school.

As he spoke with Isaac's mother, Dr. B. attempted to engage Isaac from time to time. He asked what he was building with his legos, what he liked to read, what his little brother was like. Isaac responded to these questions, despite his obvious anxiety. He rocked slightly back and forth when he spoke, and kept his eyes on his building blocks. Nonetheless, his vocabulary and use of language was above average, and the rocking stopped at one point when he was describing a building project he was working on at home. Towards the end of the hour, Isaac agreed to spend a few minutes alone with Dr. B. By the end of hour, he had agreed to come back on a weekly basis with the goal of being able to return to school.

While Dr. B. almost immediately recognized the signs of autism in Isaac's behavior—the almost total lack of eye contact, the restricted, nonsocial interests, the inflexibilities in eating and clothing, the rocking, the inability to interact normally with others—it appeared that no one else had made the diagnosis. Mrs. T. seemed to regard Isaac with benign acceptance. His physician had not diagnosed autism, nor had the school. Later, it became clear that because Isaac had superior intelligence and a quiet demeanor, and oddities that were not apparent to anyone but his mother who never thought to mention them, he had passed through elementary and high school as a shy but compliant youngster.

However, Isaac knew that he was not like other people. As he became comfortable with Dr. B., he began to reveal an awareness of his isolation, his differentness. He had never had an interest in a romantic or sexual relationship, and he knew this was abnormal. He could not tolerate crowds, make telephone calls, or even easily respond to e-mails and he knew that this, too, was abnormal. He reported that he didn't "understand how other people worked." His sense of humor was different and he was mystified by the nuances of social behavior. While he preferred to spend his time alone, he still felt lonely and apart. This feeling had intensified as he had matured.

When his father died, Isaac lost one of only three people in the world he felt accepted him exactly as he was, the remaining ones being his mother and brother. His mother, though seemingly carrying on with her work and life, was grief-stricken and more withdrawn herself. She was preoccupied with money issues and managing life for her family without her spouse's support. Isaac felt that he had "lost a parent and a half." He began to wonder what would become of him if anything happened to his mother. After all, he didn't drive, he hadn't finished college, he had no work skills, he couldn't bear to be around others very much. It wasn't surprising that he began to feel panic.

Dr. B. wondered whether it might be helpful to share the diagnosis of autism with Isaac and his family. On the plus side, there were educational and financial resources available for students with autism. Additionally, perhaps Isaac could find an on-line support group of other autistic young adults which might lessen his feeling of isolation without taxing his social skills. He might begin to understand himself better, and perhaps even gain at least partial mastery over some of his deficits. On the minus side, he or his family might resist the diagnosis and lose faith in the therapist. They might feel stigmatized or more anxious, or even hopeless. As a first step, Dr. B. consulted with Isaac's family doctor. When he shared the diagnosis, the physician said "oh yes, that makes sense. I think I missed it because he's so darn smart." With the physician on board, Dr. B. told Isaac he thought he might understand the underlying problem. He read Isaac the description of autistic symptoms found in the DSM-5 and asked him what he thought. What followed was a lengthy conversation, held over many sessions, and interspersed with discussions of immediate problems or environmental stressors. On his own, Isaac began to read about autism online. As Dr. B. suspected he would, Isaac visited a number of sites for and about persons with autism.

Gradually, over about six months, Isaac began to identify himself as autistic. He learned that many of the things he did had names: "stimming" meant rocking back and forth or humming a phrase over and over or pinching himself. Isaac didn't do this, but apparently other people with autism sometimes did. "Meltdowns" referred to massively overreacting to a seemingly mildly negative situation, like a small disappointment of some kind. He learned that these usually occurred for others after periods of sensory overstimulation—and he was able to see that the same was true for him. He watched a television show about Temple Grandin, a brilliant autistic woman who was especially able to describe her condition so that others could understand. He began to refer to himself as an "Aspie," a slang term for Asperger's Syndrome which is a kind of high-functioning autism. He began to be able to identify and feel proud of the creative and offbeat way his mind worked. He began to value his ability to amuse and keep himself interested. He was never bored. He was relieved that his condition had a name and he was grateful that Dr. B. had helped him learn about himself and connect with others who had similar challenges.

The same could not be said for his mom, though. Isaac had elected not to have Dr. B. speak with Mrs. T. about autism. He wanted to do so himself, in his own way, and in his own time. He reported to Dr. B. that she was skeptical. She felt his ability to go through public school without a hitch belied the diagnosis. She said that he was just a little shy, like she was, and could do anything he wanted if he put his mind to it. Isaac felt frustrated at his inability to explain his problem with sensory overload, his difficulty understanding social interactions, or his need for unvarying routines in his daily life to his mom, but felt that she would come around in time. Anyway, even if she didn't, she loved and cared for him and tolerated his idiosyncrasies. She rarely frightened him or made him anxious. She accepted his limitations in her own way.

Isaac's therapy went very slowly. He spent much of the time talking about his projects and concentrating on the lego structure he was building in the session. During these conversations he was animated and at ease, though his eye contact never really improved. He had much greater difficulty talking about his problems and their possible solutions. Often he became agitated, with increased rocking, tugging at his hair, and wearing a pained expression. At these times, Dr. B. took the opportunity to suggest various ways that Isaac might be able to calm himself—by breathing slowly and by trying to understand what was upsetting about the topic under consideration. Isaac came to realize that his biggest fear was that he would be asked to do something that he knew would generate anxiety, like speaking with a teacher, taking a driving lesson, or going to the bank to open an account.

Together with Dr. B. Isaac worked on breaking these tasks down to smaller components that seemed more manageable. For example, to get prepared to open a bank account, Isaac first walked by the bank over and over until he was comfortable passing it. Then he went in, accompanied by his mother, and looked around. His mother, on a separate visit, alerted the bank manager about the plan Isaac was following and why he was doing so. After several weeks of almost daily trips to the bank just to look around, he began to poke his head into the manager's cubicle when he noticed she was alone and said "hi." She responded with a friendly smile and a "hi, Isaac. Nice to see you." All of this was carefully orchestrated with Dr. B. and Mrs. T. After several more weeks, Isaac felt comfortable enough with the manager to ask her to help him open an account. She also introduced him to three of the tellers so that he would almost certainly know the person who was helping him with a transaction. This experience taught Isaac an important lesson: he could master a scary situation if he "overlearned" each of its parts. It was tedious, and it took a very long time, but it worked. He also found that he needed a period of "decompression" following a practice session. To decompress, he went to his room, and worked silently on a drawing. His mother and brother knew not to interrupt him until he came out on his own. In addition, he learned that if he waited too long in between practice sessions, the anxiety built up again, and the task was more difficult to accomplish. So he had to make a concerted effort to do each part as frequently as possible in order to make progress.

Despite making progress in limited, circumscribed situations, Isaac remained unable to imagine going back to school. At Dr. B's suggestion, and with his mother's involvement and assistance, Isaac enrolled in an on-line college in order to get an accounting degree. This worked out quite well for him. He found the work easy to master, could do it on his own, and had no trouble with the computer issues. He even found himself able to participate in on-line "classroom discussions." While the challenge of finding, interviewing for, and getting to a job remained serious issues for him, Isaac felt he had made enough progress to terminate his therapy, at least for the time being. He agreed that he might return if he felt stuck in moving forward at any time in the future.

Thinking About The Case

The case of Amy [#3] illustrated severe autism. The case of Isaac illustrates a less severely impaired, more high functioning individual. While the epidemiological data indicate, as we reported, that the prognosis for autism is quite poor, it is possible that there are many less severely autistic individuals living and functioning in the community, as perhaps Isaac will be able to one day.

Amy and Isaac's syndromes share the same core features: deficits in social skills, deficits in empathy, repetitive and idiosyncratic behaviors and interests, and susceptibility to sensory overstimulation. They differ in important ways as well. Perhaps the most important of these is language. Isaac can communicate effectively, while Amy can not, and may never be able to. Isaac relates to other people, though not without anxiety and oddities, while Amy does not. Isaac has been able to learn about his condition, to be self-reflective, to problem-solve, and to reach out to others (online). In all likelihood, Amy will not be able to do any of these things. These differences may lead to radically different outcomes.

The differences in how autism presents in these two cases reflects how difficult it will be to find the cause or causes of autism. Some researchers have hypothesized that maybe each of the core aspects have different causes. And, while genetics may play a large role in the development of the disorder (the concordance rate for identical twins is 90%), it is clear that as yet unknown environmental problems, agents, or toxins are also implicated. For example, advanced parental (particularly paternal) age is a risk factor, as are prenatal viral infection and gestational diabetes in the mother. Perhaps there are multiple routes to the multiple problems that seem to co-occur together in what we call austistic spectrum disorders.

Questions To Consider

1. Does it appear to you that Amy and Isaac have the same disorder? Why or why not? What does your answer say about classification of abnormal behavior?
2. Do you agree with Dr. B's decision to share his diagnostic conclusion with Isaac? What do you think are the pros and cons of doing so? Do you agree with his decision to let Isaac handle the issue with his mother in his own way? Again, what are the pros and cons?

CASE 5

ATTENTION DEFICIT–HYPERACTIVITY DISORDER: THE CASE OF MICHAEL C.

This case is contributed by Stephen A. Karl, M.S.W., a colleague who has had substantial experience in working with adolescents in an agency where a multiplicity of professionals and programs are available. Working together, psychologists, psychiatrists, nurses, occupational therapists, social workers, and others provide a combination of individual, group, residential, educational, and support services to youngsters with serious emotional and behavioral problems. The case illustrates how treatment of a youngster often involves more than one-on-one psychotherapy. It also makes clear that sometimes the best laid treatment plans are scuttled by outside events beyond a therapist's control. Good communication with the important people in a child's life, his parents, teachers, and doctors, among others, is essential, but not sufficient for progress to be made. Here is Michael C.'s case.

I MET MICHAEL C. FIRST WHEN HE WAS FIFTEEN, along with his mother, Linda, his stepfather, Dave, and his nine-year-old sister, Cindy. The thin, awkward boy had recently left his biological father, John, to reestablish residence with his mother. They all resided in a middle-class suburb adjacent to a moderately large city. Linda brought Michael for psychotherapy because she wanted to ensure that he would do well in school, and to avoid his becoming emotionally and physically abusive, isolated, and unemployed like his biological father, John. Michael C. freely admitted his frustration with himself and the failure he perceived in most parts of his life.

Michael's biological parents had separated when he was six. Linda had begun an affair with Dave shortly before she separated from John. Dave had provided the means for Linda to escape an increasingly abusive husband. The level of early attachment between Michael and his mother may have been limited by his mother's preoccupation with surviving the abuse dealt out by her husband and by the time and energy taken up by her affair with Dave. Also, she had a negative, although unconscious, emotional reaction to Michael, most likely because of his similarity in appearance, mannerisms, and behavior to his father.

At the first interview, the family revealed several prior attempts to obtain mental health treatment. At age three, Michael had been taken to a psychologist because he was waking several times a night, rarely sleeping more than three or four hours at a time. He was also difficult to manage during the day. He required constant monitoring to prevent him from jumping off high places or engaging in other, equally dangerous, activities. Linda reported that Michael wouldn't allow her to cuddle him or read to him. He couldn't seem to stay in one spot for more than a few minutes at a time. She felt worn out and frustrated.

After his parents separated, Michael's impulsivity in first grade increased to the point where his peers began rejecting him. He was teased or avoided by classmates who appeared to find his impulsive statements and aggressive acts intolerable. When Michael was eight, a psychologist diagnosed him as having attention deficit–hyperactivity disorder (ADHD) and recommended that his pediatrician prescribe a drug called Ritalin, a stimulant medication used to increase attention span. Linda reports having seen some improvement in Michael's behavior with this intervention, but his father was adamantly opposed to Michael's taking medication. He felt that Michael's problems were the result of Linda's poor parenting. Despite being separated from John at the time, Linda went along with his request to stop Michael's medication in order to avoid further conflict.

Dave, Michael's stepfather, had become part of the family when Michael was seven. A family therapist was engaged at about the same time that the Ritalin was started to help with the transition into a step-family. Linda told the therapist that since Dave had moved in, Michael had been crying at night and had developed a pattern of alternately engaging Dave then rejecting him. Michael appeared to become more cooperative and engaged with family members as a result of the family therapy. At the same time, the therapist worked with the school to provide tutors to assist Michael with his school work. This intervention helped Michael to focus and complete tasks.

Michael's parents commenced divorce proceedings when Michael was nine. The divorce process was difficult and drawn out for the family. Frequent accusations and court proceedings involving allegations of neglect and abuse between Linda and John persisted, and visitation and custody battles for both children continued long after. The ongoing power struggle between Linda and John seemed to result in a family that lived from one crisis to another.

Even though Linda was the main caregiver for Michael throughout most of his childhood, John had gained sole custody of Michael for two years (from age thirteen to fifteen). Michael had repeatedly voiced a desire to live with his father and the never-ending battle in the family had finally convinced Linda to let him try it. She and Dave felt they needed a break. However, they recently re-established custody of Michael because they suspected that John had been abusing him, both emotionally (frequent yelling, unpredictable expectations, irrational demands) and physically (slapping, verbal threats, and an incident of being threatened with a gun). Child Protective Services had investigated and had determined that the allegations were grounded in fact, so that custody was again awarded to Linda with paternal visitation allowed.

My evaluation began soon after Michael's return to Linda and Dave's home. His history seemed consistent with the original diagnosis of ADHD. In addition to the core features of inattentiveness, impulsivity, and hyperactivity, he also exhibited the commonly associated behaviors of defiance and aggression.

I suspected that Michael's father also had ADHD. John received Social Security Disability payments for an unspecified disability rather than seeking work. He had few meaningful relationships and a history of interpersonal conflict. He also exhibited antisocial behavior including verbal and physical aggression, frequent lying and stealing, irresponsibility, and poor financial management. These behaviors are often exhibited by adults with untreated ADHD. I felt that the following risk factors, which might predict Michael's ADHD, were in place: (1) probable family history of ADHD, (2) the likelihood of a critical maternal attitude, (3) early and excessive physical activity by the fetus while still in the uterus as reported by the mother, and (4) parental (paternal) psychopathology.

Michael's school history was also consistent with a diagnosis of ADHD. Despite having above average intelligence, he had experienced increasing difficultly in school as he went along. Prior to junior high school he had exhibited low frustration tolerance, often lost things, was impulsive and mouthy with teachers and his parents, and was fidgety and distractible, but his grades were good. Bright children like Michael are often able to keep their grades up until increased organizational skills are required in junior and senior high. By junior high, Michael's coping strategy of waiting until the end of the semester, cramming, and doing well on exams was proving increasingly less effective. Hoping that a more structured environment would benefit him, Linda and Dave enrolled Michael in a parochial school beginning in eighth grade. Between eighth and tenth grade Michael attended three different parochial schools. He failed in each of them despite average test scores because he was insolent, stubborn, and wouldn't do his homework. Not surprisingly, his teachers and parents increasingly thought of him as a lazy, procrastinating, unpleasant youngster.

Since mood disorders are frequently associated with ADHD, I requested a psychiatric evaluation to assess the possible presence of depression. Sure enough, the psychiatrist agreed that Michael was suffering from clinical depression and prescribed an antidepressant medication.

The first psychotherapy task was to engage with Michael, repair his damaged self esteem, and help his parents understand and cope with his disorder. I noticed that the family frequently displaced anger towards John at Michael, who, at fifteen, increasingly resembled his father. A Gestalt therapy technique of introducing an empty chair into the session, representing the absent father, allowed the family to vent or redirect their frustration toward John and away from Michael. I frequently referred to the empty chair when disproportionate anger was expressed towards Michael's behavior. I also tried to teach the family to recognize when Michael did something well. Children with ADHD frequently have histories of getting overwhelmingly negative feedback from others which, over time, damages their self concept and contributes to depression.

The interventions were only marginally successful. Typically, the family reported less conflict for two days after sessions and then returned to previous levels of conflict that came to include Linda's threats of violence toward Michael. After several months of increasing risk of domestic violence between Michael and his parents, Linda requested a foster care placement. Instead, I made a referral to an intensive in-home crisis intervention program in the hopes of preventing yet another residential disruption. The five-week, ten-hour-per-week intervention appeared to reduce family conflict and induce a sense of hopefulness. It also provided new coping strategies for Michael's parents, including improved communication skills, the ability to contract for desired behaviors, and the provision of immediate, logical consequences if Michael messed up. Additionally, I provided written and oral information about coping with ADHD in the family.

This intervention, along with medication and an alternative high school placement with special teachers who were knowledgeable about ADHD and behavioral management techniques, together with regular communication among providers, facilitated a ninety-day period of marked improvement. Michael showed less defiance and improved academic performance. His scores on a scale designed to measure ADHD behaviors were reduced and his relationships improved.

However, over the next three months, the loss of a girlfriend, the increased presence of John in Michael's life, and a reduction of Linda and Dave's use of appropriate behavioral techniques appeared to contribute to a worsening in Michael's behavior. He began to abuse marijuana and alcohol, increased the frequency of stealing from home, and was defiant of family norms.

Finally the increasing disillusionment and emotional disengagement by his mother and step-father resulted in Michael's return to John's home once again. Linda felt that Michael had indeed, become like his father. Her attempts to prevent it had been exhausting and unsuccessful. Her wish to protect and nurture Michael had been replaced by her wish for some peace and stability for herself, her husband, and her daughter. Although medication and specialized academic placement continue, Linda's disengagement, John's lack of cooperation, and Michael's increasingly antisocial behavior make the prognosis less than hopeful.

Thinking About the Case

The diagnosis of attention deficit/hyperactivity disorder is a controversial one. Some people feel it is diagnosed much too often, resulting in the labeling and medicating of children who are simply rambunctious or poorly parented. Parents and teachers apply the label, it is argued, to justify use of a "chemical straitjacket" for children who are hard to handle. According to this view, attentional capacities and activity levels fall along a continuum, where the cut-off point for defining a "disorder" is entirely subjective and open to misuse. The disorder, critics say, lies in the eye of the beholder.

However, others feel that ADHD is a true disorder which, if left untreated, often results in snowballing difficulties for children as they encounter ever more challenging life tasks. Many parents and teachers will attest to the startling change in a youngster's behavior and goal attainment when properly treated for ADHD. One mother described it this way: "It's like he can finally be who he really wanted to be. Before, he kept trying and trying, and we knew he didn't want to be like he was, but he just couldn't help it. Now, he can." Proponents of the diagnosis argue that even if the continuum idea has merit, children whose functioning is seriously impaired should have access to remediative treatments.

Unfortunately, there is no laboratory test that can detect the presence of ADHD. Instead, it is diagnosed on the basis of reports about the child's behavior. Most clinicians will gather data from parents, teachers, and even the child. If possible, classroom and/or home observation will be made. When the bulk of the data point to the possible presence of ADHD, a treatment plan is developed. This plan generally includes a trial of stimulant medication that improves attention span and fine motor control, education and support for family members and teachers, and training in behavioral management techniques. It may also include a specialized educational environment with a specially trained teacher and a smaller class size. Since specific learning disabilities are often associated with ADHD, additional educational services may be necessary.

The outcome for children with ADHD is extremely variable. Some respond well to treatment and learn to make adjustments in how they operate in the world to compensate for their inattentiveness and impulsivity. Their parents learn to cope with their deficits and value them for who they are. Others respond less well, live in a less supportive environment, or are perhaps less well treated. These may develop behavioral problems like Michael. In the worst case scenario, ADHD is associated with conduct disorder in adolescence and antisocial personality disorder in adults. Early detection and multimodal intervention are key to a successful outcome.

Until recently, it had been thought that children "grew out" of ADHD in mid-to-late adolescence. Typically, medication was stopped at some time during the teen years. It is now believed that ADHD is a lifelong disorder and that some adults with it could benefit from treatment with stimulant medication, while others can proceed successfully without medication, using the coping strategies they have learned during their school years. Efforts are being made to reconsider the history of adults who have problems holding jobs, exercising adequate social judgment, and containing impulses to see if they might have undiagnosed ADHD. The outcome of treatment of these adults is currently under study.

Questions to Consider

1. What were the factors that contributed to the poor outcome of treatment in Michael's case? What might clinicians have done differently along the way?
2. Can you think of a way to determine whether medication was really helping a child with presumed ADHD? If you were a parent, how would you decide whether or not to accept a recommendation for medication?
3. Some researchers have discussed the concept of "goodness of fit" to

describe the relationship between a child's innate temperamental traits and the expectations of the environment in which he lives. According to this model, if a child is lucky enough to have traits that "fit" his environment, he will do well, but if not, he will fare poorly. Can this concept be applied to Michael's case? Is this idea an alternative to the notion that ADHD is a true "disorder?"

CASE 6

ATTENTION DEFICIT–HYPERACTIVITY DISORDER, INATTENTIVE TYPE: THE CASE OF MEGAN D.

MEGAN WAS A PETITE, adorable blond fourteen-year-old when her mother first sought help for her. She looked like the daughter everyone would want to have, and in many ways, she was. She was helpful, kind, and funny, according to her mom. She loved sports, music, animals, and people. But, despite apparent good intelligence, she was in serious danger of failing eighth grade.

Megan's mother had tried everything to help her, but so far, nothing had worked. She had hired a tutor to help with homework only to find that Megan frequently failed to turn it in. She had punished her for poor grades, but that only led to bad feelings and not to better grades. Rewards for good performance had not really helped either. Megan seemed to get over her disappointment at not getting the reward inordinately quickly. Megan lied about whether she had homework, and stuffed failing tests in her dresser drawer. Since Megan had been a good student in elementary school, her mother felt sure that some emotional problem of adolescence was impairing her performance, and so she had sought a referral to a psychologist. Megan's teachers were of the opinion that she was far too interested in the social aspects of school, and could do the work if only she were motivated.

Despite her declaration that therapy was "lame," Megan couldn't stop herself from engaging with the therapist. Happily, she babbled on about her pets, her soccer team, her upcoming birthday party, and her friends. When the conversation turned to school, Megan's mood seemed to turn as well. With reluctance, she admitted that she "hated" school—at least the part that involved classwork. She liked choir, gym, art class, and lunchtime. She was bored during class, she said. She thought it was "stupid" to read the books that were assigned in English class, and "irrelevant" to learn about world history. Math was so easy for her that she didn't feel she needed the practice that homework offered. So, she often failed to do it. Mostly, she couldn't see the point of school. She wanted to be a singer, or an actress, when she grew up, so most of what they were force-feeding her in school would be of little value to her. Her statements seemed to support her teachers' view of her.

Still, not far below the surface was an undercurrent of disappointment and dismay. As she got more comfortable with the therapist, Megan admitted that she hated to disappoint her mother and her grandparents and had frequently vowed to do better, if only to make them happy and get them off her back. But something always happened between the vow and the end of the next marking period. She might keep it together for a day or a week, but then her energy seemed always to drain away into other, for her, more interesting directions.

She didn't want to fail eighth grade, either. All her friends were in her grade and she loathed the idea of having to hang around all the "babies" in seventh grade. Plus, she felt ashamed. None of her friends were failing. They didn't make a big deal out of it, but she knew that they cared about their grades. In reality, she did, too. She didn't understand why she couldn't seem to succeed no matter what she did. At this point in the interview, Megan began to cry.

The psychologist wanted specific examples of what "not keeping it together" meant. Megan and her mom reported that she would do homework but forget to turn it in or lose it in the rubble of her bedroom. She would put off homework until she had "I.M.ed" her friends or washed her hair and then never get to it. She would pass notes in class or compose a tune in her head while everyone else was focusing on a lesson. She had three folders for each class (one for homework, one for notes, and one for projects) and often couldn't find the one she needed in her locker. She lost textbooks and misplaced notes. She couldn't bear to study for more than ten minutes at a time, and even then didn't retain much of what she had studied. Generally, she had something far more important, like the school play, or her best friend's recent fight with her boyfriend, on her mind.

Mrs. D. had brought along a snapshot she had taken of Megan's bedroom for the therapist because, she said, she knew that nobody would believe her if she just described the site. It looked, literally, as if a bomb had exploded in the room. Clothes, trash, papers, food, stuffed animals, toiletries, and all the other detritus of a young girl's life were strewn haphazardly on all available surfaces. Drawers were half opened and clothes spilled out in a heap. On top of one of these open drawers was a pile of magazines, topped with a plastic soda cup. Mrs. D. said that she and Megan spent the better part of each Saturday morning cleaning up the bedroom and that this picture had been taken on Thursday evening.

The therapist inquired about Megan's family history. Megan's parents had split when she was a baby. Her father was a "pothead" with no ambition. Mrs. D., who had been a pothead herself in adolescence and early adulthood, felt the need to grow up when she got pregnant, but apparently her husband had not felt the same need. She returned, with her baby, to her parents' home where she completed almost two years of college before meeting Megan's stepfather, a long-distance trucker. That marriage was fairly short-lived. By the time Megan was eight, she and her mom were on their own again, although Megan still had a relationship with her stepfather, whom she called "dad." At the time of the therapy, Mrs. D. and Megan were living with Mrs. D.'s boyfriend, a man twelve years her junior, an electrician with steady work and an easygoing disposition. Mrs. D. had worked for a while in the office of a non-profit social welfare organization, but had been laid off when money got tight. She was trying to start up a home business, doing proofreading and editing. She also wanted to try her hand at writing children's books, but so far hadn't had any luck with publishing. The family's financial status had been precarious, until they moved in with the current boyfriend. Now they were doing better.

Mrs. D. was an old hand at psychotherapy. She had had marital therapy with her husband, and then had stayed on by herself after they split up. Since that time, she had gone back from time to time for help with "depression" and "finding a direction for my life." She wondered if Megan might be depressed.

Mrs. D. was shocked to hear the psychologist's assessment of Megan's condition. Megan did not have signs or symptoms of clinical depression, he said. Rather, she had classic symptoms of Attention Deficit-Hyperactivity Disorder, Inattentive Type. If Megan was depressed, it was in reaction to her school failure, rather than the other way around.

Mrs. D. protested: Megan wasn't hyper at all. She had seen children with ADHD at the agency at which she had worked and Megan wasn't like them at all. Those children couldn't sit still, they got in trouble at school, they had no friends—or at least no well-behaved friends. Megan never got in trouble and she had terrific friends. However, as the psychologist explained about inattention, and educated Megan and her mother about the behavioral criteria for the disorder, Mrs. D. began to warm to the idea. She had had no idea that ADHD might occur without hyperactivity and impulsivity, but Megan certainly had all the signs of inattention and disorganization. Once Mrs. D. was onboard, treatment planning could begin in earnest.

The first order of business was to educate Megan's educators about her diagnosis and her educational needs. This was not an easy job. Like Mrs. D., the teachers had seen a lot of ADHD, and they didn't think Megan fit the bill. They didn't really accept the diagnosis but they did agree to cooperate with the plan the psychologist had devised. This involved the following elements:

1 Megan would be evaluated by her pediatrician for a medication trial.
2 Megan's teachers would participate in using a "runaround sheet" detailing Megan's assignments, and whether they had been turned in, on a daily basis.
3 Megan's mother agreed to review the sheet each evening. If Megan lost it or forgot to bring it home, they would both go to school the following morning and stop at each individual teacher's to make up a new one and to get the information from the preceding day. (Megan didn't like this part of the plan at all!)
4 At the end of each week in which the runaround sheet had been brought home, filled out, and homework done, Megan received a gift certificate. (She *did* like this part.) There was no reward for a partial week, but no punishment for missed days, except having her mother go to school with her the next morning.

The hardest part of the plan, was getting Mrs. D. to do her part consistently. During the first two months, there were lots of errors and omissions. Mrs. D. sometimes forgot to check the runaround sheet and homework. Sometimes, when Megan failed to bring it home, Mrs. D. was too tired or too busy to go to school the next morning. Sometimes Megan forgot to get the teachers to sign it, and sometimes the teachers forgot as well.

Through it all, the psychologist urged consistency, and sometimes took steps to help achieve it. For example, he arranged for the school to designate a "lead teacher" who would be the liaison from the teachers to Mrs. D. and himself. If there were problems with the plan, the lead teacher was responsible for solving the school's end of it. He played the role of competent parent with Mrs. D., even as he taught her to play it with Megan. In addition, he spent time with Megan, helping her learn organizational "tricks of the trade" as he put it, and joined her in taking pleasure in each small success she attained. He worked on repairing her damaged self-image and gradually she began to give up her rationalizations about not needing school. She began to prepare to attend college as a music and drama major.

At the same time, several medications were tried and discarded until one was found that seemed to help Megan concentrate without having undesirable side effects. Despite Mrs. D.'s profound distrust of medicating her child for presumed attentional problems, even she had to admit that it did seem to make a difference. Megan's room was neater, she lost far fewer things, and she actually seemed happier overall.

Megan did not fail eighth grade, as it turned out. It couldn't be said that she passed with flying colors, but she did pass. Over the summer, Megan convinced her mother that she would not need the runaround sheet in ninth grade, but her grades during the first marking period indicated that she did, indeed, continue to need the structure provided by immediate feedback. So the loathed sheets were reinstituted, with the promise that if Megan could keep her grades above 80 for two marking periods in a row, they would be discontinued. This didn't happen until the end of tenth grade, but by then she had amassed an impressive wardrobe with her earned gift certificates.

Megan's therapy continued, although at greatly reduced frequency throughout high school. She didn't really need the sessions anymore, but she had come to count on the listening ear and nonjudgmental advice of the psychologist as she might a favored uncle. Her mother felt that this was valuable enough, given the lack of consistent adult males in Megan's life, to continue. Megan had appointments monthly, and occasionally corresponded with the therapist by e-mail until she went off to college. Her future in show business is not yet known.

Thinking About the Case

Youngsters like Megan are struggling with school throughout the Western world. Their parents, teachers, and peers tend to think of them as lazy, dreamers, willful, or just plain dumb. Rarely are they identified as having attentional problems, or as needing services, even when their report card repeats, year after year, "doesn't pay attention in class." Children who don't make trouble don't get noticed.

While Attention Deficit-Hyperactivity Disorder has been identified for many years, its name and definition has undergone some changes. Previously known only as Attention Deficit Disorder (ADD), it was thought always to include hyperactivity. However, it has become clear that attentional deficits can occur with or without hyperactivity. Thus, the disorder is now broken down into three subtypes: Combined Type (attentional and hyperactive symptoms are equally prominent), Predominantly Inattentive Type, and Predominantly Hyperactive-Impulsive Type. In each case, symptoms of the disorder must have been present by age 7 and must produce impairment in at least two settings (school/work, and home, for example). The diagnosis requires that there must be "clear evidence of clinically significant impairment," probably as a response to the charge that ADHD is overdiagnosed and overtreated with medicine.

Megan meets the criteria for ADHD, Predominantly Inattentive Type. She is disorganized in the extreme, easily distracted in school, and unable to complete assignments. She loses things and is forgetful. She can not bring herself to attend to boring tasks like homework. The impairment is clearly clinically significant in that she is failing eighth grade.

Part of what confuses parents and educators alike is that these youngsters seem to be able to attend adequately "when it suits them." They can play video games for long periods of time, for example. However, one of the diagnostic criteria reads "often avoids, dislikes, or is reluctant to engage in tasks that require sustained mental effort (such as school or homework)." Thus, the motivational problem is actually part of the diagnosis itself. These youngsters are far from "lazy" when something engages their attention, but boring, repetitive tasks are impossible for them. They may want to stay focused, but they cannot will themselves to do so. Pretty soon, like Megan, they begin to rationalize: "I don't really care anyway, school is stupid, I have better things to do."

Like Michael in the previous case, Megan's innate intelligence kept her in the game through elementary school. However as requirements for independent work, self-motivation, and organizational skills increased in junior high school, she began to falter. However, unlike Michael, she had more to fall back on. While Michael's hyperactivity and impulsivity had made him a negative stimulus for people around him, Megan was well-liked. Also, she had stayed in the same school system throughout her childhood so her educators were reasonably motivated to cooperate with her mother in putting a plan in place. The psychologist was willing to function as a case manager, keeping all the players motivated and doing their part. The clinical picture was not complicated by drugs and alcohol as it was with Michael. Megan's medical care was more consistent: no one was sabotaging the treatment plan as Michael's father had done. All of these differences lead to a difference in prognosis: Megan's chances of life success are far superior to Michael's.

Questions to Consider

1. ADHD tends to run in families. What evidence is there that Megan's mom might have similar problems? What questions might you ask Mrs. D. to help you decide? What might you do about it, if anything, if you were to discover that Mrs. D. also had attentional problems severe enough to warrant the diagnosis?

2. Do you think Megan's career goal of being a musician or actress will be significantly hampered by her ADHD? Why or why not? What sorts of careers might a person with ADHD be ill-suited for? What careers might he or she do well in?
3. Design a school tailored to the needs of youngsters with ADHD. How would children with normal attentional processes fare in your school?

CASE 7

TOURETTE'S DISORDER: A SURGEON'S LIFE

What follows is an account by the late neurologist Oliver Sacks of a Canadian surgeon who is virtually consumed by compulsive tics of all sorts—except when he is operating. Sack's two books, The Man Who Mistook His Wife for a Hat, *and* An Anthropologist on Mars, *are highly readable and full of accounts of strange and wonderful neurological anomalies: intellectually disabled individuals who can play complex sonatas on the piano, an autistic woman who designs cattle enclosures, people who can understand words but not facial expressions, a man with no memory. Read them if you get a chance, but in the meantime, imagine what it would be like to be operated on by Dr. Carl Bennett.*

I FIRST MET DR. CARL BENNETT at a scientific conference on Tourette's in Boston. His appearance was unexceptionable—he was fiftyish, of middle size, with a brownish beard and mustache containing a hint of gray, and was dressed soberly in a dark suit—until he suddenly lunged or reached for the ground or jumped or jerked. I was struck both by his bizarre tics and by his dignity and calm. When I expressed incredulity about his choice of profession, he invited me to visit and stay with him, where he lived and practiced, in the town of Branford, in British Columbia—to do rounds at the hospital with him, to scrub with him, to see him in action. Now, four months later, in early October, I found myself in a small plane approaching Branford, full of curiosity and mixed expectations. Dr. Bennett met me at the airport, greeted me—a strange greeting, half lunge, half tic, a gesture of welcome idiosyncratically Tourettized—grabbed my case, and led the way to his car in an odd, rapid skipping walk, with a skip each fifth step and sudden reachings to the ground as if to pick something up. . . .

When Bennett first came to Branford, he was regarded, he thought, with a certain suspicion. "A surgeon who twitches! Who needs him? What next?" There were no patients at first, and he did not know if he could make it there, but gradually he won the town's affection and respect. His practice began to expand, and his colleagues, who had initially been startled and incredulous, soon came to trust and accept him, too, and to bring him fully into the medical community. "But enough said," he concluded as we returned to the house. It was almost dark now, and the lights of Branford were twinkling. "Come to the hospital tomorrow—we have a conference at seven-thirty. Then I'll do outpatients and rounds on my patients. And Friday I operate—you can scrub with me." . . .

In the doctor's common room, Bennett was clearly very much at ease with his colleagues, and they with him. One sign of this ease, paradoxically, was that he felt free to Tourette with them—to touch or tap them gently with his fingertips, or, on two occasions when he was sharing a sofa, to suddenly twist on his side and tap his colleague's shoulder with his toes—a practice I had observed in other Touretters. Bennett is somewhat cautious with his Tourettisms on first acquaintance and conceals or downplays them until he gets to know people. When he first started working at the hospital, he told me, he would skip in the corridors only after checking to be sure that no one was looking; now when he skips or hops no one gives it a second glance.

The conversations in the common room were like those in any hospital—doctors talking among themselves about unusual cases. Bennett himself, lying half-curled on the floor, kicking and thrusting one foot in the air, described an unusual case of neurofibromatosis—a young man whom he had recently operated on. His colleagues listened attentively. The abnormality of the behavior and the complete normality of the discourse formed an extraordinary contrast. There was something bizarre about the whole scene, but it was evidently so common as to be unremarkable and no longer attracted the slightest notice. But an outsider seeing it would have been stunned.

After coffee and muffins, we repaired to the surgical-outpatients department, where half a dozen patients awaited Bennett. The first was a trail guide from Banff, very western in plaid shirt, tight jeans, and cowboy hat. His horse had fallen and rolled on top of him, and he had developed an immense pseudocyst of the pancreas. Bennett spoke with the man—who said the swelling was diminishing—and gently, smoothly palpated the fluctuant mass in his abdomen. He checked the sonograms with the radiologist—they confirmed the cyst's recession—and then came back and reassured the patient. "It's going down by itself. It's shrinking nicely—

you won't be needing surgery after all. You can get back to riding. I'll see you in a month." And the trail guide, delighted, walked off with a jaunty step. Later, I had a word with the radiologist. "Bennett's not only a whiz at diagnosis," he said. "He's the most compassionate surgeon I know."

The next patient was a heavy woman with a melanoma on her buttock, which needed to be excised at some depth. Bennett scrubbed up, donned sterile gloves. Something about the sterile field, the prohibition, seemed to stir his Tourette's; he made sudden darting motions, or incipient motions, of his sterile, gloved right hand toward the ungloved, unwashed, "dirty" part of his left arm. The patient eyed this without expression. What did she think, I wondered, of this odd darting motion, and the sudden convulsive shakings he also made with his hand? She could not have been entirely surprised, for her G.P. must have prepared her to some extent, must have said, "You need a small operation. I recommend Dr. Bennett—he's a wonderful surgeon. I have to tell you that he sometimes makes strange movements and sounds—he has a thing called Tourette's syndrome—but don't worry, it doesn't matter. It never affects his surgery."

Now, the preliminaries over, Bennett got down to the serious work, swabbing the buttocks with an iodine antiseptic and then injecting local anesthetic, with an absolutely steady hand. But as soon as the rhythm of action was broken for a moment—he needed more local, and the nurse held out the vial for him to refill his syringe—there was once again the darting and near-touching. The nurse did not bat an eyelid; she had seen it before and knew he would not contaminate his gloves. Now, with a firm hand, Bennett made an oval incision an inch to either side of the melanoma, and in forty seconds he had removed it, along with a Brazil-nut-shaped wedge of fat and skin. "It's out!" he said. Then, very rapidly, with great dexterity, he sewed the margins of the wound together, putting five neat knots on each nylon stitch. The patient, twisting her head, watched him as he sewed and joshed him: "Do you do all the sewing at home?"

He laughed. "Yes. All except the socks. But no one darns socks these days."

She looked again. "You're making quite a quilt."

The whole operation completed in less than three minutes, Bennett cried, "Done! Here's what we took." He held the lump of flesh before her.

"Ugh!" she exclaimed, with a shudder. "Don't show me. But thanks anyway."

All this looked highly professional from beginning to end, and, apart from the dartings and near-touchings, non-Tourettic. But I couldn't decide about Bennett's showing the excised lump to the patient. ("Here!") One may show a gallstone to a patient, but does one show a bleeding, misshapen piece of fat and flesh? Clearly, she didn't want to see it, but Bennett wanted to show it, and I wondered if this urge was part of his Tourettic scrupulosity and exactitude, his need to have everything looked at and understood. I had the same thought later in the morning, when he was seeing an old lady in whose bile duct he had inserted a T-tube. He went to great lengths to draw the tube, to explain all the anatomy, and the old lady said, "I don't want to know it. Just do it!"

Was this Bennett the Touretter being compulsive or Professor Bennett the lecturer on anatomy? (He gives weekly anatomy lectures in Calgary.) Was it simply an expression of his meticulousness and concern? An imagining, perhaps, that all patients shared his curiosity and love of detail? Some patients doubtless did, but obviously not these. . . .

Friday is operating day for Bennett, and he was scheduled to do a mastectomy. I was eager to join him, to see him in action. Outpatients are one thing—one can always concentrate for a few minutes—but how would he conduct himself in a lengthy and difficult procedure demanding intense, unremitting concentration, not for seconds or minutes, but for hours?

Bennett preparing for the operating room was a startling sight. "You should scrub next to him," his young assistant said. "It's quite an experience." It was indeed, for what I saw in the outpatient clinic was magnified here: constant sudden dartings and reachings with the hands, almost but never quite touching his unscrubbed, unsterile shoulder, his assistant, the mirror; sudden lungings, and touchings of his colleagues with his feet; and a barrage of vocalizations—"Hooty-hooo! Hooty-hooo!"—suggestive of a huge owl.

The scrubbing over, Bennett and his assistant were gloved and gowned, and they moved to the patient, already anesthetized, on the table. They looked briefly at a mammogram on the X-ray box. Then Bennett took the knife, made a bold, clear incision—there was no hint of any ticcing or distraction—and moved straightaway into the rhythm of the operation. Twenty minutes passed, fifty, seventy, a hundred. The operation was often complex—vessels to be tied, nerves to be found—but the action was confident, smooth, moving forward at its own pace, with never the slightest hint of Tourette's. Finally, after two and a half hours of the most complex, taxing surgery, Bennett closed up, thanked everybody, yawned, and stretched. Here, then, was an entire operation without a trace of Tourette's. Not because it had been suppressed, or held in—there was never any sign of control or constraint—but because, simply, there was never any impulse to tic. "Most of the time when I'm operating, it never even crosses my mind that I have Tourette's," Bennett says. His whole identity at such times is that of a surgeon at work, and his entire psychic and neural organization becomes aligned with this, becomes active, focused, at ease, un-Tourettic. It is only if the operation is broken for a few minutes—to review a special X-ray taken during the surgery, for example—that Bennett, waiting, unoccupied, remembers that he *is* Tourettic, and in that instant he becomes so. As soon as the flow of the operation resumes, the Tourette's, the Tourettic identity, vanishes once again. Bennett's assistants, though they have known him and worked with him for years, are still astounded whenever they see this. "It's like a miracle," one of them said. "The way the Tourette's disappears." And Bennett himself was astonished, too, and quizzed me, as he peeled off his gloves, on the neurophysiology of it all. . . .

Friday afternoon is open. Bennett often likes to go for long hikes on Fridays, or cycle rides, or drives, with a sense of the trail, the open road, before him. There is a favorite ranch he loves to go to, with a beautiful lake and an airstrip, accessible only via a rugged dirt road. It is a wonderfully situated ranch, a narrow fertile strip perfectly placed between the lake and mountains, and we walked for miles, talking of this and that, with Bennett botanizing or geologizing as we went. Then, briefly, we went to the lake, where I took a swim; when I came out of the water I found that Bennett, rather suddenly, had curled up for a nap. He looked peaceful, tension-free, as he slept; and the suddenness and depth of his sleep made me wonder how much difficulty he encountered in the daytime, whether he might not sometimes be stressed to the limit. I wondered how much he concealed beneath his genial surface—how much, inwardly, he had to control and deal with.

Later, as we continued our ramble about the ranch, he remarked that I had seen only some of the outward expressions of his Tourette's, and these, bizarre as they occasionally seemed, were by no means the worst problems it caused him. The real problems, the inner problems, are panic and rage—feelings so violent that they threaten to overwhelm him, and so sudden that he has virtually no warning of their onset. He has only to get a parking ticket or see a police car, sometimes, for scenarios of violence to flash through his mind: mad chases, shoot-outs, flaming destructions, violent mutilation, and death scenarios that become immensely elaborated in seconds and rush through his mind with convulsive speed. One part of him, uninvolved, can watch these scenes with detachment, but another part of him is taken over and impelled to action. He can prevent himself from giving way to outbursts in public, but the strain of controlling himself is severe and exhausting. At home, in private, he can let himself go—not at others but at inanimate objects around him. There was the wall I had seen, which he had often struck in his rage, and the refrigerator, at which he had flung virtually everything in the kitchen. In his office, he had kicked a hole in the wall and had had to put a plant in front to cover it; and in his study at home the cedar walls were covered with knife marks. "It's not gentle," he said to me. "You can see it as whimsical, funny—be tempted to romanticize it—but Tourette's comes from deep down in the nervous system and the unconscious. It taps into the oldest, strongest feelings we have. Tourette's is like an epilepsy in the subcortex; when it takes over, there's just a thin line of control, a thin line of cortex, between you and it, between you and that raging storm, the blind force of the subcortex. One can see the charming things, the funny things, the creative side of Tourette's, but there's also that dark side. You have to fight it all your life." . . .

It is difficult for Bennett, and is often difficult for Touretters, to see their Tourette's as something external to themselves, because many of its tics and urges may be felt as intentional, as an integral part of the self, the personality, the will. It is quite different, by contrast, with something like parkinsonism or chorea: these have no quality of selfness or intentionality and are always fatal as diseases, as outside the self. Compulsions and tics occupy an intermediate position, seeming sometimes to be an expression of one's personal will, sometimes a coercion of it by another, alien will. These ambiguities are often expressed in the terms people use. Thus the separateness of "it" and "I" is sometimes expressed by jocular personifications of the Tourette's: one Touretter I know calls his Tourette's "Toby," another "Mr. T." By contrast, a Tourettic possession of the self was vividly expressed by one young man in Utah, who wrote to me that he had a "Tourettized soul."

Thinking About the Case

Tourette's, named after its discoverer, the Frenchman Gilles de la Tourette, used to be nicknamed "the cursing disease" because many of its sufferers were plagued by the uncontrollable urge to curse or blaspheme, much to their own shame and embarrassment. Emerging generally before the age of fourteen, and three times more prevalent in boys than in girls, Tourette's syndrome typically involves uncontrollable head movements, accompanied by sounds, such as grunts, yelps, clicks, or words. Dr. Bennett's symptoms are particularly severe, including, as they do, movements of the limbs and torso as well as the head.

A generation ago, Tourette's was thought to represent a deep-seated psychological problem with managing hostility, and some of Dr. Bennett's experiences seem to support this hypothesis, but recent evidence suggests that the disorder is primarily neurological in origin. Perhaps the part of the brain that generates and modulates anger plays some role in Tourette's.

Still, as Sack's description makes clear, there are psychological aspects to the disorder. For one thing, why are certain words, often those which are socially unacceptable, "chosen" for tics and not others? Why are Tourette's patients often obsessively attentive to detail and order? What are the factors that make some tics feel like part of the self while others feel alien? Why are tics worse when the individual is tired or anxious? Answers to these questions are likely to come from the "psychological" rather than the "neurological" domain, if, indeed, such distinctions have real meaning after all.

Modern treatment for Tourette's is primarily biological. Medication often helps decrease the frequency and intensity of tics. Supportive psychotherapy and patient education can help the person cope with the impact the disorder may have on self-esteem and life goals. Reading about Tourette's or joining a self-help mutual support group may be of value to the individual and family.

Many tic disorders are less complicated than Tourette's, may have more situationally specific symptoms, and may yield to one or another form of behavioral therapy. One such therapy directs the person to repeat the tic behavior over and over. While this procedure often does decrease the frequency of the problem, it is not clear what mechanism is responsible. Perhaps the response satiates, or perhaps it is brought under voluntary control by repeated practice. General anxiety reduction strategies (like relaxation training or meditation) and even assertiveness training can be useful in the treatment of simple tics.

Questions to Consider

1. What personality characteristics would lead a person with Tourette's to become a surgeon? Assuming Dr. Bennett's Tourette's disorder emerged in childhood, as most do, what factors in his character or environment could account for his unusual success?
2. Tourette's disorder often co-occurs with obsessive-compulsive disorder. It is also associated with various learning disabilities and with attention deficit hyperactivity disorder (although the medication used to treat ADHD makes Tourette's worse). What do you make of all this?
3. Some people question the inclusion of neurocognitive disorders like Tourette's, dementia, and delirium in the DSM-5. How do you think we should set the boundary between psychological and neurological disorders? Or, is a boundary necessary at all?

LANAHAN NOTES

Neurodevelopmental Disorders

General characteristics

First manifest in childhood or adolescence

Involve impaired functioning in personal, social, academic or occupational functioning

Tend to be severely incapacitating, lifelong with varying degrees of impairment

The neurodevelopmental disorders often co-occur

Treatment

Community-based treatment and normalization

Behavioral techniques, special education, and parent consultation

Medications to treat symptoms

Major neurodevelopmental disorders

Intellectual Disabilities

Causes

Biological: prenatal etiologies (genetic syndromes, brain malformations)

Perinatal: complications during labor and/or delivery

Postnatal: infections, seizure disorders

Environmental: teratogens such as alcohol, other drugs or toxins (lead, mercury); severe and chronic social deprivation

Types of diagnoses (includes deficits in both intellectual functions and adaptive functioning)

Mild: the individual may function age-appropriately in personal care but need support with complex daily living; difficulty in perceiving peers' social cues; concrete and/or immature in communication and regulating emotions

Moderate: the individual can care for most personal needs with extended period of teaching; social judgment and decision-making abilities limited; some communication but much less complex than that of their peers

Severe: the individual requires support for all activities; cannot make responsible decisions regarding well-being of self or others; language may be single words or phrases; family and other relationships can be a source of pleasure and help

Profound: the individual is dependent on others for physical care, health, and safety; very limited language aside from simple instructions or gestures; limited speech

Communication Disorders

Language disorder: persistent difficulties in the acquisition and use of language across modalities such as spoken, written, sign language due to deficits in comprehension or production

Speech sound disorder: persistent difficulty with speech sound production

Childhood-Onset Fluency Disorder (Stuttering): disturbances in the normal fluency and time patterning of speech

Social (pragmatic) communication disorder: persistent difficulty in the social use of verbal and nonverbal communication; deficits in using communication for social purposes

Autism Spectrum Disorder

DSM-5 includes previously referred to disorders as early infantile autism, childhood autism, Kanner's autism, high-functioning autism, atypical autism, pervasive developmental disorder, childhood disintegrative disorder, and Asperger's disorder

Prevalence about 1% of the population

Symptoms

Typically recognized by the second year of life

Persistent deficits in social communication and social interactions, including social-emotional reciprocity (reduced sharing of interests/emotions, back-and-forth conversation); nonverbal communicative behaviors (eye contact/body language/expressiveness); developing/maintaining/understanding social relationships (imaginative play, making friends, interest in others)

Restricted, repetitive patterns of behavior, interests, or activities, including repetitive motor movements; insistence on sameness, inflexible adherence to routines; highly restricted, fixated interactions abnormal in their intensity or focus

Hyper- or hypo reactivity to sensory input

Severity ranges from requiring some support for problems of organization and planning to very substantial support in all spheres of daily living

Attention-deficit-hyperactivity disorder

Characterized by inattentive behavior (careless mistakes, lack of focus, organizational difficulties, distractions) and/or

Hyperactivity/impulsivity symptoms (fidgeting, excessive talking, interruptions, difficulty waiting)

Symptoms manifest before the age of 12 years and are present in more than one setting

Prevalence rates: about 5% of children and 2.5% of adults

ADHD is seen as a developmental disorder where motoric hyperactivity becomes less obvious in adolescence and adulthood, but other symptoms (inattention, poor planning, impulsivity) persist

Tends to run in families.

Treated with a combination of stimulant medication and behavioral therapy

Tic Disorders

Tourette's Disorders: multiple motor and one or more vocal tics of varying degree

---

Source for all of the Lanahan Notes: (2013) *Diagnostic and Statistical Manual of Mental Disorders, 5th Edition: DSM-5*. Arlington, VA: American Psychiatric Association.

CHAPTER THREE

Schizophrenia Spectrum and Other Psychotic Disorders

Most of us rely on our ability to distinguish what is real from what is not. We know the difference between our thoughts and others' voices, between our fantasies and real lives. Only in our dreams do we get a hint of what it feels like to experience the world as a person with a psychotic condition might—as bizarre, fragmented, incomprehensible.

The disorders covered in this chapter are some, but not all, of the conditions in which the sufferer cannot, at least at times, tell what is real. He or she may hear, see, smell, touch, or taste things in the absence of appropriate sensory stimulation. Or the sufferer may have thoughts or ideas that don't match reality—perhaps the radio is sending him special messages, or maybe she thinks the psychology professor is really a CIA agent sent to spy on certain students in the class.

Historically, the psychoses have been separated diagnostically into those with known organic origins from those without. Drug abuse, brain injury, and various medical conditions can induce psychotic symptoms. A case later in the book (Case #42) describes a young man who developed a brief psychosis as a consequence of drug use. But these syndromes are not the focus of this chapter. Instead, we deal here with the group of disorders that used to be called the "functional psychoses," meaning that specific organic origins could not be found. Included are schizophrenia as well as "functional" delusional disorders.

Schizophrenia is by far the most disabling, and most stigmatizing of all the psychological disorders. People think of schizophrenia as being "split personality" which it is not. People think of individuals with schizophrenia as being invariably dangerous, which they are not. In fact, they are more likely to be victimized than victimizer. People think of schizophrenia as being caused by faulty parenting, which it is not. While the environment (not just the parents) can play a role in the timing and prognosis of psychotic episodes, biochemical factors have also been implicated in the etiology of the disease. People think of schizophrenia as being rare, which it is not. Instead, schizophrenia is one of the most common and expensive of all psychological disorders. It is diagnosed in as many as one out of every hundred Americans (but striking twice as often in Scandinavia and four times as often in western Ireland, for reasons as yet unknown). A large number of people in the United States are diagnosed with schizophrenia, at a cost to society estimated between ten and twenty billion dollars a year in treatment costs, disability and welfare payments, and lost wages. And, since schizophrenia tends to strike in late adolescence or early young adulthood, the emotional costs to individuals and families who must give up or at least adjust their hopes, dreams, and aspirations are incalculable.

In this chapter, we include three cases. The first looks at the course of treatment for a young man who was progressing well in life when he developed acute symptoms of schizophrenia. The second follows the story of a young man whose illness developed gradually, and was complicated by drug and alcohol abuse. Both of these are common patterns in schizophrenia. The third case is fascinating in that a man's longstanding delusional disorder is only discovered and diagnosed in the context of his daughter's mental health treatment.

CASE 8

SCHIZOPHRENIA IN A YOUNG ADULT: THE CASE OF STEVE M.

STEVE M.'S TROUBLES BEGAN when he was a nineteen-year-old college freshman. He was a handsome and engaging young man, the second in a family of four boys. Steve's high school career had been, by any measure, successful and satisfying. He had earned letters in both football and track, had served as co-editor of the student newspaper, and had been elected president of his senior class. With high grades and SAT scores, Steve earned a place in one of the finest colleges.

Still, Steve's early life was not without tragedy. When he was four, his mother, who had had a long history of troubled behavior, committed suicide by hanging herself in the attic. Only Steve and his younger brothers were home at the time, and they found her body when they woke up from their afternoon nap. Steve's father, an attorney, struggled valiantly to provide both financially and emotionally for his traumatized sons, but, in truth, he had been severely shaken himself. Already accustomed to a cocktail in the evening after work, he began to drink more heavily after the loss of his wife and, even though he remarried four years later, he became a quiet, withdrawn alcoholic. His new wife found herself in complete charge of the household and threw herself into the task with diligence. She was determined to make up to the children and their father for the loss the family had incurred. She believed firmly that with devotion and time, she could heal the wounds. Sure enough, the children seemed to thrive under her loving and watchful eye. She was impressed by how they seemed to bounce back from the loss of their mother. If their father was still distant and uninvolved, at least he worked steadily and provided an income which allowed her to tend to the needs of the family. Mr. M. clearly loved the children, but he interacted with them only intermittently, and then with wry, intellectualized banter.

Steve did well the first semester at college, although he came home frequently to visit his girlfriend and to see his parents. He wished he could find a way to relate more genuinely to his father, but had long since accepted that this was unlikely to happen. Occasionally they fished together, or discussed the course material he was studying in philosophy, but for emotional support he always went to his stepmother.

At the beginning of the second semester, Steve's girlfriend, with whom he had been going steady since junior year of high school, broke up with him. He appeared to take the news reasonably well and began staying at school on weekends in order to begin to date. Still, in private, he found himself lonely and miserable. He really didn't know how to ask women out and didn't seem to have the knack for flirting or reading their nonverbal signals.

One day, while studying in his room, Steve had a strange sensation. He felt an ominous presence of some sort, a premonition that something dangerous was afoot. The feeling stayed with him for some hours and then it passed, but a few days later, in the cafeteria, he felt it again. This time, he looked around, and saw a knot of students across the room who seemed to be looking at him and smiling. He thought he heard one of them say, "he's queer." He couldn't understand why they would think such a thing about him—they didn't even know him. Visibly upset, he left quickly and went back to his room.

Later that week, in psychology class, his professor referred to a laboratory experiment, and suddenly Steve had a flash of insight. He understood that he, himself, was the subject of the experiment, and that his professor was trying to warn him that he was in danger. Still, he didn't know what kind of experiment he was in, nor why he had been chosen. As the class conversation continued, he began to detect hidden meaning in the remarks of the male students. The female students seemed blithely unaware of the plot against him.

Over the next week, Steve became increasingly vigilant, and increasingly agitated. He heard hints about the experiment in the songs broadcast by the student radio station. His preoccupation was so severe that he was unable to study effectively. His sleep was fitful and restless. His appetite was nonexistent—in truth, he was afraid to eat in the cafeteria, because he was beginning to feel that the food he was served had been laced with chemicals related to the experiment. He noticed that people would invariably stop what they were doing and give him strange looks as he passed them in the hall. Even his good friends began to shun him. Sometimes, in desperation, he tried to ask for help by code—using the first letter of each word he said to mean something else, but the few people he still trusted didn't seem to understand.

Finally, terrified and desperate, he decided to contact the professor who had tried to warn him. He looked up his home address in the campus directory and then, at two A.M., when no one would suspect him of being out, he broke into the professor's bedroom crying and pleading for help. The professor, who couldn't understand anything Steve was saying, was badly frightened. While trying to calm Steve, he called the campus police who took Steve to the emergency room of the local hospital for a psychiatric evaluation. Within hours, Steve was admitted to the hospital's psychiatric wing where he was administered a sedative, so that he could get some rest, and an antipsychotic medication, which, it was hoped, would lessen his delusions.

Steve was hospitalized for two-and-a-half weeks. During that time he was given medication on a daily basis. He also participated in individual therapy and group therapy. In these settings he discussed his loneliness and his grief at losing his girlfriend. He developed some plans for meeting girls and did some role playing to rehearse how he might start conversations. At the same time, his parents had a consultation with the hospital social worker, who provided a tentative diagnosis—schizophreniform disorder. This meant that Steve had a psychotic break that might signal the beginning of schizophrenia, but only time would tell. They had many questions about whether Steve should return to school, how long he would have to take medication, and what his prognosis might be, and the social worker tried to answer them as best he could. Still, they felt his answers had been frighteningly vague.

Gradually, Steve's delusions began to recede. His mood brightened and he started to take better care of himself. By the end of his hospitalization, he wondered where he could have gotten all those "crazy ideas." He was embarrassed, but eager to return to school and pick up where he'd left off. Despite the recommendation of the treatment team that he take a few courses at first rather than a full load, Steve chose to resume his formerly busy schedule. He did agree, however, to continue taking the medication to treat the chemical imbalance he was told he had, despite the fact that it made him feel sleepy and somewhat "fuzzy" in the head. He also agreed to attend follow-up appointments at the local mental health clinic.

As it happens, Steve didn't keep his promises for long. He did return to school and tried hard to do what he had practiced in the hospital. He was finding it difficult, though, particularly since everyone appeared to know he had been in the psychiatric wing. His concentration seemed impaired, and he found that he had trouble following conversations. At the end of each day he was exhausted, and socializing seemed more trouble than it was worth.

He didn't like going to the mental health center, either. The waiting room was full of people who seemed "out of it." Most of them were a lot older than he was, too. The psychiatrist spent only a couple of minutes with him, asking him the same questions each time. She seemed pleasant enough but, in truth, not very interested. Steve didn't see why he had to take medicine that made him feel worse than he felt normally, nor why he had to go to a place where nothing therapeutic seemed to happen. After two months he stopped doing either, although he felt it best not to tell his parents about his decision. He knew they would worry, but he felt sure he could "make it" on his own.

For the next few weeks, Steve felt substantially better. His mind felt clearer and he had a lot more energy. His parents commented on how good he looked when they saw him, which wasn't frequently since he was determined to develop a social life at school. He pushed himself hard to ask young women out, and he had a date virtually every other night. This meant a lot of late night study sessions, since he wasn't willing to give up the high grades he was used to.

One evening a few months later, while studying, Steve again felt the familiar feeling of foreboding. This time, he distinctly heard someone say, "you think you've fooled us. You're queer." He looked around, but he was alone. He opened the door to the hall, but it, too, looked empty. From the other end of the hall, he heard, "he's a pig, look at him," but again, no one was there. Suddenly, he realized that the experiment he had feared had occurred while he was in the hospital. A transmitter had been implanted in his head through which he was receiving these messages. Someone wanted to drive him crazy!

Without waiting to put on shoes or socks, Steve ran out of the dormitory and down the street. He planned to confront the doctors in the hospital about what they had done. He ran the two miles to the hospital, threw open the emergency room doors, and tackled the first man in a lab coat he saw. Within an hour he was readmitted to the psychiatric wing.

Steve's diagnosis was changed to paranoid schizophrenia. This time it took longer for the voices and the delusions to recede. Larger doses of medication were needed. When he began to feel better, the doctor cautioned him that he had a formidable illness, a "chemical imbalance in the brain," and that his knowledgeable cooperation with treatment was essential to his remaining well. Rather than return to school immediately, he was advised to attend a day treatment center at the hospital for a few months.

Steve was badly shaken. He didn't know what he had done wrong. He couldn't really believe that there was something the matter with his brain. The idea that he couldn't trust his ears or his thoughts was terrifying. Besides, he retained a lingering fear that the plot was real and the doctors were lying to him. Still, his mother had been dreadfully ill. Maybe he was destined to follow in her footsteps. This was the most frightening thought of all.

It is now five years later. Steve has been hospitalized three more times. Each time he had stopped his medication, twice believing himself well and once, just tired of the whole thing. In between hospitalizations, he has spent some time in the day treatment program and some time taking classes at college. He still struggles with determining what is real and what is not, but he has learned that he can check this out with people he trusts, principally his stepmother, brother, and father. His self-esteem has been badly shaken, and he no longer has a clear idea what he might reasonably hope to accomplish in his life. Some days, just getting dressed and out of his apartment (which he now shares with two other young men from the day treatment program) is a monumental achievement.

Nonetheless, some gains have been made. Steve has developed a long-term therapy relationship with a psychologist from the clinic who he sees once a week (in addition to his medication checks with the psychiatrist). Together they confront the very real challenges that his illness and the stigma attached to it pose. He is learning to set short-term goals and to modify his expectations without altogether giving up hope. His parents, through the parent-support group they have joined, are learning to do the same. Steve has learned, through trial and error, that he needs the medication to keep the irrational ideas and the voices at bay. He doesn't like the side effects of muscle stiffness and diminished clarity of thinking, but he has decided that they are the lesser of two evils. The day treatment program provides practice in socializing and classes in stress management and in independent living. He doesn't feel he really belongs there, but he doesn't feel at home on campus either. His life, though nothing like what he and his family had envisioned for him a decade before, holds possibilities for mastery and satisfaction. Still, the illusion of security is gone forever.

Thinking About the Case

Approximately one out of every hundred persons develops schizophrenia in which the core features include loss of contact with reality as manifested by delusions, hallucinations, or gross disorganization, as well as severe dysfunction in virtually all areas of life. Like Steve, most of the sufferers become ill when they are in their late adolescent or young adult years. While the illness strikes men and women equally as often, women tend to develop the disorder, on average, ten years later than men. Schizophrenia is known in all cultures throughout the world and has been around for as long as we have written records available. Interestingly, its prognosis is somewhat better in less developed cultures than in the Western world.

Just fifty years ago, Steve might have spent the majority of his adult life in a mental hospital. As a result of more effective treatment methods and a treatment philosophy that emphasizes community-based care, most people with schizophrenia can now expect to spend only a small fraction of their time in inpatient care. A host of outpatient services have been designed to assist people with major mental illnesses to live as independently as possible. These include supervised housing alternatives, like community residences that might house eight or more recovering people in a house supervised around the clock by trained counselors, or smaller apartments like the one Steve lived in, with counselors who drop by on a regular basis and are available by phone anytime. Vocational training programs, shared jobs, special college programs, and sheltered workshops (which provide fairly simple, repetitive tasks and a very low wage) are designed to offer a range of occupational alternatives, depending upon the individual's ability to concentrate and motivation to work. Various psychotherapies, including individual, group, and family treatment are also part of most treatment plans. But the backbone of the plan, for the great majority of sufferers, is medication. While not without side effects, the antipsychotic medications, of which there are more than two dozen, provide a level of control over symptoms that is not otherwise available. Most patients could not function nearly as well, if at all, without them. New antipsychotic medicines are constantly under development and coming to market. And most patients need to take them for many years because, as Steve discovered, symptoms generally return when medication is stopped.

The short-term prognosis for schizophrenia is quite variable, but generally fairly grave. While some people seem to recover uneventfully, most, like Steve, find that their lives are profoundly changed. The cognitive and social deficits associated with schizophrenia make one's progress through the life tasks of early adulthood very challenging. For example, the inability to filter out extraneous stimuli makes attending to social or occupational tasks exceedingly difficult. Residual paranoia and distrust can interfere with developing relationships. The stigma and assault on one's sense of self engendered by having experienced a psychotic episode can erode a person's ability to function independently. Multiple hospitalizations are common, and goals generally need to be revised downward.

Interestingly, data are emerging to suggest that the long-term prognosis (twenty years and more) might be substantially better. Several studies, carried out in different countries, have indicated that well over half of study subjects who had been gravely ill with schizophrenia as young adults were functioning fairly well in their sixties and beyond. Many of these subjects had experienced prolonged hospitalizations which could be expected to further impair their ability to function in the community, but even these seemed to fare well in their later years. Still, schizophrenia is one of the most seriously disabling of all psychiatric conditions. Wasting thousands of lives and costing millions of dollars each year in lost wages and treatment costs, it is worthy of substantial attention in terms of public health research priorities.

Questions to Consider

1. What were the possible contributions of nature and nurture to the development of Steve's illness?
2. What do you imagine it might be like to return to campus after going through what Steve went through? What might you worry about? How might these worries affect your recovery prospects? What might your friends do that would be helpful to you? What could you do that would be helpful to yourself?
3. What hypotheses might you entertain to explain why the short-term prognosis for schizophrenia is far worse than the long-term prognosis? Can you design a study or experiment that could test one or more of your ideas?
4. What are some reasons why the age of risk of developing schizophrenia is different for women than for men? Consider both biological and social possibilities.
5. While schizophrenia is distributed equitably by gender, the same is not true for social class. Schizophrenia tends to be diagnosed far more often in the lower social classes than in the upper ones. Why might this be so?

CASE 9

CHRONIC SCHIZOPHRENIA: THE CASE OF LENNY D.

LENNY D. IS A FORTY-FOUR-YEAR-OLD single man. He lives in a home with seven other adults who suffer from mental illness. The home is staffed by mental health counselors twenty-four hours a day. Lenny has lived here for three years. This is his story:

Lenny is the oldest of two children born into an Italian-American family in a middle-sized city. His younger sister is married and has two children of her own. She rarely sees Lenny these days, except at holidays. She probably would not see him at all, except that it pacifies her mother whose most fervent hope is that her children will be friends to each other.

As a youngster, Lenny had lots of family around—aunts and uncles and cousins. His grandparents lived only two houses down the street so he saw them virtually every day. Lenny's parents had a boisterous but loving marriage. Occasional screaming battles would be followed, a few hours or days later, by furtive giggling and quiet nuzzling.

Lenny was a handful, his mother recalls. He was an active child—bright, but into everything and going a mile a minute. He wore her out, exasperated her husband, and overshadowed his little sister. He always had friends, but they tended to be vociferous boys like himself. At the Catholic school he attended, Lenny got pretty good grades in the early years, but his behavior wasn't always the best. Still, he was a likeable boy most of the time—friendly, helpful, generous, and affectionate. He could infuriate you, Mrs. D. said, but you could never be mad at him for long.

Lenny and his dad seemed to butt heads a lot. Both were stubborn, and both had volatile tempers. Still, they had one thing in common: sports. Lenny began playing softball and soccer in elementary school, and continued for a number of years . . . until the trouble with drugs started. Lenny's dad coached his son's soccer team for the first few years, then attended all Lenny's games, even taking time off from work to do so.

School didn't go as well as sports, though. Despite his parents' interest and involvement, Lenny's grades dropped gradually throughout his later elementary and junior high school years. He seemed to have trouble staying "on task" according to his teachers. In fifth grade, he was evaluated to see if he had attention deficit-hyperactivity disorder, but it appeared that his problems were not severe enough to justify a diagnosis. He was just a rowdy kid, said the nuns, who just didn't seem to want to apply himself.

Lenny's parochial school only went to grade nine, and Lenny was unable to pass the entrance exam for the Catholic high school, so he had to transfer to the local public high school when he was fifteen. It is safe to say that he experienced a pretty severe culture shock when he got there. Gradually, his parents saw a change in his appearance and behavior. No longer uniformed as he had been as a youngster, Lenny adopted the "punk" persona in high school, with its droopy pants, backward caps, and nonchalant attitude. He got an earring, which caused a major uproar with his father, and a few months later, a tattoo, which freaked everybody out—parents, grandparents, aunts and uncles, the whole clan.

Lenny became harder to hang on to. He started lying about where he was. His new friends covered for him, so catching him became harder and harder. His parents found cigarettes in his room, and more frightening, pipes and papers. When they confronted him, Lenny said that the paraphernalia weren't his: he was keeping all of it for a friend. He got grounded, but he snuck out . . . over and over again. And when he did come home, sometimes he was drunk. Other times his glassy eyes and vacant stare made it clear that he had been smoking pot.

Meanwhile, Lenny's parents' marriage was deteriorating. His father wanted to come down on Lenny hard, but his mother felt that this would only alienate him further. She wanted to take a softer approach. Mr. D. accused her of undermining his authority. She retorted that she wasn't going to let him bully Lenny. Their arguments got more heated. The time it took to make up got longer. The atmosphere at home became icy and charged.

By this time, Lenny was missing a substantial amount of school. Not surprisingly, he failed eleventh grade. Seventeen years old at the time, he decided to drop out of school. His parents were dismayed, but there was nothing they could do. Mr. D. insisted that Lenny get a job, though, and pay rent. Lenny went to work at the car wash but he got fired after a few weeks for missing work. He also worked at a laundramat, gas station, convenience store, and on an assembly line at the local produce canning factory. Always he got fired, usually after only a few weeks. He never paid rent. Nor did he pay for the car insurance, despite his promise. Mr. D. wanted to take away the car, but Mrs. D. argued that Lenny wouldn't be able to even try to work without transportation.

In May of what would have been Lenny's senior year of school his behavior began to deteriorate even further. He stopped socializing with his friends. While this change initially heartened his parents, it was accompanied by other changes that frightened and perplexed them. For one thing, Lenny's personal hygiene got a lot worse. He stopped showering, shaving, and brushing his teeth, and he was content to wear the same clothes day after day. He slept most of each day, rising at bedtime and wandering the house at night, listening to music, watching television, and smoking cigarettes. His appetite diminished and he began to lose weight. When his parents did see him, Lenny seemed preoccupied and jumpy. He got startled by the smallest noise or unexpected movement, stared intently out the window for long periods of time, and began to mumble to himself as if he were answering other voices that others could not hear. When his parents spoke to him, he either ignored them or yelled at them to shut up. Later, he would resume his "conversations." They didn't think he was still smoking pot, because he never left the house to get any, but they were frantic in the face of the changes they saw. Mrs. D. was sure that Lenny was sick and needed help. Mr. D. felt he needed a "kick in the pants to get him moving."

The "kick in the pants" came soon enough. One day Mr. D. had had enough. He grabbed hold of Lenny's arm to get him into the shower. Lenny went berserk, grabbed a glass bottle of aftershave and brought it down on his father's head. Lenny took off out of the house, half dressed, his father pursued him and his mother, hysterical, dialed 911. The melee ended with Lenny's admission to the psychiatric wing of the city hospital. It had taken three police officers to subdue the terrified and confused young man.

Despite their embarrassment, the D.'s were relieved by Lenny's hospitalization. At last he would get help. They expected that after a short time, he would be able to pick up his life where it had left off . . . before the drugs and before the breakdown. It took nearly two decades to fully dash these hopes.

What really happened was that Lenny spent the next fifteen years in and out of hospitals, drug treatment programs, outpatient mental health centers, and vocational training programs. When he was not living at a treatment center, he returned home to his parents. The pattern was always the same. First, Lenny would get stabilized on psychiatric medications and off street drugs. Then he'd come home. For a while he'd attend whatever outpatient program he'd been assigned to. Then, he'd start missing days and hanging out with his old crowd of loser friends. He'd complain that the medicine made him sleepy and contributed to his weight gain (a few pounds a month . . . month after month). He'd become more withdrawn, more irritable, and more irrational, again responding to inner voices and entertaining unrealistic ideas.

The behavior of Lenny's family members also fit a pattern. His mother would try to cajole and plead with him to cooperate with treatment, fixing his favorite foods as a bribe. She'd root through his room, throwing out whatever drug or paraphernalia she found. His father was distant and short-tempered. He tried to keep his mouth shut, although he frequently failed. His sister, now a high school senior herself, avoided Lenny like the plague. She spent virtually all of her time at school activities or at the homes of her friends. She was deeply ashamed of Lenny, furious at the suffering he had caused her parents, and didn't want to be associated with him at all if she could help it.

The cycle always ended with Lenny's rehospitalization, although the actual precipitants were many. Twice he threatened suicide; once he kicked his mother who he had found searching his room; once he showed up at the high school, threatening the principal who, he said, had ruined his life. Once he withdrew so severely that his ability to care for himself in the most basic ways was in doubt. At each hospitalization, his exhausted parents vowed that they couldn't go through this again, but each time he recovered and voiced the wish to come home, they found themselves unable to refuse. Who, after all, would turn away a sick child? It was unthinkable.

Finally, gradually, the unthinkable became thinkable. Lenny's parents knew intuitively that what they were doing at home wasn't helping. They had also begun to accept what they had denied for so long: Lenny might get better, but he was not going to get cured.

At this point in their journey, they accepted, reluctantly, a referral to a support group composed of relatives of people with mental illness, to whom they had been introduced by the hospital staff on one of Lenny's numerous admissions. They had put off getting involved with the group for a long time. For one thing, mental illness was shameful, and in their family, shame was kept secret from strangers. For another thing, they believed, maybe Lenny would get better on his own. Besides, everybody was different; how could anybody really understand what they were going through?

Surprisingly, they found that other parents had made very similar journeys, and listening to their experiences was enlightening. For example, while they had been told of the availability of supervised living circumstances for people like Lenny, it was only when they heard of the experiences of others in the support group that they began to feel that having Lenny live in such a place would not constitute abandonment, but might be a chance for him to learn to live more independently. Gently, other family members in the support group reminded them that they would not be around forever. They needed to turn over caregiving responsibilities to someone else at some point, and Lenny's sister was not willing to take the job. Another thing they learned was how to plan for possible relapse before it happened, how to intervene early, how to access services efficiently. They learned about something called "Assertive Community Treatment, (A.C.T.)" in which a team of mental health professionals could be assigned to Lenny, available twenty-four hours a day, and willing to come to where he lived rather than wait for him to come to services. They learned how to become adept at advocating for Lenny, to make sure he got the services he needed.

The learning was slow. Over the next five or six years, they figured out how to make the system work better for them. Interestingly, in the process they became less reactive to Lenny. Mrs. D. cajoled and pleaded less while Mr. D. lost his temper less often. They both came to understand, although not without resistance and sadness, that Lenny's condition was serious and chronic. He needed long-term support, not continuous crisis-intervention. While Lenny's condition improved as the stress at home abated, he still needed hospitalizations from time to time. His parents, aging as we all do, began to realize that they wouldn't be able to take care of him forever.

Finally, three years ago, following yet another hospitalization, they refused to take Lenny home. They insisted that he accept transfer to a community residence, instead. Reluctantly, he did. While he required brief rehospitalization twice in the first eighteen months, he was accepted back into the residence at each discharge. He has not been hospitalized at all in the last year and a half. He finally seems to have settled in fairly comfortably. He has a daily routine: he takes a long walk to the coffee shop while listening to music on his walkman. At the coffee shop, where he has become a "regular," he talks with the clerk and a few of the other patrons for a bit, then walks home. After lunch, he takes a nap and plays a game of chess or checkers with one of his housemates. After dinner, he watches television and goes to bed early. He sees his parents almost every weekend. He goes out for dinner with them or comes to their house for brunch. He spends holidays with them.

Lenny still has symptoms: he talks to his voices, but quietly, and mostly when he is alone. He is sometimes restless at night and during these times he helps the night staff person do laundry and prepare food for the next day. He is not able to work, or even to attend a day program. Being around other people for any length of time seems to agitate him. Still, he has a life of some quality and he is safe. For this, his parents are extremely grateful.

Thinking About the Case

The previous case (#8) looked at schizophrenia from the vantage point of five years post-onset in a previously healthy, well-functioning young adult. This case looks at the illness almost twenty-five years post-onset in a young man who had difficulties coping with life's demands almost from the beginning. As we mentioned in our discussion about Steve M, schizophrenia can have many outcomes, but Lenny's is, sadly, not an uncommon one. Many, if not most, individuals with schizophrenia wind up chronically incapacitated to at least some extent. In Lenny's case, a number of variables may have contributed to the relatively poor outcome. First, he had early behavioral problems that were challenging for his parents to manage. Then, he lost the structure that Catholic school provided and was exposed to negative influences in public school where, one might imagine, his efforts to fit in with the "good" kids were doomed to fail. Unlike Steve, whose illness was clearly apparent in behavior that was in marked contrast to his normal level of functioning, Lenny slid gradually and almost imperceptibly into mental illness. This makes appropriate and timely diagnosis and treatment difficult to achieve. It also makes achieving family unity about what must be done quite difficult. While Steve's parents weren't confused about the accuracy of the diagnosis and the need for treatment, Lenny's parents disagreed about whether he was sick at all. Further, while Steve had years of adequate, even superior functioning, to fall back on when he began to recover, Lenny lacked these skills and prior experiences of success.

Another important variable with respect to diagnosis and prognosis is concomitant drug abuse. This is particularly true for schizophrenia, the symptoms of which are worsened significantly by marijuana use. Nonetheless, many young people with emerging schizophrenia use marijuana or other drugs. For one thing, drug use is common in the age group that comprises the greatest risk period for schizophrenia. Further, young people with incipient thought disorder of some kind may try to "medicate" their problem with drugs. Drug use also gives them an excuse for functioning poorly: virtually anyone would rather think of himself as stoned than as mentally ill. In addition, odd behavior is tolerated better in drug-abusing subcultures, so a young person with thought disorder would suffer less assault to self-esteem as a member of these groups. In Lenny's case, drugs and alcohol may well have masked, medicated, and exacerbated his developing cognitive abnormalities. Lenny and his family would have been able to rationalize his gradually worsening ability to function and timely diagnosis and treatment would have been made less likely. In a young person who abuses drugs and alcohol, an underlying psychosis is more difficult to detect.

Cases like Lenny's suggest that the "medical model" which specifies that "treatment" will lead to a "cure" may be inappropriately applied to schizophrenia. Some experts have suggested that a "rehabilitation model" is more appropriate. This model implies that "treatment" will be replaced or augmented by "services." It is not expected that a cure will be achieved or that services will be terminated at some point. Rather, interventions are designed to support as high a quality of life as the individual is capable of obtaining.

Finally, we should note that we have caught up with Lenny in the middle of his illness, not at the end. Sometimes, the acute symptoms of the illness diminish over time (the voices, the delusions, the agitation) and individuals continue to recover some aspects of their roles as citizens (such as church attendance, or volunteer or job activities, for example) well into their fifties and sixties. Without the negative effects of long-term institutionalization, much functioning can be preserved and a life of dignity and safety can be achieved.

Questions to Consider

1. We noted that Steve and Lenny had different levels of competence prior to the onset of their illness. Which of them would be better off during recovery, and why? Are there any ways in which the other would be better off?
2. We briefly described how Lenny's sister felt at certain points in time. Imagine that you had a sibling with schizophrenia who behaved like Lenny. How would his illness affect your own life? How might it change the choices you made for yourself?
3. Lenny's parents' behavior changed over time. Why might this be so? What effect might this have on Lenny's future?

CASE 10

DELUSIONAL DISORDER: THE CASE OF MR. P.

LIFE IS SOMETIMES NOT what it seems. This is certainly the case for delusional patients. They have sensations or ideas that to them seem perfectly real, but for us, their ideas have only the slightest relationship to reality. In their work, therapists and researchers may also confront a surprising reality from time to time. Consider the case of Mr. P. and his daughter, Sarah, in which the patient is not the person who is ill.

Sarah was fifteen when she was brought to the mental health clinic by her parents, Mr. and Mrs. P. Apparently, she had been running away from home every few months for the past year and a half. Her parents were totally puzzled as Sarah had been a sweet and obedient child, apparently well-adjusted in every way. Even now, she continued to do well in school, had many friends, and seemed generally happy, but still she ran away—sometimes to friends' houses, sometimes to her aunt's in a neighboring state, sometimes to hide in the woods until hunger overtook her and she came home again.

Sarah was not able to shed much light on her motives for running away. She just wasn't comfortable at home, she said, but she couldn't say why. She denied the presence of family conflict or abuse. A mental status examination and clinical interview revealed no evidence of depression, psychosis, or any other mental disorder. The therapist, nonetheless, asked Sarah to return to the clinic for a few more counseling sessions as clearly something was going on. She agreed.

Because her mother was working, Sarah's father brought her to the next session. After another pleasant, but unilluminating hour with Sarah, the therapist spoke with Mr. P., to see if he might have any insight into Sarah's problem.

Serendipity plays an occasional role in psychotherapy. In this case, Sarah's "problem" became more defined when the therapist, thinking only to make a connection with Mr. P., happened to ask him something about his job. He replied that he had recently changed jobs. Why? Well, apparently he had had some trouble at his previous place of employment where he had worked for eighteen years. He had left that job because of some conflict with the union leadership there. The conflict had been so severe, he reported, that union officials were still persecuting him. In fact, he whispered, they had implanted a minute radio receiver in his head through which they transmitted all manner of disgusting messages to him. Specifically, these messages told him to sexually molest various women, including his daughter.

Mr. P. became increasingly agitated as he spoke. The union had surrounded him with agents that tempted him. For example, a secretary at work persistently leaned over the filing cabinet in a way that suggested he was supposed to rape her. He, however, was onto their game and had resisted all of their efforts to get him to engage in these despicable behaviors. They had targeted him years ago, but he had been strong enough to ignore their behavior and to continue to work until he was able to get a new job at the same rate of pay. After all, he had a family to support.

Needless to say, the therapist was taken aback by Mr. P.'s ideas. When Mrs. P. brought Sarah in for the next session, the therapist told her what her husband had said and was surprised to find that she knew all about his delusions. She reported that she had long since stopped trying to talk him out of them, since her experience had been that he had only gotten more agitated when they discussed it. It was better, she had discovered, to gently change the subject after sympathizing with how difficult the situation must be for him. She reported that he had never behaved inappropriately, had never missed work, had never even spoken about his odd ideas to anyone other than to herself as far as she knew.

Mrs. P. and the therapist brainstormed a bit about what could be done about the situation. Sarah's discomfort at home was now totally comprehensible. They both agreed that she was probably sensing Mr. P.'s agitation, and probably even the sexual feelings he had towards her. But since he had never acted on these feelings, Sarah wasn't consciously aware of what was making her uncomfortable. The therapist advised Mrs. P. that psychotherapy was unlikely to have an impact on Mr. P.'s delusions, but that antipsychotic medication might. The problem was that since he was unaware that he was ill, he was unlikely to agree to take medication. Still, they decided to give it a try. The therapist called him back in and suggested that since Sarah's running away, combined with his new job, was clearly putting a lot of stress on him, he might want to take some medication to help him feel calmer. He seemed quite resistant, but agreed to think about it and talk it over with his wife for a week. Since Mr. P. had not acted on his delusional ideas, the therapist felt it was physically safe to let Sarah remain home while he and Mrs. P. tried to enact the treatment plan, so a session was scheduled for a few days later.

At the next session, Mrs. P. reported that her husband had continued to refuse to consider taking medicine, no matter how she had tried to convince him of its value. Since he had committed no crime and did not appear to constitute an immediate threat to anyone, involuntary treatment was not possible. Together, Mrs. P. and the therapist agreed that an alternative placement for Sarah had to be found, since she was clearly being emotionally damaged by her father's illness. Mrs. P. shared with Sarah, in the therapist's office, what she knew about Mr. P.'s illness, and the therapist filled in the gaps by explaining his diagnosis and prognosis. With her mother's help, and oddly, with her father's agreement, Sarah went to live with her mother's sister for the remainder of her high school career. She saw her parents frequently, but avoided spending time alone with her father. The family was lost to follow up, so there is no way of knowing whether Mr. P. ever received treatment or got over his bizarre ideas.

Thinking About the Case

Sadly, delusional disorder is quite resistant to treatment. Psychotherapy generally is markedly ineffective. A good example of this can be found in a book called *The Three Christs of Ypsilanti*. The author, Martin Rokeach, a social psychologist, brought together at Ypsilanti State Hospital in Michigan three men, each of whom believed himself to be Jesus Christ. Rokeach hoped that being confronted with each other might shake the men's delusions. However, each man simply modified or held fast to his delusion. One, for example, decided that there were various levels of Christ and that he was the highest level.

Some clinicians have tried a variant of Rokeach's idea, in which they attempt to engage the patient's rational faculties to confront paradoxes between his beliefs and reality, but they have generally had quite limited success. Medications are sometimes helpful in reducing the delusional ideas, but, like Mr. P., most people with delusional disorder are reluctant to take them because they have no insight that they are ill.

Questions to Consider

1. If you had a belief system that you knew to be at extreme variance with the beliefs of your friends and family, how do you think it would affect you? What do you make of Mr. P.'s ability to behave so normally in situations in which his delusions are not activated?
2. What do you think are the ethical issues involved in talking about Mr. P. behind his back to his wife and daughter? Would you have handled the case differently? How?

LANAHAN NOTES

Schizophrenia Spectrum and Other Psychotic Disorders

Symptoms of schizophrenia

Abnormalities in one or more of the following five domains: 1) delusions, 2) hallucinations, 3) disorganized thinking (speech), 4) grossly disorganized or abnormal motor behavior (including catatonia), 5) negative symptoms

Typically diagnosed when a person experiences two or more of the above, each present for a 1-month period with at least one symptom being delusions, hallucinations, or disorganized thinking (speech)

Delusions: false beliefs; usually bizarre; persistent even when the individual is confronted with contradicting evidence or proof of the false belief

Persecutory: most common; the belief that one is going to be harmed

Referential: belief that gestures or words of others are specifically directed at them; e.g., television broadcaster is speaking directly to the individual

Grandiose: they are someone of extreme importance; e.g., individual might think he or she is King of Iceland or a celebrity

Somatic: the belief that one has a foreign substance in one's body; e.g., an electrode that communicates with the CIA

Control: one's thoughts and/or actions have been taken over by some outside force

Erotomanic: someone, often famous, is in love with them

Nihilistic: a major catastrophe will occur; e.g., a major terrorist attack

Hallucinations: Sensory experiences in the absence of sensory stimuli; can affect any of the senses; most common, auditory (hearing voices)

Disorganized thinking: typically inferred from the individual's speech

Derailment or loose associations: switching from one topic to another

Tangentiality: answers to questions not related to question

Incoherence or "word salad": so disorganized as to be nearly incoherent

Grossly disorganized or abnormal motor behavior (including catatonia): "silliness" or "psychotic laughing" to unpredictable agitation; catatonia may be rigidity or even a complete lack of verbal and motor responses

Negative symptoms: the individual has an "absence" of a behavior; e.g., little emotional expression; decrease in motivated self-initiated purposeful activity; diminished speech; decreased ability to experience pleasure; lack of interest in social interactions

Onset: for men, typically 18-25 years of age; for women, 25-35

Causes of schizophrenia

Diathesis-stress model: a biological predisposition and the presence of relevant environmental stressors

Environmental factors: developmental injury; birth complications; maternal malnutrition; possible maternal exposure to virus during pregnancy; challenges of adolescence and young adulthood

Biological: no one "schizophrenia" gene found but one or cluster of genes suspected

Brain chemistry/dopamine hypothesis: inferred since using drugs to alter the level of the neurotransmitter dopamine reduces symptoms of the disorder

Treatment

Antipsychotic medication: drugs act on either dopamine or a combination of neurotransmitters, including serotonin; unpleasant side effects, e.g., muscle rigidity, tremors, restless agitation, peculiar involuntary postures, flatted affect, memory loss

Psychotherapy and/or psychosocial interventions; used after individual is stabilized with drugs; goals include educating patient and family members about the illness, social skills training, supporting 'healthy' adaptation to the challenge the illness presents

Outcomes: vary widely; women seem to respond better to treatment with less chronic symptoms than men; schizophrenia is generally a life-long disorder

Other Psychotic Disorders

Delusional disorder: presence of one (or more) persistent delusions; functioning not markedly impaired; behavior not obviously bizarre or odd

Brief psychotic disorder: duration of psychotic symptoms less than a month Schizophreniform disorder: symptoms of schizophrenia but duration is less than 6 months

Schizoaffective Disorder: a major mood episode (major depressive or manic) concurrent with schizophrenia criteria

CHAPTER FOUR

Bipolar and Related Disorders

In this category, DSM-5 includes disorders characterized by unusual and often extreme shifts in mood, energy, activity levels, sleep, and the ability to carry out day-to-day tasks. These disorders are by no means rare; it is estimated that as many as ten million Americans experience a disorder in the Bipolar spectrum. Because bipolar disorder is often associated with high energy and creativity, it is not surprising to find that many accomplished people have been diagnosed with it.

In this section we have chosen to include three cases. The first two are examples of Bipolar Disorder Type I. Type I disorders include diagnosable manic conditions in which the person has markedly elevated mood and energy levels. While these can lead to increased productivity and creativity, they frequently also lead to inappropriate and impulsive behavior resulting in both personal and interpersonal problems. Individuals with Type I Bipolar Disorder also experience episodes of severe depression, marked by low mood and energy, social withdrawal, and inability to manage life's tasks. We have included two cases in order to illustrate the change in treatment of this illness over time.

We have also included a case of Bipolar Disorder Type II. In this form of the disorder, diagnosable depressive episodes are interspersed with periods of what is called "hypomania," that is, periods of elevated but not extreme mood. Type II may be difficult to diagnose and often hard to treat appropriately as the periods of elevated mood may be subtle and difficult to discern. The category also includes Cyclothymic Disorder in which both the highs and the lows are less extreme though the cycling of mood is considered abnormal.

CASE 11

BIPOLAR DISORDER TYPE I: THE CASE OF NOREEN W.

THE CASE REPORTED HERE is more than forty years old. While it had an eventually positive outcome, years of the patient's life were consumed by her illness. Had she been diagnosed today, her prognosis would be greatly improved. This case illustrates both changes in treatment and the vagaries of diagnostic fads and fashions.

Noreen was nineteen years old when she first became a resident of the state hospital. As it turned out, she was to live there, off and on, for over seven years. Her first admission was occasioned by an episode in which she was discovered dancing naked outside the church where her parents had been founding members. Had she been first spotted by church members, she would have been taken home where her parents would have tried, no doubt unsuccessfully, to calm her, to get her to eat something or to rest. Instead, she was noticed by a police officer cruising by. He took her to the hospital for evaluation, and she was admitted that same day.

During the evaluation, Noreen spoke rapidly, shifting topics every few sentences, seemingly unable to maintain a single stream of thought. Her mood was labile, ranging from laughter to agitation to anger. One moment she would be shouting obscenities at the admissions officer, the next she would be seductively pleading with him to take her to his home. She was unable to sit still. She paced about the interview room and at one point suddenly burst into song, causing even the doctor to break into a giggle. Noreen told the doctor that she was planning a career on the stage. She said that her family did not understand her, that they were plotting to keep her prisoner so that she could not go to New York as she had planned.

Noreen's parents provided additional data when they arrived at the hospital a few hours after Noreen's admission. Apparently, she had been a model youngster, quiet and well behaved until about fourteen months previously. She began to develop a certain moodiness that her parents found distressing, but thought was probably typical of her age. At times she was withdrawn and listless, at others more outgoing than usual, seemingly tirelessly engaged in countless school and church-related activities.

Of more concern to her parents was her developing interest in young men. From time to time, she seemed especially keen on getting male attention, and there had been frequent arguments of late about what she wore and how she behaved in public. Since the church the family belonged to was quite conservative, her flirting was particularly embarrassing for the W.'s. They could also ill afford the money she spent on clothes. She had even "borrowed" her mother's credit card and come back from the store with over five hundred dollars worth of clothing, most of it entirely inappropriate for her to wear. Mrs. W. was able to return the clothes, although not without difficulty.

The W.'s were at their wits' end. They had been told by their minister that Noreen was possessed by the devil, and the congregation had been praying for her regularly for some months. Everybody's patience was running thin, and Noreen was in danger of being removed from the congregation which would, in essence, mean that she would be disowned by her family.

Mr. and Mrs. W. were quite wary of the hospital. They considered Noreen's problem to be a spiritual one, not a medical one. They did not wish her to have intimate contact with the secular world. Besides, then as now, state hospital admission carried with it a permanent stigma. Still, they were exhausted and fresh out of ideas about how to contain, let alone help, Noreen. They were even a bit afraid of her, they admitted reluctantly. Twice recently she had tried to hit her mother, and her father had had to physically intervene.

Noreen's diagnosis on admission was schizophrenia, paranoid type. Her anger, her disorganization, the inappropriateness of her emotions, and the apparent presence of delusional ideas all contributed to this formulation. Indeed, the great majority of patients admitted to the state hospital in those years were diagnosed with schizophrenia.

Noreen was treated with an antipsychotic medication, and after a couple of weeks, she seemed more like her quiet, compliant self. She appeared genuinely embarrassed and contrite about her inappropriate behavior. She felt so ashamed that she did not know how she would be able to return to her community and face her family, friends, and neighbors. Gradually, over the course of the next few weeks, she fell into a depression, which seemed to the hospital staff to be a reaction to her previously psychotic behavior. She cried frequently and was full of self-recrimination and remorse.

The hospital had a full working farm at which she could spend some time, a pool and bowling alley, a hairdresser, a canteen, a used clothes center, occupational therapy, and movies. Noreen was so immobilized by guilt and shame that she was unable to make much use of the hospital's activities. Staff had to lock her out of the dormitory in the morning and press her to do even the most mundane of personal chores for herself, like showering and dressing.

Gradually, over the next several months with a compassionate therapist and support from other staff, Noreen's depression lifted. As her psychotic thinking seemed to be under control, Noreen was discharged to her family's care. They, however, were hesitant to take her back. Without her, their home life had returned to some semblance of normality, and they were just beginning to overcome the discomfort they felt around the minister and others in the church congregation who had seemed silently to blame them for Noreen's bizarre behavior. They had seen little of her while she had been hospitalized since the staff felt that their visits were potentially upsetting to her, and they had had virtually no contact with her doctor, her therapist, or others involved with her care. They didn't know what her diagnosis was or what they could do to prevent her from having further difficulties.

To make matters worse, the Noreen they were presented with was a far cry from the Noreen they had raised. This Noreen was twenty pounds heavier, moved slowly, and seemed uncharacteristically subdued and tentative. Still, she was docile and seemingly eager to do anything she could to regain their trust and respect.

When she left the hospital, Noreen was scheduled for a visit to the local outpatient mental health center one month after her discharge and given a month's supply of medication. However, within a week Noreen had stopped taking her medication. She felt it made her sleepy and heavy and fuzzy in the head. She had only taken it in the hospital because she had had no choice. Her parents agreed with her decision—the side effects of the medication were all too apparent, while the benefits, if there were any, were subtle and harder for them to detect. They felt that, with their support and that of the congregation, Noreen would turn over a new leaf. The church was going to give her one more chance, and Noreen was determined to use it well.

All did go well, for a while. About six months after her discharge, Noreen was readmitted, this time having cut her wrists in an attempt to kill herself. At the admission interview, Noreen was nearly mute. She did convey that she believed herself to be damned by God for sins too numerous and too horrendous to recount. She heard God's voice telling her that she had to die by her own hand as expiation. In this way, she could keep her family safe from harm.

Safe in the hospital, away from the judgmental eyes of family and friends, and placed on an antidepressant medication, along with the antipsychotic that had been prescribed during her first hospitalization, Noreen gradually recovered from this episode. Again, she was returned home, this time more demoralized and doubtful of her chances to succeed than before.

Over the next several years, this pattern was repeated five more times. Sometimes Noreen was suicidally depressed, sometimes she was filled with bizarre and grandiose plans. There were times in between when she seemed like her old self, but these were fleeting. Always, she was diagnosed, with hardly a second thought, as having schizophrenia—until her seventh hospitalization.

During the years that Noreen was in care, standards for diagnosing schizophrenia had gradually changed. It had been known for some time that schizophrenia was diagnosed far more often in the United States than in Western European nations where patients with similar symptoms were being diagnosed as having affective disorders: depression or bipolar disorder (then known as manic-depressive illness). In the state hospital where Noreen was being treated, psychiatric interns were being trained in the admissions unit. Their lack of experience and expertise was balanced by their knowledge of the most current research findings and by their capacity for viewing problems with few preconceptions. One of these young interns suggested that perhaps Noreen really had manic-depression and might benefit from lithium carbonate—a relatively new medication that was proving itself to be helpful specifically for this disorder. As you might have guessed by now, he was right. When Noreen was treated with lithium at the proper dose (as measured by blood levels), her mood stabilized, her delusional ideas subsided, and her behavior returned to normal. More important, the lithium had a prophylactic effect: it prevented further episodes of either mania or depression.

It took several more years for Noreen to really recover. Once, she stopped taking her lithium to see what would happen—what happened was a manic episode. This proved to her and to her family that she really did need the medicine. She stayed in therapy for some time, trying to work through what the illness had done to her life. She had virtually lost seven years. Socially, academically, and psychologically, she had fallen behind her peers. She felt she had to prove herself to everyone, but the illness had eroded her confidence that she could succeed at anything. She kept worrying that she would get sick again. She had been told that stress could precipitate an episode, even with the lithium, so she wasn't sure what she could attempt and what she shouldn't try.

Still, as they say, time heals. As Noreen went through the subsequent years, without serious setbacks, she gradually regained her confidence as she gained the respect of those around her.

Thinking About the Case

A patient like Noreen would be treated much differently today than she was twenty years ago. Now, the diagnosis of bipolar disorder would likely be made much more quickly. While a manic episode and an acute episode of schizophrenia share many features—among them delusional thinking, grandiose ideas, possible hallucinations, inappropriate emotions, particularly irritability, pressured or rambling speech, and distractibility—clinicians are far more sensitive to the timing of psychotic episodes, and the individual's level of functioning in between in making diagnoses. Noreen's alternating periods of manic elation with profound depression are consistent with a diagnosis of bipolar disorder. An individual with schizophrenia would be less likely to experience such marked shifts in mood, and would be likely to continue to have some symptoms, even between acute episodes.

Of course, even a diagnosis of bipolar disorder is not always clear. Some individuals have very mild depressions or manic episodes, so that the cycling of mood is not always readily apparent. Still others seem to have genuinely schizophrenic symptoms, even between episodes. For these we have the diagnosis "schizoaffective," referring to a disorder midway between bipolar disorder and schizophrenia.

Despite our advances in diagnostic clarity, we still get "stuck" in diagnostic ruts from time to time—a diagnosis once made is unlikely to be changed even in the face of new data. We simply organize the data differently now than we did forty years ago. We will organize it in yet a different way forty years hence.

The role of the state hospital has changed enormously in these last thirty years. When Noreen was ill, state hospital residence for long periods, sometimes life-long, was the norm for young people who developed serious mental illness. We had far fewer effective treatments and a dearth of supervised therapeutic living environments in the community. Now, Noreen would be treated episodically in the psychiatric unit of a full-service hospital. Her stays would likely be fairly brief, a few weeks at most, while medication was stabilized. At discharge she would have other options besides returning home to her family. These would include group homes and supervised apartment living. Much of her therapy would take place on an outpatient basis.

Deinstitutionalization, the movement responsible for these changes, has not been without its drawbacks. A substantial percentage of the homeless population suffers from serious and persistent mental illness. This group remains on the street because under the law, they can not be hospitalized against their will unless they represent an immediate danger to themselves or others. Many others find their way into jails and prisons where they receive little if any treatment. Community mental health facilities are neither plentiful nor aggressive in reaching out to those who do not seek treatment on their own. Many patients who have been discharged from inpatient care "fall through the cracks" once they are on their own. They fail to keep their appointments, stop taking their medications, and drift onto the streets, or into harm's way. Still, the development of community-based alternatives to inpatient treatment allows newly-diagnosed patients to engage in treatment without shredding the fabric of their lives. Social connections and skills in community living can be better preserved.

Another way in which modern treatment focuses on preserving natural supports involves viewing families as partners in treatment. Today, Noreen's parents would be provided with information about her diagnosis and treatment. They would be invited to treatment planning meetings. They might be referred to a family education or support group for additional help. State hospital treatment tended to isolate and stigmatize families, often leading to their withdrawal from the treatment system and from their loved one who was ill. Families still sometimes complain about lack of communication with mental health professionals and about insensitive clinicians who make them feel guilty and incompetent, but these complaints have diminished greatly in recent years.

Questions to Consider

1. Imagine yourself as Noreen's younger sister or brother. What effect do you think her abnormal behavior would have on your life as a preteen, a teenager, and as a young adult? What feelings might you have about her? About yourself?
2. Some patients with bipolar disorder are resistant to taking medication that controls their abnormal moods. Aside from the possible presence of distressing side effects, what are some other reasons why this might be so?

3. Psychoanalytic explanations for bipolar disorder suggest that manic episodes constitute a defense against depression. What sorts of data might help you decide whether this hypothesis is true?
4. Many people with bipolar disorder are treated, like Noreen was, involuntarily. In trying to balance individual civil liberties, protection of people who are not thinking clearly, and society's right to be protected from potentially harmful people, what criteria do you think should be met before a person could legally be treated against his or her will?

CASE 12

BIPOLAR DISORDER TYPE I: THE CASE OF CARLA P.

CARLA WAS A BRIGHT, engaging seventeen-year-old high school senior when she first began to experience mental health problems. At first, it seemed as if she was just overwhelmed with activities and obligations. Like many youngsters her age, she seemed to be on the go from early morning until late in the evening. In addition to school she played soccer and basketball, was in the school play, and took dance and horseback riding lessons on the weekend. How she found time for her ten hour per week part-time job was anybody's guess. Still, up until about January she seemed to manage quite well.

But as the days grew shorter and darker Carla found she had less and less energy. She seemed to want to sleep all the time, but no matter how much she slept, she still woke up feeling tired. Her concentration started to wane, and her normally stellar school performance slipped. Her family noticed that she was becoming increasingly irritable, frequently bursting into tears for no apparent reason, and then apologizing profusely—way more profusely than was necessary.

Carla and her parents agreed that Carla had probably bitten off more than she could chew and that when basketball season and the school play were over she would take some time for herself. But several weeks later, she wasn't feeling any better. If anything, she was worse. She didn't have the energy to socialize with her friends and began to dread going to school. When she tearfully told her mother that she could hardly bear to get up in the morning and sometimes just wished that she wouldn't wake up, her parents decided that a doctor's visit was in order.

In short order, Carla had an appointment with her family physician who diagnosed her as being depressed and prescribed an antidepressant. He also referred her for counseling to help her find more effective ways to balance her interests and responsibilities and to help her learn stress management techniques. However, before she could get an appointment with a counselor, Carla's condition changed dramatically.

At first, everyone thought the change was for the better. Within a few days, Carla had increased energy and her mood seemed to improve dramatically. However, soon it was clear that something was drastically wrong. Carla began sleeping only a couple of hours a night. She called and e-mailed her friends at all hours to the point where their parents began to complain. She talked incessantly about her plans for college and beyond, and the talk seemed increasingly unrealistic—she would complete four years in two, she would take a medical degree along with her undergraduate degree, she was already at work on a chemical formula that would cure macular degeneration, a progressive disorder leading to blindness from which her grandmother suffered. If anybody tried to get Carla to be more realistic, she became uncharacteristically hostile, yelling and swearing. After getting into an argument with her chemistry teacher that ended with Carla's pushing him so hard that he fell against a desk, she was involuntarily hospitalized in the psychiatric wing of the local university hospital. Carla's parents were devastated. They brought their lovely, accomplished daughter to a ward with locks on the doors, and as they walked away, they heard her screaming, cursing, and crying.

In the hospital, Carla was evaluated by a psychiatrist who diagnosed her as having bipolar disorder. He changed her medication, stopping the antidepressant and adding a mood stabilizer and an antipsychotic drug to normalize her thinking. In addition to the change in medication, Carla spoke with a therapist each day and attended group therapy as she was able. The unit social worker interviewed Carla's parents within the first few days, both in order to get relevant history from them and to explain to them the diagnosis and treatment options. He became their liaison with other unit staff, including the primary therapist and the doctor.

When, after several weeks, Carla's condition had stabilized, discharge planning began in earnest. Carla and her parents met with the social worker to develop strategies for relapse prevention. They spoke about the need for continuing medical treatment and the advisability of ongoing psychotherapy. The social worker also introduced the family to various self-help organizations for people with bipolar disorder and their families, some of them national and one local. She also gave them a list of articles and books about the disorder. The social worker offered Carla admission to the hospital's day treatment unit where she would have additional time away from her daily activities to recuperate and additional group support and education about her disorder, but she elected to return to school immediately so that she could finish high school on time and get on with her life.

Not surprisingly, Carla and her parents were dazed and confused by her hospital experience. Carla didn't entirely believe the diagnosis she had been given. She thought that she had just had a bit of a "breakdown" because of stress. Besides, she didn't like the antipsychotic medication at all. It had made her feel lethargic and weighed down. Her psychiatrist had told her that she could get off it eventually, but she felt that she was ready now. She was home no more than a few days when, after arguing unsuccessfully with her parents about it, she took matters into her own hands. She started throwing pills away, rather than swallowing them. This was the first time in Carla's memory that she had lied to her parents.

Carla also faced the immediate problem of what to tell her friends, teachers, and other people. Her best friend had visited her in the hospital, but was sworn to secrecy. She had talked over the issue with her therapist while in the hospital, and now added the opinions of her parents and her best friend to the mix. In the end, she decided to tell people that she had had a "breakdown" (the truth, anyway, she thought) and try to leave it at that.

Meanwhile, her parents weren't sure about how much Carla could handle. Should they insist that she quit her job? Should they set a curfew for her so that they could ensure that she got enough rest? What should they tell other family members about Carla's condition? How could they balance Carla's need for privacy with their need to be kept informed about her condition? Should Carla still plan to go to college out of town, or would it be safer for her to attend school close by and live home for a while longer?

Unfortunately, this last question became moot. Although Carla graduated with her class, in August she experienced another episode of mania and, while her parents recognized the early warning signs, Carla did not. Again she was hospitalized, this time after making a scene at a local bank. Carla was forced to accept a one-year deferment offered by the college she had chosen to attend. This time, Carla accepted placement in the hospital's day treatment program for six weeks. Chastened and saddened, she began to accept her diagnosis. Typical for her, she took on learning about bipolar disorder as if it were an advanced placement course. Throughout the Fall, Carla worked with her therapist and her parents on planning to live with the disorder as she now understood it. She also came clean with the psychiatrist about her feelings about medication, and they began to work more cooperatively, eventually finding a combination of medications she could tolerate.

By January, Carla felt ready to take some courses at the local community college in preparation for the start of her undergraduate program the next autumn. Not without trepidation, her parents let her go, realizing that risk was a part of life. They had been helped to this realization by attendance at parents' support group meetings that had been part of Carla's day treatment program. Everybody agreed that, with proper monitoring and treatment, Carla's prognosis was good. And life went on.

Thinking About the Case

As this case illustrates, much has changed in the treatment of bipolar disorder over the last several decades. Like most people with depression, Carla first saw her family physician. His original diagnosis of simple depression was understandable, if ultimately incorrect. What happened next is not uncommon. In people with a predisposition for manic episodes, treatment with an antidepressant medication can sometimes stimulate such an episode. This is one of the reasons why a careful assessment of family and personal history is crucial. By the time Carla was hospitalized, the diagnostic picture had clarified itself: she had now had both manic and depressed episodes and therefore met the criteria for Bipolar Disorder, Type I.

Type I disorder indicates that at least one genuine manic episode has occurred, with or without diagnosable depressive episodes. Type II disorder is diagnosed when only hypomanic episodes can be documented. A hypomanic episode is a persistently elevated, expansive, or irritable mood that is different from the person's normal mood, but is not severe enough to cause the marked impairment in an individual's functioning that is characteristic of manic episodes.

Note that Carla's treatment involved a lot more patient and family education than did Noreen's (Case #11). It has been clearly demonstrated that such education is an important tool for recovery and rehabilitation. When Noreen was ill, there was no information available for the general public about most mental illnesses; now there is a great deal. Further, when Noreen was ill, parents were considered part of the problem and were generally kept at arm's length by the treatment team. Now they are more likely to be included as part of the solution. This more modern approach helps preserve the family as an integral part of the support network. In addition, education has reduced stigma somewhat. While Carla was initially hesitant to accept her diagnosis and its implications, the availability of information and social support allowed her to use her formidable intellect to help overcome the disabling effects of the illness.

The outcome of Carla's illness was benign, but this is not so for all individuals with bipolar disorder. Sometimes, medications don't work well in controlling symptoms, and sometimes patients fail to take their medication consistently, either because of unpleasant side effects or because they enjoy the manic symptoms. A substantial percentage of individuals with bipolar disorder have other diagnoses as well. The presence of concomitant substance abuse and/or personality disorder are particularly problematic, making the course of the disorder far less benign. Many individuals with bipolar disorder experience some amount of disability for many years if not for a lifetime.

Questions to Consider

1. Long stays at state hospitals had profound effects on patients' lives. In the last twenty years, these institutions have all but disappeared. What are the pros and cons of having "asylum" available to the mentally ill?
2. Both Noreen and Carla struggled with how to explain their behavior to family and friends. Both were, to some degree, self-stigmatized by the illness. What might the effect on self-esteem be of having bipolar disorder? How might this complicate recovery?
3. Manic episodes are frequently characterized by grandiose beliefs. People believe themselves to have marvelous powers and to be able to achieve great things. How might this complicate recovery?

CASE 13

BIPOLAR DISORDER TYPE II: THE CASE OF BERNIE B.

BERNIE IS A FORTY-NINE YEAR OLD engineer. He is married with two school-aged children. His wife has finally convinced him to schedule a mental health evaluation. She has been asking him to do it for at least ten years, but up until recently he has refused.

About a month ago, while they had been arguing over the new boat that Bernie had bought without consulting her, he pushed his wife so hard that she fell against the kitchen table and bruised her hip. His wife was hurt and frightened, and Bernie was dismayed and consumed by guilt. He had immediately called his physician for a referral, and by the next day he was paralyzed with depression.

The depression was not new. Bernie had been experiencing episodes since adolescence. They came on without warning for the most part. Once in a while they were stimulated by something that had happened or that he had done, like this one. When he was depressed, Bernie could barely get out of bed. He didn't shower or brush his teeth unless his wife insisted. He lost his appetite and dropped pounds quickly. Because he worked from home on his computer, he had managed to hold his job, but barely.

When he was depressed, Bernie had trouble concentrating and would often not start work until early afternoon. Still he managed to meet his deadlines through sheer white-knuckled effort. In the evenings when he wife and children were around, he would withdraw to the bedroom and sleep in front of the television. It seemed he could sleep fifteen hours a day and not feel rested. He hated himself and felt that his family would be better off without him. When in the grip of a depressive episode, Bernie believed that he would always feel as horrible as he felt at that moment. He often ruminated about how he might end his life.

But the depressions always came to an end. One morning after some weeks—generally three to eight weeks—Bernie would awaken feeling better. He did not experience the generalized dread that marked his depressed awakenings. He felt hopeful, more energetic, alive . . . finally. He resumed intimate contact with his wife and interest in his children's activities. He worked with zest and vigor, making up for lost time, he felt.

His wife had another interpretation. She reported that her husband's recoveries were not normal either. While she concurred that his work and relatedness improved, she felt that at times he was irritable and self-centered. During these times he talked non-stop, started projects he never finished, and frequently came up with some "cock-eyed" idea that he would follow without consulting with his wife. That is what had happened with the boat.

Bernie had bought the boat without even mentioning it to her. It cost more than they could afford. In fact, they already had some credit card debt to repay. He said that he wanted it for "family recreation," but the closest body of water was over an hour away, and his children had sports activities that took up most of their summers. His daughter had pretty severe motion sickness and wouldn't likely be able to enjoy boating at all.

Bernie's wife insisted that buying a boat was impulsive and poorly considered. Her husband, now chagrined, had to agree. He could only say that it had seemed like a marvelous idea at the time, and he had been sure that his wife would be delighted with the surprise. He had been confused, hurt, and angry when she had objected.

Previous "surprises" included buying a large dog (despite his son's allergies) that had to be given away, buying the materials for and starting to build a deck—still unfinished after three years, and buying a pick-up truck—not a very convenient vehicle for a family of four.

Bernie's wife said that these purchases were out of character for Bernie. When he was "normal," he was a thoughtful man who communicated well with his wife. She couldn't reconcile the Bernie she loved and whose depressions she had accepted, with the "crazy Bernie" he sometimes would become. This Bernie she could not live with, though his children and his friends seemed to like this Bernie quite a bit. He was charming, outgoing, and funny, though prickly and exhausting. Being his wife was difficult in the extreme. Mrs. B was worried because it seemed to her that the periods between depressions and "crazy Bernie" were becoming fewer and briefer.

The psychologist elicited a family and social history as a matter of course. Bernie was one of five children raised in an intact family. Bernie's father had abused alcohol and complained about depression. Sometimes he would leave the family for days at a time. Bernie's mother assumed that he was on an alcohol binge during these absences, but he denied this was so. He did drink some, he admitted, but mostly he was just "seeing the world." He always returned home, dirty and sometimes bruised. After a long sleep, he would resume his daily routine as if nothing out of the ordinary had happened. One of Bernie's brothers had been treated for depression. He had had a period of being unable to work, but seemed fine now. His sister seemed chronically oppressed by her life but she had never sought treatment. His mother and other two siblings did not appear to have any mental health problems.

Bernie's depressions had begun in college just before his freshman final exams. He became so "stressed" by the pressure of studying that he "collapsed." He could barely get out of bed, and he stopped eating. His roommate notified school authorities who notified his parents. He took a medical leave of absence, came home to "rest" for the Summer, and resumed school in the Fall. He graduated a year late, but had no further problems academically. His second major depression occurred after graduation and delayed his getting a job by about six months. Again, a period of "rest" seemed to help him recover. He met and married his wife when he was twenty-six. He had another depression in the second year of their marriage, and had had one about every eighteen to twenty-four months thereafter. They lasted several weeks and were very debilitating. In each instance, he recovered spontaneously.

The psychiatrist whom Bernie has consulted had no difficulty making a diagnosis: Bipolar Disorder, Type II. She recommended that Bernie and his wife educate themselves about the illness by consulting reputable medical sites on-line. She prescribed a medication which she predicted would help stabilize Bernie's mood and she recommended that both he and his wife seek counseling to help them understand and cope with his illness, both individually and as a couple. She said that if they followed through on her suggestions and Bernie took his medication as directed, their lives would improve dramatically.

Thinking About The Case

Bipolar Disorder, Type II is diagnosed when depressions are present as are episodes that are characterized by elevated and/or irritable mood along with increased energy and activity. These episodes do not reach the incapacitating level of true manic episodes, and are, therefore, called "hypomanic." "Hyper" refers to more, and "hypo" to less. In other ways, it is quite similar to Bipolar Disorder, Type I. Its onset usually occurs by the teens or early twenties. It is diagnosed six times more often in people who have parents or siblings who have been diagnosed with Bipolar Disorder than in people with no family history of mood disorder. Some people cycle between depression and hypomanic episodes, while others, like Bernie, also have periods of normal mood in between.

Bipolar II is often misdiagnosed as Recurrent Depression, since hypomanic episodes may go unnoticed and untreated. Sufferers do not experience the elevated mood as a problem, so unless there is a spouse or other person affected by the person's behavior and able to explain it sufficiently to mental health care providers, the diagnosis may be inaccurate. The distinction is important, since unipolar depression is treated with antidepressant medications, generally without mood stabilizers. These medications have been shown to precipitate hypomanic or even manic episodes in some people, generally those who actually have some form of Bipolar Disorder. Sometimes, a diagnosis of Bipolar Disorder is only made after a person has been treated with an antidepressant, and has had a manic or hypomanic episode as a result. When manic or hypomanic episodes are present, antidepressants are prescribed only with great care, and are almost always accompanied by a mood stabilizer.

Bernie's treatment was better than average in that counseling was suggested in addition to medication. Sometimes providers fail to consider the effects of the illness on family members or the effects of family members' reactions to the symptoms on the person with the disorder. Mood disorders are often extraordinarily difficult to live with, especially if symptoms are misinterpreted as selfishness or lack of caring. Both depression and mania present challenges to relationships. Counseling and education about the disorder can go a long way towards addressing these challenges.

Questions To Consider

1. Do you think Bipolar Disorder lies on a continuum with ordinary moodiness? Why or why not? What kinds of evidence would help you answer this question?
2. Bipolar I and II are currently considered two separate but related disorders. Does this make sense to you? Why or why not? Again, what data would be relevant to your answer?
3. Bipolar Disorder is diagnosed much more often than it used to be. Almost everybody knows somebody so diagnosed. Why might this be?
4. Should Bernie's children be included in counseling? Why or why not?

LANAHAN NOTES
Bipolar and Related Disorders

Many people suffer some sadness or intense elation: How do we distinguish these individuals from those who are bipolar?

Indications of a Mood Disorder

Person's emotional reactions are greatly out of proportion to the events causing the reactions

Person's daily functioning is impaired

Bipolar Disorder (once known as manic-depression)

Characterized by the presence of distinct phases of mania and depression

Manic symptoms

Thoughts: skewed cognitions, inflated self-image, unrealistic plans, poor judgment, racing thoughts, distractibility, and impulsivity

Feelings: abnormally elevated, expansive or irritable mood

Behavior: decreased need for sleep; increased mental and physical energy

Note: mania in bipolar disorder can be mistaken for schizophrenic symptoms

Depressive symptoms

Thoughts: worthlessness and guilt; diminished ability to think or concentrate; indecisiveness; sometimes thoughts of suicide

Feelings: sadness, hopelessness; anhedonia (diminished pleasure in activities)

Behaviors: fatigue, sleep disturbance (insomnia or hypersomnia), weight changes (loss or gain), psychomotor agitation or retardation

Categories of Bipolar Disorder:

Biopolar I disorder: diagnosed when criteria are met for at least one manic episode; manic episode may have been preceded by and may be followed by hypomanic (less intense mania) or major depressive episodes

Biopolar II disorder: diagnosed when there are recurrent major depressive episodes interspersed with hypomanic episodes

Cyclothymia: characterized by less intense mood swings

Who Gets Bipolar Disorder?

About 1 percent of the population

No significant gender difference

First episodes usually occur in individuals in their late teens-early twenties

Runs in families: likely strong genetic and biochemical basis

Causes of Bipolar Disorder

Genetic factors: bipolar disorder can run in families; not conclusive

Neurochemical factors: dysfunction of certain neurotransmitters, possibly levels of norepinephrine, serotonin, and others

Environmental factors: a life event or even alcohol or drug abuse may trigger a mood episode in a person with a genetic disposition for bipolar disorder.

Medication-triggered mania: some medications such as antidepressants can trigger a manic episode in people susceptible to bipolar disorder.

Treatments

Drugs: Antidepressants, anticonvulsants, and antipsychotic drugs: used to treat actual symptoms

Lithium carbonate and other mood stabilizing medications: can reduce the frequency and severity of mood swings, but blood levels must be closely monitored

Psychotherapy: helps patients and families deal with the practicalities of living with bipolar disorder

CHAPTER FIVE

Depressive Disorders

Next to anxiety, sadness is probably the most common human emotion. None of us escapes loss in our lives, and loss inevitably leads to sadness. But when does sadness, a normal feeling, shade into depression, a clinical condition? The DSM-5 answers this question by specifying that mood disorders must be of sufficient duration and intensity that they cause significant subjective distress or dysfunction in one or more of life's roles (relationships, work, school).

Depression is an all-encompassing condition. Its accompanying physical symptoms include changes in sleep, appetite, activity level, and the ability to experience pleasure. Cognitive changes include thinking of the present as bleak and the future as hopeless. The past seems marred by errors that one is helpless to rectify. Concentration and motivation are impaired. Emotional changes include despair, emptiness, and often guilt. Social changes include socializing less and feeling short-tempered and ill at ease. It is no wonder that depression is associated with an elevated risk of suicide.

The good news is that depression is often self-limiting and is, in most cases, a highly treatable condition. Both biological and psychological interventions have been shown to be effective in ameliorating the symptoms of depression and in preventing relapse.

In this section we begin with two cases that illustrate the different complexity, intensity, and course that depression can take. In the first (Case #14), episodes are severe but intermittent. Treatment is multifaceted and prognosis is good. In the second (Case #15), symptoms are less severe, but more persistent. This type of depression tends to have a more guarded prognosis.

We then go on to examine how stage of life may be relevant to the development of depression. One case (#16) examines depression in a teenager, and the other (#17) discusses the treatment of an elderly man and his wife, each of whom is diagnosed with depression.

Taken as a whole, these cases show that co-morbidity and the use of multiple and eclectic treatments is common. Depression is ubiquitous, and how it presents itself is affected by biological, environmental, and interpersonal factors—a true biopsychosocial syndrome.

CASE 14

MAJOR DEPRESSIVE DISORDER: THE CASE OF HANNAH H.

HANNAH H. IS A VIBRANT, GREGARIOUS fifty-two-year-old naturalized American citizen. She was born in Hungary towards the end of World War II. Her parents divorced when she was a baby and she was raised, primarily, by her mother and grandmother, although her mother did remarry when Hannah was eight. Hannah did not know who her biological father was until she was eleven, when her mother confessed that a man who had functioned as a family friend and sort of "uncle" to Hannah was actually her father.

Hannah's mother, Mrs. P., was a prominent woman in the business community in the city where they lived. She had a good bit of money and Hannah went to the best schools and dressed in the best clothes. On the surface, her life seemed serene. However, appearances can be deceiving. Hannah's mother was a difficult, demanding, and judgmental woman. She controlled Hannah's every move, never allowing her an independent thought or movement. She berated her daughter constantly for being fat, stupid, ugly, or selfish. No matter what Hannah tried to do to please her mother, nothing worked.

But this was not the worst of it. Mrs. P. had a serious mental illness in which she had recurrent bouts of suicidal and homicidal feelings. Hannah vividly remembers an incident that occurred when she was about five or six in which her mother was holding her hand as she walked them both into the river near their home, apparently planning to drown them both. Hannah remembers her mother saying, "It's alright, it won't hurt, it will be very peaceful." She remembers crying and struggling, saying, "I don't want to die, mother, please don't." She doesn't remember why her mother stopped, but she thinks it was because she remained upset and wouldn't calm down. In those days mental illness carried even more of a stigma than it does today. Mrs. P.'s family attempted to cover up her illness rather than seek treatment, although Hannah remembers that her mother did spend some time in a sanatorium at some point during Hannah's childhood. She can't remember exactly when or for how long, though.

Hannah's misery was not exclusively in the hands of her mother. When she was ten, her stepfather began to undress and fondle her when no one was around. He went upstairs into her room at night, while her mother and grandmother sat reading or crocheting in the living room, and exposed himself to her, forcing her to rub his penis until he ejaculated. After about a year of this, Hannah worked up the nerve to tell her mother, who became hysterical and swore she would divorce him. However, after confronting her husband, she became enraged at Hannah and accused her of behaving seductively. She stayed married but saw to it that Hannah was never alone with her stepfather again. Oddly, though, Hannah felt less protected than ostracized.

While this account makes it sound as if Hannah's childhood was an unremitting disaster, this is not so. She had an unusually loving and trusting relationship with her grandmother. Even though she was Mrs. P.'s mother, Hannah's grandmother could not have been more different in temperament and behavior. She was there to comfort Hannah after her mother or stepfather had verbally or physically abused her. They laughed together and played together. From her grandmother she learned how to keep house and how to love another person. Her grandmother always tried to keep Hannah connected to her mother by making excuses for her or urging Hannah to forgive and forget. Hannah believes that her grandmother's presence saved her life, both emotionally and in reality.

Hannah also had a good life at school. While a bit shy, she was a good student and well liked by both teachers and peers. Her outward success was about the only thing in which her mother took any pride, so Hannah strove as hard as she could. She felt that if only she could be a better student, a better daughter, a better person, then her mother would be able to love her.

Nobody in the community ever reacted to the abuse Hannah suffered at home. She believes people must have known about it because she often came to school with bruises on her face and arms from her mother's beatings. In those days, she says, people minded their own business, and what parents did to children was a private matter.

From age ten or eleven on, Hannah suffered from symptoms of panic disorder. These were characterized by difficulty breathing, pain in the chest, and lightheadedness. She was terrified of dying. Gradually these attacks, which lasted from minutes to hours, became more frequent and longer in duration. Despite her suffering with these symptoms for years, she was never taken for treatment.

Not surprisingly, Hannah married young. At nineteen, she married a young man who turned out to be physically abusive. She had two daughters from that marriage, and after she divorced him, her husband dropped out of sight. A year later, Hannah met and soon married a young American soldier stationed in Hungary. He seemed kind and considerate, and, best of all, he planned to take her and her daughters back to the States to live. This marriage has lasted twenty-five years, although it, too, was not without its share of troubles.

Mr. H., Hannah's second husband, had a violent temper, as had her mother, stepfather, and first husband. In the early years of their marriage, he beat, choked, and shoved her whenever she displeased him. When she cowered or tried to run or hide, he beat her worse. She says he seemed to enjoy her terror. The beatings only stopped when Hannah began therapy, and with the help of her therapist, decided to call the police when her husband attacked her. She had him jailed once, which, though it infuriated him, stopped him from laying hands on her again. She also stopped cowering. Instead, she learned to hold her ground and tell him that if he touched her, he would go to jail. Apparently, he learned that she meant it.

Why did she stay? Hannah says she didn't find what she was living with particularly odd. She had always been beaten. Besides, her husband was a good provider, often fun to be with, and he treated her two girls exactly like the three children they subsequently had together. In fact, he was a wonderful father to all of the children. She loved him, and she felt fairly certain that he loved her as well.

Hannah first requested mental health treatment when she was thirty-six years old. She sought treatment for her panic symptoms and was seen for a few sessions. She had a few more sessions for the same problem when she was forty. Then, three years later, following the birth of her fifth child, she suffered a serious post-partum depression. Her mood gradually worsened, she had difficulty sleeping, and she was horrified to find herself thinking of killing the baby. Because of the concern that she might hurt her child, Hannah was hospitalized in a psychiatric unit of a general hospital for about two weeks. There she was treated with antidepressant medication as well as individual and group psychotherapy. Her thoughts of harming her new son receded, and she continued to do well with medication and outpatient psychotherapy. Two years after this episode, Hannah's therapist left the mental health center. Hannah had difficulty attaching to the new therapist that had been assigned to her. Since she had felt well for some time, she gradually stopped going to the center and taking her medication.

Hannah remained essentially symptom-free for three more years when, in the midst of some family turmoil, she began to again display the symptoms of depression: early morning awakening, lack of interest in her appearance or her usual activities of daily living, and the reappearance of suicidal and homicidal thoughts—again directed towards her son, whom she adored. In a panic, she called her primary care physician who prescribed Prozac, one of the newer antidepressant drugs at that time, and referred her for psychotherapy. Her therapist requested a consultation from a psychiatrist, reasoning that a psychiatrist's involvement would be necessary if hospitalization should become necessary. The therapist also wanted to see whether, in view of Hannah's history of relapse, lithium carbonate should be added to the medication regimen. This medication has been found to be effective in treating bipolar disorder (previously known as manic-depressive illness), and seems to prevent relapse in a substantial number of patients. The psychiatrist agreed the lithium carbonate might be useful and this was prescribed by the primary care physician.

While her depression continued for some time, Hannah's suicidal and homicidal thoughts disappeared when she began taking the antidepressant again, so she was able to avoid hospitalization during this episode of illness. A month later she was essentially symptom free. Her depression appeared to have lifted. She reported sleeping well, having increased energy, experiencing a return of her sexual drive (often diminished during depression), and rediscovering her sense of humor. If anything, she appeared mildly elated, causing her therapist to worry that she might develop a manic episode, as sometimes happened with people who have an underlying bipolar disorder not yet diagnosed.

This did not come to pass, though, and Hannah's mood has ranged from mildly depressed to normal ever since. She stopped taking lithium carbonate about one year after she started, because she felt it made her somewhat lethargic and sleepy. In addition, she suffered from annoying diarrhea as a side effect. She understood that she ran some risk of relapse, but decided that the benefits of the medication were uncertain while the side effects were known and unpleasant. She did, however, elect to remain on the Prozac given the clear and convincing evidence that it relieved her depression. She was particularly fearful that her homicidal thoughts would return without medication, and these were so horrifying to her that she would do anything to stop them.

Hannah also elected to remain in psychotherapy, essentially indefinitely. She sees her therapist approximately twice a month, and they discuss the various stresses in her life—problems with or concerns about the children or her husband, unresolved feelings about her mother, who is still alive in Hungary, upset feelings brought about by television shows or some news event related to child abuse or neglect. They also monitor carefully how she is sleeping and how her energy level is, because they know from experience that problems in either of these areas can be warning signs of impending relapse. They are working on two fronts at once: they hope to increase her psychological resistance to environmental stress, and to intervene earlier, should she begin to suffer a relapse. Hannah has not only survived, she is a loving and protective mother, a loyal and devoted friend, and a productive citizen of the community. She demonstrates the resilience of the human spirit, the redemptive value of the care and protection of even one loving adult in the life of a child, and the benefits conferred by modern mental health treatment.

Thinking About the Case

Hannah's case is not unusual in its multiplicity of diagnoses and pathways to illness. Hannah's primary diagnosis is recurrent depression, characterized by saddened mood, lack of energy and initiative, inability to take pleasure in previously enjoyed activities, oversleeping, and suicidal thoughts. These are hallmark symptoms of the disorder. The homicidal thoughts are somewhat unusual, particularly because they were not experienced as consistent with her depressed mood—"life is so awful that my son would be better off without it." Rather, they were experienced as intrusive, unwanted, compelling ideas, more in the nature of a compulsion. One could have been led to diagnose her as having obsessive-compulsive disorder, but the bulk of the symptoms supported the diagnosis of depression.

Hannah also suffered from panic disorder, although she doesn't have the symptoms at present. She does have symptoms of post-traumatic stress disorder, characterized primarily by nightmares about being held against her will by her mother, and by her strong avoidance of and emotional overreaction to stimuli associated with child abuse. Thus, she has at least three mental health diagnoses. Research indicates that each of these three disorders may share some neural pathways in the brain (primarily involving the neurotransmitter serotonin), so Hannah's symptoms may all be related to a common disturbance.

It appears that Hannah's medication provides some protection against depression. It may also be of value in treating the panic symptoms. The post-traumatic symptoms seem relatively unaffected and are treated more by the support that psychotherapy has to offer. They seem to come and go, depending upon whether her children have contact with their grandmother, thus stimulating her thinking about her own childhood.

This case also has material for both nature and nurture supporters.

Hannah appears to have symptoms similar to those her mother had. This may indicate a genetic predisposition, although since she was raised by her mother, modeling may play some role. The onset of depression was post-partum, so hormonal forces may be implicated. Women undergo massive hormonal changes after childbirth. Naturally, the traumatic aspects of her childhood could be expected to have contributed to her psychological distress.

Rather than choose between heredity and environment, the widely accepted "diathesis-stress model" allows us to combine features of both. According to this model, mental illness occurs in people who have a built-in genetic or constitutional vulnerability combined with environmental stress of some kind. Whether the vulnerability (the "diathesis") must be specific for a particular illness, or whether the stressor must be of a specific kind for a particular illness is, as yet, unknown. According to this model, Hannah inherited a predisposition to develop depression with suicidal and homicidal features from her mother. In the face of her stressful childhood, combined with the hormonal, physical and emotional stresses of having a new baby, the predisposition manifested itself. The model states that both the diathesis and the stress are necessary for the illness to occur. It is likely that some individuals have a very strong predisposition to illness, such that little if any stress is necessary. Others may have a weaker predisposition, requiring extraordinary stress to trigger an episode of illness. Hannah appears to have had a hefty dose of each.

The prognosis for depression is variable. About one-third of patients seem to recover from a single episode of depression without any long-term effects. Another third recover well, but relapse after some time has passed. The last third, appear to experience only a partial recovery, struggling with a milder form of the disorder on a more chronic basis. Hannah appears to fall within the second group, recovering well, but prone to relapse.

Questions to Consider

1. The question of whether adult mental health disorders can be prevented by early intervention is being studied by researchers worldwide. Do you think Hannah's depression could have been prevented by mental health intervention earlier in her life? Why or why not? If your answer is "yes," what sorts of interventions would you have wanted to see done?
2. Post-partum depression is usually thought to have at least a partially hormonal etiology. Can you think of some psychological rea-

sons why a woman might become depressed following the birth of a baby?

3. Apply the diathesis-stress model to your own life. Do you have familial predispositions for depression or other psychological disorders? Have you experienced relevant stressors? If you answer is yes to either of these questions, what steps might you take to reduce your risk?

CASE 15

PERSISTENT DEPRESSIVE DISORDER: THE CASE OF BONNIE D.

BONNIE WAS A THIRTY-EIGHT YEAR OLD legal secretary when her primary care physician referred her for psychotherapy. In the first interview, she complained of having little energy and wandering concentration. She said that she felt tired a lot of the time, and could sleep as many as twelve hours a day on the weekends if left to her own devices. She was concerned that she didn't seem to be able to enjoy things the way other people did. Often, she went through the motions of happiness without really feeling it. She didn't think much of herself either. She felt fat and ugly (despite being within the normal range for women of her height and age), and believed that she was boring to be around. "I wouldn't want myself for a friend," was how she put it. Bonnie reported that she had been experiencing these symptoms off and on for as long as she could remember. Sometimes they were worse and sometimes a bit better, but she could not recall ever being really joyful or even happy for a sustained period of time.

Married for fifteen years to a building contractor, Bonnie led an outwardly normal and even satisfying life. The couple had enough money and they were on good terms with Mr. D.'s parents and three siblings who lived nearby. Bonnie's family lived in a neighboring state, and they all got together on holidays when they could. Bonnie described her husband as a good man, if a bit of a "workaholic." She felt badly that she was often irritable with him for no apparent reason, and that she rarely felt like having sex. Her irritability seemed to roll off his back, although they did argue about the frequency of sex from time to time. They generally spent leisure time separately—he in hunting and fishing and she in knitting and sewing.

Bonnie said that she felt lonely much of the time, and had never been very good at making friends. She didn't think people liked her much, although she couldn't say why. When asked about her work, she admitted that she seemed to get along well enough with co-workers, and always got good performance reviews. Still, her colleagues seemed to socialize with each other outside of work, but she was never included. They sometimes asked her to go to lunch with them, but since she always brought a sandwich, she generally refused.

Bonnie's history was fairly unremarkable. She was the third child out of four in a middle class family. Her father, now nearing retirement, was a computer software salesman, and her mother was also a legal secretary. The couple separated when Bonnie was twelve. There hadn't been any real warning. Arguments between her parents had been rare. Bonnie seemed to recall that the marriage was more of a partnership than a love match. In fact, she said, expressions of affection, either physical or verbal, had been uncommon in her household. Shortly after the divorce, Bonnie's father married a woman he had worked with for years. Bonnie came to believe, as did her mother and siblings, that her father had been having an affair with this woman during the last several years of the marriage, although he never admitted this to anybody. Bonnie and her two brothers stayed with her mother (her oldest sister was, by the time of the divorce, in college), but her father stayed in regular contact with the children.

Bonnie recalled being very upset about the divorce. She cried herself to sleep many nights for many months. She was embarrassed to tell anyone about it, and for quite a while kept a distance from her friends lest they ask her what was wrong. She couldn't figure out how to feel about her father, whom she loved but with whom she was furious. Her mother seemed preoccupied and didn't take much note (or perhaps didn't have the energy to deal with) Bonnie's emotional reaction.

When asked what she had been like as a youngster, Bonnie described herself as a somewhat shy child, without any strong interests. She had a few friends in each grade, played flute in the school band, and was a solid B student. She couldn't remember much of her childhood, but she thought it had been fairly normal prior to the divorce. There had been a few family trips, holidays with extended family, the usual sibling squabbles. Nothing much really stood out. She had dated some in high school, although not much. Upon graduating, she elected to attend a local business school because she had no burning interest in academics and couldn't really see spending four years at college. Through an acquaintance at school she had met Mr. D. They dated for fourteen months and then became engaged. Within a year they had married. Even at her wedding,

Bonnie recalled feeling strangely "blank." Though she was relieved that she had found someone who seemed to love her and glad that she wouldn't have to grow old alone, she didn't feel the joy that she imagined others felt in similar circumstances. This was, in a way, a marker for her life experience: good times were marked more by an absence of negative feelings than by the presence of positive ones.

Bonnie had tried psychotherapy and medication before. She had begun to see a therapist during business school, prompted by feelings similar to those she had now, but then she met Mr. D. and life seemed to improve. Five years into her marriage she tried an antidepressant, prescribed by her family physician. At first she felt like it might have been helping, but then her sex drive diminished even further, she began to put on weight, and the bleakness returned. She had agreed to try therapy once more only because her doctor said she hadn't given it enough of a try the last time. She really didn't think it would help. She was much like her mother, she said, and she didn't think there was anything she could do about it.

The therapist began by identifying two areas for exploration: lifestyle issues and psychological issues. Under the first heading, the therapist listed two problems: lack of regular physical exercise and lack of socialization activities. Under the second heading, she listed poor self-esteem and an inability to invest sufficient meaning in life. The therapist said that Bonnie was going through the motions of living, without feeling that any of her activities were worthwhile or important. Bonnie agreed.

By the time several sessions had passed, Bonnie and her therapist had fashioned a therapeutic contract in which they agreed that half of each future session would be spent setting behavioral goals and reviewing progress under the lifestyle heading, while the other half would be devoted to examining what kind of a person Bonnie wanted to be, what she wanted to accomplish with her life, and how she would like to be thought of by others.

Bonnie liked the therapist and was initially quite hopeful. Within the first few visits, her spirits had lifted and she felt more optimistic than she had felt in a long time. However, she found it difficult to follow through with goals that she'd set for herself. She couldn't find the time to walk (her exercise of choice) and when she did, her feet hurt. She would do it for a few days, then stop for several more. Only at the therapist's urging would she begin again. She couldn't see how it would make a difference, she said. She had tried exercising before and it hadn't helped.

Socializing was no better. She had difficulty identifying anyone with whom she would like to socialize. There were no particular activities she enjoyed doing that might bring her into contact with others. She didn't have time or energy for volunteering, what with working full-time and keeping house. She didn't want to go out to eat with her colleagues every day because restaurant meals were way too fattening. Besides, the other women in the office all had families, so they weren't free to do things outside the office anyway.

After about eight visits, Bonnie began to miss sessions. First she had the flu, then a few weeks later her boss wouldn't let her leave work early. Finally, she left a message canceling an upcoming appointment saying that she had gotten very busy shopping for Christmas, and she would call the therapist after the holidays for another appointment. She never did.

Thinking About the Case

Persistent depressive disorder (also known as dysthymic disorder) describes a form of depressed mood that is less severe but more prolonged than major depression. In order for dysthymia to be diagnosed, the symptoms must have been present for at least two years. Bonnie had a number of the common signs and symptoms: poor self-esteem, overeating and oversleeping, low energy, reduced concentration, diminished capacity to feel pleasurable feelings, and a sense of hopelessness. It is not uncommon for dysthymia to erupt into a major depression, usually in response to a stressor or loss of some kind. This is called "double depression," where major depression is superimposed on an underlying dysthymia. Dysthymia can also co-occur with anxiety disorders, substance abuse disorders, and somatoform disorders. In these cases, the depressed mood and lack of energy tend to complicate treatment of the associated disorders.

The cause or causes of dysthymic disorder are unclear, although it is virtually certain that a number of different pathways, particularly when they converge, can lead to the disorder. Moderate heritability has been shown for the disorder. It tends to occur more often in families in which the same or other mood disorders are diagnosed in other family members. In Bonnie's case, her mother seems to have experienced dysthymia as evidenced by her inability to connect with her children and general lack of positive emotionality. Temperament may play a role as well. Bonnie was a somewhat shy child, with few talents or traits that would counteract her natural tendency to stay on the sidelines. She had weak goal orientation, evidenced by lack of interest in any specific activities or career possibilities. She appeared also to have only average, or even below average persistence—the capacity to stick to a course of action in the face of difficulties or barriers.

Modeling and parental reinforcement may also be a factor. If parents are joyfully committed to work, or play, or family, or church, or, community, or indeed, anything outside themselves, they are more likely to have children who are able to do so as well. Bonnie had few childhood models for this type of commitment. Her father's one attempt to take hold of life came in the form of an affair. Her mother seems never to have experienced much pleasure.

Finally, childhood loss is implicated in virtually all forms of depression. One might speculate that the breakup of Bonnie's parents' marriage changed her ideas about what one could expect from significant others. To the extent that she identified with her mother, she may have come to the (probably unconscious) conclusion that she was unworthy of another's full affection and permanent commitment.

Unfortunately, dysthymic disorder is difficult to treat. Bonnie's case illustrates one of the common outcomes: multiple attempts at treatment with initial improvement, followed by reversion to baseline. As a rule, the longer that psychiatric symptoms have been present, the less likely they will be to remit. The symptoms become incorporated into the person's self-image, a part of who one is. This is accompanied by a sense of hopelessness about the possibility of change and a diminution of persistence in pursuing change. Bonnie was unable to sustain hope that any of the changes that she might make would lead to feeling better. Her own experience had taught her that this was highly unlikely, and thus, a self-fulfilling prophecy was created.

Questions To Consider

1. The therapist in this case focused a lot of initial effort on behavioral changes, especially exercise and socializing. Might this have been a mistake? Why? What might you do differently? Why?
2. It has recently been suggested that people's baseline happiness level is pre-set, with some people being naturally fairly contented and others being naturally less so. Events may change one's happiness level, these researchers believe, but only for brief periods of time, followed by a reversion to baseline. Does this seem true to you, given your everyday experience? Outline a study that might help you find out whether this is so. What implications might this fact (if it is a fact) have for psychotherapy efforts?
3. The therapist in this case suggested that Bonnie's depression might be related to a lack of meaningful engagement in her life. Do you agree? What activities or beliefs shelter you from depression?
4. Take your insights and ideas about the development of Bonnie's dysthymia a step further. What might parents do, if anything, to inoculate their children against depression of this kind?

CASE 16

DEPRESSION IN AN AFRICAN–AMERICAN TEENAGER: THE CASE OF TAKISHA LANDRY

The case presented here is from "Dealing With Cross-Cultural Issues in Clinical Practice," a book chapter written by Harriet Lefley, Ph.D., in P.A. Keller, and S. R. Heyman, (eds.), Innovations in Clinical Practice: A Sourcebook *(Sarasota, FL: Professional Resource Exchange, 1991). It is included here with Dr. Lefley's introduction, comments, and treatment plan to illustrate the role that cultural and socioeconomic factors can play in the diagnosis and management of psychological problems. After you read the case, but before you read the "Comments" section, stop and consider how you might conceptualize Takisha's problems, and what you might do to resolve them. Then, compare your ideas with Dr. Lefley's in the following case:*

TWO CRITICAL ERRORS EMERGE in therapy with persons who are culturally different not only in racial/ethnic background, but also in socioeconomic status. One is the misinterpretation of behavioral cues that are linked to specific cultural values. The other is the tendency to impose unwarranted psychodynamic meanings on some basic realities of living at or just above the poverty line. These are exemplified in the following case example. It is presented in some depth to show patterns of cultural misinterpretation, reassessment of need, and treatment planning geared toward empowering both parent and child while restoring psychological stability to an economically stressed family system.

Takisha Landry (a pseudonym), a female, African-American, 12-year-old sixth grader, was referred to the school counselor for evaluation. Previously a fine student, Takisha's grades had slipped in the last year, and she was now in danger of repeating sixth grade while her peers moved on to a higher level. During the past 4 months she had seemed tired, preoccupied, and increasingly depressed. The counselor tested her on the WISC and obtained a Full Scale IQ score of 118. She denied any trouble at home.

Takisha's mother came to school for a conference and indicated she was not aware of any trouble at home, did not see particular changes in Takisha's behavior, but was concerned to learn that her child's school performance was decreasing. When Takisha and her mother met together with the counselor, Mrs. Landry spoke sharply to Takisha and ordered her in no uncertain terms to shape up in school or she would be punished. Takisha looked down at her hands and said nothing. The counselor observed that there was not eye or body contact between the two, no touching or overt affection. Takisha, she noted, seemed either afraid of her mother or distant from her; she addressed her only as "yes ma'am" and "no ma'am." Later, however, when Takisha returned to class, Mrs. Landry asked to speak privately with the counselor. She seemed genuinely puzzled and concerned. Takisha was a good child, dependable, honest, and a great help to her. The mother wanted Takisha to finish school and go to college. She would do anything she could to help.

Takisha was referred to a child guidance clinic for psychotherapy. Because of her previously fine school performance, which indicated a high level of intelligence and motivation for learning, she was considered a good candidate for psychotherapy and was assigned to a young psychology intern from a midwestern white Protestant background. Mrs. Landry received a letter asking her to come in for a preliminary conference. She called the clinic and asked to reschedule an 11:00 A.M. conference to an earlier hour; her voice seemed harassed and short-tempered. When she spoke with the interviewer, she again could recall nothing that would explain Takisha's behavior, was annoyed at the questions, and finally said sharply it was the clinic's job to "fix Takisha up," because raising children was just too hard. She was very disturbed that the clinic had scheduled Takisha's sessions for just after school, saying she didn't know what she would do with the younger children, but that she would try to arrange for a neighbor to take care of them as long as it was for only a few weeks or so.

In the first three sessions Takisha was depressed and spoke in soft, reluctant monosyllables, but the following story came out. She was the main caregiver for her three younger brothers and sisters, aged 5 to 8. Their father had left long ago. They lived in the projects, and in addition to picking up each of the children from their various schools and walking them home, Takisha was required to prepare their meals, monitor them, and keep them from playing outside because it was too dangerous. She also had to do laundry and housework. The children wanted to play outside and were getting increasingly harder to handle. Their mother was always away from home working, because she refused to be on welfare. About 6 months ago, a man had moved in with them, but he stayed only briefly, maybe a few months.

The therapist thought Takisha's depression was tied into that particular time frame—to the man's coming and leaving. He questioned gently about abuse, particularly sexual abuse, but Takisha denied any. Ultimately it came out that, following the man's departure, Takisha's mother had taken a second job; she worked from 3:00 P.M. to 11:00 P.M. as a hospital aide, then went on a midnight to 8:00 A.M. shift at an all-night restaurant. It was only after four sessions that the therapist began to understand why the mother had seemed so short-tempered about the clinic's scheduling of appointments for herself and her daughter—schedules that were for the convenience of the clinic rather than responsive to Mrs. Landry's needs for sleep and her job responsibilities as a breadwinner. The enormity of Takisha's role as a parental child, whose tasks extended from early morning to night, from getting the children up to putting them to bed, also began to take on significance. The therapist thought that the only time the mother seemed to assume her proper parental role was on Sundays, when the family spent the entire day and evening in church.

The therapist still thought that strained relations between mother and daughter were at the root of Takisha's depression. The mother was viewed as harsh and demanding, insensitive to Takisha's needs as a child, and emotionally distant. All of this went into the case record. Takisha was approaching puberty and had had no life as a child. The treatment goal was to remove the yoke of parental child, to allow her time to study, and to give her some play experience with children her own age. To accomplish this, the therapist hoped to validate Takisha's separation from her parenting role by counteracting her need for maternal approval. He would substitute unconditional positive regard within the therapeutic alliance. He gently normalized: "Sometimes we all get mad at our parents, at the things they expect of us." Takisha looked startled. He continued: "I used to get angry at my mother all the time. I was just about your age when I realized that parents don't know everything!" But instead of responding, Takisha looked terrified. The therapist decided there was really something profoundly disturbing going on between Takisha and her mother. However, the more he tried to explore this, the more withdrawn and depressed Takisha became, and after six sessions they seemed to be getting nowhere.

Comments

Given the therapist's perceptions, a psychodynamically oriented treatment approach is doomed to failure because the "insight" he is seeking is based on incorrect premises. First, let us consider some realities of cultural life in the lower income African-American community. The sharpness heard in Mrs. Landry's admonitions to her daughter, and the child's seeming passivity, are culturally normative in ghetto life. For centuries, beginning with the harsh realities of slavery, children have learned to accept the withholding of praise and the strictures to behave obediently—often reinforcing submissiveness and passivity with elders—that were essential for survival in earlier times. Children learned to accept these parental behaviors without missing the underlying love and approval that are typically invisible to cultural outsiders. The passive response does not mask anger, but indicates acceptance of culturally normative parent-child interactions and perhaps a tacit understanding of the meaning of the behavior. A child's avoidance of eye contact with an adult still connotes respect, in American Indian as well as in African-American cultures. Lack of tactile contact between a mother and 12-year-old daughter does not in any way indicate that affection is missing; as a baby, Takisha was undoubtedly cuddled and held on the laps of numerous adults. But hugging in front of strangers is not commonly done.

Finally, criticism of one's mother is unacceptable in its overt form, in both black and Hispanic lower income life. This is such a powerful tool for insult and metaphor that it has become transmuted into an art form in ghetto life: games such as "playing the dozens" are based on insults to another's mother. The most penetrating attack on another person's integrity comes through insulting his or her mother. In the black community, for a child to acquiesce in criticism of his or her mother is called "flying in the face of God." It defies the most powerful of cultural taboos, and can be harmful to subject and object. It is inappropriate for an adult authority figure to give a child permission to express anger toward the mother. In some belief systems, anger can harm the mother and in some cases even cause her death. Nor is depression always the obverse side of object-related anger; in this particular case, a child is trapped in an impossible situation, and this is reason enough for her dysphoria.

Treatment Plan

This particular case calls for involving the mother in a collaborative role in treatment planning. From a structural viewpoint, the mother's authority should be reinforced and redirected, not undermined. There is no reason to think the underpinnings of this case are psychodynamic conflict between mother and daughter; it is rather a matter of reality needs, cultural expectations, and the daughter's approaching the age of puberty when the burdens are becoming overwhelming.

. . . The therapist cannot and should not remove the parental role in a family where this is necessary for survival. Rather, the therapist helps redistribute the burden by alerting the family to alternative resources. In Takisha's case, the best therapeutic option is to work with the mother in solving the problem. Mrs. Landry realizes her daughter has no life; she just cannot see her way out of the situation. The therapist works with the mother and children to draw on the social network of available helpers. A relative, neighbor, or friend, perhaps available before but unsolicited, is now asked to help out. If necessary, the family's pastor and church are enlisted. The therapist works with the school to assign special help, perhaps a tutor. A specified amount of time is set aside for Takisha to do her homework, and a specified number of hours to spend on her own or with friends. The younger children are assigned tasks. The therapist praises Mrs. Landry for her hard work in keeping the family together—it is legitimate praise—joins with Takisha in admiring her mother, and joins with the mother in admiring Takisha's contribution to the family. Finally, since Takisha is nearing puberty, the therapist may give the mother instruction and reading materials so she can share with Takisha the functional aspects of menstruation and prepare her for her approaching role as a woman. In this process the mother's directive role is reinforced, mother-daughter bonding is reinforced, and Takisha is endowed with a more adult female identity that will legitimate and ease her needed role as a caregiver to the young.

Thinking About the Case

Depression is, by far, the most common psychological problem of adolescence. Takisha exhibited its most prominent symptoms, dejected mood and lack of pleasure in previously enjoyed activities (called "anhedonia"), as well as decreased concentration, lethargy, and declining school performance.

This case illustrates the importance of considering the context in which a disorder is manifested, both in terms of understanding the causes of the disorder and in planning treatment. Models of mental illness are not culture-free. Freud's view of neurosis developed out of his experiences with middle-class women in late nineteenth-century Vienna. Skinner's view that reinforcement is the primary (if not only) factor in the development and maintenance of behavior comes out of the radical environmentalism of mid-twentieth-century America. The current emphasis on biological bases of behavioral disorders is, no doubt, related to technological developments in brain-imaging equipment as well as to ongoing turf battles between the medical establishment and non-medical mental health practitioners. In attempting to understand any individual case, it is useful to be aware of one's own biases and to keep an open mind with respect to alternative perspectives. The perspective of the patient (in medical terminology) or client (in non-medical language) is particularly important. Studies indicate that feeling understood may be the primary feature of a successful therapeutic relationship. Interventions which are based on models that are substantially different from that of the person being treated are unlikely to be successful.

Questions to Consider

1. If you have encountered Martin Seligman's Learned Helplessness model of depression in your text or lectures, what might it say about Takisha's problems?
2. Does this case make an argument for matching patients and therapists along cultural dimensions? Why or why not? What about same sex versus opposite sex therapist/patient matches? Are the arguments the same?
3. Suicide is the third leading cause of death among adolescents (behind accidents and homicides). But the rate is substantially lower for African Americans than for Caucasians. Why might this be so? There is also a difference between males and females, with males completing suicide more than twice as often as females. Why might this be so?
4. The rate of suicide in adolescents has increased over 200 percent since the 1950s? Why might this be so? What could be done about this?

CASE 17

SITUATIONAL DEPRESSION IN THE ELDERLY: THE CASE OF MR. A.

MR. A. IS A SEVENTY-SIX-YEAR-OLD married father of three. He grew up the oldest son of immigrant parents in a large East Coast city. Under his parents' stern and watchful eye, he did well both academically and in schoolyard sports and graduated from high school at sixteen, then going on the road to learn the sales trade with his uncle. He married at nineteen and fathered a son, but the marriage did not survive his almost constant absence and single-minded focus on making money. He and his wife divorced after three years. For some years he kept in touch with his son, but squabbles with his ex-wife over money and visitation gradually eroded his emotional ability to stay involved. His ex-wife wanted him out of their son's life and finally she got her way.

Mr. A.'s apprenticeship with his uncle was interrupted by a three-year stint in the Navy during World War II. He was at sea in the Pacific for most of that time. He recalls playing lots of poker on board the ship and making friends with the cooks and bakers so that he ate as well as the officers. With his poker winnings, he paid other sailors to do his laundry, make his bed, and even, occasionally, take his watch. Still, he was always at his place during battles and earned an honorable discharge at the war's end.

Mr. A.'s self-confidence and charm made him a natural salesman. It didn't take long, upon his return from the service, to develop his own business. Over the next forty years, he made (and occasionally lost) lots of money, married his secretary and fathered two more children, joined a country club, and generally lived the good life.

He did not, of course, escape his share of heartache. He went bankrupt twice (but bounced back quickly), his parents died—first his father, and then his mother less than six months later. His second marriage, relatively happy for the first decade, gradually disintegrated over the next twenty years into one in which bickering and sniping outweighed loving and communicating. His wife complained that he was totally self-centered and had an unreasonable temper. He felt she nagged, belittled, and blamed him. His wife often thought of leaving him, but, having two children and no independent source of income, she stayed, resentfully, in the marriage.

Mr. A. was without diagnosable mental health problems until a series of catastrophes befell him in his seventy-third year. It began with his falling one day. His wife felt that his complaints of weakness in his leg were "in his head," but after the third fall, spinal stenosis, a narrowing of the spinal openings through which nerves pass, was diagnosed and surgery recommended. Mr. A. had every possible complication of surgery. His pacemaker (installed some years before following coronary bypass surgery) failed immediately after the incision was made so the surgery had to be aborted and a new pacemaker inserted. He developed a potentially dangerous blood clot in his leg. He suffered a post-surgical psychosis in which he thought that the doctors were engaged in a plot to sell drugs. In a panic, he tried to tear out his intravenous tube and had to be sedated. His diabetes, previously under fairly good control, became unstable and several times he went into insulin shock. His wound failed to heal properly and had to be reopened, cleaned out, and reclosed. This involved days of painful packing of the open wound. Every time it appeared that he had stabilized, something else happened.

In the midst of all of this, an unrelated event made his medical problems seem minor in comparison. Mrs. A., having gone to her husband's office to clean it out and prepare it for subletting, found a loveletter written to Mr. A. by a woman acquaintance. Confronting him with this, she discovered that he had had an affair with this woman. She could never get clear exactly when and for how long the affair had lasted, but what she learned was enough to devastate her.

Mr. A.'s presumed fidelity was the one trait that had allowed Mrs. A. to remain attached to him over the years, despite what she felt were his serious flaws. At least, she reasoned, he was faithful to her. With this presumption shattered, she had nothing left. For days she refused to visit him in the hospital or speak with him on the telephone. She decided that he probably had had other affairs and had visited prostitutes during his years of traveling. Whether this was true or not, her pain was intense. She cried continuously and told the hospital social workers that she would not bring him home from the hospital. But since Mr. A.'s financial condition did not make him eligible for Medicaid, and with nursing home costs being what they were, she really had no choice. She brought him home, and took care of him in stoney silence. Over the next two years, Mr. A.'s medical condition deteriorated gradually. His heart had been severely stressed by the traumas he had recently survived, and he was hospitalized several times in acute heart failure. Each time, he lost weight—and strength. His back surgery, ironically, had come too late to prevent nerve damage, and he was not able to regain much use of his leg, despite physical therapy. Finally, wheelchair bound and demoralized, he was placed in a nursing home, much to Mrs. A.'s relief and Mr. A.'s chagrin.

By this time, Mrs. A., having entered psychotherapy herself, had come to some peace about Mr. A.'s infidelity. She was no longer enraged at him, but neither did she feel love or loyalty towards him. She was, however, loyal to her own sense of duty and continued to provide some caretaking for Mr. A. She supervised his care at the nursing home, visited him almost daily, and brought him whatever he needed. She engaged him in casual conversation as best she could but her coldness was unmistakable.

Mr. A. was a much changed man. Having been voluble, social, and optimistic all his life, he was now silent, withdrawn, and depressed. He took all his meals in his room and refused to participate in any therapeutic or social activities at the nursing home. He complained bitterly that the nursing aides treated him disrespectfully and that the food was intolerable. He cried easily and spent his days staring, unseeing, at the television. He neither told nor laughed at jokes. He was unable to engage in conversation of any kind. He continued to lose weight even after he recovered from the acute heart failure. He seemed prepared to die in that life offered no pleasure.

Mr. A.'s physician at the nursing home recognized the signs of depression. While Mr. A.'s family thought his behavior was normal for an old, sick, disappointed man, the doctor felt that his mood might improve if he were treated with an antidepressant medication. Within ten days after treatment was begun, his appetite began to improve, and he stopped complaining about the food. A week later, he allowed himself to be talked into eating in the communal dining room where he found a table of men who became his regular mealtime companions. Gradually, his sense of humor returned. So did his ability to charm. He went from being the bane of the staff's existence, to being one of their favorites. He got to know them, joked with them, wheedled special favors from time to time. One of the nursing aides took to sharing her "garlic chicken," his favorite Chinese food, with him whenever she got it. He began to act more like his old self—optimistic and gregarious. He was appreciative for what his wife had done for him. In his optimism, he even talked himself into believing that she really stilled loved him and that, in time, she would forgive him. It appeared that whatever life would be left to him, despite his limitations, he would live with gusto and zest.

Thinking About the Case

Depression in the elderly is often undiagnosed. Like Mr. A.'s family, we tend to think that people who are old, limited, and who have suffered losses and setbacks must necessarily feel sad and demoralized. Anybody who has to suffer the indignities and loss of freedom of living in a nursing home would be depressed, we reason. Anybody whose wife now despised him after fifty years of marriage would be depressed.

As this case illustrates, "it ain't necessarily so." Brain biochemistry may be an important intervening variable. It is likely that external events affect the relative balance of neurotransmitters in the brain, which then affects mood. With treatment, the nursing home food tasted better, the nursing staff were perceived as more friendly, and even Mr. A.'s wife seemed more loving to him. His longstanding emotional resilience, his ability to make the best out of any situation, was restored.

Could psychotherapy have produced the same result? Perhaps. The literature is equivocal about the comparative benefits of antidepressant medication versus psychotherapy. Two forms of psychotherapy in particular have been shown to be effective in treating depression: interpersonal psychotherapy, which focuses on the critical relationships in the person's life, and cognitive psychotherapy, which works on changing the distorted thinking patterns often exhibited by depressed people. Other forms have not been systematically tested, but may also be effective. Mrs. A. was treated with psychotherapy and improved significantly over the two years she was in therapy. She didn't achieve the sunny optimism of Mr. A., but then, she'd never had it before.

It's likely that some people respond better to psychotherapy and others to pharmacological interventions. Psychological-mindedness, the ability to form a trusting therapeutic relationship and a model of symptoms that lends itself to "the talking cure," are probably prerequisites for achieving a good psychotherapy result. Some people distrust and fear medicines, which would also make them candidates for a psychotherapeutic approach. Others don't have the patience for psychotherapy, don't wish to or can't share their feelings with another person, don't have very good capacity for insight, or believe that medication will cure them. These people would be good candidates for pharmacological treatment.

In practice, many people who are depressed receive both psychotherapy and medication, since we do not yet have any real way of knowing who will benefit from what. While most of these improve significantly, the relative benefits of combined treatment compared with single treatment have not been scientifically sorted out.

Questions to Consider

1. If you became depressed, what sort of treatment would you be inclined to seek out? Why would you choose that treatment over the alternatives?
2. Learned helplessness is a model of depression on which much of cognitive therapy is based. How would the model apply to Mr. A.'s experiences? What kind of therapeutic intervention would be dictated by this model?
3. Depression is diagnosed much more frequently in women than in men. What are some reasons why this might be so?

LANAHAN NOTES
Depressive Disorders

As with the NOTES in Chapter Four, Bipolar and Related Disorders, we can ask the same questions regarding depressive disorders: What is normal sadness versus depression? Many people suffer some sadness: How do we distinguish these individuals from those who are clinically depressed?

Indications of major depressive disorder:

Person's emotional reaction is greatly out of proportion to the events causing the reaction

Person's daily functioning is impaired

Characteristics of depressive disorder

mood: sad, tearful, unable to experience pleasure

physiology: negative changes in sleep patterns, appetite, weight, energy, activity level

cognition: diminished concentration, indecisiveness, feelings of worthlessness and guilt, and thoughts of death and suicide

can be single episode or recurrent

Other depressive disorders

Disruptive mood dysregulation disorder: severe recurrent temper outbursts inconsistent with developmental level; persistently irritable or angry between outbursts

Persistent depressive disorder (dysthmia): a chronic, but less severe form of depression lasting for at least two years (1 year for children or adolescents)

Premenstrual dysphoric disorder: depressive symptoms, mood swings and/or irritability; symptoms are typically present in the final week before the onset of menses; improvement within a few days after the onset of menses; minimal or absent in the week postmenses; 5–8% of women experience such symptoms

Not otherwise specified: depressions not meeting criteria for more specific syndromes

Seasonal affective disorder (SAD): people—particularly those who live where there are fewer hours of sunlight — get depressive symptoms particularly at winter

Who gets major depressive disorder?

7 percent of the population

18–29 year olds 3 times more likely than 60-years old or older

Women are 1.5–3 times more likely than men to be diagnosed, but considered a controversial statistic

Causes of major depressive disorder — biopsychosocial model

Biological: genetics; depression runs in families as possible biochemical defect.

Behavioral-cognitive (learned helplessness theory): patients learn that they have no control over their situation; they feel helpless; depression can follow

Cognitive: depressed individuals tend to have distorted thoughts (cognitions) out of sync with actual experience

Modeling: depressed behavior may be modeled from parent

Environmental: childhood loss may predispose to adult depression.

Treatment

Medications: affect the brain's biochemistry; alleviate the depressed mood

Selective serotonin re-uptake blockers (SSRIs)

Tricyclics act on the level of the neurotransmitter, serotonin

MAO inhibitors, though dangerous when certain foods (cheese, red wine) are consumed

Interpersonal psychotherapy: helps the person handle relationship issues better.

Cognitive therapy: can "re-order" the client's distorted thoughts

Behavioral therapy: rewards clients for small, then larger positive actions; individuals learn that they can gain increasing control over their situations

Electroconvulsive therapy (ECT): sometimes used to relieve very serious deep depressions that cannot wait for drug and behavioral-cognitive therapies to take effect

Marital or family therapy: helpful if the depression seems to evolve more from interpersonal factors or has interpersonal effects.

Light therapy: a new therapy that effects a chemical change; some success with seasonal affective disorder

Note on therapy evaluation: drugs, interpersonal psychotherapy, and cognitive therapy treatments have all been shown effective in large controlled clinical trials undertaken by NIMH

CHAPTER SIX

Anxiety Disorders

It is likely that fear is among the most commonly experienced of human emotions. None of us is a stranger to it. The heart pounds, muscles tense, pupils dilate, sweat glands secrete, and one experiences a strong urge to escape. Often, fear is a functional response: if a tiger is at your heels, being afraid motivates running away. However, decades of research have demonstrated that the fear-response pattern is highly conditionable. That is, neutral stimuli can come to elicit fear if they are paired, under certain circumstances, with painful, emotionally charged events. So, a wide variety of non-noxious situations can come to produce dysfunctional fear responses—responses that aren't useful and may, in fact, be harmful. Housecats may resemble tigers in some ways, but running from them isn't necessary and may even prevent you from going where you might otherwise like to be. Yet, some people with phobia react in this very way.

Fear has a specific object. Anxiety, fear's more nebulous cousin, is a feeling of apprehension or dread for which no specific stimulus is apparent. When we are anxious, we are generally unable to say exactly what we are afraid of. Or if we can, we are painfully aware that others do not feel the same way. Like fear, anxiety is a commonly experienced emotion.

When fear or anxiety seem out of proportion to the stimulus, when they cause significant distress or dysfunction in the sufferer, one of the anxiety disorders is diagnosed. These disorders are extremely common. It has been estimated that, in any given year, more than 15% of adults in the United States have one or more anxiety disorders. The annual cost to society in the form of lost productivity, suicide, and treatment expenses of anxiety disorders is estimated to be in excess of $42 billion dollars. Clearly, anxiety disorders constitute a major public health problem.

The DSM-5 lists eleven anxiety disorders. We have chosen four for inclusion here: simple phobia, panic disorder with agoraphobia, social anxiety disorder, and generalized anxiety disorder (GAD).

The first case is about a man who had a phobia he didn't even know about until he had to submit to an MRI (magnetic resonance imaging) test for a physical problem. He was treated successfully as are most people who seek treatment for simple phobias. This is a good example of behavior therapy at work.

The second case concerns a woman who has spent years suffering from panic disorder with agoraphobia, in which attacks of overwhelming fear, seemingly coming out of nowhere, caused her to become virtually housebound. The case is particularly instructive because the woman had several different kinds of therapy before she recovered. It is fascinating because she recovered despite the fact that her history of sexual abuse was never disclosed or discussed in therapy. This patient actually participated in writing up her own story for this volume.

The third case introduces us to a boy from a chaotic family who also has a physical disability. He experiences social anxiety, not surprisingly, when he enters school and develops a host of behavioral problems to try to cope. His case illustrates the real-world complexity of psychological disorders and the role of ongoing or new stressors in maintaining symptoms. In the previous edition of this book, this case was included in the section "Disorders First Manifest in Childhood or Adolescence," which no longer exists. It was used to illustrate school phobia, a diagnosis that no longer exists. Thus are the vagaries of diagnostic practices.

The fourth case, describing a woman with a lifelong history of generalized anxiety disorder, illustrates treatment with cognitive therapy. She learns to identify and modify the thoughts that lead to her anxiety, with good results. Generalized anxiety disorder is also treated with medications, and the relative efficacy of the two types of intervention is still uncertain.

CASE 18

SIMPLE PHOBIA: THE CASE OF PHILIP B.

PHILIP B HAD EMBARRASSED himself terribly. He didn't know how he could face them, but he knew he had to. So he went to a therapist, even though that, too, embarrassed him. Here's what had happened:

Philip, a university professor, had been scheduled for an MRI (magnetic resonance imaging) examination to assess the feasibility of surgery for back pain that he had been experiencing for some time. He had known what an MRI was, and, in general, what the procedure entailed. The patient lies on his back on a table. The table slides him into the MRI machine, a large hollow tube that encases the patient quite closely. When the machine is activated, the patient hears loud banging noises, somewhat like construction site sounds for the duration of the test which can last approximately forty-five minutes.

In the weeks approaching the test, Philip had not been particularly nervous about it. However, a few seconds after being moved into the machine, Philip found, to his dismay, that he was having trouble breathing. In an instant, he panicked and began to try to inch his way out. The technician, seeing that Philip was in distress, interrupted the procedure and brought Philip out.

At this point, Philip was taking rapid, little gulping breaths. His face and hands were clammy. His heart was beating wildly. His throat had tightened and he could barely speak. Philip was mortified . . . and mystified. Nothing like this had ever happened to him before. It was totally unanticipated. The technician tried to calm him, saying that many patients became anxious in the MRI machine. Perhaps he might want to try it again in a moment when he had calmed down. Indeed, he did want to try it. Philip was quite sure that he could stay in control if he set his mind to it. After a few minutes, back he went into the bowels of the machine. Philip tried to breath evenly and keep his eyes closed so he wouldn't see how close to his face the lid of the machine was. But it was no good. He felt, he later said, like the machine was a coffin and he had been buried alive. He couldn't stay inside, and quickly signaled the technician to let him out. Deeply chagrined, Philip was led out to the office nurse who gently suggested that he see one of the three psychologists whose names she had written down for him. Then he went to the appointments secretary where he was rescheduled for another MRI a month later.

The psychologist took a careful history. Philip was the youngest of three sons born to a pair of high school teachers. There was no history of substance abuse or emotional disorder in his family. However, when asked whether he had had any childhood experiences that might be related to his recent difficulties, a startling memory resurfaced. In their bedroom, his parents had had a trunk at the foot of the bed. Apparently, his father had used it during the war, and now it kept extra blankets for cold winter nights. Philip and his older brothers would often play in his parents' room and once, when he was about four years old, his brothers had put him in the trunk and sat on the top so he couldn't get out. As he related to the psychologist how he had gone from joyfully participating in the game to frantically screaming and pounding on the trunk and calling for his mother, his anxiety began to mount, there, in the office. Astonished, he found himself almost as frightened in the telling as he had been in the doing. Philip didn't think it had taken his mother long to come and let him out, but in that time he had become convinced that he was going to die in that trunk for lack of air. By the time she got him out, he had been almost unable to breathe from crying so hard.

This recollection released a number of related thoughts and feelings. Philip became aware that he had been mildly uncomfortable on his friend's boat, when everyone went into the cabin to look around. He had come out quickly, feeling strangely relieved to be out in the air again. He didn't much like going up into the cedar closet where he and his wife kept their winter clothes during the summer months—he tended to ask his wife to go up there when he needed to retrieve something. Come to think of it, he didn't even really feel comfortable in restaurant booths, preferring a table always. He hadn't ever been troubled by these minor "quirks," but now he wondered if they were all linked to the episode (or episodes, he couldn't really remember) in the trunk.

Philip wondered if, now that he knew what had caused his fears, he might no longer have them. The psychologist suggested he check this idea out by going into the cabin of his friend's boat. At their follow-up appointment the next week, Philip reported that his experiment had gone poorly. He had, indeed, gone into the cabin as he had agreed, with every expectation that he would be quite comfortable, but he hadn't been comfortable at all. Within short order, his breathing became rapid, his heart started to pound, and he began to feel a strong need to get out—which he did, much to his dismay.

The psychologist explained to Philip that, while insight wasn't generally enough to cure a phobia, the condition was highly treatable with a procedure called "systematic desensitization." In this procedure, Philip would be taught how to relax deeply, and then would apply these relaxation techniques during a series of increasingly anxiety-producing situations. With repeated exposure to the feared situations, the anxiety response would gradually give way to the relaxation response. Philip readily agreed to participate.

With the therapist's help, Philip was taught how to use a 0–100 point scale to rate the amount of anxiety he felt in any given situation. Then, as a homework assignment, he was asked to list all the situations that caused him any anxiety at all, rating each one using the scale. At the next visit, Philip and the psychologist constructed a hierarchy of feared situations, beginning with the least feared (sitting in a booth in a restaurant, rated 30) to the most feared—the dreaded MRI, rated 95. To give Philip the opportunity to practice his relaxation strategy in a situation that would approximate the closed-in feeling of the MRI, the therapist came up with a clever simulation. He had Philip lie first under the dining room table (rated 40), then under the coffee table (rated 65), and finally, under the bed (rated 95—the same as the MRI).

The procedure for learning the relaxation response included progressively tensing and relaxing various muscle groups, along with deep, restful breathing and imaging a relaxing scene at the beach. Philip was amazed to find that he was actually tense much of the time, but that he could learn to relax on cue. Sent home to practice the relaxation response, he began, on his own, to work through his hierarchy of feared situations. By the time of his next visit, he was able to lie under the coffee table for indefinite periods of time without any noticeable anxiety. In fact, during his last practice session, he had fallen asleep! Philip reported to the psychologist that he didn't feel he needed any more sessions. He had confidence in his anxiety-fighting techniques and was certain he could undergo the MRI after spending a few hours under his bed, which he intended to do after work that same day. The psychologist reminded Philip to keep practicing and to make sure he did not slip back into small avoidance behaviors in the future, because anxiety tends to recur if given an opening. Ten days later, the psychologist got an e-mail from Philip. He had survived the MRI just fine—and had joined his friends for dinner in the cabin of their boat!

Thinking About the Case

Fears are extremely common. Phobias, fear reactions that are greatly out of proportion to the reality of the danger, are also quite common, occurring in about six percent of the population. They are also quite amenable to treatment based on learning or behavior theory as this case illustrates. According to the principles of classical conditioning, closed in spaces have become conditioned stimuli (CS) which are related to, or signal, the presence of the unconditioned stimulus (UCS), in this case, being locked in a trunk. The unconditioned response (UCR), panic at being locked in the trunk, is replicated as a conditioned response (CR), in this case, ranging from mild anxiety to panic. Previously neutral stimuli now evoke fear. Note that this accounts for the fact that phobias expand. Philip is not only afraid of situations that closely resemble being locked in a trunk, but also situations which are more distantly reminiscent, like sitting in restaurant booths. The CS signals the UCS in some way, but not in all ways.

The behavioral model also accounts for the persistence of phobias: extinction of the phobias cannot occur because people usually avoid the situations that are difficult for them to handle. Therefore, they do not find themselves in situations in which the CS occurs without the UCS, which is the condition that allows extinction of the CR to occur.

Treatment creates situations in which extinction can occur. Patients are taught to remain in the presence of the CS (in Philip's case, using relaxation as a means to do so) until they can "learn" that the UCS will not occur. Other methods that can achieve this goal have also been used successfully. One is called "flooding," in which the patient is simply prevented from leaving the feared situation until the fear is extinguished. The other is "modeling" in which the patient watches and then imitates a person who engages in the feared behavior. In each of these, exposure to the CS, the feared situation, in the absence of the UCS, the traumatic event is necessary for extinction of the phobia.

Most phobias are readily amenable to treatment if, and this is an important "if", the patient is well-motivated. Because each of the treatments requires the patient to do exactly the thing that he or she has most feared, it generally requires tolerance of at least some measure of anxiety. If the patient is more motivated to avoid anxiety than to master the situation, treatment resistance will present a major obstacle.

Questions To Consider

1. Why do you suppose that knowing that a situation is not objectively dangerous doesn't cure phobias? Why must Philip actually sit

in a booth in a restaurant over and over to "learn" that it is safe to do so?

2. Some phobias are much more common than others. Virtually nobody is afraid of chairs, but lots of people are afraid of animals, or heights, or closed in spaces, like Philip. Why might this be?
3. Some phobias, like Philip's, occur through "one trial learning" whereas Pavlov's dogs needed to have the bell (the CS) paired with food (the UCS) repetitively to produce a salivary response (CR) to the bell. Why might this be so?
4. There is some evidence to suggest that phobias run in families. If phobias are classically conditioned through experience, what is it that is being inherited?

CASE 19

PANIC AND AGORAPHOBIA: THE CASE OF SANDY J.

SANDY J. IS A PETITE, lively, forty-three-year-old woman. She has been happily married to the same man for twenty-three years and has two healthy, successful young adult children. She and her husband manage an apartment complex in a small college town in Maryland. She also founded and is still active in an organization that cares for and finds homes for stray cats. Recently, she has been driving a friend, who had been injured, to physical therapy appointments. But for years, she could not drive at all. In fact, she had been virtually housebound. Here's how it happened.

Sandy was one of five children in a two-parent, working-class family. She had a twin brother, two older sisters, and a younger sister. Her father was a machinist who had left school in the tenth grade, and her mother was an office worker who had completed high school. Sandy reports there was heavy drinking, possibly alcoholism, in the males on both sides of her family in her grandparents' generation. Her parents, though, were both teetotalers. She describes her maternal grandfather as emotionally disturbed. She remembers him as being unstable, jealous, and full of insecurities. He panicked easily. She recalls that he was deathly afraid of thunderstorms and used to make the family hide in the basement until they passed over. She says he was both physically and verbally abusive to other family members.

Sandy believes that her parents were good providers but were "distinctly lacking in nurturance." She describes them as "not good at coping with life." Rather, they were "easily overwhelmed" and "seem to me, in retrospect, terribly frightened in just trying to manage life." She describes her father as somewhat distant and her mother as a "wrathful disciplinarian" who went after the children with hairbrushes, flyswatters, and whatever else was handy. Sandy remembers that her mother once broke her sister's nose with a blow of the brush. Sandy feels one key to her later problems may be related to the fact that while her mother often "flew out of control," the children were not allowed to express any anger. She believes she grew up without a role model for the appropriate expression of feelings, and without tools to help her manage her own feelings. The children's anger was managed by insisting they sit absolutely quiet in a chair until they apologized, at which point their mother would refuse to accept the apology and make them sit some more.

Sandy describes herself as a child as shy, introspective, self involved, and often afraid. She remembers being afraid that airplanes would mistake the flat roof of her house for a runway and try to land on it. She became frightened of carbon-monoxide poisoning after a neighborhood girl died while necking with her boyfriend in a parked car. She was most especially afraid of drawing attention to herself by speaking in front of the class at school. Despite this fear, she was able, with encouragement from her parents and teachers, to perform the lead role in the school play as a high school senior.

Sandy's childhood and young adulthood were marred by a number of terrifying sexual experiences which, although remembered, did not seem particularly important to her until years later. From about the age of eight until her early to mid-teens she was regularly molested by neighborhood boys who lived as foster children with a family up the road from her house. None of them had intercourse with her, but they fondled and rubbed up against her to the point of their having orgasms. She can't remember why or when the abuse stopped. However, this was not the end of it.

When she was sixteen, her father kissed her—hard—on the lips when no one else was home. He never did it, or anything like it again, but when she talks about it now, she says, "it took him ten seconds to destroy our relationship." A couple of years later, Sandy lost her virginity through date rape. "What's so bizarre," she says, "is that the relationship went on for six months after that. I can't understand why I let that happen." Over many years, Sandy has told virtually no one except her husband about these experiences, and even he doesn't know about her father. She doesn't know whether her sisters were also molested by the neighbors or sexually approached by her father, although one of her sisters doesn't like her father and no one seems to know why.

Despite her private hardships, Sandy appeared, for a while, a model youngster who was moving successfully through life. She graduated high school and looked forward to college. However, on the first day of her freshman year, her grandmother, "the one I really loved," died suddenly of a heart attack. Her sister came to campus to tell her, and then, unaccountably, she left without Sandy and went back home alone. Sandy attended college orientation and then, by herself, went to the funeral, all in the same week. Freshman year, she recalls, "was doomed to failure." At its end, she took a leave of absence, and went to work.

In October of what would have been her sophomore year, she met her future husband, Donald. By November she was pregnant, and they married in February. Fourteen months after the birth of their first child, they had another. It was then that Sandy had her first panic attack. Out of the blue, and with no apparent precipitant, her heart began to pound intensely. It felt as if it were going to jump right out of her chest. She broke out in a cold sweat and felt as if she were suffocating. She remembers thinking that she was going to die. While that attack abated after several minutes, it was not to be her last. Doctor's visits, tests, and examinations revealed nothing physically wrong, despite her growing apprehensions that she had heart disease, a brain tumor, or a host of other diseases. She became acutely sensitive to every bodily sensation, examining each for cues of disease. Her doctor gave her Valium, an anti-anxiety medication in the benzodiazepine class, which helped some but still the attacks continued and expanded. They seemed to occur most often when in the car—the farther from home, the more likely and the more severe the attack. Gradually, Sandy developed the symptoms of agoraphobia—avoidance of places in which an attack might occur. She began to curtail driving by herself. After an attack occurred in the grocery store, she stopped going to that store. Since she felt safer if Don were around when she had an attack, she stopped going out except when he could accompany her. Within a couple of years, she was completely housebound. She begged Don not to leave the house, and when he had to go, she would go from window to window, trying to keep sight of him for as long as possible. She was distraught until he returned. Don became her only source of safety. The symptoms seemed manageable in his presence, but without him, she felt they would "swallow me up, eradicate me."

Sandy went to a psychiatrist for a few visits, but found them unhelpful. She can't now remember what they spoke about. A year and a half later, as her symptoms worsened, she began treatment with a clinical social worker who seemed to focus on the dynamics of the marriage as the cause of the symptoms. Towards the end of the treatment, the therapist tried some hypnosis, but that didn't seem very useful either. Sandy stayed in treatment about ten months that time.

Finally, after another year had passed, she tried therapy again, this time with a psychologist who took a cognitive approach, helping her identify the thoughts that were leading to her fear, and helping her learn to modify those thoughts in a more realistic direction. For example, she learned to recognize her symptoms as being related to anxiety, rather than illness. She learned to question her belief that fainting or being embarrassed would be catastrophic. She learned to ask herself the question, "what's the worst that can happen?" She learned not to say, in her mind, "I can't stand it," but rather to say "I prefer that it be different."

For the first time, she got a label for the disorder and soon learned that many others suffered from similar symptoms. Reading about agoraphobia, joining a therapeutic support group, and subscribing to a newsletter from a national phobia-support organization helped as well. She began to set behavioral goals for herself and practice them each day. Don was her support person, encouraging her and accompanying her on her practice when necessary. He also consulted with the psychologist from time to time, so that his questions and concerns could be addressed. Sandy says the therapy taught her that she really could make choices for herself, and it helped her to view her "baby steps" towards confronting and mastering her fears as victories. She also feels it was immeasurably helpful to "be viewed with respect [by her therapist] in the midst of a paralyzing disorder" instead of being treated like a "sick" or "weak" patient.

After a couple of years of individual and group therapy, Sandy was functioning at a much higher level. She had resumed driving, although she was still wary of the expressway into the nearby city. She was doing all her local chores—shopping, banking, and the like—by herself. Don was able to go about his business without worrying that she would be unable to do without him. She decided to terminate therapy and continue to work on her own with the "tools" she had been given.

Now, some eight years later, Sandy is virtually symptom free, although she says her progress to this point has been, at times, "inexorably slow." She reports she now has an "absolute feeling of emotional integrity," which is entirely new for her. She has gone back to college and has finished her undergraduate degree. She is immeasurably grateful to her husband and children for their support and believes it significantly aided her recovery. She is also convinced that getting involved with the "kitties" was key, in that it focussed her attention outside of herself and increased her self-esteem. Of therapy, she says, "when I was ill, it seemed my emotional landscape was illuminated by candles, each one lighting only a small portion of the field at a time. On the other hand, therapy was like halogen lighting, wonderful for reading, but almost too bright." Describing the present, she says, "now I have a GE softlight, with a rheostat that's under my control."

Thinking About the Case

This case is illustrative of the typical development of agoraphobia. First come a series of panic attacks. While they often begin during a period of time when the individual is under significant stress, they generally are perceived as coming "out of the blue," with no immediate precipitant at hand. With racing heart, pain in the chest, nausea, dizziness, and a sensation of choking, the sweaty sufferer has the strong sensation that she is having a heart attack or going crazy—in either case, losing control.

The attacks are so painful and so frightening that sufferers are highly motivated to avoid them, so they start to avoid situations in which attacks have occurred, reasoning that there must be something in the situation that stimulated the attack. If an attack occurs in a grocery store, the individual begins to be wary of going shopping in that store. If another occurs there, the person may begin to avoid the store altogether. If an attack then occurs when shopping in a different grocery store, the person may begin to avoid shopping altogether. As you can see, it doesn't take long for the sufferer to develop a "fear of fear." When this happens, attacks begin to occur with increasing frequency in situations in which the person feels unprotected. Examples include being in places where exit without embarrassment is difficult, like church, restaurants, checkout lines, or being some place without a "safe" person, one who could protect the sufferer if something terrible did happen. Desperately, the individual further restricts activities. In the worst cases, like Sandy's, people become virtual prisoners in their own houses.

Sandy's illness occurred at a time when the treatment for agoraphobia was changing. Psychoanalysis and psychodynamically oriented psychotherapy, which had been the treatment of choice for all the anxiety disorders for years, had proven fairly ineffective with panic and agoraphobia, although some professionals still relied heavily on those methods. Some practitioners, like the social worker Sandy saw, were beginning to look for the etiology of the disorder in the social relationships of the patient. For Sandy, the focus on her marital relationship seemed to have quite limited value in modifying her symptoms. At the same time, medical practitioners were researching medicines that could potentially block the panic attacks from occurring. Several of these medications were available at the time Sandy sought treatment, but because of their side effects and her desire to control her own progress, she elected not to take any of them. Still other therapists, like the psychologist, were beginning to use behavioral and cognitive strategies to modify the "fear of fear" and address the avoidance component of the disorder. This approach proved to be most helpful to Sandy.

Most striking about this case is the fact that, although the trauma history was virtually neglected in therapy, Sandy made substantial progress anyway. It is hard to imagine that the sexual abuse she endured did not predispose her in some way to psychological disorder, but it appears that analyzing this aspect of her past was not necessary in order for her symptoms to improve greatly. In retrospect, Sandy believes that she had not been ready to discuss her abuse history at the time of her treatment. Rather, overwhelmed by her symptoms, she apparently had needed to focus directly on reducing her level of dysfunction. Interestingly, she reports that thoughts and memories of the abuse have grown "more vivid" in recent years as she has recovered emotional stability. Perhaps she will find that a course of more exploratory, psychodynamically-oriented psychotherapy aimed at resolving some of her feelings related to the abuse would interest her in the future.

Questions to Consider

1. According to learning theory, agoraphobia combines elements of both classical and instrumental conditioning. Can you identify the components of each in Sandy's case?
2. Some people have panic attacks but never go on to develop agoraphobia. Can you imagine some reasons why this might be?
3. Are there elements in Sandy's history that might particularly predispose her to panic and agoraphobia, as opposed to other psychological disorders? What might these be?

CASE 20

SOCIAL ANXIETY DISORDER: THE CASE OF TIMMY R.

TIMMY HAD BEEN DEALT A VERY bad hand in life. He was born with spina bifida, a disorder in which the spinal column is incompletely formed and nerve damage of various sorts results. For Timmy this meant that he had no control of his bladder or bowel functioning. At six years of age and in first grade, he also walked with a slight limp and his speech was difficult to understand. The latter was not much of a problem, however, because Timmy rarely spoke. He stayed to himself and, according to his teacher, didn't seem to be interested in the other children in his class. She said that he reminded her of Tiny Tim in *The Christmas Carol*—small and thin, with a "pinched little face."

Timmy's father was a binge drinker and heroin user who had difficulty holding a job. The family lived in poverty and despair. They rented a trailer in a run-down park. Much to the park owner's consternation, the R.'s had several vehicles (or parts of vehicles) littering their small yard. Inside, they had mattresses on the floor rather than beds, but it didn't matter much—Timmy said that people in his family rarely went to bed. Instead, they tended to fall asleep watching television at night.

Mrs. R. was a thin, worn-looking woman. Missing her two front teeth and dangling a cigarette from her mouth, she looked two decades older than her actual age of thirty-two. She worked a part-time job making minimum wage and had her hands full at home. Timmy required lots of care and she didn't get much help from her older daughter, Cheryl, age twelve, who had lots of needs of her own. Still the house, though dreadfully furnished, was clean and neat, at least when the school's counselor made a visit.

Cheryl, a spare child with a pasty, acne-ridden complexion, had needed special education services throughout school. Often coming in just to talk, she liked to spend time with the counselor, who found her to be a needy, affectionate youngster. However, her speech was decidedly odd and difficult to follow. She switched referents in the middle of sentences so you could never really know what she was talking about. She drifted from topic to topic, getting distracted by a detail that took her in a new direction altogether. She talked a lot about animals, but her stories about them always revolved around injury or death. Her cat got hit by a car; a neighbor's gerbil was found dead in its cage; a friend's dog was poisoned. Her other main topic centered on her own illnesses and injuries. Her teacher said, "if she had half the things wrong with her that she says, she'd be the sickest kid on the planet." She talked about her neck "splitting" and bleeding. She had "locked" intestines. She had pain in her knees. She also saw and heard things that nobody else perceived. Despite being approached several times, Mrs. R. was resistant to having Cheryl evaluated by a mental health professional. Her own mother had had voices and visions, she said. It was no big deal. Cheryl was fine. It was Timmy that she had to worry about.

The counselor never met Mr. R., but her contacts with the three other members of the family left her with the feeling that they all felt that the family had been singled out for misfortune. Their sense of burden, mistreatment, and misery were almost palpable.

Despite his disabilities, Timmy had seemed to make an adequate adjustment to his half-day kindergarten when he was five. He had had some initial problems adjusting, but seemed to make out okay. He got along fairly well with the aide who was assigned to change his diapers and assist him in accomplishing his tasks. Timmy didn't make out as well with the other children in kindergarten. Prior to school he had been isolated, interacting only with his family, doctors, and other caregivers. He couldn't move about as quickly as his peers, and he couldn't communicate as well. He kept mostly to himself, but didn't seem particularly unhappy.

However, he began to miss a lot of school in first grade. A new aide had been assigned who neither he nor his mother liked very much. He began throwing fits in the mornings, and his mother didn't seem to try very hard to make him go to school. His teacher reported that Timmy had no friends, and while she was on the lookout, she couldn't entirely keep other children from teasing him. He never stood up for himself. She thought he didn't know how. His response was to withdraw more and more until he barely spoke at all. On days when he did get to school, he spent most of his time making up illnesses and insisting that his mother had to be called.

At first his teachers ignored his constant complaining, gently refocusing him back on the task at hand. Then he escalated—pretending to throw up in the boys' room. He disrupted the class every ten to fifteen minutes with a physical complaint, a request that he be sent to the nurse, or that his mother be called. Finally, when they could stand it no longer, his teachers started sending him to the front office several times a day.

Mrs. R. reluctantly attended a school conference only after she was threatened with legal action if she did not. At the conference, she was informed that she was legally obliged to get Timmy to school and that he could be removed from home if she did not. A deal was cut: Mrs. R. would get Timmy to school if they would refrain from calling her during the day about his complaints. The counselor recommended that Timmy receive mental health therapy from the local mental health center, but Mrs. R. seemed uninterested in the suggestion.

For a while after that, things seemed to improve. Timmy got to school almost every day. His complaints and interruptions diminished under a behavioral plan devised by the counselor and administered by his teachers. According to this plan, Timmy earned a gold star for every fifteen-minute interval during which he did his work and did not interrupt the teacher. Ten stars earned him ten minutes of play time with the counselor.

All seemed to be getting better. But, unfortunately, in the spring of his first grade year, Timmy had to have surgery to attempt a partial repair of his spina bifida. He was out of school for some time, receiving in-home tutoring services to keep him up with his class. When he returned to school after six weeks of recuperation, his behavioral problems escalated again. His mother reported that he would become so upset at the idea of coming to school that he would hold his breath until he passed out. This frightened and dismayed her, and she didn't know how to respond. Getting him to school was just not worth the battle.

Individual sessions with the school counselor, now provided daily, didn't seem to improve the situation any. Timmy asked to have his sister come in to the sessions with him, but this, too, seemed to go nowhere. While he was content to play quietly in the counselor's office, he balked at going back to class, and the counselor found that she, like Timmy's mom, did not have the energy to resist his vociferous demands.

School officials were between a rock and a hard place. They could ask the family court to remove Timmy from his home to a foster care or residential setting in the hopes that this might improve the situation, or they could provide home tutoring on a long-term basis. As of this writing, Timmy is being tutored at home.

Thinking About the Case

Timmy's symptoms might be subsumed under several diagnoses. He might be diagnosed with separation anxiety disorder, which is marked by developmentally inappropriate and excessive anxiety concerning separation from home or from major attachment figures (usually the mother). He might be diagnosed with somatic symptom disorder since he complained of physical symptoms which almost certainly had psychological origins. He might be diagnosed with having attention deficit hyperactivity disorder since he appeared distractible and had difficulty controlling his impulses to disrupt the class. However, at base, Timmy was insecure around other people, particularly his peers. Certainly, he came by this honestly given his lack of experience and the social implications of his physical disability.

Social anxiety disorder is not rare. However, it is likely underdiagnosed with many of the people who meet the criteria for the disorder labelled simply "shy." And, since gregariousness and shyness lie along a continuum, the issue of when a psychological disorder is actually present is cogent. As always, DSM-5 requires that the symptoms cause significant discomfort and/or interfere significantly with day-to-day functioning for a diagnosis to be made.

Timmy's case illustrates the use of behavioral techniques in treatment, including modelling, coaching, and reinforcement. It also reminds us that if treatment is interrupted prematurely, gains can be lost. Timmy's anxiety returned when he was out of school following surgery, and he was more resistant to working on the problem when he came back to school. Medications are also used to treat social anxiety disorder, but without exposure and mastery of the feared situations, change is unlikely.

Questions to Consider

1. Why do you think Mrs. R. was so resistant to getting outside help for her children? Do you think she played a role in the development of Timmy's social anxiety? If so, what was it? What might have been done differently to develop a more cooperative alliance with her?
2. What do you think were the contributions of Timmy's family environment to the development of his school problems? Do you think his physical handicap also contributed? In what way?
3. Develop a comprehensive treatment plan for Timmy, choosing any or all of the six treatment options listed in our discussion above. Justify your choice. How successful do you think your plan would be in this particular case? Why?

CASE 21

GENERALIZED ANXIETY DISORDER: THE CASE OF DAWN D.

DAWN, A FORTY-FIVE-YEAR-OLD married school nurse, appeared for her first psychotherapy consultation immaculately attired in a navy blue wool suit with matching shoes and handbag. Her hair was perfectly done and her makeup was flawless. She looked around in dismay, and finally perched on the nearest chair when the therapist told her to sit wherever she liked. She spoke softly and somewhat hesitantly, answering questions clearly but without excess verbiage. She was there, she said, because she "worried a lot," and her grown daughter had finally extracted a promise from her that she would seek help.

Dawn was worried, it seemed, about virtually everything. She worried every workday about making mistakes—those she had made, those she might make in the future, and those she imagined she might have made. She also worried about what the teachers and principal at her school thought of her. She wondered if maybe they didn't think she was stuck up because she didn't enter easily into the teachers' lounge banter. She didn't think she had very good social skills.

Dawn worried also about the health and wellbeing of her family. Her husband, a stockbroker, was mildly overweight and a bit of a couch potato. Dawn worried daily that he would have a heart attack or stroke. She was at him all the time to eat better and to exercise. She wanted him to see the doctor three times a year for "checkups." She worried about his driving to his job, forty-five minutes away, particularly in bad winter weather. She often called him at the office to see if he'd gotten in all right. She had a secret worry about him as well: she worried about whether she loved him enough. Sometimes when she looked honestly into her own feelings, she wasn't sure if she actually loved him, or just felt responsible for him. She wondered anxiously whether these feelings were "normal," but she suspected they were not. Perhaps she was deficient in her capacity to love.

Dawn worried about her two children as well, and this "drove them crazy," as they had so often told her. She worried about their health, their morale, their relationships, their travel plans, their future, and all of the myriad dangers to which they were exposed every day. She worried also about what other people thought of her children—were they good citizens, had she been a good mother? Then, too, she felt guilty for being so dependent on the evaluation of others. She knew that her children needed to live their own lives, but she could not restrain herself from calling each of them almost every day, just to see how they were, and to offer her advice on various matters. Tearfully, she reported that her son and his wife spent more time with her daughter-in-law's family than with her and her husband. They seemed uneasy in her company, though she tried harder than anyone could know to have everything perfect for them when they came for dinner.

In fact, preparing dinner for company or having extended family stay in the house for a few days generally sent Dawn into paroxysms of cleaning and "obsessing." For these occasions, she spent hours preparing menus, shopping, and cooking. She had flowers in every room that she had arranged and rearranged over and over. She worried that everyone would think her home was "tasteless." Dawn admitted that for several nights before having company she slept fitfully, if at all, and was irritable in the extreme with her husband.

Dawn described her life as "joyless." "I feel like I'm always carrying the weight of the world on my shoulders, and I can't seem to set it down," she said. Generally, she felt tired and listless, and sometimes she was so preoccupied that she could barely concentrate on what she was doing.

Dawn, it seems, had been this way since she had been "knee-high to a grasshopper." The youngest of three children born to Russian immigrants, she had had a pleasant childhood. Her father, a tailor, was a kind and gentle man. Her mother was the more forceful of her parents—the glue that kept the family on track. In fact, her mother had been "a bit of a taskmaster," as Dawn recalled. Mom expected good grades from each of the children, at least one sport and one other extracurricular activity, and exemplary behavior in public at all times. Her mother often talked with pride about how her children spoke, looked, and acted like "real Americans." Every Sunday, when they attended the Russian Orthodox Church, each family member was dressed, scrubbed, and behaved without flaw . . . or "there was hell to pay when we got home!"

Dawn had been a good student, although she had been socially inhibited. Even as a youngster, she had been sensitive to what others thought of her, and often wondered if she was dressed appropriately, had studied enough to do well on tests, or had made a "dumb" remark. She was especially sensitive to the possibility of embarrassing her mother, whom she loved and wanted very much to please. She had always tried very hard to make her mother proud of her, which was not easy to do since her mother's standards were high and praise was hard to come by. At the same time, she was embarrassed by her mother's inadequate command of English and slept poorly on the nights before parent-teacher meetings, or school open-houses. On top of that, she felt guilty for feeling this way, but she couldn't seem to shake it.

Still, Dawn had had a group of friends in school, and had acquitted herself well enough to get into the nursing program at the teaching hospital where she earned her RN degree. It was during this time that she had met her husband-to-be. She had been attracted to his looks, his ambition, and his work and family-oriented values. He had been attracted to her maturity and good sense, as well as her apparent wish to please him. After dating for fourteen months they married, and had been married, peacefully, ever since. Mr. D. clearly loved his wife, although she wondered why this should be so, given how annoying her worrying was, not to mention her secret inability to love him "properly" in return. He was generally thoughtful with her, and had been a loving father to their children. It struck Dawn as "selfish" and "stupid" that she should feel so ill at ease all the time when her life was one that most people would envy.

The therapist offered Dawn three courses of action. The first was medication. The therapist could consult with Dawn's internist who could prescribe an anti-anxiety medication for her to try. If her internist ran out of choices, she could consult with a psychiatrist for other medical options. The second was psychotherapy, aimed at identifying and modifying the thoughts that were maintaining her anxiety, a procedure called "cognitive therapy." The third option was to do both at the same time.

Dawn was wary of medicines, and elected the psychotherapy option. She felt that she could add medication later if need be. The first step was the most difficult. Dawn found that it was hard, at first, to identify the thoughts associated with her anxiety. She was so focused on how she felt that she hadn't really noticed what she was thinking. She agreed to keep an "anxiety journal" to help her become more aware of her thinking processes between therapy sessions and with practice she became more adept.

When she did examine her thoughts, Dawn was surprised to find that they often didn't make much sense. For example, one of Dawn's thoughts was the following: "if my house isn't perfect when my children come, they won't think I value them, and then they won't love me, and then my life wouldn't be worth living." With the therapist's help, Dawn was able to see that 1) it isn't possible for her house (or anyone else's) to be "perfect," 2) the odds of her children thinking that she didn't value them, in light of all the data to the contrary was vanishingly small, 3) since her children had seen the house "imperfect" on many occasions and appeared to still love her, the premise that this would mysteriously change in future was unlikely to be true, and 4) there were many things that made life worth living, the love of her children being only one (albeit an important one) of them.

Over time, Dawn began to see patterns to her anxiety-producing thoughts. She became aware that she demanded perfection of herself (but tolerated all manner of mistakes in others), that she overgeneralized from "one" situation to "all" situations, that she presumed to read other people's minds and what she "read" was always bad, and that she catastrophized, "making mountains out of molehills" as her mother used to say. The therapist taught her strategies to question or counter these beliefs. For example, she learned to question whether a particular expectation she had of herself was the same as she expected of others, or whether she had "special rules" for herself. "Must other people look absolutely perfect with not a hair out of place for me to think they're worthwhile, or only me?" She learned to ask herself "what's the worst that can happen" when she discovered that she had made an error, and to distinguish her fantasies ("I'll get fired") from the reality ("I might get corrected" or "my supervisor might be annoyed with me for a while"). She learned not to rush to judgment about what other people were thinking ("she didn't say hello—she thinks I'm an idiot" to "she didn't say hello—perhaps she was preoccupied, or perhaps she is annoyed with me but this may pass"). She discovered that it was possible that other people were thinking all manner of things and that she really didn't have a clue much of the time.

In each of the first half dozen visits, Dawn used her journal to jog her memory about situations in which she had been anxious during the week. She and the therapist would identify the thoughts, pick out the irrational ones, and modify them. Dawn became aware that each time she did this, she felt less anxious. During the next dozen or so visits, Dawn moved to doing more and more of the "therapeutic" work between sessions, using the visits to refine her skills or to work specifically on situations in which she had gotten "stuck" and hadn't been able to reduce her anxiety on her own. By the twentieth visit, Dawn felt ready to terminate therapy. Her anxiety symptoms were greatly improved, and she felt that she had the "tools" to keep working on them on her own.

Thinking About The Case

Worry is a ubiquitous feeling. Everybody worries about something. And virtually everybody has had the experience of being somewhat incapacitated or preoccupied with worry, at least for brief periods of time. However, when worry is constant, diffuse, and overwhelming, the diagnosis of generalized anxiety disorder (GAD) is appropriate.

It is unclear whether GAD is really a disorder distinct and separate from the other anxiety disorders. In fact, most of the people who are diagnosed with it also meet the criteria for one or more simple phobias, social phobia, or panic disorder at some time in their life. Possibly, GAD represents an "anxious biology," with the other disorders superimposed when circumstances are right.

This disorder often begins in childhood or adolescence and continues throughout life, waxing and waning, but present at some level virtually all the time. Many patients, like Dawn, are so used to their anxiety that only the urging of others gets them into treatment. Others become debilitated, unable to sleep or to function during the day, and therefore seek treatment on their own. Some patients with generalized anxiety self medicate with alcohol, pain medications, or over-the-counter sleep aids.

Not surprisingly, generalized anxiety disorder often co-occurs with various forms of depression, particularly dysthymic disorder. In fact, the most common clinical presentation is one of mixed anxiety and depression. In these cases, the anxiety disorder may well be primary and the depression secondary. It is not difficult to see how functioning over time with severe anxiety could be depressing in and of itself.

While anti-anxiety medications do exist and have been shown to be fairly effective, anxiety tends to return once the medication is discontinued. In addition, medications that are most effective in moderating anxiety also present a moderate risk of addiction. Interestingly, the selective serotonin reuptake inhibitors, normally used to treat depression, have also been shown to be effective in treating generalized anxiety disorder. These medications are not addictive, but must be taken for fairly long periods of time in order to achieve a therapeutic result. The effectiveness of the antidepressants in treating anxiety raises the issue, once again, about whether anxiety and depression might not be separate disorders at the biological level.

Cognitive therapy, of the kind that Dawn chose, has also been shown to be moderately effective, and when successful, produces much more permanent change than does medication. Progressive relaxation, in which muscle groups are systematically tensed and loosened until the muscles are wholly flaccid, can reduce the physiological component of anxiety and is often included as a part of treatment. Mindfulness, in which the person learns to observe thoughts and feelings without judgment, noting their impermanence, complements relaxation strategies.

Questions To Consider

1. How might the presence of fairly constant anxiety affect a person's self-image and social development? Contrast this with how a person with a very low level of general anxiety might develop. What would be the major differences?
2. Give an example of a study designed to find out whether the overlap between anxiety disorders and depression reflected similar neurobiology or rather some environmental or adaptational processes.
3. If you experienced the symptoms of GAD, would you opt for medication or psychotherapy or neither? Why? Most insurance companies require much higher out-of-pocket payments for psychotherapy than they do for medication management. Would your decision be affected by these financial considerations?

LANAHAN NOTES
Anxiety Disorders

Symptoms of Anxiety

Physical: pounding heart, sweaty palms, lightheadedness, nausea, shortness of breath, tingling feelings, chills

Cognitive: racing thoughts or blank mind: fear of going crazy or losing control

Behavioral: retreat, avoidance, freezing

Question: Everybody experiences these or similar symptoms. When do they constitute a disorder?

symptoms must be prolonged

symptoms must markedly interfere with the individual's functioning

Types of anxiety disorders

Separation anxiety disorder (formally known as school phobia): fear of being separated from an attachment figure

Selective mutism: failure to speak in specific social situations despite speaking in other situations

Specific phobia: debilitating fear of particular situations, being in elevators; or of objects, like snakes, dogs

Social anxiety disorder (social phobia): fear of being embarrassed in social situations

Panic disorder: with or without agoraphobia; avoidance of places where an attack of severe anxiety symptoms might occur

Generalized anxiety disorder: at least six months of excessive anxiety and worry about multiple events/activities

Others: related to medical conditions, substance abuse, or not specified

Who gets anxiety disorders?

maybe up to 18 percent of the population

women often diagnosed (especially with phobias) more than men, approximately 2:1

Note: display of fear is more acceptable for women than for men in society

Causes

Behavioral theory: anxiety (classical conditioning and modeling) and avoidance (instrumental conditioning and modeling) are learned

Cognitive theory: one's distorted or misinterpreted thoughts, images assumptions can produce anxiety

Biological theory: some anxiety disorders run in families; predisposition might be (partially) inherited

Evolutionary (preparedness) theory: combines behavioral and biological theories; individuals are prepared to learn certain fears

Psychodynamic theory: Symptoms are symbolic or partial expressions of unacceptable impulses (generally sexual or aggressive). Repression is fundamental defense; not often empirically studied, validity in doubt

Biopsychosocial model integrates several of the above theories

Treatment (many approaches have reasonable success)

Behavioral therapy: good outcome for several anxiety disorders

Some behavioral methods:

- systematic desensitization
- exposure
- flooding
- modeling
- response prevention

Cognitive therapy: targets the irrational ideas that produce anxiety; teaches patient to re-label bodily symptoms; good results

Psychodynamic approaches: uncover repressed conflict; mixed results

Biological approaches: medications can block panic; some have high addictive potential or annoying side-effects; usually used in combination with cognitive and/or behavioral approaches

Self-help techniques: mindfulness, relaxation, meditation, yoga, exercise, and support groups can be very useful

CHAPTER SEVEN

Obsessive-Compulsive and Related Disorders

As the name suggests, obsessive-compulsive disorders have two related sets of symptoms. Obsessions are repetitive, intrusive thoughts or images that the person is unable to banish. Real-life examples include feeling that one has hit someone with his car, despite evidence to the contrary, images of hurting someone one loves (or oneself), or even persistently thinking of penises. Generally, obsessions are what is called "ego-alien," that is, they are unwanted and not in keeping with the person's values and sense of self. Often they have to do with sex or violence.

Compulsions are strong urges to engage in (or avoid) some specific, repetitive behavior. Often this behavior is experienced as magically warding off some catastrophe. Remember the childhood rhyme "step on a crack, break your mother's back." For example, a woman might feel that avoiding words ending in "S" will protect her children from harm, or a man might feel that entering doorways backwards will keep him from developing cancer. A person goes back home time after time to make sure that the oven is turned off, while yet another spends hours washing his hands, interfering with his ability to get to work, and causing his hands to become raw and painful. Sometimes, compulsions simply ward off feelings of dread, rather than being designed to prevent a specific horrific outcome.

Many of us engage in rituals that could be considered minor compulsions. We brush out teeth with the same number of strokes each day; we check our pockets for keys even though we know we've put them there a few minutes prior; we need to have the spoons nested together and facing the same way in the silverware drawer. These compulsions give us a sense of safety, and we don't think much of them. If questioned, we would say that they are logical and useful. In short, they are ego-syntonic. In addition, they don't bind a great deal of anxiety—that is, if we were prevented from doing them we might experience minor discomfort, but not more than that. However, in obsessive-compulsive disorder, not being able to carry out certain rituals is accompanied by a great deal of emotional distress.

[OCD used to be classified among the anxiety disorders. In this latest version of the DSM-5, they stand alone as a category of their own. Future research will tell us if this distinction is, in fact, valid.]

This chapter includes not only obsessive-compulsive disorders, but also body dysmorphic disorder (the false belief that some part of the body is horribly flawed,) hoarding disorder, trichotillomania (hair-pulling) disorder, and excoriation (skin-picking) disorder. These disorders are now grouped together in DSM-5 because they all have some obsessive and/or compulsive trait at their core. We have included an example of three of these five. In the first, we borrow a case from Dr. Judith Rapoport's book about OCD, called *The Boy Who Couldn't Stop Washing*. In the second, we encounter a college student who believes his perfectly normal face is "hideous." In the third, we tackle hoarding, a disorder which has become somewhat of a media phenomenon in recent years, with reality television shows devoted to individuals whose lives are ruined by the inability to discard anything.

CASE 22

OBSESSIVE-COMPULSIVE DISORDER: THE CASE OF DR. S.

Dr. S. is a psychologist in his mid-forties. He suffers from obsessive-compulsive disorder (OCD) as do his paternal grandfather, his father, his two brothers, a nephew, and his son. His case is reported in The Boy Who Couldn't Stop Washing: The Experience and Treatment of Obsessive-Compulsive Disorder, *written by Judith Rapoport, M.D., a clinician-researcher at the National Institute for Mental Health. Here, in his own words, is a description of one of Dr. S.'s OCD attacks.*

I'M DRIVING DOWN THE HIGHWAY DOING 55 MPH. I'm on my way to take a final exam. My seat belt is buckled and I'm vigilantly following all the rules of the road. No one is on the highway—not a living soul.

Out of nowhere an Obsessive-Compulsive Disorder (OCD) attack strikes. It's almost magical the way it distorts my perception of reality. While in reality no one is on the road, I'm intruded with the heinous thought that I *might* have hit someone . . . a human being! God knows where such a fantasy comes from.

I think about this for a second and then say to myself, "That's ridiculous. I didn't hit anybody." Nonetheless, a gnawing anxiety is born. An anxiety I will ultimately not be able to put away until an enormous emotional price has been paid.

I try to make reality chase away this fantasy. I reason, "Well, if I hit someone while driving, I would have *felt* it." This brief trip into reality helps the pain dissipate . . . but only for a second. Why? Because the gnawing anxiety that I really did commit the illusionary accident is growing larger—so is the pain.

The pain is a terrible guilt that I have committed an unthinkable, negligent act. At one level, I know this is ridiculous, but there's a terrible pain in my stomach telling me something quite different.

Again, I try putting to rest this insane thought and that ugly feeling of guilt. "Come on," I think to myself, "this is *really* insane!"

But the awful feeling persists. The anxious pain says to me, "*You Really Did Hit Someone.*" The attack is now in full control. Reality no longer has meaning. My sensory system is distorted. I have to get rid of the pain. Checking out this fantasy is the only way I know how.

I start ruminating, "Maybe I did hit someone and didn't realize it . . . Oh my God! I might have killed somebody! I have to go back and check." Checking is the only way to calm the anxiety. It brings me closer to truth somehow. I can't live with the thought that I actually may have killed someone—I have to check it out.

Now I'm sweating . . . literally. I pray this outrageous act of negligence never happened. My fantasies run wild. I desperately hope the jury will be merciful. I'm particularly concerned about whether my parents will be understanding. After all, I'm now a criminal. I must control the anxiety by checking it out. Did it really happen? There's always an infinitesimally small kernel of truth (or potential truth) in all my OC fantasies.

I think to myself, "Rush to check it out. Get rid of the hurt by checking it out. Hurry back to check it out. God, I'll be late for my final exam if I check it out. But I have no choice. Someone could be lying on the road, bloody, close to death." Fantasy is now my only reality. So is my pain.

I've driven five miles further down the road since the attack's onset. I turn the car around and head back to the scene of the mythical mishap. I return to the spot on the road where I "think" it "might" have occurred. Naturally, nothing is there. No police car and no bloodied body. Relieved, I turn around again to get to my exam on time.

Feeling better, I drive for about twenty seconds and then the lingering thoughts and pain start gnawing away again. Only this time they're even more intense. I think, "Maybe I should have pulled *off* the road and checked the side brush where the injured body was thrown and now lies? Maybe I didn't go *far enough* back on the road and the accident occurred a mile farther back."

The pain of my possibly having hurt someone is now so intense that I have no choice—I really see it this way.

I turn the car around a second time and head an extra mile farther down the road to find the corpse. I drive by quickly. Assured that this time I've gone far enough I head back to school to take my exam. But I'm not through yet.

"My God," my attack relentlessly continues, "I didn't get *out* of the car to actually *look* on the side of the road!"

So I turn back a third time. I drive to the part of the highway where I think the accident happened. I park the car on the highway's shoulder. I get out and begin rummaging around in the brush. A police car comes up. I feel like I'm going out of my mind.

The policeman, seeing me thrash through the brush, asks, "What are you doing? Maybe I can help you?"

Well, I'm in a dilemma. I can't say, "Officer, please don't worry. You see, I've got obsessive-compulsive disorder, along with four million other Americans. I'm simply acting out a compulsion with obsessive qualities." I can't even say, "I'm really sick. Please help me." The disease is so insidious and embarrassing that it cannot be admitted to anyone. Anyway, so few really understand it, including myself.

So I tell the officer I was nervous about my exam and pulled off to the roadside to throw up. The policeman gives me a sincere and knowing smile and wishes me well.

But I start thinking again. "Maybe an accident did happen and the body has been cleared off the road. The policeman's here to see if I came back to the scene of the crime. God, maybe I really did hit someone . . . why else would a police car be in the area?" Then I realize he would have asked me about it. But would he, if he was trying to catch me?

I'm so caught up in the anxiety and these awful thoughts that I momentarily forget why I am standing on the side of the road. I'm back on the road again. The anxiety is peaking. Maybe the policeman didn't know about the accident? I should go back and conduct my search more *thoroughly*.

I want to go back and check more . . . but I can't. You see, the police car is tailing me on the highway. I'm now close to hysteria because I honestly believe someone is lying in the brush bleeding to death. Yes . . . the pain makes me believe this. "After all," I reason, "why would the pain be there in the first place?"

I arrive at school late for the exam. I have trouble taking the exam because I can't stop obsessing on the fantasy. The thoughts of the mystical accident keep intruding. Somehow I get through it.

The moment I get out of the exam I'm back on the road checking again. But now I'm checking two things. First that I didn't kill or maim someone and second, that the policeman doesn't catch me checking. After all, if I should be spotted on the roadside rummaging around the brush a second time, how in the world can I possibly explain such an incriminating and aimless action? I'm totally exhausted, but that awful anxiety keeps me checking, though a part of my psyche keeps telling me that this checking behavior is ridiculous, that it serves absolutely no purpose. But, with OCD, there is no other way.

Finally, after repeated checks, I'm able to break the ritual. I head home, dead tired. I know that if I can sleep it off, I'll feel better. Sometimes the pain dissipates through an escape into sleep.

I manage to lie down on my bed—hoping for sleep. But the incident has not totally left me—nor has the anxiety. I think, "If I really did hit someone, there would be a dent in the car's fender."

What I now do is no mystery to anyone. I haul myself up from bed and run out to the garage to check the fenders on the car. First I check the front two fenders, see no damage, and head back to bed. But . . . *did I check it well enough?*

I get up from bed again and now find myself checking the *whole body* of the car. I know this is absurd, but I can't help myself. Finally . . . finally, I disengage and head off to my room to sleep. Before I nod off, my last thought is, "I wonder what I'll check next?"

While some symptoms of OCD may have existed in his childhood, Dr. S.'s disorder began in earnest when he was in his early twenties. He found himself needing to check to make sure that various awful things hadn't occurred—that he hadn't left a light on that might start a fire, that he hadn't poisoned someone with insecticides that he may have touched, that the figures for his research hadn't been incorrectly computed. His doubts were endless and the hours he spent compulsively checking and rechecking seemed equally endless. About one year following the first onset of his illness, Dr. S. consulted a psychiatrist. Together they worked on finding and eliminating any possible emotional source to the illness and in developing ways that Dr. S. could adapt to his symptoms. They paid particular attention to Dr. S.'s angry and aggressive feelings, since many of his compulsions seemed designed to ward off the possibility that he had caused someone harm. Dr. S. also began taking the anti-anxiety medication Valium, which provided minimal relief from the emotional suffering but made him feel tired and gave him headaches.

At about the third year of therapy, Dr. S. experienced a partial remission, as he put it "not perfect, but substantially improved." However, with the birth of his first child, the symptoms returned in force. While he was able to perform his public responsibilities quite well, in private he was consumed by intrusive, frightening thoughts. Everyday tasks took him twice to three times as long to do as they would have taken someone else due to the ritualized checking he had to perform over and over. He felt exhausted, and his wife felt frustrated and sometimes furious with him. Still, with a great deal of motivation and sacrifice, he was able to hide his illness from most people who knew him, although the private toll taken by his obsessions and compulsions was enormous.

After ten years of therapy, Dr. S. begged his psychiatrist to consider a medication trial. The psychiatrist prescribed imipramine, a drug that had been used for many years to treat depression. The medication was gradually increased from 25 mg. to 200 mg. per day. One month after Dr. S. began the 200 mg. dose, his symptoms suddenly receded. While he still had obsessive doubts, they no longer had the force they once had. The overpowering need to act on them had disappeared. The attacks gradually decreased in frequency from daily, to weekly, to monthly. Once the attacks of severe symptoms stabilized at a frequency of once every few months, the medication was gradually reduced to a maintenance dose of 100 mg. For the last several years, Dr. S. has been essentially symptom free. Both his brother and son have also experienced marked relief from their OCD through the use of imipramine.

Thinking About the Case

It is ironic that obsessive-compulsive disorder, which has often been cited to illustrate the psychodynamic principles of altered representation of unconscious wishes, has been the least amenable to change through psychodynamically oriented psychotherapy. As in Dr. S.'s case, years of psychotherapy often left the symptoms essentially unchanged.

Today, neurobiological substrates are presumed to underlie OCD. Using brain imaging techniques, researchers have identified abnormalities in the functioning of the basal ganglia in OCD patients. The basal ganglia is an area of the brain that is related to how individuals organize and respond to information from their senses, and possibly, to how individuals formulate the complex functions of "purposiveness" and "will." Further support for the biological model comes from the fact that OCD is often accompanied by various tic behaviors (brief, spasmodic movements or sounds that are not under the individual's voluntary control), and is often co-diagnosed with Tourette's disorder, in which facial and vocal tics are prominent symptoms. Finally, recent advances in psychopharmacology have given OCD sufferers new hope. Dr. S.'s case is atypical in that imipramine, a tricyclic antidepressant, is not generally helpful for OCD patients. However, a new class of antidepressants, called SSRI's (selective serotonin reuptake inhibitors) is at least somewhat effective for about 70 percent of OCD patients. The very popular antidepressant, Prozac, is an SSRI, as is its newer pharmacological cousin, Paxil, although the drug of choice for OCD is a related compound called Anafranil.

The essentials of modern therapy for OCD include medication, education of the patient and the family about the illness (known as "psychoeducation"), and, particularly in cases in which compulsive behaviors play a prominent role in the symptom picture, behavior therapy. The behavioral techniques of modeling, flooding, and response prevention are generally combined. If, for example, the patient is afraid of contamination by germs, the therapist will set up a series of gradual "confrontations" with the alleged "germs." First, the therapist may begin by having the patient watch her smear dirt on herself. Then, the patient will be encouraged to dirty herself, and to tolerate the anxiety that arises when she resists the urge to wash. In effect, the avoidance behavior becomes extinguished as the patient becomes desensitized to the anxiety-producing situation associated with dirt. Note that this is essentially the same as the "exposure therapy" used with phobias, in which the person is encouraged to remain in the phobic situation until the anxiety diminishes.

In practice, behavior therapy is often combined with cognitive-behavioral techniques in which the therapist will help the patient identify and dispute irrational, "catastrophizing" beliefs that contribute to the maintenance of the compulsions. In Dr. S.'s case, this might include helping him recognize that even if his data were incorrectly analyzed (an infinitesimally small possibility), the result would not be catastrophic, but only unpleasant or unfortunate. The therapist might also help Dr. S. develop more rational ideas about the probability of the various events he fears. Supportive therapy, relaxation training, and stress management may also be part of the main pharmacological, educational, and behavioral treatments.

Questions to Consider

1. OCD is often co-diagnosed with depression. What are some reasons why this might be so? Can you devise experiments that might decide which hypothesis is correct?
2. The content of OCD obsessions and compulsions appears not to be random. Generally, obsessional ideas have to do with aggression, contamination, or sexuality. Compulsions include cleaning, counting, checking, and repeating. What do you make of this? Does it suggest a role for nonbiological factors in the way the illness expresses itself?

CASE 23

BODY DYSMORPHIC DISORDER: THE CASE OF AARON W.

"I DON'T KNOW WHY I'M HERE," Aaron told Dr. R. "I don't need a shrink. I'm not crazy. I need a plastic surgeon. I don't understand why my doctor doesn't agree. How can he expect me to go on looking hideous when it can be corrected so easily?" Despite the sunny August weather, Aaron was wearing a knit cap pulled tight over his ears and hadn't removed the reflecting sunglasses which shielded his eyes. "There's no reason that people should be subjected to looking at me, no reason at all." With this, Aaron burst into tears.

Aaron, a twenty-one year old college student, had been referred by his family physician who was completely baffled by Aaron's insistence that he needed "a new face." As far as the physician could tell, Aaron's face was completely normal. His features were regular and the overall effect was pleasant, nondescript. Aaron had agreed reluctantly to see a psychologist one time only. Dr. R. asked Aaron to describe how he had come to view himself as "hideous," and how he had coped with it.

Aaron said that he had had a normal childhood. He was the only child of two school teachers. He had been a good student, had participated in basketball, and sang in the school choir. He had had a group of buddies throughout elementary and high school. He described himself as kind of shy with girls. He had some girls as friends, but had not really dated.

Aaron had not noticed anything different about himself until he began college. Away from his lifelong friends and thrust into an unfamiliar situation, he felt odd and isolated. He was assigned to a suite with five other guys, and three of them had known each other from high school. Naturally, they hung together. They invited Aaron and the other two guys to hang with them, but Aaron felt uncomfortable when he did.

One morning, about two weeks into the semester, he noticed, while looking in the mirror, that his face looked strange. His ears were huge, his nose enormous and crooked, and his eyes were different sizes and shapes, the left being large and round and the right being smaller and almond shaped. He looked monstrous. Panicked, he couldn't believe that he hadn't noticed this about himself before. How had he gone out, hung out, without realizing how bizarre he looked? He tried to calm himself: he had friends at home, people seemed to like him, it couldn't be so bad, he thought. But when he looked back into the mirror, he saw only a misshapen, ugly face. Aaron had to come out of the bathroom, and eventually he did. He put on a cap to cover his ears. He fished around in his drawers until he found his summer sunglasses, and he put them on. He went to class.

Over the next few weeks, Aaron was agitated and upset most of the time. He checked himself constantly, looking in every mirror he could find, running his hands over his ears and eyes to see if he could feel the deformities. It was excruciating to be out and about, though, oddly, people seemed to treat him normally. Still, in class, if he happened to glance at somebody, he noticed that sometimes the person was looking right at him. He figured everybody was drawn to stare at him, as you would stare at a car accident when passing one. But they were too polite to do it overtly. Instead, they snuck glances when they thought he wouldn't notice. He almost teared up when he realized how kind everybody had been to him, never mentioning his looks, acting like everything was normal. But he understood now why he had never attracted girls. It was absurd to think anyone would ever go out with him.

Aaron's roommate asked him why he'd taken to wearing the cap all the time, even indoors. "Cover my enormous ears," he replied. "There's nothing wrong with your ears, man. Get over it. Lose the cap" retorted his roommate. But no way was that going to happen. His roommate was just trying to make him feel better.

Aaron tried and tried to refocus himself, to concentrate on his studies, to act normal with the guys, since they acted normal with him. Yet, his concentration declined as his preoccupation with his looks increased. And he began to keep to himself even more than before. He found excuses to avoid his suitemates—he had to go to the library, he had to study. Really, he was just hiding.

At Thanksgiving vacation, Aaron went home. He was incredibly relieved to be back in his old, secure environment. But he was still miserable. He avoided his old friends, and wore his cap and glasses continually.

It didn't take his parents long to see that something had changed, that Aaron was not himself. His father came into his room one evening and asked whether they could have a talk. He had only to ask "what's wrong, son?" and Aaron burst into tears. "You know what's wrong! Why have you never done anything about it?" Aaron cried. "About what?" asked his puzzled father. "This!" Aaron cried, tearing off the cap and glasses. "This!" he repeated. "Son, I still don't understand. What's troubling you?" asked Mr. W. "This face, these ears, these eyes, this hideous nose—what don't you understand?" Mr. W. said quietly "son, your face is fine. You're a fine looking, perfectly normal young man. Not movie star handsome, but fine."

Aaron looked at his father incredulously. "You love me, I know. And maybe you don't even really notice anymore because you love me. But I'm hideous. Everybody has treated me as if I was normal. I'm grateful for that, I really am. But I know what I see. I'm hideous."

In the months that followed, Mr. and Mrs. W. tried to reassure their son that he was a normal looking person. They even enlisted his life-long friend to talk to him, but nothing made a dent. Aaron thanked everybody for loving him and protecting him, but he knew what he knew. He could see it quite clearly in the mirror.

Finally, his parents asked him if they could make an appointment for him with their family physician, and Aaron gratefully agreed. Their agenda was to see if Aaron needed medicine or psychiatric help while his agenda was to seek a referral for plastic surgery. Neither really understood what the other expected from the visit. Aaron came out of the visit frustrated and confused. His doctor, whom he had known since childhood, had denied that his face was misshapen. He had thought doctors were sworn to tell the truth to patients. He wondered briefly if his parents had somehow convinced the doctor to lie. In the end, he understood that the doctor would discuss plastic surgery only after Aaron was seen by the mental health specialist. Grudgingly, he had agreed.

Dr. R. inquired about family history of psychological disorders, but Aaron didn't know of any. Nor did he admit to any previous mental health problems himself. At the moment, he admitted, he was agitated and depressed, but other than that, he felt he had had good mental health.

Gently, Dr. R. suggested that sometimes stress could influence a person's self-perception. Perhaps the stress of going away to school, to a new social environment, had triggered Aaron's feelings about his looks. Aaron, admitted to the stress, but said that he knew what he knew about his face. Dr. R. wondered aloud why, if Aaron was so ugly, he had not noticed it before college. Aaron said that he had been puzzled by that too, but he figured he'd just not really given his looks much thought until recently.

Dr. R. also noted that nobody else had ever commented on Aaron's looks or had seemed to avoid him. Aaron chalked this up to people not wanting to hurt his feelings. Again, he knew what he knew.

By the end of the interview, Dr R. and Aaron were at an impasse. Aaron had no therapeutic agenda. He wanted Dr. R. to write a report supporting Aaron's request for plastic surgery, but Dr R. said he could not do so. Instead, he offered to work with Aaron to help him come to terms with his feelings about his face, so that he might feel less depressed, might be able to concentrate better, and might not isolate himself so much. Aaron wasn't interested. He felt that he was doing the best he could under the circumstances, and anyway, he couldn't really connect with Dr. R. How could he connect with a man who couldn't or wouldn't see what was in front of his eyes? He declined the offer of a follow-up interview, and Dr R. did not see or hear from him again.

Thinking About The Case

Most of us have something about our appearance that we don't like. But for the most part, we can get on with our lives without having it affect us too much. However, people with body dysmorphic disorder (BDD) are preoccupied with one or more perceived defects or flaws in physical appearance that are either not observable or appear slight to others. They may spend hours a day thinking about the defect. They are unable to control the thoughts with distraction. They can't be reassured by others, though they may seek reassurance ceaselessly. They experience severe emotional distress because of the perceived defects and, like Aaron, often withdraw from others, can not concentrate on their normal activities, and may become seriously depressed, even suicidal.

BDD occurs in about one percent of the population and generally has its onset in adolescence, though it can make its first appearance in childhood or early adulthood as well. It affects young men and women about equally.

BDD often co-occurs with other anxiety disorders, and is thought to be related most closely to obsessive compulsive disorder (OCD) with which it is now classified in the DSM-5. In fact, OCD and BDD may run in the same families, and may even occur in the same person.

Treatment of BDD rests on the level of insight manifested by the sufferer. Aaron experienced virtually no insight that his thoughts and feelings might be abnormal rather than his appearance. Therefore, he could not develop a trusting relationship or a mutual agenda with a psychotherapist. However, other people with the disorder have greater or fluctuating insight. They are willing to entertain at least the possibility that they may be misperceiving or overreacting. In these instances, cognitive behavior therapy targets irrational beliefs and perceptions, and gives the individual tools to combat these. Dr. R. tried a few cognitive interventions, for example, by attempting to get Aaron to see the illogic in his "suddenly" noticing such a severe deformity that had apparently been present all along, but these did not work.

As with OCD, selective serotonin reuptake inhibitors (SSRI's) can be helpful in treating BDD. After a few weeks on a therapeutic dose of medication the person may notice that his or her preoccupation with the perceived defect begins to lose strength. The individual may not spend as many hours worried about it. He or she may begin to feel more optimistic in general. Over time, the preoccupation may disappear almost entirely, floating into the person's mind from time to time, but without the ability to grab and hold his or her attention. Again, insight is crucial in order to get the individual to agree to a trial of medication at all.

Without treatment BDD is a fairly chronic condition. It can wax and wane in intensity, but it generally persists over a long period of time. With treatment, the prognosis is much better—not for the disorder to disappear entirely, but for it to interfere much less with the person's functioning, self-esteem, and mental health.

Questions To Consider

1. This case illustrates how important insight is in developing a successful treatment plan. This is true for many other disorders as well: schizophrenia, alcoholism, and anorexia nervosa among them. A new field called "Motivational Therapy" aims to get clients ready to participate in psychotherapy. Can you think of some strategies that might work?
2. Do you think that Dr. R could have done a better job of convincing Aaron to return for another visit? If so, how?
3. What role do you think psychosocial factors played in the development of Aaron's disorder? Do you think he might have developed any disorder, or was he predisposed to this specific one?
4. There are a number of disorders in which the sufferer has a fixed, but false idea—paranoid schizophrenia, anorexia, BDD, OCD, and illness anxiety disorder. Yet they are not classified together. Why might this be so? Does it make sense to you?

CASE 24

HOARDING DISORDER: THE CASE OF SUSAN O

SUSAN IS AN ARTIST. At fifty-eight years of age, she plays guitar and lute, sings, composes songs, writes poems, knits and crochets beautiful gift items, cooks and bakes restaurant quality food and sometimes sells a wedding or graduation cake. She refinishes antique furniture, reconditions antique jewelry, and builds custom birdhouses. She paints and draws beautifully. She loves animals and currently has five cats, though she feeds many more that come to her porch each morning and evening.

Susan has lived, until recently, with her mother. Now, following her mother's death two years ago, she finds that she does not have enough money to maintain her house. She must move to an apartment. There is one great problem with this plan, however. Susan's home is filled, top to bottom, with all sorts of things that she can not bear to part with. It is a large home, with four bedrooms and a front and back parlor. Each and every room is full to bursting with stacks, bags, and boxes.

Susan has to wend her way through the piles to get to the kitchen, where she has to clear space to prepare food. She has hundreds of serving pieces, collected at antique stores and garage sales. She has thirty sets of flatware and as many sets of dishes and glasses. The shelves hold many dozens of jars of spices and rubs and sauces. The drawers hold more than a hundred dish towels, collected from all over the world, and every type of kitchen implement you can imagine. She has copper pots and stainless steel pots. She has pots with no lids, and some with burned bottoms. She has been planning to convert them to planters for the garden but hasn't gotten around to it yet. The kitchen counter is covered with piles of fabric that she has recently acquired. She plans to make a quilt for her niece. On the kitchen chairs are stacks of magazines from which she has been collecting cooking and home decorating ideas for all of her adult life. She plans, one day, to go through them and cut out the articles she wants to save and throw the rest away. This, too, is a project for another day.

At bedtime, Susan has to step over and around mounds of stuff to get to the bedroom. The sitting rooms are filled with furniture, sometimes stacked two or three pieces high. Many of these pieces Susan had collected with her mother, who also enjoyed antiques. Their habit was to spend each Saturday, when the weather allowed, browsing yard sales within a fifty mile radius of their home. Susan can remember where and when they acquired each piece. Often, she can tell a story about a piece's provenance or about the family from whom she acquired it. On every surface sits a frame with a picture of a family member or friend. The frames were lovingly acquired over the years as well. Next to the frames, in tall piles, sit many more photographs. They are meant to go in albums . . . some day. There are also hundreds of collectibles, small china figurines of animals and angels. Her mother loved angels.

Susan has only one chair she can sit in. The others are covered in newspapers or fabric or laundry or craft projects at various stages of completion. Next to her chair is a little table with a stack of books she is reading. There is room for a cup of tea. She loves her chair and feels completely comfortable there.

To get to the bedroom, Susan has to navigate the stairs, which are also covered with laundry, books, and whatever else needs to go upstairs. In her room, every inch, even most of the bed, is covered with clothes, rugs, paintings, musical instruments, towels, blankets, and jewelry boxes. As you might have guessed by now, Susan collects jewelry. Most of it is costume, but she has a few good pieces that she bought when her mother was alive and she had money. She has more than six dozen rings and many more bracelets, necklaces and earring sets. And she has scarves, probably two hundred of them.

Susan has come to a therapist because she has been utterly unable to make her house presentable for sale. She has been carting around bolts of cloth and various crafting materials in her car which she calls her "traveling shop." Sometimes her friends will buy some of the items she's toting. She has brought some of her jewelry to a gold wholesaler. The $800 she got will pay to heat her house for the next several months, but it cost her many sleepless nights and much misery as she had such a difficult time choosing what pieces to part with and actually getting herself to drive to the appointment. She has gifted her son and several of her friends with certain pieces of furniture or an antique instrument or some other item she knew would be especially appreciated and understood by the recipient. This is as far as she has gotten. She is utterly stuck. She sleeps much of the day, is depressed and anxious when she is awake. She has been withdrawing from friends and losing interest in her many projects. She admits to wishing she could "just go to sleep and not wake up," though she has no plans to harm herself.

The therapist decides to use cognitive therapy to help Susan explore the blocks she has placed in the way of progress. She discovers that Susan fears that the distress she feels when she has to choose an item to get rid of will only grow and expand over time. Together they plan an experiment in which Susan rates her distress before, during, and after giving away several items. She finds, to her surprise, that the upset only lasts for a few hours and is generally almost gone by the next day. It peaks at the moment she chooses an item, holds pretty steady until she has actually disposed of it, and then diminishes over the next several hours. Often, she even feels some relief, particularly if she feels that she has made a good choice of recipient for whatever she has parted with. She learns to repeat to herself "this will only hurt for a little while and then I will feel better."

The therapist also discovers that Susan feels her memories of her mother are stored in her possessions. She is secretly afraid that she will somehow forget her mother or dishonor her by getting rid of stuff. She and the therapist discuss this idea at length and Susan begins to understand that her memories of her mother are in her mind and she can draw on them, even if they are not stimulated by seeing things around her that remind her of her mother. Over the course of time, she sorts through the pictures and creates a "memory book" in remembrance of her mother. It is lovingly done with pictures, poems, stories, drawings and bits of fabric or jewelry embedded in its pages. The completion of this project helps her feel less attachment to all the other mementos with which she has surrounded herself. She learns to remind herself, when she is feeling anxious, that she can remember her mother at will. After all, she is able to tell her therapist story after story without the aid of possessions. She doesn't need them in order to remember.

Other issues arise over the course of therapy. Apparently, Susan's son, who lives several hundred miles away, is not so sure that she actually needs to sell the house. He is attached to it as well and hates the idea of having to see his mother in some strange setting. He thinks that she should get a job and work nine to five. This only makes Susan more anxious. She has never held a structured job in her life. She has few marketable skills, despite her enormous talent, and no work history. She has back problems and finds it difficult to stand or sit in one position for very long. She current gets publicly funded health insurance, and if she were to get a minimum wage job she would be, in some ways, worse off than she is now. She doesn't think work is a viable solution to her problem, and her therapist reluctantly agrees.

At the therapist's suggestion, Susan invites her son for a visit. She schedules an appointment for them with her accountant so they can go over the financial situation and options together. They also have a visit together with the therapist in which Susan is able to share how depressed and anxious she has been and how worried about issues related to financial security. Her son is not in a position to help her, nor is he willing to invite her to come live with him and his wife. She doesn't want to, anyway, as she has a comfortable group of friends, and is secure in her well-traveled environment.

Reluctantly, he agrees that she cannot really work full-time, and part-time work won't solve the problem—and might create more. He agrees that she must reduce her expenses, particularly the risk of unexpected expenses like a new roof or furnace. He agrees to her selling the house. He offers to come and help her prepare for an auction when she is ready, and to help her move when the time comes. He also makes a plan to return in the next month with a rental truck so that he can take whatever he wants out of the house.

Another issue that arises is Susan's lack of organizational skills. Even when she becomes more willing she remains unable to develop a plan for disposing of possessions. She is simply overwhelmed by the task. She and her therapist work on breaking the task into smaller parts—working just on fabric, for example, or taking one room at a time. But Susan can't bring herself to complete these assignments. Together, they agree that Susan needs help. In discussion, they identify which of her friends has the best skills to help her, and Susan offers her friend a trade: a handmade sweater for twenty hours of organizing help. Her friend says that she would help Susan as many hours as necessary, and doesn't need payment, though she won't turn down the sweater that she knows will be lovingly and beautifully made.

After eight months of therapy, slow progress is being made. Susan continues to avoid tasks much of the time, but when her friend comes over, they are able to organize and make choices. Susan decides to end therapy. She says "I know what I have to do; I just have to do it." A year later, Susan sends her therapist an e-mail: she has identified a rent-controlled apartment and she is preparing to move. The auction of her furniture and other antiques will be held in a couple of weeks. Her son and his wife will come to help. So will her friends. Her son has agreed to rent a storage unit for $50.00 a month because there are some things that neither she nor he can stand to let go, but neither can fit into their homes. This is their compromise. Though sad, she is relieved beyond measure.

Thinking About The Case

Collecting is a hobby. Hoarding is a disorder. The difference between the two lies in the extent to which the behavior causes problems for the individual. Hoarding is a newly recognized disorder, and is categorized for the first time in DSM-5. Interest in hoarding has increased to the point where reality shows about it appear on cable television channels. Perhaps this is because hoarding represents a normal impulse to acquire and save gone wild. Perhaps we see the possibility for hoarding in ourselves and we are fascinated by the excess.

Hoarding can be accompanied by good insight, as is the case with Susan, but it can also occur in individuals who are in complete denial that their behavior or its consequences are problematic. Even in Susan's case, had she not believed she needed to vacate her home, she might not have developed insight into the dysfunctional nature of her behavior. She had accommodated to stumbling up and down the stairs, sleeping in a small corner of her bed, having only one small space in which to place a tea cup. This illustrates the point that insight is not entirely innate—it can be affected by circumstances. A person might have insight at one moment and lose it later. It waxes and wanes. Insight is a necessary precondition for therapy to take place, and so many hoarders go untreated, just as many substance abusers or other individuals with dysfunctional behavioral patterns may go untreated for the same reason.

Hoarders generally have one or more of several rationales for their behavior. First, like Susan, they attach meaning in an abnormal way to objects. Discarding objects associated with loved ones feels to hoarders like discarding the loved person. The individual is afraid that he or she will forget or lose contact with loved people unless the object, which acts as a sort of talisman, is preserved.

Secondly, hoarders may be abnormally fearful that they will not have an object at some point in the future when it is needed. This leads to saving piles of papers, scraps of material, parts of appliances, or anything else that might be put to use in the future. Not only is the estimate of the usefulness of these items distorted, but the gravity of having once had them and then let them go is magnified out of all proportion. Hoarders believe it would be catastrophic, rather than simply unpleasant, to find that they have use for an item that has been discarded.

Thirdly, hoarders procrastinate. Like Susan, they have plans for much of what they have acquired—it will be sorted, it will be organized, it will be made useful or beautiful. Only each of these plans goes by the board as another plan takes its place. Soon, there are simply too many projects, too much to do, nowhere clear to start, and the individual gets paralyzed into inaction.

Hoarding is difficult to treat. Treatment relies, not only on insight, but on the individual's capacity to tolerate the massive anxiety associated with changing the behavior. Since hoarding rests on a number of irrational beliefs, cognitive therapy has been the treatment of choice, and it has moderate success when the patient is sufficiently motivated. However, as Susan's case illustrates, cognitive therapy alone is not always enough. Here, family therapy and consultation about family issues, as well as use of a therapy aide (in the person of Susan's organizing friend) to work in the home on behavior change are essential for progress to be made. Many cognitive therapists have found that they must, indeed, go into the individual's home to help them begin to learn that the anxiety associated with getting rid of possessions can be managed and overcome.

Medications do not play a large role in the treatment of hoarding. Sometimes, antidepressant medications or antianxiety medications will be used as an adjunct to treatment, but these are not generally helpful in the absence of a cognitive-behavioral and behavioral retraining component. However, as Susan's case illustrates, hoarding can often co-occur with serious depression. In her case, the depression lifted when the hoarding began to come under control. In other cases, depression may need additional treatment.

Questions To Consider

1. Susan's mother and her son show at least some of the signs of hoarding disorder. What are some reasons this might be so?
2. Our culture equates acquisition with success. Do you think hoarding disorder might vary from culture to culture? In what ways? Devise an experiment or study to evaluate your hypothesis.
3. Hoarding is classified with obsessive-compulsive disorder along with trichotillomania (in which patients compulsively pull out their hair or eyebrows) and excoriation disorder (in which patients can not stop picking at their skin). What are the common features? Can you imagine some common underlying etiology? What might it be?

LANAHAN NOTES

Obsessive-Compulsive and Related Disorders

Definitions

Obsessions: repetitive, intrusive, inappropriate ideas or images

Compulsions: repetitive, ritualistic behaviors that the person feels driven to perform to alleviate the distress brought on by the obsessions

Obsessive-compulsive disorder

Clinically significant distress caused by recurrent and persistent thoughts, urges or images (obsessions)

Repetitive behaviors or mental acts aimed at reducing the distress, anxiety (compulsions)

Behaviors are developmentally inappropriate

Onset typically about 19 years of age; 25% of cases start by age 14 years

Prevalence is about 1.2% of the population

Body Dysmorphic Disorder

The obsession is that one has a physical defect or serious flaw

The resulting compulsion may include mirror-checking, camouflaging (excessive make-up or tanning); reassurance seeking behaviors, or even seeking plastic surgery

Prevalence in the U.S. is about 2.4%

Hoarding Disorder

The obsession is the excessive emotional value of holding onto possessions or the idea that discarding the items would have consequences, feelings of loss, distress, disappointment

The compulsion is the inability to discard possessions regardless of their usefulness to the individual; the resulting clutter substantially compromises active living areas to the point that basic activities such as moving through the house, cooking, cleaning, personal hygiene and even sleeping are difficult, often to impossible to achieve

Prevalence is approximately 2%–6% of the population

Greater prevalence among males than females

Hoarding symptoms are more likely to appear in older (55–94 years) adults

Trichotillomania

Characterized by hair-pulling usually from the scalp, eyebrows, eyelids; sometimes any body site where hair grows

Excoriation

Characterized by excessive skin-picking mostly from the face, arms, hands often at minor skin irregularities (pimples, scabs); sometimes at healthy skin usually with fingernails but some may use tweezers, pins, objects

Onset of both trichotillomania and excoriation most commonly coincides with or follows the onset of puberty

Both disorders are common in individuals with OCD or first degree relatives with OCD

Prevalence rates are about 1–2% of the population

Causes

Genetics: familial rates are as high as 50–60%; co-morbidity rates with anxiety and depressive disorders are high

Temperamental: greater internalization and inhibition of emotions; negative emotionality and indecisiveness

Environmental: high stress sometimes associated with childhood abuse or neglect

Treatment

Medications: selective serotonin reuptake inhibitors (SSRIs) alleviate symptoms;

since depression is co-morbid, both disorders are targeted with medication; medication should be coupled with therapy to improve results

Cognitive Therapy: Exposure and Response Prevention (ERP); involves not performing the ritual (the compulsion) exposes the person to the full force of the anxiety provoked by the distressing stimulus (the obsession); the exposure results in the extinction of the conditioned response (the anxiety)

CHAPTER EIGHT

Trauma- and Stressor-Related Disorders

Who among us has not experienced stress? And who among us has not experienced the consequences of acute stress: sleeplessness, preoccupation, loss of appetite, and difficulty concentrating among others? A stress-related disorder is diagnosed when the reaction seems out of proportion to the stimulus either in intensity or in duration or both, or when it interferes with functioning. This category is new in DSM-5. It reflects the idea that symptoms which are brought about by stress may have more in common with each other than they have with disorders with which they have previously been grouped (for example, anxiety disorders or disorders first manifested in childhood).

Completely new is the diagnosis of acute stress disorder. These symptoms would previously have been classified as post-traumatic stress disorder. The new diagnosis acknowledges that some symptoms and short-term disability may be expected in the wake of severe trauma, like war or sexual assault. As an example, we include the case of Miss F. that we have left intact, but simply renamed.

Next we consider a case of true post-traumatic stress disorder of the kind common in survivors of armed conflict. In these cases, symptoms often persist well past the point at which the trauma has ended, sometimes for a lifetime. It is as if the nervous system has been permanently changed by exposure to the trauma. And not only is the nervous system damaged, but so are self-image, social relationships, and occupational functioning. In our example, George G. improved a great deal. Sadly, many do not. Many develop drug or alcohol problems, probably in an attempt to self-medicate their symptoms. A substantial percentage of homeless people have faced combat, so severe are their symptoms and deficits upon returning home.

Finally, we include a case of reactive attachment disorder which occurs in some children whose early nurturing was severely disrupted by inadequate caregiving or perhaps multiple changes in caregivers at a crucial point in the child's emotional development. These children are thought to be persistently unable to attach to and trust adult caregivers. They may exhibit inhibited emotional responsiveness to others, lack of positive affect, and behavioral problems in social situations.

Taken together these cases help us understand the range of emotional, behavioral, and social problems that can be caused by stress. They also help us understand that the context in which stress occurs can have a profound effect on how an individual copes.

CASE 25

ACUTE STRESS DISORDER: THE CASE OF MISS F.

MISS F. WAS A TWENTY-FOUR-YEAR-OLD graduate student in psychology at the University of Pennsylvania. She had been born the eldest of three children in a two-parent, middle-class family. Her father had been married previously and had had a daughter from which he had become gradually estranged. Although he worked long hours and was often away, he doted on Miss F. She grew up a happy and successful child, perhaps a bit bossy to her siblings and friends, but bright and active. During high school she participated in a plethora of school activities, garnered the drama award at high school graduation, and went on to study psychology at the University of Pittsburgh where she worked a part-time job, took honor classes, and graduated Phi Beta Kappa.

Like most graduate students at Penn, she lived in an apartment in West Philadelphia which, like most urban university environs, was not the safest place to live. One early spring evening, while her fiancé, with whom she lived, was out playing bridge, the doorbell rang. Peering through the crack in the door, she saw a young man who appeared to be in his late teens or early twenties. "Is Mr. B. here?" he asked, "he was supposed to tutor me tonight." Mr. B. was an instructor at a nearby college and might, for all she knew, have been providing special assistance to one of his advisees. Miss F. told the young man that Mr. B. must have forgotten the appointment, because he was out playing bridge, and when he asked whether he might leave his phone number, she unlatched the door and let him in. When she returned with a pad and pencil, she found him standing in front of the now latched door, with his right hand in his pocket. Evenly he said, "if you scream, you're dead." At that moment, Miss F. seemed to step into an alternate universe, from which she watched the ensuing events with detached calm, as if she were watching a television show. As he walked her into the bedroom where he raped and sodomized her, she thought clearly about whether she should scream or try to break away. She could hear her upstairs neighbors' stereo playing loudly, so she judged that they were unlikely to hear her if she screamed. She assumed her attacker had a knife in his pocket, and he was certainly larger and stronger than she, so fighting him off seemed hopeless. In the end, she judged that her best chance of staying alive was to submit. When he was finished, he tied her hands behind her back with wires he had ripped off the stereo, took $100 that she had in her purse, told her to count to one hundred before she tried to get out, and warned her that he would come back and kill her if she called the police.

When he left, she lay quietly for some time wondering why he hadn't killed her. She tried to get his face firmly fixed in her mind, because, despite his threat, it never occurred to her not to call the police. Finally, she extricated her hands from the wire cuffs, threw on a robe, went upstairs to her neighbors, and told them she had been raped and robbed. She then called the police, who warned her not to shower until after she'd been examined. She also called her fiancé, and asked him to come home from the bridge game. She seemed so calm and collected that her neighbors were astonished. She only said that she was amazed that she was still alive. She didn't see why her attacker hadn't killed her to prevent his ever being identified. A few minutes later a police detective arrived. He took her to the city hospital where she was examined, treated prophylactically for venereal disease, and seen briefly by a psychiatric resident. He tried to get her to say how angry she was, but all she could say was that it had been a very strange interaction to have with another human being. She didn't feel angry. Actually, she didn't feel anything.

After the examination, the detective came back in to take her home. She asked him to take her to the police station so she could look at mug shots, but he said that she needed some rest and could do it the next day. "No," she said, "I can feel his face slipping out of my mind. I need to do it now. By tomorrow I won't remember what he looked like." "Lots of women feel like that," he said. "If you see him, you'll remember."

Miss F. elected not to return to her apartment right away. That night she and her fiancé went to the home of a professor they knew—a household full of children. She felt she needed to feel "lots of life" around her. A few days later, her apartment was broken into and vandalized. Oddly, this seemed to frighten her more than the assault had. She wanted never to return to the apartment, feeling that she could never be safe there again. Her fiancé went back, packed their belongings, and they moved into a house with some friends.

In the first week or two after the assault, Miss F. talked about it a lot with friends. She told what had happened, explained why she hadn't cried out, and described how oddly detached she had felt. She almost never described the experience as frightening, more often she described it as "odd" or "interesting." She cooperated with the police investigation, even typing out her own statement, because the detective was a much worse typist than she. She had been right, though. She looked at thousands of mug shots and hadn't a clue whether any of the men resembled her attacker. She felt she'd be able to walk by him on the street and not recognize him.

To everyone she knew, she was a picture of mental health. She was able to talk dispassionately about her experience and seemed to be functioning well at her daily routine. However, the feeling of unreality that began at the moment she realized that she was in danger had persisted. She found herself sleeping ten to twelve hours a day, and after some months her fiance' complained that she seemed emotionally unavailable, short-tempered, and distant. While her actual sexual response was unimpaired, she wasn't very interested in sex. She was troubled by occasional nightmares, in which she was walking to her house, aware that she was being followed by someone who was going to hurt her. Always he caught up with her just as she was at the door, fumbling with the lock, and she awoke, terrified. She was generally able to be alone, even at night without difficulty, but sometimes, without warning, as she was walking down the street, if a young man of about the same age and body build as her attacker approached from the opposite direction, her heart began to pound out of her chest, her throat tightened up, and she felt overcome by panic. For months, she replayed the scene at the apartment door over and over in her mind, trying to figure out what she might have done differently, trying to undo what had been done. She felt guilty about not having protected herself better at the same time that she felt proud of having survived, both physically and emotionally.

Miss F. did not receive any formal therapy. But over the first couple of years, she found reasons to tell her story over and over, to muse aloud about her reactions to it, to receive the support of people who were impressed with her ability to talk about it, to feel a sense of mastery, to reassure herself that "that was then, this is now." Gradually, her sleeping and emotional distance abated, as did the nightmares and occasional panic episodes. Now, twenty years later, she speaks of it less, although she can talk about it when appropriate. She finds herself avoiding movies, television shows, books, or plays in which rape plays a part in the plot. On the rare occasions when she thinks about what happened, she distracts herself from the unpleasant memories fairly quickly, but without panic. She is probably more careful than most people when she goes into urban areas, locking her car doors, and staying with other people. She feels she has mostly mastered the experience, but she notices, as she writes this account, a distinct feeling of queasiness in the pit of her stomach.

Thinking About the Case

The classic features of acute stress disorder are present in this case: intrusive reexperiencing of traumatic feelings and memories, avoidance of stimuli associated with the trauma, numbing of general responsiveness, and symptoms of increased arousal. One might speculate whether this syndrome, or constellation of symptoms, is a "disorder" at all, in that it is hard to imagine anyone who has experienced a severe trauma not having some of these symptoms.

The most salient of Miss F.'s symptoms is emotional numbing. The psychological defenses employed are repression, suppression, and intellectualization. An example of repression is the automatic, involuntary forgetting of the assailant's face that Miss F. experienced. Suppression is voluntary and can be seen in her active avoidance of media presentations which would stimulate recollections of the rape. Intellectualization includes conceptualizing her experiences as a "case," from which she could learn something about human behavior. Defense mechanisms like these, which serve to shield the individual from painful feelings, often are considered pathological by psychodynamic theorists on the grounds that they distort or deny reality. True recovery is thought to be possible only if traumatic memories are reunited with the feelings of terror, guilt, and shame that are presumed to have been present. However, it could be argued that in Miss F.'s case, these powerful defense mechanisms protected her from being overwhelmed initially and led to gradual mastery of the traumatic event.

This case is also interesting in that substantial recovery occurred in the absence of formal therapy of any kind. Researchers and clinicians who study trauma (traumatologists) suggest that telling and retelling the traumatic event in an atmosphere of safety and support can facilitate recovery. While this process is often confined to the therapy room because people may be ashamed or otherwise inhibited from telling their tale to others, it can sometimes take place within the natural support system as well.

Questions to Consider

1. Some people seem to recover from trauma more quickly or more completely than others. What factors might contribute to these dif-

ferences? What aspects of the person's personality, history, or phase of life might be relevant? What aspects of the traumatic situation or events might be relevant? What aspects of the support network might be relevant?

2. What are the pros and cons of being diagnosed with a "disorder" after suffering a life-threatening trauma? In what ways might it be helpful? In what ways might it be hurtful?

CASE 26

CHRONIC POST-TRAUMATIC STRESS DISORDER: THE CASE OF GEORGE G.

GEORGE G, A FORTY-FIVE-YEAR-OLD married father of two teenage children, entered marital therapy with Violet, his wife of twenty years. Although he graciously shook the therapist's hand at the beginning of the meeting, it was clear that George was there under duress. He sat at the edge of the sofa with his arms wrapped around his middle, looking down at his wristwatch. He spoke rarely and appeared to be holding himself in check somehow. Violet answered most of the therapist's questions.

Violet and George were on the verge of divorce. She loved her husband, she said, but she could no longer live with him. Her major complaint was that George seemed to be vacant and distant—"just like he looks now." He was uncommunicative, wouldn't answer her questions, wouldn't speak to her at all for days at a time with no apparent reason. He had terrible fits of rage over minor frustrations, and she could never tell when he would erupt. He seemed "paranoid," expecting the worst of people and refusing to socialize except with his war buddies. She was glad he had these friends because George was otherwise so isolated, but she was concerned about their favorite pastime—drinking. She also suspected George and his friends of using marijuana because she had found empty baggies and cigarette papers. He had denied this on several occasions, so she had given up asking about it years ago. She knew that George loved her and the children, but she couldn't take "the cold shoulder" and the occasional verbal abuse any longer. Sadly, she reported, this wasn't the George that she had married. This was, instead, the George that had returned from Viet Nam.

George responded to the therapist's questions tersely and in a guarded manner. He had been the middle of three children born into a rural farm family. His father, who had died a couple of years previously, had been a hard worker, but moody and difficult for the children to warm up to. His mother kept the books for the farm and worked part-time as a hairdresser. George reported that he was fond of his mother, but Violet pointed out that he rarely called her or went to see her unless Violet reminded and urged him to do so. One of George's brothers still worked the farm, and he and George were pretty close, while the youngest child, a girl, had married and moved to a neighboring city. George and Violet saw her and her family at holidays.

George had been a fair student, had played football in high school, and had had a lot of friends. He had played in a band on weekends, smoked, drank some, and generally had a good time. He had met Violet in sophomore year of high school, and neither had ever really seriously dated anyone else. The couple married in the September following their graduation from high school and in August of the next year George was drafted into the army and sent to Viet Nam.

George had been proud to go to Viet Nam. While he had not looked forward to being drafted, and he hadn't enlisted, he hadn't any other plans, really. He didn't want to go to college, and he didn't want to work on the farm. At the time he was drafted, he was working in a local auto parts store, but wasn't enjoying it much and didn't see a future in it. George, like many young men, had a need to prove himself, to find a direction, to develop some self-esteem. Perhaps, he thought, serving his country would serve these purposes as well.

George spent three years in Viet Nam, much of it on the front lines. He was wounded once by shrapnel, but returned to duty following a brief stay in a M.A.S.H. unit. When he first arrived, his letters to Violet had been long and detailed—describing the scenery, his buddies, his thoughts about the experience. But as his stay lengthened, the letters became shorter and less frequent. Their tone and language changed, Violet said, becoming "hard," and full of nasty words that George had never used before. For the last six months before his discharge, George would sign off each letter with "from the bloody asshole end of the world, love, George."

When George returned from Viet Nam, he found a world far different than the one he had remembered. Instead of being welcomed with honor, he found himself a pariah among his former friends, many of whom had been heavily influenced by ever increasing body counts, reported war-related atrocities, and increasing distrust in the United States government. Some people even challenged him about having chosen to serve. The genuinely courageous thing would have been to refuse, they said. Even worse for George was the discontinuity between his life in Viet Nam and his life at home. The bright lights, the overflowing grocery shelves, television, skyscrapers, everything felt jarring and artificial to him. He felt like he was walking through a dream and that Viet Nam had been "more real." He found himself having trouble relating to Violet, whose talk of family and friends, clothes and children seemed trivial to him. Neither she, nor anyone else at home seemed to have a clue about what "real life" was all about.

At first during therapy, George refused to talk in any detail about his war experiences. Frequently, he simply sat silently in response to questions. However, over the next few sessions, as he got to know the therapist a bit, he did admit, upon gentle questioning, that some of his experiences were so horrific that he wanted more than anything to not think about them ever again. But he was troubled by nightmares and on the days after these dreams, his experiences would replay in his head over and over. He knew he was "a bear" to live with at these times. He couldn't stand to have anybody around, and he couldn't stand to be alone with his thoughts. He felt like a powder keg on the verge of exploding, and it took all his energy to maintain self-control. He didn't want to be that way. He knew that Violet was right and that he was the problem, but he simply didn't know how to handle his feelings. He just hadn't been able to "get on with life." Instead, he felt "stuck in a dark fog."

The therapist suggested that George try an antidepressant, but he refused. A series of therapy visits was offered as well, but again George refused. He didn't see how talking to somebody who hadn't been there would help. Finally, the therapist suggested that George attend a Viet Nam veterans' therapy group facilitated by vets who had been in Nam themselves, had attended the group as participants themselves, and had had training in counseling for post-traumatic stress disorder. Initially, George hesitated. He already had his own support group—his buddies from Nam. But, as the therapist pointed out, George and his buddies mostly drank and watched sports on television. They didn't ever talk about their war experiences.

Talking about his experiences was the last thing that George wanted to do. Talking would stimulate the nightmares, he felt sure. Talking would make him worse. The therapist agreed that talking might initially stir up a lot of painful memories and feelings. But he told George that, just as courage had been required to get the job done in Viet Nam, it was needed now for George to get well. "If you can do three years in Nam, you can do six months in this group," he said. This way of putting things struck a chord with George, and he agreed to attend the group for six months.

George stuck to his word. He attended the group each week. At first, he dreaded the meetings, and he came home angry and hostile. His drinking increased over the first several weeks, until he made a pledge to the group to refrain from drinking until the six months were up. As time went on, encouraged by the group, he began to share a few of his war experiences with Violet. When George went into therapy, Violet began attending a wives' support group and, prepared for the time when George would begin to talk about the war, she listened respectfully and quietly. Sometimes, George would cry in her arms after telling her about some particularly harrowing experience. These times were not easy for Violet, and she might have responded quite differently, had she not been coached and supported by other wives in the group.

At the end of six months, George came to three important decisions. First, he would visit the Viet Nam memorial in Washington, D.C. Second, he would continue to abstain from alcohol because he had become aware that drinking had as often intensified his painful feelings as banished them. Besides, he didn't want to be a poor role model for his children who were at an age when decisions about their own drug and alcohol use would have to be made. Third, he would continue in the group long enough to become a facilitator himself. In this way, he could give something back for what had been given to him.

George was changed by his therapy experience in many ways, but he was not "cured." He still had moody times in which he became withdrawn. He still sometimes had nightmares. He still had a temper. However, he and Violet had discovered ways to cope with these times together. She didn't nag him to socialize when he was "in his cave," but instead let him know that she could see that something was wrong. Generally, this was enough to prod him to take stock of himself and figure out what was bothering him. He then shared what he had learned with Violet, even though doing so still was difficult. Sometimes the process took days, but it rarely took weeks anymore. While George was still less social than Violet, he was more tolerant of social situations, more responsive to her needs to be with people, and less hostile towards people outside of his inner circle. He related better with his children, more patient and less judgmental. In general, Violet said, he seemed to have "softened." George agreed. He said he didn't feel so much like he needed to keep his guard up as he'd used to feel. He didn't feel like a powder keg about to blow. He felt more able to feel tender feelings.

George felt that becoming a therapy group facilitator had been the real turning point for him. It continually reinforced that he had to talk about what was bothering him, rather than ignore it. In being a role model for the new guys and in explaining the rationale for confronting rather than running from painful memories and feelings, George kept renewing his own motivation and shoring up his own confidence that the emotional work had a payoff. This experience had such a profound and enduring effect on George that he and Violet eventually began a couples' group which has now become part of the therapeutic offering at the Veteran's Outreach center George attends. They co-facilitate the group every third week, alternating with two other couples that they trained.

Thinking About the Case

The casualties of war don't end with the last serviceperson to leave the field of battle. Nor are they confined to severed limbs and lost eyesight. Psychological damage caused by war may be more subtle, but can be just as severe and persistent. Chronic post-traumatic stress disorder, illustrated by this case, occurs in a substantial proportion of veterans who have seen action. Fifty percent of Viet Nam veterans who saw intense action experienced PTSD. The wars in Iraq and Afghanistan have, no doubt, produced another generation of psychological casualties, among them PTSD patients. The disorder can also occur in people who have been traumatized in other ways, for example, by famine, flood, childhood abuse, poverty, loss of a spouse or child, or living in a dangerous urban community.

Chronic PTSD is diagnosed when symptoms last longer than three months. Delayed PTSD is diagnosed when symptoms begin at least six months after the stressor ends. This form of the disorder is common among children who have been subjected to chronic abuse. For these youngsters, symptoms of PTSD may emerge in late adolescence or adulthood after the actual danger has passed.

As George's problems illustrate, the symptoms of chronic PTSD often go beyond the reexperiencing of and avoidance of stimuli related to trauma, although these are present. More generalized changes in physiological and emotional reactivity, as well as interpersonal behavior often occur. Sufferers may experience virtually permanent changes in overall anxiety level, irritability, and concentration. They may have difficulty with love relationships of all sorts; they tend to experience more divorces and estrangements than people without traumatic histories. They often have occupational difficulties. They may, like George, struggle with substance abuse. And, like George, they may not seek treatment for trauma-related symptoms either because they are unaware that their symptoms are related to the trauma or because they do not want to discuss the traumatic events.

It is instructive to compare George's case with the previous case (Miss F.). Why do some people develop long-standing symptoms while others do not? Studies indicate that some people are predisposed to symptoms by a generally lower level of mental health prior to the trauma. Genetic heritability has also been demonstrated: identical twins show a greater concordance for PTSD when exposed to trauma than do fraternal twins. Further, the more severe and prolonged the trauma, the greater the likelihood of experiencing symptoms.

Other factors, like the availability of a support network or how the trauma changes one's perception of oneself or of the world in which one lives, may also be relevant. One can imagine that George's experiences changed his view of human nature and possibly his own nature more profoundly than did Miss F.'s. Miss F. was accorded the benefits of the victim role immediately, while George initially was treated by his friends and his society as a perpetrator. She saw viciousness in one human being; George saw it in many, including his closest comrades.

Chronic post-traumatic stress disorder is quite difficult to treat. As George's case illustrates, symptoms tend to be long-lived indeed. Prolonged exposure therapy, in which individuals repeatedly imagine the traumatic events and describe them to therapists in the present tense, has been shown to have moderate success. Indeed, research indicates that those who talk about the trauma fare better, both physically and psychologically, than those who do not. Thus, PTSD is a disorder in which early intervention may, in fact, reduce the probability and severity of later symptoms.

This case also illustrates the importance of including significant others in the treatment plan. Not only did Violet choose not to leave George, but she functioned in a therapeutic role during his treatment. In order for this to happen, she herself needed support and training. One can imagine how different the outcome of this case would have been had the couple separated.

Questions To Consider

1. Under what circumstances might a self-help group be more effective than professional intervention?
2. Have you, or a good friend or family member, experienced a traumatic event? What symptoms did you (or the other person) display and for how long? What factors contributed to recovery?
3. Consider the phenomenon of violence in public schools. What might a PTSD prevention program look like? Who would be targeted? What would the interventions be? How would outcomes be measured?
4. Studies show that therapists who treat people with severe PTSD often develop symptoms of PTSD themselves. Why might this be so?

CASE 27

REACTIVE ATTACHMENT DISORDER: THE CASE OF SONJA S.

SONJA WAS AN EIGHT-YEAR-OLD second grader when her parents brought her to the child guidance clinic for evaluation and therapy. They reported that she had severe tantrums on an almost daily basis, sometimes biting or scratching herself or whoever was closest to her. She was irritable in the extreme, and could not or would not be comforted by either of her parents . . . or anyone else for that matter. In fact, she disliked being cuddled or hugged. Oddly, when she was hurt, for example, if she fell and skinned her knee, she was stoic. She did not seem to react to pain in a normal way.

Sonja exhibited problems in daily living skills. She would not brush her teeth, and bathed only when her parents absolutely insisted. Bathtime was usually a trigger for a tantrum. She hated having her hair washed or combed or even brushed. Left to her own devices, she would be smelly and disheveled.

Sonja was cruel to her younger sister and consistently lied about her behavior when caught. She stole from her peers at school and from her parents and sister at home. No consequences or punishments seemed to matter. Her parents had tried grounding, taking away social media and television time. In extreme distress, her mother had even swatted Sonja on the behind a couple of times when she had physically hurt her sister. Even this had had no effect. In fact, Sonja had seemed almost to enjoy her mother's loss of control. When it was over she had "sauntered" to her room where she played peacefully for the rest of the afternoon.

In school, Sonja did well. She was clearly bright, though not very motivated. She did not seem to respond to praise, but did her homework because she enjoyed it. If she faced a task which she did not enjoy, she simply didn't do it. But this happened rarely. Socially, she did not fare as well. She had no close friends. She was known as a thief, so of course, that didn't help. She was on the soccer team and seemed to get along fairly well there, though she generally sat apart when after-game pizza parties occurred. She never complained about a lack of friends, though she did complain that other children were stupid or slow or just "idiots." She seemed impervious to the opinion of others in general.

The intake counselor asked for a social history and learned the following: Sonja had been adopted from China when she was twenty-eight months old. Her biological mother had gotten pregnant accidentally. Since her parents already had one child, they placed Sonja in an institution for unwanted children shortly after birth. The institution provided a clean, orderly environment, and adequate physical care. However, the ratio of caregivers to children was low. Each infant got a minimum of individual attention—just enough to ensure he or she was clean and fed. There were day care services of course, and once the children were old enough, these centered on learning the rudiments of language, reading readiness, and other appropriate cognitive tasks, like color learning, object sorting, and the like. By the time Sonja could walk, she was eating and washing up with a group of other children. Adults were distant, unemotional figures.

Sonja's adoptive parents met her for the first time when they arrived in China to take her home with them. They had picked her picture out of an album provided by the adoption agency. They were assured that she was healthy and had no significant developmental delays. The adoption process had been arduous—tons of paperwork over a two year period. They had been unable to conceive a child of their own, and they had enough money both to adopt and to raise a child well, and they were eager to do so. Ironically, soon after they returned home with Sonja, they conceived her sister. They were thrilled. Now they would have a real family!

At first, Sonja seemed the model child, quiet and obedient. She seemed to adapt to her new environment remarkably quickly, exhibiting little distress. And she was independent, almost to a fault. She seemed indifferent to her new sister, at first, but as time wore on, her behavior towards the little one became intolerant and nasty. She would snatch toys and push the toddler over if she got in the way of Sonja's activity. Mr. and Mrs. S. had become so concerned about Sonya's behaviors that they had come to the clinic for advice and help.

Sonja was diagnosed with reactive attachment disorder. Her parents were told that, while no definitive treatment had been discovered, a stable, secure environment characterized by compassionate, consistent limit-setting would help Sonja progress. While her parents participated in weekly parental consultations designed to provide them emotional support and help with limit-setting, Sonja was treated in a social skills training group composed of other children her age, with various diagnoses. An attempt was made to help her develop skills in interpersonal empathy and relating, but it was hard-going as Sonja didn't care what the other children thought of her.

Despite her parents' best intentions, and despite the help they were receiving from therapists at the clinic, tragedy struck about four months into treatment. One day, in a rage at her sister for entering her bedroom without permission, Sonja shoved her sister out the bedroom door, and pushed her again . . . down the stairs. Her sister broke her collarbone. Sonja was sent first to a child psychiatric unit and from there to a residential treatment facility for children. Her parents were both furious and heartbroken. They could not afford to put one child at serious risk at the hands of another, and they refused to take Sonja back home. Sonja was lost to follow-up: when the clinic tried to contact her parents six months later, the phone calls were not returned.

Thinking About The Case

Reactive attachment disorder (RAD) is diagnosed when there is a pattern of emotionally withdrawn behavior towards caregivers accompanied by minimal social or emotional responsiveness towards others, limited positive emotionality, and /or episodes of unexplained irritability, sadness or fearfulness. People with this disorder exhibit difficulty forming lasting relationships and lack of empathy for others. Often they have great difficulty with trust, and may not develop a conscience.

Critical to making the diagnosis of RAD is a history of insufficient care in childhood, either through institutionalization, repeated changes of primary caregivers (for example multiple foster placements), or extremely inattentive caregivers (for example, drug-addicted parents). Without this specific history, this diagnosis can not be applied.

The disorder is a controversial one, in that symptoms overlap with other behavioral and developmental disorders. Communication and social deficits may be extreme enough that the disorder is confused with autism. Unwillingness to abide by social norms and lack of feeling for others suggests antisocial personality disorder.

The disorder has also spawned a controversial treatment: "holding therapy." This approach involved holding a child so closely that movement is impossible and holding this position for an extended period of time. It was thought that this would induce in the child a feeling of containment and safety which had been presumed missing in the child's rearing environment. This "treatment" is now widely considered ineffective and abusive.

To date, no specific therapy has been shown to be efficacious for RAD. Providing a stable, secure environment is key so removing a child from a chaotic or insufficiently nurturing environment may be necessary. When symptoms persist after such an environment has been provided for a period of time, as was the case for Sonya, treatment usually focuses on helping the caregivers manage the child's behaviors in a consistent and compassionate manner. No one has any idea how many children with RAD benefit from treatment. Many of those so diagnosed go on to live chaotic lives, abusing drugs, breaking rules, behaving violently.

Questions To Consider

1. Why might RAD persist even after a stable, nurturing environment is provided?
2. Foreign adoption is a risk factor for RAD. If you ran the adoption agency, could you think of any measures you could take that might ameliorate the risk? What might they be?
3. Not all children raised in inadequate environments develop RAD. Why might this be?

LANAHAN NOTES
Trauma and Stressor Disorders

These disorders share a relationship with anxiety disorders, obsessive-compulsive and related disorders, and dissociative disorders

Causes of trauma and stressor disorders

Traumatic events, e.g., experience of war

Continual stress situations, e.g., long-term neglect during childhood

Related causal factors: the amount of stress, duration, timing, genetic make-up, family history, temperament

Reactions to Stress

Physical: pounding heart, sweaty palms, lightheadedness, nausea, shortness of breath, tingling feelings, chills

Cognitive/emotional: racing thoughts or mind blank, fear of going crazy, fear of losing control

Behavioral: retreat, avoidance, freezing

Question: everybody experiences these symptoms. When do they constitute a disorder? Symptoms must be prolonged and the symptoms must markedly interfere with the individual's functioning

Types of trauma and stressor disorders

Reactive attachment disorder: typically evident before age 5, the child displays a consistent pattern of inhibited, emotionally withdrawn behavior by:

lack of comfort seeking or response to comforting when distressed

persistent social emotional disturbance characterized by:

minimal social and emotional responsiveness to others

limited positive affect

episodes of unexplained irritability, sadness, fearfulness

Disinhibited social engagement disorder

Evident when the child has reached at least 9 months

The child has reduced or absent reticence in approaching, interacting with, going with an unfamiliar adult.

These first two disorders, the child has insufficient attachments that result from social neglect in childhood such as insufficient parenting, multiple foster care placements, rearing in institutional settings with high child-to-caregiver ratios

Posttraumatic stress disorder (PTSD)

Caused by exposure to a traumatic event: threatened death/injury/violence; exposure can be actual experience or witnessing the event happening to others

Intrusive symptoms: memories, dreams, and/or flashbacks often accompanied by physiological reactions

Avoidance of stimuli associated with the event (people, places, conversations, objects, etc.)

Negative alterations in cognition and mood such as dissociative amnesia, exaggerated negative beliefs (I am bad, the world is dangerous, etc.) and emotions (guilt, anger, etc.)

Alterations in arousal and reactivity such as anger outbursts, hypervigilance, exaggerated startle response, etc.

Onset is typically within the first 3 months of the trauma; diagnosis may be delayed for weeks, months or years

Acute stress disorder

Similar to symptoms of PTSD

Symptoms must occur and resolve within a 1-month period after the trauma

A diagnosis of PTSD is given if symptoms persist

Adjustment disorders

Characterized by marked distress out of proportion to a non-life-threatening stressor

Individual will show symptoms of depressed mood with or without anxiety, disturbance of conduct, mixed disturbance of emotions and conduct

Often caused by a significant change (stress) in one's life, a single event or multiple events, e.g., termination of a romantic relationship, job-related difficulties and the like

Who gets these disorders?

Everyone has exposure to stress in life; age, duration of exposure, severity of traumatic event all play a role; Some risk factors:

previous diagnosis of mental illness in self or family members
lower socioeconomic status
exposure to childhood adversity
lack of a social support system

Treatment

Similar to treatments for anxiety disorders.

Prolonged exposure: client imagines the traumatic event in a safe environment or in vivo exposure to safe situations that have been avoided

Cognitive processing: focus on challenging and modifying maladaptive beliefs

Eye Movement Desensitization Reprocessing (EMDR):

The client revisits an emotionally arousing memory along with negative belief of self

Recognizes the related emotions and bodily sensations while simultaneously attending to external stimulus, most commonly directed lateral eye movements

Clients are taught to replace negative cognitions with positive ones

CHAPTER NINE

Dissociative Disorders

Dissociative disorders are among the most fascinating of all the phenomena we will study. How can it be that a person can be blind, although his eyesight is normal? How can several "personalities" inhabit a single body? How can a person be "outside" her body, watching herself behave?

Among those who have attempted to answer these questions was Sigmund Freud. Freud developed his theories about the psychodynamic origins of maladaptive behavior from studying the dissociative symptoms found in young, middle-class Viennese women of his day. His interpretation of their repetitive accounts of childhood abuse as a symbolic account of their own fantasies and repressed wishes was a critical (and, critics would say, a terribly erroneous) turning point in the development of Western theories about abnormality.

In this chapter we have included a case in which the dissociative disorder is fairly subtle. This is much more common today than the complete blindness, deafness, and paralysis that Freud encountered in his time. We have also included a fascinating first-person account of a psychiatric nurse who has struggled with multiple personality disorder for many years.

CASE 28

DEPERSONALIZATION / DEREALIZATION DISORDER: THE CASE OF MARIE O.

Marie O., a separated fifty-five-year-old woman, sat rigidly in the high-backed chair in her therapist's office. Her voice had become faint and she spoke very slowly. She seemed to be taking an inordinate amount of time to process questions and formulate answers. When her therapist asked her what she was experiencing, she became completely mute. After ten minutes of silence, she resumed her previous train of thought, as if the bizarre episode had not happened. Patiently, the psychologist commented on these "absences" in a curious, but nonjudgmental way after Marie recovered from them, and gradually the patient was able to describe her experiences.

During those times, Marie explained, she was not in the room. Rather she was on the other side of the door. At times, she was relatively nearby, so that she could hear what was being said, although the sounds were slightly muffled. Sometimes she was far away, as if several football fields separated her from her therapist. At times the distance was so great that she was unable to hear or see anything at all.

Marie explained that being "way back in my head" occurred automatically when she began to experience emotional distress. There, she was calm and safe. Many things could trigger it—being on a bus with teenagers who were loud and mildly menacing, the smell of alcohol on someone's breath, conversations in which a violent or abusive act was mentioned. It had been going on as long as she could remember. Marie understood that these states were not normal, and while she valued the sense of safety they provided, she wished they were more under her control. Her therapist agreed that this would be one of their therapy goals.

As the weeks went by and trust developed in the therapeutic relationship, Marie naturally disclosed more of her history in the sessions. She had only vague memories of her childhood, but what she did remember was enough. She was raised in a devoutly Catholic home. Her only sibling, a younger brother, is now a priest. Her mother managed to go to church daily, despite holding down a full-time job. Marie doesn't have any images of her mother, save those of her praying or leaving the house for work. As she spoke, Marie's therapist noted that the image of Marie's mother putting on her coat had triggered a mild "absence."

Unfortunately, Marie's memories of her father were more vivid. A verbally and physically violent alcoholic, Mr. O. dominated family life with his unpredictable, demanding presence. Mealtimes were grim, frightening affairs in which Mr. O. quizzed the children about biblical passages or lectured them about God, sin, and hellfire. He had almost always had several drinks by the time they sat down to eat. A wrong answer meant no dinner, but sometimes being banished from the table was a blessing in itself. Marie reported experiencing several days of feeling "spacey" following the session in which she first spoke about her father.

Marie describes herself as a shy, obedient child. She was not allowed to participate in school activities and therefore had no real friends, despite being well enough liked by other children. Not surprisingly, she was a pious child, full of guilt and shame about the smallest infraction, error, or untruth.

Sometime during her teenage years, Marie can't remember exactly when, her father began to molest her. While she had never fully repressed these experiences, she had great difficulty describing them in therapy. She was often mute for long periods of time and upon returning seemed disoriented and a bit dazed. She remembered what she had been talking about but experienced a sense of inhibition so strong that she could barely speak. Still, she persevered and gradually recounted what she could. It appeared that her ability to psychologically remove herself had developed as a way to emotionally survive the abuse and continue on with her life in a "normal" way.

By the time the sexual abuse started, Mr. O.'s relationship with his wife had completely soured—they survived in economic partnership together, nothing more. Marie cannot remember them ever laughing, hugging, or even touching—except, of course, when her father got angry and knocked her mother around. Unable to protect her mother, Marie practiced "removing" herself during these situations as well.

Mrs. O. worked second shift, from three P.M. to eleven at night. Marie's brother was often out of the house, either at sports or church. As a boy, he had much more freedom of movement then she was allowed, even though he was younger, and he used it to keep away from their father whenever possible. Mr. O. got home from work at four, shortly after Marie got home from school. He began drinking immediately, and after four or five beers would come looking for Marie. What began as fondling and deep kissing, ended as mutual masturbation and forced fellatio. Throughout, Mr. O. talked to Marie, sometimes telling her that she was a slut and a whore, at others declaring that he loved her, and at others explaining that he was preparing her for sex with her future husband—teaching her what her duties would be. Marie had been taught to be a dutiful child, and despite knowing that what they were doing was horribly wrong, she was unable to resist her powerful father. She knew her mother would be unable to protect her, and she couldn't imagine what would happen to their family if she let the terrible secret out. She felt that perhaps her father was right: she was the sinful one. Otherwise, why would God allow her to suffer such torture?

Marie solved the problem the way many young women do. She married immediately upon graduating from high school. Her husband was from an enormous and dysfunctional family in which violence was the preferred mode of interaction. Shortly after they married, the couple moved several hundred miles away in order to be closer to her husband's family. While she was initially relieved to be away from her father, she missed her mother and brother and she felt intimidated by her husband's thirteen siblings and their families. Not surprisingly, in the bosom of his own family, Marie's husband's behavior began to deteriorate. Soon he, too, began to slap and push her when he got angry. Like her father, and like his own brothers, his drinking began to increase. Marie, already adept at surviving abuse through dissociating, used these skills to cope with her husband's abusive behavior as well.

A few years into the marriage a tragedy occurred. One day, a neighbor's car broke down in front of their home. Marie asked her husband to come out and help move it off the road. In the course of doing so, he was struck by a passing vehicle and lost an arm. Marie blamed herself for the accident, and her husband seemed willing to allow her to do so. From the time of the accident forward, his drinking and abusiveness escalated without respite. Marie used to believe that he had no control over his temper, but in talking with the therapist, she realized that he never hit her with his prosthesis—the doctor had admonished him to be careful of it, lest it get jammed up into his arm and damage him further.

In any case, Marie's life was harsh. Her husband earned meager wages as a worker on a dairy farm. She found herself raising three children with little money left over for groceries after her husband's hunting equipment and liquor were taken care of. She had begun to take Valium, an anti-anxiety medication, shortly after the accident. Neither seeing nor asking about the context in which Marie lived, her family physician simply thought that she was "a bundle of nerves" and needed a prescription to calm her.

After a decade or so of trying to balance her mostly grim life with Valium, Marie had a "nervous breakdown." She was unable to stop crying. She felt that insects were crawling all over her. She couldn't eat.

Her husband was characteristically unsupportive. In fact, in his frustration at her inability to function, he beat her and poked at her eyes when she "looked at him funny." However, her daughter, now a young woman, insisted she be taken to the hospital where she was first diagnosed as having a psychotic depression. One of the attending psychiatrists had a different hypothesis. He felt that her overuse of Valium over a long period of time might also have produced her symptoms, and indeed, when she was gradually withdrawn from the Valium, her symptoms lessened and finally disappeared.

Marie found it harder to tolerate the beatings without the Valium. Finally, after her husband cracked three of her ribs, she left him and went to a battered women's shelter. There, she was helped to get a job and find a therapist. She also developed a support system of women who had been through similar experiences and who remained her friends from that time on. By the time she entered therapy, she was working for an elderly woman as a companion. This afforded her room and board and a small living stipend. She had one brief romance but had found that her companion's beer drinking triggered her "absences," so she terminated the relationship.

Marie remained in psychotherapy off and on for about five years. She would go regularly for six months or so, then take a break for some months, returning when a significant life change occurred or when she felt like she wanted to work on a particular issue. In therapy she recounted details of her father's abuse for the first time, affirming out loud that it had really happened. She learned to manage the pain and rage that these experiences provoked in her. She talked about the guilt and shame she had felt and, with her therapist's help, came to realize that she was not responsible for her father's behavior.

Over the course of therapy, the frequency of her dissociative episodes diminished as she became better able to manage the anxiety that caused them. Her sense of herself as "damaged goods" changed to an image of a decent person who had been victimized as a child by circumstances outside of her control. She began to see that as an adult she had personal skills and resources—in short, she was no longer helpless. Her self esteem and ability to care for herself increased. She became more independent, and showed better judgment in managing her affairs. She became more assertive and self-protective.

Marie has not seen her therapist recently, although she sometimes calls her for reassurance, particularly if something has really unsettled her. She has begun "dating" her husband again. Old habits are hard to break, and the romantic prospects for a fifty-five-year-old woman are not wonderful. Things are different now, though. She does not allow her husband to drink when she visits, nor does she tolerate even the most subtle hint of verbally abusive behavior. She especially enjoys having holiday dinners together as a family with him and her children. She says she's happier than she's ever been. Her therapist worries what will happen to her when the woman she is caring for dies. Marie has never really lived alone. But she will cross that bridge when she comes to it.

Thinking About the Case

Dissociative symptoms are marked by alterations in the normal, integrated functions of a person's identity, memory, or consciousness. All of us have experienced the phenomenon of awakening from a particularly compelling dream in a state of disorientation and confusion. Where am I? Am I awake or asleep? Some of us have had the experience of watching ourselves behave, as if from a vantage point outside of our own bodies. These are the dissociative experiences of everyday life. When these symptoms are prolonged and interfere with normal functioning, as they do in this case, dissociative disorder is diagnosed.

Dissociative disorders are among the most dramatic psychopathological syndromes, particularly when they occur in the form of multiple personality disorder. We have all been fascinated by *The Three Faces of Eve*, or *Sybil*, or claims by criminals like the "Hillside Strangler" that an alter-ego actually committed the crimes. Some of these cases are so spectacular that observers have wondered whether they might be faked, particularly when strong motivation in the form of reduced culpability or stealing the limelight exists. As a result, professionals have been reluctant to diagnose multiple personality disorder. More recently, though, the possibility of the disorder being more prevalent is being taken more seriously. Whether more cases actually exist, whether clinicians are simply more prone to properly diagnose them, or whether more suggestible clients are feigning them is a matter of some dispute.

Most actual clinical cases of dissociative disorder are, like Marie's, somewhat less dramatic. Commonly, the dissociation is incomplete. Marie had not completely repressed her horrific memories, nor was she a different person when "absent." Nor were the absences total, except in very rare instances. Rather, she often experienced a sense of distance, called "depersonalization," or of functioning as if in a dream ("derealization") that she referred to as feeling "spacey."

Marie's case, like many, has its origins in trauma. It appears that the mind is capable of protecting itself from unmanageable anxiety by blocking out the memories of situations that evoke the terror. For example, one type of dissociative disorder, called "fugue" (for "flight") is diagnosed with some frequency in soldiers exposed to combat. Under the stress of battle, they simply walk away, losing their memories for the war situation, and taking up a new life elsewhere. Often, a person who has been in a fugue state will wake up suddenly, remembering his past life, but not recent events that occurred when in the altered state. For Marie, her mind "walked away" from extreme distress by blocking her perceptions (hearing and sight) enough to reduce her discomfort to manageable levels.

Not all dissociative experiences are related to trauma, however. Interestingly (and perhaps reassuringly for you at this moment), mild and fleeting episodes of depersonalization are common in adolescents and young adults and appear not to represent a history of chronic trauma or any serious psychopathology. Perhaps as many as 70 percent of young people report brief out-of-body experiences or spells of being in a dreamlike state. These are sometimes precipitated by acute stress, like an illness or accident. Generally, there are no long-term negative outcomes, although in a small minority of cases, these spells can be the precursors of a more chronic dissociative disorder or even a full-blown schizophreniform illness.

Questions to Consider

1. What would psychodynamic theory have to say about why one symptom versus another is chosen in response to the severe and overwhelming anxiety associated with trauma? What would learning theory have to say about it? Might biological or genetic factors be relevant to the issue of symptom selection?
2. What are some reasons why only a subset of children who are severely abused develop dissociative disorders?

CASE 29

DISSOCIATIVE IDENTITY DISORDER: THE CASE OF ANONYMOUS

Multiple personality disorder seems such an exotic disorder. It's hard to imagine anyone who has it functioning in everyday life. The nurse who wrote up her own case describes how she managed at work and at home despite her occasionally having several distinct personalities. She also talks poignantly about how the stigma and skepticism associated with multiple personality disorder affects her.

The sad part about being a multiple
is that no one knows.

In the fall of 1984, when I was 39 years old, I went into therapy for symptoms of depression. For years I suffered ghastly outbursts of anger. They came so fast that I only could be stunned by the words coming from my mouth. I had a violent side and a hateful nature. I was unable to make decisions. I had been a "good girl" growing up, however, and never gave my parents a moment of trouble. From where was this behavior coming?

The day before I began therapy, I had no idea that there was more of me than I was aware. I had no idea I would be seeing a psychiatrist for the next 9 years for supervision of my medication, and that I would soon meet the therapist who would start me on the path to self-discovery. I knew only that there was something terribly wrong with me. I was not like other people; I was miserable.

After 2 years of therapy fraught with emotional pain and upheaval, I was stuck in a desolate place where I could move neither backward nor forward. Although my therapist was nurturing, she was unaware of my dissociation. I began again with a second therapist, a psychotherapist (PhD) specializing in sexual issues. It was this therapist who after a year made the diagnosis of multiple personality disorder (MPD). Thus began the long, difficult treatment process . . . the search . . . the journey into sorrow.

Painful Years

Growing Up Looking back, I can see that I was not comfortable when alone with men, and I made sure that situation rarely occurred. The few dates I had in high school resulted in sweaty palms and anxiety attacks. I could not bear the thought of being near anyone of the opposite sex, and holding hands was out of the question. It was not worth it. It was difficult, and much too frightening.

As a young teenager I became preoccupied with religious beliefs. There was a deep-seated feeling that I was a bad person, yet I was not aware of ever doing anything wrong. To compensate, I became pious. I meditated, sang in the church choir, read the Bible, and prayed daily. I hoped that although I failed at being good, trying would count for something. I was lost in a great, dark pit.

Nursing School I had suicidal thoughts while in nurses' training. Many times I despondently stood on the roof of my dormitory, seven floors up, and considered jumping. I had no idea why I wanted to jump—it did not make sense. I had friends among my classmates, but none was close. I was forgetful; my math skills stopped developing in the 4th grade. As a result, I had difficulties in some of my nursing classes.

Family Life After graduation, I gathered my courage and married a handicapped man introduced to me by a friend. I loved him and he was "safe." He was a gentle person with a sparkle in his eyes and a positive attitude toward life. His physical limitations made it possible for me to approach him without feeling threatened.

The first year of our marriage, I went into a sudden rage—without warning—and threw the Christmas gifts given to us by our families into the garbage can on Christmas Eve. I threw them, smashed them, and screamed at my husband—I was beside myself, not knowing why I was doing what I was doing. I was horrified as he sat watching in disbelief.

We became foster parents. Part of me loved it; part of me hated it. Friends said, "There is a special place in heaven for you"—I thought hell was more like it. What they did not know was that at times I lost control and physically abused the children. I hated myself for doing this—but no matter how hard I tried, I could not stop. How was I to know that it was not actually me?

I had no idea when I might "lose it." One alter would decide, "This is the last child. I HATE KIDS! You're CRAZY and shouldn't be doing this." Another alter would lovingly accept the children and anticipate their arrival. Still another would pray for forgiveness and ask God to let the children forget the cruelty. I would rock them one day and then hit them the next. Why was I so different inside?

My internal struggle continued as child alters fought with my own children, screaming at and hitting them. I heard myself shout that I hated them and that they were not mine. They stood staring at me with huge round eyes. Part of me cringed and hurt for them. One alter cursed loudly. Alarm bells clanged. Babies wailed in my head. Internal arguing went on during the nights. Insults from within pelted me.

My husband became my "daddy." One alter married him; others hated him. I could not bear for him to look at me during sex, so I hid my face under a pillow in shame.

Career I am a certified clinical psychiatric nurse and have worked the past 10 years on acute crisis stabilization units. It was important that I function on the job; not only to help my family financially, but also to pay for therapy. In the beginning of therapy, working became my focus; for this I developed an alter who went to work for me. She was industrious and well liked by co-workers and patients.

Getting to work was often difficult because I would lie in bed unable to get up. My body felt eight sizes too big and too heavy to move. Inside, little girls would sigh, tired of being in bed. They wanted to play outdoors. One of them would get me up and most times appropriately dressed for work.

When my key slid into the door of my unit, a "switch" immediately took place and my working alter would be there—smiling and ready to begin. My work alter loved her work. She was gentle and sensitive to those in her care. She was especially perceptive to persons with MPD. She recognized their "switching" and acknowledged each alter with respect.

Working with inpatient MPD patients can be emotionally draining for a "normal" nurse. Working with MPD patients while having MPD is extremely draining. In my situation, most of our MPD clients had the same physician that I did. When he came onto the unit I cringed and headed for the medicine room and hid in acute embarrassment. I studiously avoided charting on his patients and felt much shame.

During office visits, he reassured me that I was an excellent nurse. His patients did well with me and they felt that they could trust me.

It was difficult to have therapists treat MPD clients on the unit; some of them knew I was in therapy for MPD. Nevertheless, we worked together, in and out of seclusion rooms, and during "Amytal interviews" with their clients. Two of these therapists saw me, as a client, for psychiatric assessment and verification of my MPD diagnosis. The situation felt unreal.

At work MPD patients often triggered switches in myself. There was strong countertransference toward their child alters. My work alter was strong and no one guessed my distress. If I got overinvolved, and I sometimes did, my peers smiled and said I was a wonderful, caring person. Other staff members instinctively came to me for advice, not always knowing how to talk to alters. I pointed out switches and, for those nurses who were interested, I encouraged developing a trusting relationship between patient and nurse.

At the end of the 8-hour work shift a reverse occurred. When I turned the key in my car's ignition, a depressed, confused person—an empty shell—would drive home and go to bed exhausted and relieved that another day was done. In my head I heard plaintive cries of, "Mommy . . . mommy! Oh God . . . Oh God! I want to die!"

I knew I could not hurt myself in ways that would show because I had to continue working and appear normal. When the need to cut came, an aggressive alter named *Abusive* drew blood from my arm. In my room with the door locked, I splashed the blood, warm and sticky, onto art paper; when it dried I projected pictures onto it. The pictures were of ghoulish men torturing little girls; little girls with mouths open in silent screams, trying to get away. Like wisps of smoke, figures of little girls rose from the screaming children; alarm etched on their faces.

I cut my feet with a utility knife to punish myself for being such a miserable excuse for a human being. At work my feet hurt. Bandages and ointment covered the cuts. I wore socks to my therapist's office and would not permit her to see my feet.

If my co-workers had any suspicions about me, then they did not voice them. It is a wonder they did not; I thought my MPD was obvious. One year I received a teddy bear in a Christmas gift exchange—with the sheepish explanation, "When I saw it, I thought of you." I was amazed and pleased with the giver's perception.

I was forgetful. I blanked out in the middle of conversations with my colleagues at the desk. I would flicker in and out, catching bits and pieces of social chatter. I became a master of changing the subject. I covered my memory lapses by making jokes about how forgetful I was. I remembered details of MPD clients from one admission to the next, however. I remembered the names and characteristics of their alters, and they remembered me.

Therapy

Denial As months of therapy slowly turned into years, I continued to deny the diagnosis of MPD. It could not be right. I had no memories. I was resistant to treatment. Some alters felt threatened and were hostile toward my therapist. The babies were scared . . . she was trying to "get inside" and she wanted to make them cry. Angry alters wanted to vandalize her office. "WE DON'T CRY!" they yelled. In my dreams they threw books on the floor and shattered her glass doors.

I was evasive. I intellectualized. Fortunately, my therapist refused to give up. Of particular value to me was her patience and ability to talk me through my doubts. My confusion was immense at times and, as a result, I must have tried to quit therapy 100 times. To my chagrin, however, I found myself back in my therapist's office each time.

I was encouraged to read—and read I did. I read everything I could find about dissociative disorders. When I forgot what I read I read it again . . . and again. Contrary to the belief that reading about MPD encourages MPD symptoms, I read to compare myself with textbook MPD cases and prove that I did not have MPD. I treated myself to day-long workshops on MPD and other dissociative disorders, earning many continuing education credits. I was privileged to have heard lectures by such renowned experts in the field as Dr. F. W. Putnam and Dr. Roberta Sacks.

Realizing the Truth Studying helped me to confront the truth. The MPD diagnosis fit. I wrote; I kept journals. Alters wrote and drew pictures. They fussed, fumed, and fought.

Having MPD hurts. It makes one feel shameful and exposed. Memories are confusing and doubts are many. There is pain, despair, panic, and hiding. Resistance is difficult to overcome. It feels "crazy." Everything feels out of control. Having MPD made my thoughts spin round and round. My body jerked at night, leaving me feeling like I had been kicked in the stomach. My heart raced and my limbs ached.

I learned, through recurring pictures in my mind, what happened to me. These pictures, or memories, were of unhappy little girls, frozen in time, in pain and isolation. In the beginning I did not know what these memories were. As I learned—through trancing and hypnosis—I experienced abreactions, body memories, weight loss, weight gain, crying, resistance to crying, and the odd feeling of standing beside myself while listening to my voice speak.

Among the most frightening experiences was being unable to move . . . not an eye, not a finger . . . while another alter was out, usually a child, crying. Inside, my heart pounded and I screamed for my therapist, "Get me out! Please, please get me out!" When I "came out" my face was drenched with tears. During "real" time I was constantly bombarded by feelings and behaviors that I had little control over. This situation was ongoing in therapy and at home, while I continued to work. I truly was split. Work was my refuge and the source of my sanity.

Although I worked, I was lonely. I confided in two non-nursing friends and watched them back away because of a lack of understanding. This response reinforced my "don't trust anyone" stance. For several years, however, I wanted to trust a fellow nurse with my struggle with MPD. Some of my alters wanted to come out to be with her. Sometimes they did, briefly, and she never knew. She was amazingly comfortable to be around. I had a shy teenage alter who adored her and envied her for her free spirit and honesty.

I worked with this nurse closely for years. I dropped hints, venturing out slowly; fear kept me from fully revealing myself to her. I finally told her and we both cried. She believed me and did not think that I was crazy. She is now my dear friend, and she guards my secret.

A Turning Point The opportunity arose for me to join a group of women who were recovering from MPD. A kind and "safe" therapist facilitated the group. She created a protected environment in which she watched over us carefully. With uncanny perception and sensitivity she and the others helped me to accept my dissociated selves and believe in myself. Before joining, I made certain that I knew none of the others and they knew nothing of me. I was afraid because of my occupation as a psychiatric nurse.

It was a growing time and a relief to have a safe place to dissociate. Dissociating with others like myself at last! I have great admiration for the women in this group for displaying their courage and willingness to face their unknown terrors. They are intelligent and sensitive; I love them and have a permanent place in my heart for them. I thank them for sharing themselves with me. I was, and still am, deeply touched by them.

Now that I am integrated, I realize that I have come to love all my alters and grieve their loss. Each of them protected me over the years. They creatively kept me from losing my mind. They took the abuse for me. They hid for me, ran for me, became numb for me, and provided refuge for me. They married for me, had children for me, and got me through nurses' training.

All the alters wanted to be validated and they were. Each was listened to by my therapist. Each was heard. Each was loved and accepted. After the telling and the feeling, the anger went away—and each one said goodbye. I am proud of myself for completing this difficult task.

The Help of Others

I thank my beloved therapist, without whom I would not be free today. She gave me my life—and even more importantly, she helped me salvage my soul. She held me when I cried. She covered me when I felt naked. She listened to cries of, "I am real . . . I am real!" She was patient. She never wavered in her belief in me. Babies sat at her feet and held the hem of her dress. Alters who in sheer frustration banged their heads on her table and struggled with her found out she cared. She was strong and kept boundaries clear. Through visualization she brought color into their dark world, covered them with healing colors of the rainbow, and opened windows to outside. She was gentle; she comforted me and treated me with compassion. I learned a great deal from her during therapy.

I also want to thank my doctor for his support and assurance that I "wasn't crazy," when I felt otherwise. He was understanding of my predicament.

What can I say about my family? For 25 years my husband loved and supported me—no matter how dreadful my behavior was. He was both father and mother to our children when I could not be there for them. He cooked, cleaned, and went to school programs and conferences. Though hurt and confused, he helped the children deal with their hurt and confusion. He was, and is, my solid rock.

I also am fortunate to have an older sister who was vital to my acceptance of myself as an MPD sufferer. Her memory of events, people, and places verified my scattered memories, as the pieces of the puzzle fell together in a perfect fit. She was, and still is, supportive of me.

Skepticism and Injustice

I hope some day to come out of hiding and reveal who I am. As long as I have to keep it secret that I once had MPD, I will be hiding. I fear that I would lose my job were my secret known. I would be labeled, UNSTABLE . . . *Do Not Hire!*

The skepticism of co-workers prevents me from revealing my history. Recently, a colleague said to me, "Integration doesn't work. Multiples always come apart at the first sign of trouble." I looked at her disappointed, and thought, I am an integrated multiple. I worked 9 years at becoming whole. It is people like you who make it impossible for multiples to be open.

Unfortunately, I have seen much injustice done to individuals with MPD in the mental health field. I have seen disbelief, skepticism, misunderstanding, lack of knowledge, and hostility. I have been saddened by witnessing ineffective electroconvulsive therapy, misdiagnosis, undermedication, and overmedication. The terms *multiple personality disorder* and *borderline personality disorder* often are used interchangeably.

I have heard such comments as, "They're borderline . . . "; "She just wants attention . . . "; "Therapists create multiples, they are a status symbol . . . "; and "It's the 'in' diagnosis." These statements cause disbelief, confusion, and hurt. Such comments reinforce the resistance and denial that we fight so hard to overcome.

I personally can vouch that most persons with MPD think that they are "making up" the alters. They are not trying to be "in." We try to conceal our symptoms. We try to appear normal. We struggle every day with doubt and denial—many times right up to integration.

Please do not judge us. Every person with MPD is different. We are your friends and neighbors. We have different life experiences, and different doctors and therapists. We have different families, different support systems, and different abilities to cope.

Although I do not have the education or credentials to teach about MPD, I do have personal insight into the disorder. I have shared some of my experiences and feelings of having had MPD while working as a psychiatric nurse. Although I am whole, I continue to recover from MPD. I say *continue* because I will be recovering for the rest of my life.

Thinking About The Case

Multiple personality disorder (MPD) is a complex and controversial condition. It is defined as a severe form of dissociation in which two or more distinct personalities, each with its own age, gender, race, memories, style of speech, and characteristic mannerisms, are able to independently control the behavior of a single person. In a few reported cases, some of the personalities have been imaginary creatures or even animals. Usually there is a "host" personality who may be unaware of the other personalities. The host may, therefore, experience lapses in time and amnesia for the periods in which alternate personalities are controlling his or her behavior. Since the alternate personalities are usually hidden from the host, the disorder may take many years to diagnose: it has been reported that the average time from first complaint to diagnosis is seven years. MPD is associated with many other symptoms or syndromes. Among these are depression and suicidality. It has been reported that more than seventy percent of people with MPD have attempted suicide or have been plagued with suicidal ideas. Additionally, sufferers report sleep disorder, anxiety and panic symptoms, compulsions and rituals, substance abuse, eating disorders, and, occasionally, hallucinations.

MPD seems to be associated with severe childhood abuse, generally before the age of nine. Ninety percent of sufferers report such abuse. It is thought that the child learns to dissociate to protect him or herself from the psychological consequences of the abuse. Different personalities emerge to protect the individual. For example, a blind personality may emerge who is unable to see a parent being beaten by a partner. Or, a combative personality may emerge who will fight to protect him or herself. "Switching" from one personality to another occurs when the individual needs the protection of an "alter." As an adult, switching seems to occur often in response to stress, but may occur spontaneously as well.

Some mental health researchers and practitioners are skeptical that MPD really exists. They note that sufferers are extremely responsive to suggestion. They are easily hypnotized and alternate personalities can multiply in number dramatically when interest is shown by a therapist. Some case reports have documented over a hundred personalities in an individual sufferer. Therefore, some believe that MPD is "iatrogenic," that is, caused by therapeutic intervention. Some studies have purported to demonstrate that brain activity changes when "alters" appear. This is taken as evidence that the syndrome is real.

Another group of therapists believe that MPD is a form of chronic post traumatic stress disorder.They note the overwhelming presence of abuse in the history of these patients. Yet, others feel that MPD is really a variant of borderline personality disorder since impulsive and self-destructive symptoms occur in both, as does a history of abuse. Indeed, virtually all of the associated symptoms we listed above are also common in borderline personality disorder.

While many questions remain, MPD remains among the most vivid and mysterious of all the psychological syndromes.

Questions To Consider

1. What are some reasons that severe childhood trauma might result in MPD for only some of the children who experience it?
2. What are some ways that researchers could explore whether MPD is, indeed, a bid for attention rather than a real syndrome? Do you think the brain studies answer the question for certain?
3. What are the implications of the overlap in symptoms of MPD and borderline personality disorder? What does this say about treatment?
4. Hypnosis in the treatment of psychological disorders has a checkered history. Memories can be implanted and transformed under hypnosis. What implications does this have for diagnosis and treatment?

LANAHAN NOTES
Dissociative Disorders

Characteristics of dissociative disorders

Disruption of and/or discontinuity in the normal integration of
- thoughts = memory & identity. Consciousness & perception.
- emotion = feelings
- behavior = motor control

Unrelated to medical condition such as traumatic brain injury, seizures, etc.

Types of dissociative disorder

Dissociative identity disorder (formerly, multiple personality): presence of one or more distinct personality states resulting in alterations in thoughts, emotion, behavior

Dissociative amnesia: inability to recall important autobiographical information, generally of a traumatic or stressful nature

Depersonalization/derealization disorder: persistent or recurrent experience of unreality/detachment of self (depersonalization) and/or surroundings (derealization) while reality testing remains intact

Dissociative disorder not otherwise specified: other dissociative syndromes

Causes and risk factors

Exclusively related to severe stress or trauma; basis of much of Freud's theories about neurosis: symptoms are a way of managing unbearable anxiety

Biological factors: increased sensitivity to pain may produce a permanent change in autonomic functioning leading to a more chronic course for trauma-induced disorders

Early traumatic experiences: violence, abuse, deprivation; esp. emotional

Learning theory: modeling and serendipitous experiences (e.g., discovering that being ill brings care-giver affection)

Cultural: in some cultural settings, fragmented identities may take the form of myths and religious significance; possession-form dissociative identity disorder can be distinguished from culturally accepted possession when the fragmentation causes individual distress, interference with and violation of expected social standards

Treatment

Psychodynamic: explores underlying conflicts in attempt to reduce the necessity for symptoms; caution needed as patient can sometimes become fixated on the traumatic abuse and see themselves as a perpetual victim

Cognitive: review and rework deficits in schemes and changes in view of self and others associated with trauma

Eye movement desensitization and reprocessing (EMDR and related therapies): used to rework in enhanced information processing and healing

Medications: sometimes helpful in combating anxiety and depression

Prognosis

Guarded: treatment may be long-term; improved functioning but not "cure" is the rule

Controversies

How much conscious control does the individual have over symptoms? The line between somatization disorders, factitious disorders, true dissociation, and malingering is often difficult to ascertain; some clinicians don't believe that multiple personality disorder even exists.

Is trauma a necessary precondition for dissociation?

Is the use of hypnosis in the diagnosis and treatment of dissociative disorders appropriate given that studies clearly indicate that highly hypnotizable individuals are prone to developing false as well as real memories while in the hypnotic state?

CHAPTER TEN

Somatic Symptom and Related Disorders

We have examined many cases in which underlying physical factors including genetics and brain biochemistry have contributed to the development of psychological problems. In this section, we examine the obverse: cases in which psychological factors cause or contribute to an individual's physical suffering. Everyday examples of this phenomenon abound: we feel stressed by an upcoming exam; we develop a headache or stomach cramps. When symptoms are severe and debilitating, a somatic symptom disorder is diagnosed.

These disorders are among the most frustrating disorders to treat. Sufferers usually do not acknowledge that their problems are of psychological origin, so the basic task of developing a mutually agreed upon therapeutic agenda becomes a formidable challenge. How do "psychological" problems come to be reflected in "physical" symptoms? We examine this question with two cases: one in which both physical and psychological factors contribute to a young woman's pain, and the other in which unreasonable fear of having a dread disease becomes the focus for a man's anxieties.

This second patient would have previously been called "hypochondriacal," a term that is still used in common parlance to refer to someone who interprets the most benign or mild physical symptoms to be reflective of a dread disease.

CASE 30

SOMATIC SYMPTOM DISORDER: THE CASE OF LISA L.

LISA L. IS A TWENTY-SIX-YEAR-OLD, married mother of three children. She had the first child out of wedlock, when she was not yet eighteen years old. The birth of the second coincided, within weeks, with her marriage at the age of twenty-three. The third is a newborn. Lisa has a history of psychological problems dating back from the time she was a young adolescent. She has had many different diagnoses—the most recent being Pain Disorder. Here is her story.

Lisa is the second of three children. She grew up in a small town where everybody knew everybody. Her older brother was always in trouble as a youngster and suffered a severe break from reality at the age of seventeen. While drug use was certainly a factor, his condition did not seem to improve much when drugs were withdrawn, and he was finally diagnosed with paranoid schizophrenia two years later. He had a difficult decade, with several psychiatric hospitalizations and a stay in a drug rehabilitation center, but he is now fairly stable. He is married and has a job and a child. Lisa's younger sister had some problems with drugs as well—mostly marijuana and amphetamines, but she, too, has "cleaned up her act" in recent years. She is attending college and working part-time.

Lisa's parents seemed to get along well. She also had her grandparents nearby, and was especially close to her maternal grandmother. Despite an apparently warm and supportive family, Lisa was a fearful child. She remembers being afraid of dying from an early age, often calling out to her mother seeking relief from her panic when she awoke in the middle of the night. Thunderstorms scared her, too, as they did her mother and grandmother.

Lisa had difficulty separating from her mother to go to kindergarten and seemed to be ill frequently through her school years. Several years in a row she missed more school than any other student, which prompted her first visit to a psychotherapist when she was twelve and in the sixth grade. Therapy ended at the end of the school year, after about two months of weekly sessions. She seemed to relate well to the therapist, but her school attendance was essentially unchanged. Like many youngsters, Lisa's obedience and attachment to her parents waned markedly as she approached thirteen and fourteen. She began to experiment with marijuana (helpfully supplied by her big brother) and cut school to hang out with friends in the empty field behind the drug store. Her grades, previously beyond reproach, dropped, but not enough to put her in danger of failing. She seemed desperate to fit in with her peers and unsure of herself in social situations.

At the age of fifteen, Lisa lost her virginity to a boy who barely spoke to her afterwards. Devastated, she slept poorly and lost her appetite for several weeks. Her parents, however, seemed unaware that anything was amiss. They had enough on their hands trying to cope with her brother. Several of Lisa's friends noticed that she had lost weight and commented favorably. She then entered a period of restricting her food intake in an attempt to lose ever-increasing amounts of weight. She supplemented this regimen with occasional use of diet pills and laxatives. When she fainted in school, another course of psychotherapy was begun.

This time, Lisa expressed a wish to die side by side with her continuing fear of death. She starved so that people would see that she had the willpower to deprive herself, but she knew that she might die and she didn't care. In fact, she would have been proud of having been able to exhibit the ultimate restraint by dying of starvation. Still, she sometimes awoke in panic, afraid that she, or her mother, or her grandmother would die. Lisa worked with her therapist for the better part of a year, meeting weekly to talk about her feelings of insecurity, her anger at her brother for "driving everybody crazy," and at her parents for focussing all their attention on him. Gradually, her symptoms receded and therapy was discontinued.

Lisa was next seen when her first baby was about four months old. She was still thin, but not taking diet pills or laxatives. She thought she was fat, but tolerated it for the baby's sake since she was breast-feeding. She came to the therapist's office without outside prompting because she was afraid she might hurt her baby, whom she loved dearly.

The thoughts of hurting the baby came suddenly, without warning when she was tired, frustrated, or lonely. Sometimes she imagined how sorry people would feel for her if her baby were injured. Sometimes, she just felt enraged and almost unable to control herself. She described in some detail thoughts of cutting the baby with a knife or tying her, upside down, to a light socket. These thoughts horrified her, she said, although the therapist silently noted that she talked about them with great gusto.

In therapy, Lisa expressed fury at the baby's paternal grandfather who had talked his son out of marrying her when she got pregnant. Now, none of his family would acknowledge the baby as theirs. Her family, shocked at first, had accepted her pregnancy fairly easily. They were still dealing with her brother's continuing hospitalizations, and pregnancy seemed manageable compared to that. Her mother loved the baby and was willing to babysit while she finished high school and later, when she decided to go to college. During the course of this therapy episode, Lisa's baby's pediatrician called the therapist, concerned that Lisa brought the baby to the office more than was necessary. She had been Lisa's pediatrician, too, and voiced the thought that Lisa had tended to use illness to "get attention" and "now, she's doing it through the baby."

Lisa and her therapist met intermittently for several years. During that time, Lisa mostly attended to going to school and raising her daughter. She had virtually no love life. However, she did have one brief relationship, and, as bad luck would have it, contracted herpes.

For most people, herpes is fairly treatable, with long periods of remission interspersed with brief outbreaks of sores, accompanied by some discomfort. For Lisa, however, it was a nightmare. She had outbreak after outbreak, seemingly uncontrollable by medication. The pain worsened continuously until she had to be hospitalized so that she could receive intravenous pain medications. She had pain even without external evidence of sores. Her behavior ranged from lethargic and depressed to agitated and angry. She was short-tempered with her child and unable to continue at college.

Lisa hounded her physicians for pain medicine and voiced suicidal ideas when it was not forthcoming. The doctors were worried that she might become addicted and would need ever increasing dosages to control the pain. Given her history, they also wondered how much of the pain had psychogenic origins, particularly in the absence of visible herpes lesions.

Lisa sought and received second and third medical opinions. She found a neurologist who told her that sometimes herpes affected neural pathways, and thus could lead to a prolonged pain syndrome, although this condition was exceedingly rare. This pronouncement naturally intensified Lisa's anger at her primary care physicians and seemed to increase the stridency and frequency of her demands for medication. Everyone involved had their own opinion about how much of the pain was "real."

A course of treatment at a specialized pain center didn't seem to help much. Lisa felt they had nothing to offer her that her psychologist hadn't already taught her.

In the midst of this chaos, Lisa became pregnant by the young man she later married. He was younger than she and eager to take on the responsibilities of a family, although few people who knew him felt he would be capable of such a large undertaking. Lisa knew that pregnancy would be dangerous for her and for the baby. Vaginal delivery would put the child at risk for contracting herpes, so a cesarean section was scheduled. Lisa had debilitating pain throughout her pregnancy, leaving the care of her child and home to her mother and future husband. Somehow, all of them survived and Lisa delivered a healthy son.

Lisa continued to complain of severe pain for the next year, going into the hospital every three or four months for two or three days of intravenous medication and rest. Then, without warning, her mother died. Lisa was actually in the hospital at the time and had to be released on a pass to attend her mother's funeral.

Over the next six months, Lisa found herself literally shocked into health. Her pain, oddly, receded, but her grief was intense. So was her investment in caring for her father, who seemed withdrawn and lifeless. Following a flurry of psychotherapy sessions aimed at working through her profound sense of loss, Lisa terminated them, saying that she had to concentrate on her father, her siblings, and her children, and could no longer spend time focusing on herself. She has not returned to treatment, despite the birth of her third child, which was apparently without incident.

Thinking About the Case

Somatic symptom disorder is invariably frustrating for patients, their families, and clinicians. Since the experience of pain is private, subjective, and affected by a host of intrapsychic and interpersonal factors, both diagnosis and treatment can be difficult. Often physicians and patients find themselves at odds about whether and how much psychological factors are contributing to the person's discomfort. Generally, the suggestion that psychotherapy may be beneficial is received by the affected individual as confirmation that the doctor doesn't believe the pain is "real," but instead feels it is "all in my head."

Complicating the problem is the fact that some people do actually fake pain in order to receive some benefit—usually financial in the form of governmental or insurance disability payments. These people are called "malingerers," and they may be hard to distinguish from people who are genuinely experiencing pain. Many thousands of job-related injuries resulting in claims of disabling, chronic pain occur each year. These claims result in millions of dollars worth of lost wages, disability payments, and medical and rehabilitation bills. Generally, the longer the pain has lasted and the more the individual stands to gain from its continuation, the more difficult treatment becomes.

Lisa's case is typical in that the pain has a possible biological basis, but appears to be out of proportion to the physical stimulus. This is the most difficult type of pain problem to diagnose properly. She has some history of having more than the usual amount of illness in childhood, suggestive of the presence of secondary gain in the form of parental attention and nurturance. She has pre-existing psychological problems which indicate that her general strategies for coping with stress are not as good as they might be. Note, too, that this history might predispose a clinician not to take her claims of pain as seriously as those from a patient with less psychiatric history. The very presence of known psychiatric disorder tends to disqualify to some extent the patient's subjective account of symptoms.

What is known about chronic pain sufferers? First, the syndrome often co-exists with depressive disorders and, although to a lesser extent, with anxiety disorders. It is difficult to tell, in these cases, which is the chicken and which is the egg: does the pain cause the depression or vice versa? Second, the susceptibility to suggestion seems to be a predisposing factor in pain disorder, as it is in many of the somatoform disorders. In fact, suggesting that the pain will disappear in a specified period of time is often a useful treatment strategy.

What can we say about Lisa's prognosis? While Lisa's focus of attention shifted from her pain to the emotions and practical problems associated with her mother's death, it is probably safe to say that her symptoms are unlikely to be gone for good. Most psychogenic pain syndromes wax and wane in severity, sometimes with years of symptomfree functioning interspersed with protracted dysfunctionality, but they rarely disappear permanently.

Questions to Consider

1. List all the psychological disorders with which Lisa might have been diagnosed at one point or another. What does the shifting pattern of symptoms suggest to you about psychological distress and dysfunction? Which models would best explain the presence of different disorders over time?
2. What do you make of Lisa's "flight into health" following her mother's death? Would you predict that she would be likely to have

further psychological problems in the future? Why or why not? If you think she would be prone to future problems, what might these be? What is the basis for your predictions?

3. How would a psychodynamic therapist explain and treat Lisa's pain? Contrast this to a behavioral approach. Which would you have more confidence in? Might you combine them? Why or why not?
4. If an insurance company were paying you to tell them whether a patient was experiencing genuine, debilitating pain or not, what strategies would you employ to try to answer the question? How confident would you be in your answer?

CASE 31

ILLNESS ANXIETY DISORDER: THE CASE OF HARRY P.

HARRY P. WAS CERTAIN THAT he had stomach cancer. The pain in his gut had been almost imperceptible at first, an occasional dull ache or pulling sensation. Then, sneaking up on him gradually over several months, the sharp pains took over. Paralyzed with fear in the face of the dawning certainty that he had cancer, Harry had put off going to the doctor's for months. Finally, he did go. After the inevitable battery of tests—upper and lower gastrointestinal exams, blood tests, and colonoscopy—Harry received a diagnosis that should have been comforting but was not. He didn't have cancer. In fact, he didn't have any organic illness so far as his doctor could tell. What he had, he was told, was "stress."

Harry was incredulous. The pain was real—he wasn't making it up! Of course, he had stress, but no more than other people. His father had died of cancer at age fifty-two, about the same age Harry was now. He was convinced that he, too, had the dread disease. Harry sought a second and then a third medical opinion. Both confirmed the diagnosis, or lack of one, of his own physician. Finally, against his better judgment, but with no better ideas of his own, Harry accepted a referral to a psychologist.

Harry's behavior during his first interview was cooperative, even ingratiating, despite his lack of confidence in psychotherapy and his discomfort with self-disclosure. He answered questions as honestly as he could, but was curiously unable to describe his feelings in relation to situations or events. He could say he felt "bad" or "happy" about something, but he seemed to have no other feeling words in his vocabulary.

Harry impressed the psychologist as a private, emotionally-controlled person who focused his attention on tasks rather than on feelings. He had been employed for virtually his entire twenty-two-year career by the same *Fortune* 500 company, where he had moved up through the ranks to the mid-level supervisory position he now held. He was a loyal and hard-working employee who worked many hours of unpaid overtime and carried a large briefcase full of work home each evening, although he often managed to get through very little of it.

Harry's wife, a nurse, sometimes complained that he worked too many hours and spent too little time with her and his two teenaged children. However, she, too, had a strong work ethic and produced a long list of chores for herself and Harry to accomplish each weekend. Harry didn't spend much time with the kids, he admitted, although he had dutifully participated in scouts when his son joined a pack, and had gone to each and every dance recital in which his daughter had participated. He seemed wistful about how quickly his children had grown and how little he had known them, but he had no idea how to connect with them on a deeper level. He loved his wife and was satisfied with his marriage. He had been a virgin when he married and had never had a close relationship of any kind with any other woman. He felt that his wife was a good "partner," although, of course, there were times when they got on each other's nerves.

Over the first few psychotherapy sessions, Harry related some of his history. He had been the only son of Scandinavian immigrants. He could not remember ever having seen his parents argue. Neither could he remember having seen them hug or kiss. Like Harry, his father had worked for the same company for his entire career. Harry remembers that during the time his father lay dying with cancer, he had expressed the wish to have done more, to have had a wider range of experiences within his lifetime. Sometimes, Harry worries that he will feel this way, too. Harry feels that his parents treated him well, although there was not much warmth in their interactions. In turn, he was a respectful and dutiful son, caring for both his parents until their deaths.

Harry can't remember much about his childhood. He says he was "a regular nerd" throughout school. He got good grades, although he was often quite anxious about his academic performance. He didn't participate in any sports. He had a few friends, but remembers feeling somewhat lonely and isolated. He did not begin to date until college, where he met his wife. They married the summer after graduation. His wife went to work, and Harry worked part-time while he went to graduate school to earn a Masters' degree in business administration. They have both always worked hard and are grateful to have reaped the benefits—a secure living, a lovely home, the ability to send their children to college.

Harry spoke a great deal about his stomach pain and thoughts of cancer in the first few months of therapy. His therapist had to gently refocus him on talking about his sense of isolation and oppression. His supervisor at work, a woman, was known in the office as a "ball-buster." Harry got along well with her, he thought, but she demanded a great deal and he always felt that he was not quite measuring up to her standards. She had no loyalty to anyone, he reported, and if necessary would "throw me overboard in a minute." Still, he admired her strength and ruthlessness and expressed the wish that he could be more like her.

Gradually, as he became able to talk about the stresses in his life and how he felt about them, his talk of cancer diminished. After nine months, pain-free and no longer worried about dying, he was discharged from the psychologist's care with the admonition to return if symptoms reappeared.

The psychologist didn't hear from Harry for two years, but then he did return, this time having been rushed to the hospital with chest pains. Panicked about the thought that he must have heart disease—again despite negative test results, he was just as skeptical about the value of psychotherapy as he had been the last time, even though he had appeared to benefit from it. He seemed to have unlearned what the therapist had taught him about paying attention to his feelings, allowing himself to experience them, and even talk about them, and giving himself permission to relax and spend some time in "nonproductive" pursuits.

This time, his preoccupation with his health seemed even more severe, interfering with his capacity to pay attention at work and to relate to his wife. He reported sleeping fitfully, losing some weight because of worrying, lacking sexual interest, and feeling overwhelmed and "foggy." The psychologist felt that Harry might be clinically depressed and suggested a consultation with a psychiatrist. Harry agreed and received a prescription for antidepressant medication to be used while he continued in psychotherapy. However, Harry was extremely anxious about what the medication might do to him. During the first week of medical treatment, he called the psychiatrist six times, worried that the medicine was causing one or another physical effect—drowsiness, dizziness, nausea, balance problems, blurry vision, stomach cramps. Despite attempts to cut back on the dosage, Harry was unable to take the medication without extreme agitation. After two-and-a-half weeks, he discontinued it.

Continuing in psychotherapy, Harry made slow but steady progress as he had done the last time. His fear of heart failure began to recede, and he was again able to see these concerns as symptoms of his feeling stressed and isolated. This time, Harry and his therapist decided not to terminate therapy as soon as he was feeling well. Instead, they continued to meet every other week, working on helping Harry learn to identify and talk about his feelings, and to make some significant changes in his lifestyle.

Two significant things happened during this course of therapy. Harry asked for and received a transfer to another job assignment within the company, and he had an affair. The transfer was an undeniably smart move: the new job was less stressful, allowed more creativity and autonomy, and best of all, allowed Harry to work for a different, more supportive supervisor.

The affair was less indisputably positive in its effects. Harry had become more and more aware of the lack of intimate connection in his marriage as therapy had progressed. Yet, he had found himself entirely unable to change the situation. He knew his wife well, he told the psychologist, and she didn't like weakness. She had problems of her own. She wouldn't want to hear about his. She expected him to solve his own troubles. She wouldn't understand. She would tell his secrets to her sister. She would use them against him in an argument. Harry turned aside his therapist's suggestion that he try some marital therapy. Instead, encased in a wall composed of his own preconceptions, Harry began to confide in a co-worker, a woman who was, herself, in an unhappy marriage. Harry felt himself powerfully drawn to this woman, and almost before he knew it, he had arranged to spend a weekend with her, having told his wife that he had to be away on company business.

Harry's feelings after the weekend were decidedly mixed. It had been wonderful, exhilarating. He had never felt that close to anyone, except his therapist (interestingly, also a woman). On the other hand, he felt deeply guilty and embarrassed. If his wife should ever find out, he would be mortified. He wondered how he could have been so stupid as to risk his marriage for an affair that obviously had no future. Over the next several weeks, the balance of his feelings shifted towards the ashamed side. He broke off the relationship with his co-worker and reinvested his energy in his marriage, which seemed to benefit from his renewed interest. After six months more of therapy, aimed at understanding the feelings that led to the affair and finding some more appropriate ways of meeting the needs he was beginning to identify, Harry again felt ready to terminate treatment.

However, this time, the hiatus was even more short-lived. Harry returned to the psychologist's office seven months later, convinced that he had contracted AIDS from his affair. "I was a fool to think I could get away with it," he whispered. "If you play, you pay. Isn't that what they say?" Harry was distraught. He could not bring himself to get a blood test because even if it was negative, he knew he would not believe it. Besides, he was certain that it was going to be positive and he just didn't think he could handle having the actual objective evidence in front of him.

In the psychologist's office, Harry could hardly sit still. He kept poking himself under the arm to feel for swollen glands. His nails were bitten down to the nub and he had clearly lost weight. The only positive note was that this time he had come to the therapist's office himself, without having been referred by his physician. This time he seemed to have some dim awareness that his AIDS obsession might reflect a psychological rather than a physical problem, although this awareness was certainly not fully conscious.

As before, therapy was successful at helping Harry identify the psychological underpinnings of his fears. As he did so, the fears themselves receded. Three months into treatment Harry felt able to ask for an AIDS test, but by this time he felt he no longer needed one. Instead, he added a regimen of exercise and meditation to his daily schedule, and began to attend church, something he had done as a child with his parents, but had given up as an adult. He still had difficulty communicating with his wife, now more than ever because he had to protect his secret. But he was able to share with his therapist how sad and sorry he was to have created this additional block to intimacy. He was also able to see that the affair had had some value for him and that it had not irrevocably damaged his marriage. His black-and-white style of thinking was beginning, slowly, to allow for shades of gray. Harry and his therapist decided, faced with the evidence of his multiple relapses, that ongoing, if less intensive, therapy might be of use. They agreed to meet monthly for the foreseeable future in the hopes that they might be able to head off future problems before they became severely debilitating.

Thinking About the Case

Harry's symptoms are quite typical of illness anxiety disorder (hypochondriasis). They are longstanding, but of variable intensity. They worsen in response to stress—in Harry's case, the difficult work situation, the anniversary of his father's death, the guilt over the affair. They are accompanied by a generalized focus on and distress about bodily sensations, as evidenced by Harry's inability to take medication. Harry's personality and style of being in the world are also typical of hypochondriacal patients. He has limited ability to identify and manage his feelings. He even exhibits "alexithymia," an inability to use words describing feelings, which has been shown to increase the susceptibility to somatoform disorders.

Illness anxiety, while sometimes seen as a syndrome itself, can also occur as a symptom of another disorder, most typically depression, obsessive-compulsive disorder, or panic disorder. Actually, Harry confessed to obsessive-compulsive symptoms when examined closely—he sometimes felt that he had to engage in certain ritualized behaviors, like cleaning the bathtub using three sponges, three dabs of soap, and groups of three swipes at a time, so that his son would be protected from harm. These thoughts were so much a part of him and engaging in the rituals caused him so little distress that he hadn't thought to mention it himself.

Harry also had symptoms of depression, at least at some times. The psychologist noted over the years that Harry's symptoms tended to worsen in fall and improve in spring. Some people have seasonally sensitive depression, thus strengthening the hypothesis that perhaps Harry was clinically depressed. Interestingly, some of the same medications that are used to treat depression are also used to treat obsessive-compulsive problems, so Harry may have benefitted doubly if he could have tolerated the medication that the psychiatrist had prescribed.

Historically, most explanations of somatic symptom disorders have been psychodynamic. According to this model, the physical symptoms and fear of illness provide a focus for anxiety which is actually caused by an unconscious conflict revolving around unacceptable impulses. The presence of alexithymia in many patients suggests, instead, a communicative rather than a defensive function for the symptoms. According to the communicative model, emotions that cannot be expressed in words are expressed in physical symptoms. The fear of AIDS, for example, can be seen as an expression of guilt and remorse over Harry's affair, emotions to which he has little access and little ability to express in other ways.

Questions to Consider

1. If the fear of AIDS has symbolic meaning for Harry, might the other two diseases he thought he had also have meaning? What might they mean?
2. What features of a person's biology or personal history might make him or her susceptible to somatizing disorders?
3. What kind of theory might explain why talking about feelings generally relieves hypochondriacal concerns? How might silence affect the body's functions?
4. Does learning theory have anything useful to say about the origins, maintenance, or treatment of hypochondriasis?
5. What might therapists of different theoretical orientations do when Harry expresses thoughts about having an affair? What would you do if you were the therapist? Why? What does this tell you about the values you hold about the psychotherapy process?

LANAHAN NOTES

Somatic Symptom and Related Disorders

These disorders illustrate an intimate relationship between psychological and physical well-being.

Characteristics of somatoform disorders

"Soma" is Greek for "body"

These disorders have the following symptoms

distressing physical symptoms

plus

abnormal thoughts, feelings, behaviors in response to these symptoms

Symptoms cannot be explained fully by a known physical or neurological condition and are not under voluntary control

Sometimes, but not always, the patient appears indifferent to the diminution in functioning

Sometimes a physical condition is present, but is not serious enough to explain the symptoms

Often difficult to distinguish from real medical problems or faking

Types of somatic symptom disorders

Somatic symptom disorder

many physical symptoms occur; chronic impairment; long duration (more than 6 months) in functioning

thoughts: regarding the seriousness of one's symptoms

feelings: persistent high level of anxiety

behaviors: excessive time and energy devoted to these symptoms/concerns

High comorbidity with depressive disorders

Illness anxiety disorder (hypochondriasis)

belief that one has a serious disease based upon a misinterpretation of bodily symptoms

thoughts: preoccupation with having or acquiring a serious disorder

feelings: persistent high level of anxiety

behaviors: excessive time and energy devoted to these concerns or maladaptive avoidance (e.g., avoids doctors appointments and hospitals)

Key difference with somatic symptom disorder is that symptoms are not present, or if present, only mild in intensity

Conversion disorder (functional neurological symptom disorder):

symptoms or deficits affecting voluntary motor or sensory function (like ambulation, sight, or sound)

frequently diagnosed soon after a traumatic event

Factitious disorder (Munchausen syndrome):

an individual intentionally feigns psychological or physical signs and symptoms in order to derive the emotional benefits inherent in the sick role

may result in multiple hospitalizations and even surgeries

distinguished from malingering (faking illness) by having psychological rather than economic goals (Note: malingering is not a psychological disorder)

responds poorly to treatment; psychodynamic orientation most common

Who gets these disorders?

prevalence rates run about 5%-7%

diagnosed more often in women than men (perhaps the sick role is more allowable for women as women are more victimized across culture/religion)

Causes and risk factors

Genetic: tends to run in families; also runs in families with antisocial or substance abuse disorders; also associated with anxiety/depression disorders

Environmental: sometimes associated with severe trauma (for example, sexual abuse); childhood experience with pain or illness is a risk factor (modeling); operant conditioning; "sick role" Seen more frequently in low educational/SES status

Cultural: relationship between numerous somatic symptoms and depression appears to be very similar around the world and among different cultures within one country

Treatment

Psychotherapy: get patients to become more aware of underlying emotions/conflict; engage family physicians about these disorders and teach how to manage patients

Note: somatoform disorders tend to be chronic and difficult to change

CHAPTER ELEVEN

Feeding and Eating Disorders

This category groups together all disorders related to human ingesting. It includes disorders like pica, which is the ingestion of non-nutritive substances like hair, or ice, or dirt, and also regurgitation disorder in which food is regurgitated repeatedly (and then may be re-chewed, reswallowed, or spit out), but this category is composed mostly of the eating disorders that are recognizeable to us all: restrictive food intake disorder, anorexia nervosa, bulimia nervosa, and binge-eating disorder. Taken together these disorders are exceedingly common—estimates are that thirty million people in the United States alone have suffered from an eating disorder. They are also exceedingly dangerous: they have the highest mortality rate of any psychological disorder. They cause an enormous amount of suffering. One in five anorexia deaths is a suicide. They are expensive, both in lost productivity and in treatment costs.

In this section, we have included two cases. The first is written by Hilda Bruch, a pioneer in the study of anorexia nervosa which is probably the most dangerous of the eating disorders. In this case, the patient's pathological enmeshment with her parents seemed to Dr. Bruch germaine to her eating disorder. In Dr. Bruch's time, it was common to indict parents for the psychological disorders of their children, but today these views have fallen into disrepute. We should point out that eating disorders can arise from many sources—a chance remark by a sports coach to a gymnast desperate for success, the pressures of a modeling career, or as a response to self-imposed perfectionism. The culture with its emphasis on unnatural thinness can not be left out of the equation, either.

The second case illustrates binge-eating disorder which is by far the most common eating disorder among adults. It is likely also the most underdiagnosed as estimates suggest that only about five percent of people who have symptoms that meet the criteria for binge-eating disorder ever receive a diagnosis. And unlike the other eating disorders, it occurs more evenly among men and women, rather than being very heavily skewed towards women. Binge-eating disorder was not considered a separate diagnosis in DSM-IV-R. Rather it was subsumed under the diagnosis of bulimia nervosa. However, over the past twenty years, more than one thousand research papers have confirmed that it is a syndrome which has specificity, reliability, and validity. In this way, the diagnostic system evolves.

CASE 32

ANOREXIA NERVOSA: THE CASE OF GAIL

Hilde Bruch, M.D., a psychiatrist, was one of the first clinician-researchers to study eating disorders. Her case descriptions remain among the most vivid and powerful available. The case she relates here from Eating Disorders *(Basic Books, 1973), illustrates the incredible power struggle that anorexia can provoke between the patient and other family members. While the case is forty-five years old, it is still fresh. Gail would not now be treated with extended inpatient hospitalization, but her prognosis would still be considered quite grave. Here's her case:*

THE CASE HISTORY I AM going to present may sound to some of you like a dramatic exaggeration. It is not. On the contrary, I regret that my literary ability is not adequate to convey the full flavor of the grotesque atmosphere of mutual coercion and violence that surrounded the whole development of the patient whom I shall call Gail. She entered the New York State Psychiatric Institute in October, 1959, at the age of 20. Gail was a slim, well-groomed and fashionably dressed young lady. Her doctor had made arrangements for hospitalization several weeks earlier but Gail had refused to sign the application for voluntary admission. Her weight was 96 lbs, a sacred figure to which she had rigidly clung for the past 4 or 5 years. And thereby hangs the tale—how she had managed to maintain her weight.

Up to the age of 13 she had been plump, a fate for which she blamed her parents. Her weight had reached nearly 140 lbs and had earned her the nickname of Two-Ton Tilly. When Tilly was 11 years old the parents had sought help at a child guidance clinic because she was unmanageable at home. There was no improvement during a year of treatment of mother and child, and a boarding school with treatment facilities was recommended. Tilly went there under violent protest, saying her parents wanted to get rid of her. At the school she felt terrified and would not dare eat anything. Her fear of eating was so great that she thought if she took as little as a glass of water she might get out of hand and become even fatter. Instead a miracle happened—she began to grow thinner. When the weight loss became visible, she decided also to get rid of the much-ridiculed name Tilly, and choose for herself a new name, Gail. She continued to protest against being at the boarding school, talked about running away and wanted to go home. The parents finally gave in to her protestations, feeling guilty about the accusation of having gotten rid of her and believing her promise of better behavior. She came back weighing 96 lbs and was determined not to get fat again.

Her absolute insistence on remaining at this magic weight of 96 lbs led to her dominating the household with enforced rituals. Her parents were forced to shop three times a day because she would not permit food in the home between meals. Any food left over after a meal had to be thrown away, since she feared that she might succumb to the compulsion of eating it and thereby spoil her magic weight. She entered high school and obtained very good grades by studying religiously. In order to study she had to have absolute quiet around the home and her parents were not allowed to be there when she worked. The parents were unable to cope with the situation. They again sought psychiatric help and Gail consented to see a psychiatrist, though on her terms.

Things went along this way, with many outbursts of violence, until Gail's graduation from high school. She did not want her parents to come to the graduation and refused to get tickets for them. The mother insisted they would go just the same; Gail asked: "How? How?" When the mother refused to tell, Gail became more and more frantic in her questioning and finally grabbed a pair of scissors and attacked her mother, threatening to kill her. The mother ran out of the house to the father's store; they called the police and Gail was taken to a city hospital. She was cowed by the hospital experience and returned home with the best intentions but then was unable to control herself. She stayed at a private hospital for six months where she was kept quiet with medication; no effort at psychotherapy was made. After her return home she saw a psychiatrist regularly and became very dependent on him. She also began to work and was out of the home a good deal. For a year and a half she kept jobs as a salesgirl, lasting in any one place approximately three or four months.

Throughout this period her behavior at home was unchanged, and she still controlled the family with her demand for a restricted diet. The father suggested that now that she was earning money she should have an apartment of her own. Gail's response was: "You can't get rid of me that easily." She quit her job and just stayed home. Her behavior was so violent that within two months her parents moved out into a furnished room, the address of which they kept a strict secret. Even now, after Gail has been in the hospital for over a year, they have not moved back to their old apartment. The mother does not dare to live there; it reminds her of her daughter's violence with every piece of furniture and fixture marred and half destroyed from these battles. In fits of anger Gail had carved initials into the furniture, and the bedroom door was covered with hammer marks made when Gail had tried to invade her parents' room after they had locked themselves in in desperation. After the upholstery had been destroyed the mother had bought slipcovers but Gail had cut them into ribbons. She also had torn down the shades and drapes from the windows. The parents had put up with all this because Gail's psychiatrist implored them to be patient. The parents said that the doctor had complied with Gail's request not to talk about certain topics, for instance, the word *food* was absolutely forbidden. He also urged the parents never to talk about food, but just to obey the patient.

Gail only left the apartment to go to her doctor's office three times a week. She also had the privilege of phoning him whenever she felt anxious. Otherwise she kept entirely to herself, except for phoning the parents at the store to give them orders. This stage of affairs lasted one and a half years, the parents coming in three times a day and bringing her prepared food. This food had to be the exact amount that would keep Gail from gaining weight. If she gained as much as half a pound she would create a violent scene.

It became apparent that not only was no progress being made but that the whole situation had deteriorated, and Gail became more and more withdrawn. But she absolutely refused to enter the hospital as a voluntary patient. This was just one more of her parents' schemes to get rid of her. Things stayed in this stalemate until one day the mother reacted to her violence and began shouting and throwing things. This was so terrifying to Gail that she consented to hospitalization. "I did not know what was happening to my mother." She felt she must have done something wrong because she had caused this terrible outburst and felt she was no longer in control of her mother.

During the first few months at the hospital the effort to keep her weight under control remained her chief preoccupation. Since people in the hospital did not submit to her dietary demands, this was a strenuous task. She had brought her own scale and weighed herself every day and did not eat if she had gained an ounce. Things changed when an attractive young male patient spoke to her. This indicated to Gail that he was going to fall in love with her. She set out to accomplish this with all her manipulative skills, with the result that he fled and openly rebuffed her. Even now, many months later, she is indignant and bewildered that he did not want to love her even though she was at the perfect weight of 96 lbs and could be glamorous whenever she wanted. Actually she dressed up or was well-groomed only a few times during their brief relationship. Then she became conspicuously sloppy, expecting that since he knew she could be well-dressed if she wanted to be, he should admire her beauty even when she was dirty and neglected. Immediately after this rebuff she began to gain weight rapidly, reaching 150 lbs, within 2 or 3 months. She dressed now in maternity clothes with the expressed intent of creating the impression of being pregnant. This to her was less shameful and aroused less guilt than appearing fat. The idea of intercourse and pregnancy, however, was revolting to her. If it were not painful she would have had her uterus removed, just to be safe.

I became familiar with Gail only after her first physician had left this hospital. She had greeted her new physician with a sarcastic outburst: "I hate you already. You can never be Dr. X. I can see with one look that you are inexperienced, impervious and do not know much psychiatry." These accusations persisted through several treatment sessions. Her new doctor felt discouraged, and with justification. In spite of therapeutic efforts for eight or ten years, including one year at the Psychiatric Institute, the course had been downhill. He asked for help in evaluating the situation, for supervision if it was felt that anything could be done.

In reviewing the previous treatment approaches it became apparent that they had been conducted according to the principle of avoiding past errors, be it that of the parents or the previous psychiatrist, and of confronting the patient with her manipulative behavior and power struggle. The underlying conceptual delusions about herself and all human relatedness had *not* been recognized and therefore had remained unexplored and uncorrected. Actually Gail was unusually clear on this point—but the significance of her frequent statements had been missed. In a conference together with her parents she burst out: "I tried to remake my parents all through my life. I wanted to put them in a different role, make them warm and understanding so that they could raise me better. It is their fault that I am not a good child. What I am now, my parents have created. I'm the product of their creation. The reason that people don't like me is because I am no good; but that is because my parents did not know how to raise me. It is all their fault." There was a note of despair when she added: "Don't they see how much I suffer, don't they see how unhappy I am about being a brat, always fighting and arguing." Being thin was one way of being something in her own right, not quite her parents' product. They always had pushed food on her and wanted her to be fat. Now she is quite heavy and she is infuriated when her father greets her: "Oh, you look so much better now."

The patient was quite concrete in her assumptions (and her parents shared her delusion) that a child remains the parents' property and creation. The mother had been very devoted and attached to a little niece, Gail's five-year-old cousin. She had adored this child, a cuddly and plump baby. When Gail was born, the mother was dreadfully disappointed because her baby was long and stringy, not plump at all. She set out to change her into this dream child and it became her desperate life's work to make her skinny child plump and pleasant.

The result was this tragedy of mutual blame and guilt. I have called the interaction of this family the Frankenstein Theme. The daughter, conceived of as her parents' creation, had turned monster-like against her creators, but appearances notwithstanding, basically not in aggression, but in a desperate effort to change her parents so that they would undo their errors and recreate her in a better mold. The deep conviction of her own helplessness was vividly acted out in the dieting arrangement, which in turn must be conceived of as a consequence of her inability to recognize correctly hunger or satiation; hence the urgency with which she demanded control over her own bodily needs through the parents.

It is too soon to say whether this new orientation toward her problems will be successful. There has been a decided change in her attitude toward treatment; there seems to be a glimmer of hope that she can become a better person without having to change her parents first. I have reported on this patient, although I have many others whom I know more intimately, because she expressed with startling and dramatic directness what I have come to recognize as crucial issues in many patients with serious eating disorders, namely *the basic delusion of not having an identity of their own*, of not even owning their body and its sensations, with the *specific inability of recognizing hunger as a sign of nutritional need.* Whatever we know about regulatory centers in the midbrain, these patients act as if for them the regulation for food intake was outside their own bodies.

Thinking About the Case

Anorexia and the companion disorder bulimia are dangerous conditions that can cause emaciation, loss of menstruation, and possibly death from cardiac abnormalities. They occur almost exclusively in girls and women, with onset generally between the ages of twelve and twenty-five.

The central feature of anorexia is an extreme fear of obesity coupled with the often absurd complaint that one is fat. While some anorexics, like Gail, restrict their food intake, others induce vomiting or take laxatives to remove whatever calories they have ingested. Anorexia is often associated with other psychological disorders, including depression, anxiety, post-traumatic stress disorders, substance abuse, and personality disorders. Today, Gail would probably be diagnosed as having borderline personality disorder primarily, with anorexia as a secondary diagnosis.

Bruch's interpretation of this case is psychoanalytic in orientation. Disturbed mother–child interactions during the early years of life were presumed to cause Gail's disturbed behavior decades later. Most modern researchers agree with Bruch that family dynamics may play a role in the development of some eating disorders, and that anorexia tends to occur in young women who, for some reason, lack a sense of power and autonomy in their lives. However, factors other than disturbed family relationships can contribute to this sense of disempowerment—for example, a substantial percentage of anorexics and bulimics have been sexually abused. Others may find their lives careening out of control because they have taken on too much and approach tasks too perfectionistically. Researchers are also discovering that there might be a genetic contribution as well.

In addition, western culture incorporates extreme thinness into its notion of female beauty and success. As the old adage has it, "You can't be thin enough or rich enough." While few women can look like the models in fashion magazines (among whom, not surprisingly, there is a high rate of anorexic behavior) many are brainwashed into believing that they should. No doubt cultural notions are relevant to overall rates of eating disorders.

In any case, anorexia is often difficult to treat. Many women, even those who are seriously emaciated, deny that they have a problem. Such a woman proclaims that she has a right to weigh whatever she likes and that others should stop trying to control her. Besides, she says, she is still fat, as anyone who is telling the truth would agree. When others tell her she looks sick, she often feels triumphant, thinking that they mean that she looks thin. When she feels ill, she may paradoxically rejoice, because that means that she is achieving her goal.

Long-term psychotherapy is often indicated in the treatment of anorexia. Cognitive-behavioral strategies like helping the anorexic to identify and change distorted cognitions about food intake, weight, and body shape may be combined with stress management training. Exploration of family dynamics, self-image, and issues of autonomy are also included. Antidepressant medication helps some people, but is virtually never enough on its own. Both family therapy and group therapy also have a role in the treatment of eating disorders, as does brief hospitalization when the patient's health is failing rapidly. Still, anorexia is often intractable, with a mortality rate that is estimated to be from five to fifteen percent.

Questions to Consider

1. Research has shown that self-starvation (although not necessarily with the pursuit of thinness as a goal) exits in all cultures and times while bulimia (normal weight bingeing and purging) only exists in wealthy nations. What does this suggest to you?
2. Studies reveal that anorexic women often describe their mothers in unflattering terms: excessively dominant, intrusive, and overbearing. Does this constitute evidence for a psychodynamic view of the disorder? What other explanations are possible?
3. Research indicates that African American teenagers are less focused on thinness as a central attribute of beauty. These girls are less dissatisfied with their bodies than are Caucasian girls, and attribute sexual attractiveness more to personality traits than to physical ones. Why might this be so? What effect might this have on their overall mental health? On their vulnerability to anorexia?
4. Can you design a study to figure out whether anorexia is really an affective disorder (like depression)? What data might convince you that such a hypothesis had merit?
5. Have you known anyone whom you suspected of having an eating disorder? If so, what did you do about it? How did your intervention turn out?

CASE 33

BINGE-EATING DISORDER: THE CASE OF SHEILA A.

SHEILA WAS A TWENTY-FIVE YEAR OLD single mother. She doted on her two-year-old daughter, Michaela. She remained on cordial, though strained terms, with Michaela's father whom she described as a very bright and charming con man. She worked as a nurse's aide and had managed, by prudent money management and self-control, to maintain a small apartment for herself and her son, as well as a car. She had no debts and was currently saving money for nursing school which she intended to enter when Michaela began kindergarten. She had figured out the finances and had a plan to pay for nursing school while incurring a minimum of debt. She was currently dating a prison guard, but was unsure that he would make a responsible partner and father figure for Michaela. He liked to drink with his buddies and resisted making definite plans with Sheila. He was warm and loving, but not ready to settle down. She felt she didn't have time to waste if the relationship wasn't going anywhere.

Sheila was on quite good terms with her parents who lived nearby. They often kept Michaela while Sheila worked, and they allowed her to do laundry at their home. She was close with her older brother and younger sister as well. All of them liked her boyfriend and hoped the relationship would become permanent. His parents hoped so as well.

Sheila requested a referral to a therapist from her physician. She felt she had a problem with binge-eating, and she wanted to "nip it in the bud" before it got entrenched. She wanted to live a healthier life and set a better example for her daughter. She arrived promptly for her first appointment, related sincerely and directly, and approached the tasks set for her enthusiastically. She described "bingeing" when she was at home alone with her daughter and sometimes, much to her shame, when she was at a client's home. Once, she reported, she finished a half gallon of ice cream through the night while on duty. She felt like she had "stolen" from the client, even though she had been told that she could eat or drink whatever she liked.

Despite being questioned closely by the therapist, Sheila remained vague as to what constituted a "binge" for her. Once, she'd finished a whole pie, bit by bit, through an afternoon. She "just ate and ate" sometimes and felt she couldn't stop. But she couldn't really describe what she might have eaten on any given occasion. When her therapist commented on this, she said that it made her uncomfortable and anxious to think about it. She tried hard not to do so. So, it was very difficult for her to accept her therapist's first suggestion which was to keep a journal of her eating. The journal was not only to note what had been consumed and in what amount, but also when and where and with whom. It was also to include any observations Sheila might have about her mental or emotional state while eating, particularly if she considered the episode of eating a "binge."

Sheila returned for her second appointment about a week later. Dutifully, she had kept her journal. In fact, she had purchased a lovely notebook and decorated its cover. She wrote in it every day often when her daughter took a nap. She was surprised to report that she felt better already. She had discovered that she was more likely to binge when she was tired or sleepy—which occurred frequently. While her daughter napped, she did laundry, read books and articles in preparation for nursing school, did yoga. But what she really needed was a nap. In her therapy session she agreed to try napping when her daughter did if she felt sleepy at that time.

She also noted that she was more likely to eat despite not being hungry when she missed her boyfriend, was waiting for a his call, or hadn't heard from him when she expected to do so. She felt that with this insight, she could refrain from unhealthy behavior at these times and turn towards more productive activities.

The therapist's insights were somewhat different. She noted that what Sheila called a binge was generally an instance of mild to moderate overeating. She would finish off the leftovers of a pie rather than just having a slice, and might follow it with some ice cream. She had two or three bowls of cereal rather than one. She would eat half a pizza rather than two slices. However, like most binge-eaters, her lapses generally involved carbohydrates, fats, and sugars. And, like most binge-eaters, she was filled with shame and remorse about her lapses from healthy eating. Again, typical of binge-eaters, these lapses occurred while she was alone.

The therapist also observed that Sheila was perfectionistic by nature, and had very strict and high standards for herself and others. Her boyfriend and coworkers often failed to meet her expectations, as she did, herself. She was a tough task-master. For her, healthy eating involved small portions of natural, unprocessed, fruits and vegetables, and low-fat dairy. She ate little red meat, but allowed herself moderate portions of fish and chicken cooked simply. She knew, intellectually, that small amounts of "unhealthy" foods were fine, but she felt uneasy, nonetheless, when she consumed them. Paradoxically, the feeling of failure that this engendered caused her to eat more of the forbidden food. Her all-or-none thinking was that once she "blew it," she might as well keep going as the damage was already done. The therapist offered Sheila some "reality-testing" by telling her that her binges were relatively mild by clinical standards. This helped Sheila feel less panic, and she became even more optimistic about being able to "control" her problem.

Over the next several sessions, Sheila began each hour by reading excerpts from her journal. Gradually these were less and less about eating and more and more about her life. She and her therapist discussed her feelings about her relationships with her child, her boyfriend, her parents, her daughter's father, her coworkers and supervisor. They talked about her goals, her past and present decisions. They focused on the standards she set for herself as the therapist hoped to get her to let up a little and get a bit better balance between work and rest, between striving towards her goals and "just being."

By the sixth visit, Sheila was hard-pressed to find a journal entry that addressed eating concerns. Occasionally, she noted, she ate something that wasn't strictly healthful, but it wasn't often and it wasn't huge amounts—even by her standards. Of course, by now her standards had changed somewhat. She wondered aloud whether she should stop therapy at this point. Together, she and the therapist decided to begin by spacing out the visits, first to biweekly, then to monthly. They would then decide whether to continue infrequent "maintenance" visits, or stop altogether. In any case, Sheila knew that she could come back to therapy or increase the frequency of visits if she felt she needed to.

Thinking About The Case

Binge-eating is defined as recurring episodes over a period of at least three months of consuming large amounts of food in a short period of time. Binge-eating is generally accompanied by a feeling of lack of control and marked distress. It must contain three of the following four behaviors: 1) eating faster than normal, 2) eating until uncomfortably full,

3) eating large amounts of food when not hungry, and 4) eating alone due to feelings of guilt and shame about the eating behavior. Sheila definitely exhibited numbers 2 and 4. She believed herself to exhibit number 3, though her definition of "large amounts" was not exactly the same as her therapist's. She did not exhibit behavior 1, often nibbling or continuing to eat well after she was no longer hungry. Sheila's behaviors did meet the criteria for diagnosing the disorder, but would be considered a relatively mild case.

Binge-eating is the most common of the eating disorders, affecting nearly three million U.S. adults. Its frequency is about the same in most industrialized countries. Its prevalence is twice that of bulimia and anorexia combined. It is different from those disorders, too, in that the prevalence of women to men is much less one-sided. Bulimia occurs in five times as many women as men, but binge-eating occurs in only twice as many women as men.

Binge-eating disorder often co-exists with other psychological disorders, most often anxiety disorders, depression, bipolar disorder, substance abuse and obesity. With respect to obesity, while the correlation is substantial, fewer than half of binge-eaters meet the criteria for obesity. Many more are mild to moderately overweight. Normal weight binge-eating like Sheila's is relatively less common. Lifetime comorbidity for binge-eating is estimated to be almost eighty percent for one other psychiatric disorder and almost 50 percent for three or more disorders.

The biopsychosocial models applies well to binge-eating. It is theorized that there may be a neurobiological basis for the problematic behavior in the brain's reward system or in its impulse-regulation properties. Certainly, there are some genetic risk factors, though these are not huge. Environmental and social issues have been shown to play a role as well. A large percentage of binge-eaters report abnormal levels of stress and/or recent trauma. We can hypothesize that Sheila lived with a relatively high stress level: She supported herself and her child alone on a limited income; dealt with a manipulative ex-husband; regularly got less than a normal amount of sleep; and managed a less than ideal romance.

Specific medication for the treatment of binge-eating does not exist, though medication might be used to treat co-occurring anxiety or depression. Two kinds of talk therapy have been shown to be successful with this disorder: cognitive-behavioral therapy which addresses dysfunctional ideas that may be supporting bingeing and interpersonal therapy which helps the individual to address and manage problems in important personal relationships. In practice, the two approaches are often combined as they were in this case. The therapist helped Sheila address her unrealistic, perfectionistic ideas and modify her expectations. In the interpersonal realm, Sheila finally terminated the relationship with her boyfriend, and began a search for a more compatible mate. She also consulted an attorney to limit unsupervised and unscheduled visitation for her ex-husband with Michaela. Individual and/or group therapy may be used in treatment. Additional help may be accessed through self-help materials both in print and on-line.

Questions To Consider

1. What factors in Sheila's case led to her good outcome? Are these biological, psychological, social, or some of each?
2. Consider your own eating habits and those of your close friends. Do you or they ever binge? How do you define a binge for yourself? How would you know if you had a binge-eating problem?
3. Binge-drinking is common among college students. Does this seem similar to binge-eating to you? In what ways are these behaviors similar? In what ways are they different?

LANAHAN NOTES
Feeding and Eating Disorders

Major types of feeding disorders

Avoidant/restrictive food intake disorder:

individual does not eat due to lack of interest in eating or food

avoids food because of the sensory characteristics of food

individual may be concerned about aversive consequences of eating

seen equally in both males and females

risk factors include anxiety, autism, OCD, ADHD, children of mothers with eating disorders

Anorexia Nervosa:

individual does not eat for intense fear of gaining weight

disturbed perception of body weight or shape

individual might eat only tiny amounts or may binge-eat then purge (vomit)

typically peaks at older adolescence

more females than males are afflicted [10:1]

risk factors include anxiety, obsessional traits in childhood, culture where thinness is highly valued, esp., in industrialized nations

Bulimia nervosa:

individual has recurrent episodes of binge-eating often eating a large amount of food in a short time with a sense of lack of control

this is followed by compensatory behaviors to prevent weight gain, e.g., self-induced vomiting, misuse of laxatives, excessive exercise, etc.

typically peaks at older adolescence

more females than males are afflicted [10:1]

risk factors: physical or sexual abuse in childhood, depression, anxiety

seen mostly in white industrialized nations

Binge-eating disorder:

differs from bulimia in that the individual attempts no compensatory behaviors to prevent weight gain

more females than males are afflicted [1.6:0.8]
runs in families

Treatment

Avoidant/restrictive food intake disorder: typically seen early in life and frequently associated with neurodevelopmental disorders (autism spectrum, intellectual developmental disorder); treatment is incorporated into a holistic plan of behavioral goals; dependent on the cognitive abilities of the individual

Anorexia nervosa, bulimia nervosa, and binge-eating disorder:

Treatments for these disorders often assume that the afflicted individuals have a deep need for autonomy, often as a result of some important aspect of life out of their control, e.g., over-controlling family environment, physical or sexual abuse, overwhelming social and cultural pressures to be thin; weight then becomes the one thing they can try to control

Psychodynamic orientation: generally plays some part in the treatment; usually long-term; therapy identifies underlying control issues; helps individual find healthier ways to achieve independence

Cognitive-behavioral orientation: identifies and changes distorted thoughts about food and eating; helps individual identify environmental triggers for bingeing

Group therapy (sometimes modeled after AA): can be very helpful

Family therapy: used especially when the person is a young adolescent

Medications: antidepressants have been shown to be helpful for some

Hospitalization: used when the person is dangerously thin

CHAPTER TWELVE

Sleep-Wake Disorders

Good sleep is necessary for good mental health. Sleep problems can be associated with depression, anxiety, poor concentration, irritability, and a host of other psychological and behavioral issues. It is also true that some mental illnesses feature sleep problems as core symptoms. Bipolar and unipolar depression come to mind as examples. And yet, poor sleep is ubiquitous, as evidenced by the number of television commercials advertising sleep aids.

DSM-5 includes many sleep disorders that have clear physiological causes, including breathing-related sleep disorders (various forms of sleep apnea), some that seem primarily physiological (narcolepsy, circadian rhythm sleep disorders, restless leg syndrome, and medication-induced sleep disorder), and those that have mixed or variable etiologies (nightmare disorder, sleepwalking, night terrors, and insomnia). All may have psychological consequences, even if they do not have psychological causes.

We have included a case of insomnia because it is the most common sleep disorder and because it is so often associated with other psychological disorders. The case illustrates nicely the problem of cause and effect in the study of emotional disorders.

CASE 34

INSOMNIA DISORDER: THE CASE OF MAISEY K.

MAISEY IS A FORTY-NINE-YEAR-OLD unemployed woman. She has lived with a cousin for the last five years. Prior to that, she had a live-in relationship that lasted three years and ended badly. She has moved around a lot.

Maisey has been in therapy for several years now. She was originally referred by the department of social services because she and her partner had come to blows over issues involving the partner's children. Upon entering therapy, Maisey reported that she had had a history of problems with alcohol, but indicated that she drank only rarely at present and then only one beer during an evening. However, her partner drank daily and was neglectful of her two children. Maisey felt attached to the children and responsible for them. She wanted her partner to change and argued with her incessantly. Her partner saw her as controlling and verbally abusive. After several months of involvement with social services and weekly therapy designed to help her realize that she could not control her partner's behavior, she had her final huge row with her partner and moved out.

Now living with her cousin, Maisey takes on home-remodeling projects for various neighbors. She collects public assistance and works for "under the table" cash. She complains of severe neck and spinal pain, and says that she can not work regularly or for many hours at a time. She and her cousin have had some problems living together. The cousin is not good with money, and they have had difficulty paying the bills. The cousin is messy and Maisey is neat. The cousin loves socializing, and Maisey needs time alone. Maisey feels the cousin "acts like a child," and the cousin has occasionally threatened to throw Maisey out if she doesn't "get off my case." Still, they seem to need each other and often enjoy their life together.

Currently, Maisey comes to therapy once every other week. She has been diagnosed with post-traumatic stress disorder, persistent depressive disorder, and panic disorder with mild agoraphobia. She also complains of persistent, and virtually life-long insomnia. She is unable to fall asleep most nights until four or five in the morning. She can not sleep in the dark. Naturally, she has a great deal of difficulty getting up in the morning, and often sleeps until noon or later.

Maisey's life has not been an easy one. She is one of five children. She never knew her father and two of her siblings have different fathers. She was sexually abused by her maternal grandfather from the time she was about three until she went into foster care at age eight. She describes her mother as "a piece of work." She says her mother is cruel, distant, manipulative, and untruthful. She beat Maisey many times during Maisey's childhood, often for nothing more than "folding my sweater the wrong way." Maisey recalled that if she cried, her mother would laugh and call her names. She has tried living with her mother as an adult from time to time, but it has always ended in her leaving in a rage or being thrown out. She knows that her relationship with her mother has left her insecure, distrustful, and unable to feel that she "fits in" anywhere.

Maisey spent second grade through fifth grade in foster care. She came to love her foster mother, but was taken from the home when her biological mother requested that she be returned, and had fulfilled the tasks set for her by the department of social services. The old cycle of abuse and humiliation resumed until Maisey ran away from home at seventeen. From that time on, she lived with a variety of relatives or lovers, worked a variety of jobs but none for very long. Her ability to support herself financially has eroded gradually with the onset of chronic physical symptoms, and her confidence in her ability to manage her life independently has diminished as well. Maisey had not been permitted to remain in contact with her foster mother, though when she reached adulthood she found the kind lady and stayed in touch until she died about five years ago at age seventy-eight.

Maisey's sleep disorder significantly interferes with her functioning. She feels woozy and lethargic during the day. If she hasn't slept more than a few hours for several nights running, she becomes "paranoid," thinking people are whispering about her, seeing darting mice scurrying out of the corner of her eye, waiting for something dreadful to happen. She also becomes clumsy and has trouble working on her projects. Her brain seems to slow down, so she can't think, take measurements, avoid mistakes. At these times she isolates herself and becomes irritable and even angry if anyone tries to intrude.

Maisey used to drink alcohol to induce sleep, but discovered that it didn't help in the long run so she stopped. She has been prescribed sleeping medications more than once, but these did not help so she never refilled any of the prescriptions. Opiate pain medicines helped somewhat, but she knew they could be addictive. She tried not to take them more than a couple of times a week. Maisey refused, steadfastly, to take antidepressants or any other psychoactive medications suggested by her physician. She was afraid of them because she had read terrible things about them in on-line chat rooms; she preferred to "tough it out." She also refused a referral to a psychiatrist, though she had agreed to talk therapy.

Maisey has been in therapy for some time now. It took her almost a year to come to trust her therapist, an older woman whose calm demeanor and steady support has served as what is known as a "corrective emotional experience." She functions, in some ways, as the mother Maisey never had. Together, they have been able to stave off more residential instabiity by keeping Maisey's expectations for and behavior towards her cousin reasonable. They have succeeded in helping Maisey identify her "hot buttons," and respond more mindfully when they are pushed. Maisey is now able to drive a car independently which she had been afraid to do for the last several years. She can socialize with neighbors without having panic attacks and the strong urge to flee. She is beginning to feel connected to these neighbors and "not so out of place." She has refrained from creating chaos by searching for acceptance from her mother or sisters—a repetitive and destructive habit in the past. She is more stable than she has ever been.

However, the insomnia has not really changed. She has tried working on "good sleep hygiene,"—going to bed at the same time every night, avoiding naps, avoiding caffeine or screen time in the evenings, using the bedroom only to sleep, and getting up and reading if she hasn't fallen asleep in fifteen minutes. She finds these guidelines difficult to follow with any regularity. She and her therapist have talked at length about childhood events that may have impaired her sleep, particularly the sexual abuse which occurred in her bedroom at night. Despite understanding the probable roots of her insomnia, she still sleeps poorly most nights. She makes therapy appointments for late afternoon because she has no confidence she will show up or be able to participate if she has to come earlier. Needless to say, this problem, along with her physical pain, makes the prospect of a regular job or even keeping to a reliable schedule for her projects fairly remote. She doubts she will ever be able to work again, and worries about her financial future every day.

Thinking About The Case

Insomnia may be the most commonly experienced problem described in the DSM-5. There may not be a person on the planet over the age of three who hasn't experienced it. In order to meet the criteria for insomnia disorder, the sufferer must have had difficulty with sleep for at least three nights per week for at least three months. Even so, surveys indicate that more than fifty percent of the United States population report having had symptoms that meet this criterion.

Insomnia disorder is characterized by dissatisfaction with the quantity and/or quality of sleep associated with at least one of the following: difficulty falling asleep, difficulty staying asleep, or waking extremely early in the morning. Insomnia may be primary, meaning that it is not caused by another disorder or it can be secondary to another disorder. Maisey's case is typical in that long-term insomnia rarely occurs in a vacuum. In Maisey's case insomnia is certainly associated with post-traumatic stress disorder, caused by sexual abuse by her grandfather, but it has persisted for many years beyond the stressor and in spite of therapy designed to address the stressor. Therefore, while it may have been secondary in origin, it appears to be primary at this time. Such a situation is not terribly unusual. For example, problematic drinking may have begun in response to a stressor, but once the pattern is deeply embedded, alcoholism becomes a primary problem and must be treated as such. It will not respond to treatment aimed at the original precipitating causes. Maisey's insomnia is also supported by current stressors and by her difficulty managing anxiety in general.

Maisey's case illustrates some of the common sequelae of chronic insomnia. She is unable to work on a regular basis as her cognitive functioning is impaired by lack of sleep. Her mood is affected as are her relationships with others. At its worst, insomnia affects her grasp on reality.

Acute insomnia, the kind we have all likely experienced can be caused by stress, illness, an uncomfortable or unfamiliar sleep environment, emotional or physical discomfort, alcohol, caffeine, nicotine or medications, too much screen time too close to bedtime, or changes in sleep cycle (for example, working night shifts). Exercising too close to bedtime, having an argument, doing challenging puzzles, and even sex can impair sleep temporarily.

Chronic insomnia can be related to chronic stress and worry, depression and anxiety disorders, chronic pain or discomfort, menopause, or prostate problems among other issues. Once experienced, anxiety about the insomnia itself can worsen the problem. Maisey experienced this: much of her planning was based on how she perceived her sleeplessness would likely affect her life on any given day. She described many nights of checking the clock every fifteen minutes despairing that she would ever fall asleep. Ironically, this was more likely to happen when she had a project planned for the next day or when she had a morning appointment scheduled.

Insomnia tends to worsen with age. Older people experience less restful sleep and more wakefulness. Their sleep cycle may shift causing them to become sleepy much earlier in the evening and to wake earlier in the morning. They also may be less active and this can worsen sleep problems. Age-related changes in health like arthritis, menopause, sleep apnea, or restless leg syndrome may impair sleep. And older people take more medications, many of which can affect the quantity and quality of sleep.

Treatment for insomnia disorder may combine behavioral, supportive, and biological approaches. Sleep medications are not recommended for the long-term, but may be helpful for brief episodes. Good sleep hygiene is important. It is usually suggested that the bedroom be kept dark and cool, that it be used only for sleep or sex, that the person refrain from caffeine, nicotine, alcohol, heavy meals, vigorous exercise, or very hot showers close to bedtime. The person should refrain from napping if at all possible, and should try to keep a regular schedule of going to sleep and waking. If he or she is unable to sleep after fifteen or twenty minutes, the person should get up and engage in a relaxing activity. Cognitive therapy can lessen the anxiety associated with sleeplessness. Both cognitive and supportive psychotherapy can address the psychological issues that may be maintaining the insomnia. Relaxation training and sleep-restriction therapy can also be tried.

Behavioral methods and good sleep hygiene are generally helpful for insomnia, though it is rare for the problem to disappear entirely. But chronic insomnia may become more intermittent, and the person may be helped to function better in spite of sleep difficulties. As with other disorders, the greater the level of current stressors and the larger the number of associated mental or emotional disorders, the worse the prognosis.

Questions To Consider

1. Think back to the last time you had insomnia. What were the factors that induced it? How did it affect you? Did you do anything about it, and if so, what?
2. Do you have good sleep hygiene? What factors might you change to ensure a good night's sleep?
3. Watch the movie "Insomnia" starring Al Pacino. How did his insomnia affect his functioning?
4. Do you think that something as common as insomnia deserves to be called a "disorder?" Why or why not?

LANAHAN NOTES
Sleep-Wake Disorders

Major types of sleep-wake disorders

Insomnia disorder: individual has great difficulty falling and/or staying asleep; anxiety, depression, stress may underlie the disorder; disorder may also contribute to anxiety

Hypersomnolence disorder: individual experiences gradual but excessive sleepiness during the daylight hours; causes one to fall asleep during work, driving; also associated with depression, bipolar disorder, alcohol use

Narcolepsy: characterized by a 'sleep attack'; one suddenly falls asleep often while performing everyday activity, e.g., work, driving; may be caused by a dying off of hypocretin cells which regulate the wake-sleep cycle

Treatment of sleep-wake disorders

Medications can sometimes help regulate sleep-wake cycle

Cognitive-behavioral therapy can help if the underlying cause is anxiety or stress, or poor sleep hygiene habits

CHAPTER THIRTEEN

Sexual Dysfunctions

Our sexuality is probably the most value-laden of human behaviors. Bound up as it is in social mores, religious values, dating and mating, and self-image, it is a powerful producer of psychic pleasure and pain. While most people experience some transitory sexual problems at various times in their lives, when these problems are longstanding or severe, a sexual disorder is diagnosed.

The scientific study of sexuality dates back only to the mid-1880s. However, substantial progress in understanding the variants, both normal and abnormal, of human sexuality has been made since then. For example, masturbation, once considered to be both abnormal and harmful, is now known to be widely prevalent and apparently harmless. The notion that women had two separate kinds of orgasms, vaginal and clitoral, has been disproved.

While Freud and other psychodynamic theorists spent a great deal of energy exploring human sexuality, learning theory has also made major contributions to the understanding and, in some cases, successful treatment of sexual problems. Keep in mind, though, that no study of sexuality can proceed without reference to the cultural context in which it occurs, since what is considered normal sexual behavior can change dramatically.

DSM-IV-TR lumped all disorders related to human sexuality together. DSM-5 teases them apart into three separate categories: sexual dysfunction, gender dysphoria, and paraphilias. In this section we examine sexual dysfunctions. These include disorders of interest/arousal for both genders, and disorders of performance. For males, performance disorders include erectile dysfunction and delayed or premature ejaculation. For females, they include orgasmic dysfunction and pain during intercourse.

We have included two cases in this section. In the first, a woman's difficulty achieving orgasm is related to a number of other issues in her life, and in the second, a man experiences lack of sexual desire. Both illustrate well the interplay between nature and nurture and between psychological, physiological and relationship issues.

CASE 35

FEMALE ORGASMIC DISORDER: THE CASE OF SUSAN C.

Susan C. is a thirty-eight-year-old woman who likes to look like she's nineteen. She wears her blond hair in two ponytails, and sports short shorts and midriff-baring tops in the summertime. On entering her therapist's office, she characteristically curls up on the chair, dropping her shoes to the floor as she comes in.

Susan came for therapy because she was upset over her relationship with her boyfriend, a married man with whom she had been sexually involved for a little over a year. Recently, she related, he seemed preoccupied and distant. He no longer wanted to hear the details of her day. His quick calls just to tell her that he loved her had decreased in frequency. Worst of all, he seemed to be delaying leaving his wife, which he had promised to do from almost the beginning of the affair.

Susan had been having trouble sleeping, had lost her appetite, and was losing weight from her already thin frame. She was barely able to concentrate at her job as a bank teller and found herself breaking into tears for virtually no reason—sometimes more than once a day.

Over the first few therapy sessions, Susan related some of her family history. She was the middle child of three. She had an older sister and a younger brother. Both of her parents had been heavy drinkers. They quarreled frequently, although nonviolently, and didn't seem to have much energy left over to apply to their relationships with their children. At least this is how Susan saw it. She said that her sister thought that Susan was overly sensitive and that their parents had done a good job. In any case, her parents divorced when she was thirteen. Her father quickly found a new girlfriend (who, perhaps, had been in the picture before the breakup) and was remarried within six months of the divorce. He had two more children from that union. Susan's mother did not remarry. Instead, she seemed to withdraw further into the bottle and the television. Susan's sister was married and seemed reasonably happy. She and Susan often failed to see eye to eye on things and weren't close. Susan's brother was a heavy drinker and had difficulty holding jobs. He hadn't married, although he did have a son whom he rarely saw.

Susan herself had been married twice. She had two teenage children from her first marriage to an alcoholic and verbally abusive man. Following her divorce after six years of marriage, she had married a man who was very different—older, gentle, responsible. She became bored with him after a few years, and they, too, were divorced. She had raised her children essentially alone after that, dating from time to time but not having a sustained relationship until she met her present lover on the tennis court. She felt that he was the genuine love of her life—the man she was destined to be with. Her life revolved around pleasing him. She waited by the phone for him to call and refused all invitations if she thought he might want to be with her. Often, she cruised by his house or place of business to see if his truck was there. She was obsessively and insistently interested in his every thought and movement.

While Susan's presenting problem was not specifically sexual, it emerged during the course of therapy that Susan had never had an orgasm while with a man. For her, sex was an opportunity to demonstrate her prowess and desirability. She took great pleasure in being hugged and cuddled. She adored being told that she was a wonderful lover and that her lover could not live without her. She thought about making love constantly, but found herself strangely removed during the act itself. Sheepishly, she told her therapist that she only had orgasms occasionally—and then by a method that was so embarrassing she could barely speak about it. Apparently, she had discovered quite by accident years ago that rubbing up against a door jamb could produce an orgasm. Oddly, she had never figured out (or perhaps she was too inhibited to try) that other methods might work as well. So, for almost twenty years, sex with men was for show, while she engaged in her private practice when physical need became overwhelming (often following a visit by her lover when she had become aroused but not satiated). Needless to say, she had become quite expert at faking orgasms (many of them, in fact) with her sexual partners.

Despite her profound shame, Susan was relieved that she had spoken with her therapist about sexuality. She agreed that this was an area on which she wanted to work. Initially, Susan's therapist did two things: first, she asked Susan to read a book on women's sexuality and to begin to experiment with other masturbatory techniques for attaining orgasm. Second, she began helping Susan identify the blocks to being more honest in her sexual relationships.

Susan soon realized that she felt profoundly inadequate, except in her ability to attract and seduce men. If she were less than the siren she pretended to be, perhaps no man would want to be with her—and then she would be worth nothing indeed. Susan realized these feelings had been with her for a very long time, and she linked them to her father's emotional unavailability, despite her desperate attempts as a child to gain his love and approval. Trying to take a candid look at herself, Susan was able to identify some of her positive traits which included loyalty, a sense of humor, keen intelligence, lots of energy, and a wide range of interests. She was able to acknowledge, at least in principle, that men might be attracted to these qualities, in addition to her showy sexuality. Additionally, she asked herself for the first time whether a man who was only interested in her (often faked) sexuality was really worth keeping.

Susan did not feel that she could take the risk of confiding in her boyfriend that her orgasms had been faked and that she had been so focused on his sexual pleasure that she had neglected any attention to her own. However, she did agree to begin to pay attention to her own physical sensations during lovemaking. This led to the discovery that when she did so, her own natural responses, which included verbalizations and body movements, heightened her lover's ardor. After a few weeks of actually experiencing sex, rather than simply going through the motions as she had been, Susan had an orgasm while her boyfriend was engaging in oral sex. Over the next several months, she had additional orgasms, some during mutual masturbation, and some during intercourse with additional manual stimulation. While, like many women, Susan did not have orgasms during intercourse alone, she was more than satisfied with her sexual responsiveness. She reported no longer feeling like a "fake" and a "freak."

Ironically, the more sexually responsive and confident she became, the less Susan felt dependent on her lover's admiration. Therapy continued its exploration of Susan's intense need for approval and adoration. Almost a year after therapy started, Susan terminated her affair. Not long after, she also terminated therapy, resolved to seek a more suitable partner and to widen her focus to include other sources of pleasure and self esteem: friends, family, sports, and finishing her college undergraduate degree. She had come to grips with her parents' limitations, grieved their inability to be as attentive as she had wished them to be, and ceased to hope that they might some day change. This process had caused her some sadness, but it resulted in a greater sense of peace and freedom.

Thinking About the Case

Susan's orgasmic disorder occurred in a wider context which included her family history, her ideas about herself and others, and cultural notions about gender relationships. In this, her case is typical of virtually all of the sexual dysfunctions. Note that Susan could have been given multiple diagnoses including adjustment disorder with depressed mood (clinically significant symptoms of depression in the face of an identifiable stressor), and, possibly, histrionic personality disorder (a pattern of excessive emotionality and attention-seeking).

The case is also fairly typical in that the sexual disorder is not the presenting problem but, instead, emerges during the course of treatment. It is common for people to be ambivalent about discussing sexual concerns with a stranger. Gaining confidence in the therapist is a prerequisite for self-disclosure. In addition, the sexual concern is often not the most pressing problem. Susan was more concerned initially about possibly losing her boyfriend than she was about her orgasmic dysfunction.

Susan's therapy was truly biopsychosocial in nature. The reading and masturbation assignments were designed to give Susan a fuller understanding of the physiological aspects of arousal and orgasm. Cognitive therapy techniques were used in helping Susan question her assumption that she only had value as a sexual object. Clearly, this work was informed by an understanding of how women are socialized by the culture to think of themselves in certain ways. However, cultural expectations are interpreted through the family (as well as through television, literature and other sources). A psychodynamic perspective led to the exploration of the familial roots of some of Susan's ideas about herself. While these various schools of therapy seem quite distinct in principle, they are often used together in practice, as they were in Susan's case. Most therapists practice a kind of therapeutic pragmatism, using whatever might be helpful, rather than a therapeutic purism, relying solely on one technique. Research has not yet shed any scientific light on whether such pragmatism actually increases the chances for success, although studies have shown that experienced therapists from different schools behave more similarly than do inexperienced therapists. Apparently, clinical wisdom supports therapeutic pragmatism.

Questions to Consider

1. In this case, the therapy went beyond the presenting complaint. Do you agree with the therapist's decision to do so? Why or why not?

What factors would you consider in reaching such a decision yourself?

2. Sex and gender, while different, are intimately connected. How did gender role expectations affect the development of sexual disorder symptoms in Susan?
3. Can you diagram this case (US, CS, UR, CR) as a learning theorist would?
4. Most psychodynamic explanations of mental disorder tend to focus on the mother-child relationship, yet this case seems to suggest that a child's relationship with the father might also be important. What are the ways in which a mother's and father's influences might be different, but important? Are these differences also related to gender roles?
5. This case illustrates that therapeutic pragmatism rather than therapeutic purism reigns in the day-to-day world of psychotherapy. What implications does this have for theory and for research?

CASE 36

HYPOACTIVE SEXUAL DESIRE DISORDER: THE CASE OF SEAN D.

SEAN WAS THIRTY-TWO YEARS OLD when he presented himself as a candidate for psychotherapy. He was married, a college professor, the only child of two dour, elderly midwesterners. He was slightly portly, somewhat formal, well educated, and well-spoken. He came to his first session with his wife and asked that she be included in the first interview. In fact, she did most of the talking.

Mrs. D. was presently a stay-at-home mother. She had been the head librarian for the university where they were both employed until shortly after their marriage. She explained that the couple had been married for six years after dating for two. She had had a brief prior marriage with no children, but this was Professor D.'s first marriage. In fact, she noted, Professor D. had been a virgin when they began dating. The couple had one child, a boy aged four. Mrs. D. said that her husband was a good father, hard-worker, steadfast, and loyal. However, the couple had not had sex in over seven months, despite her willingness to do so. Her husband had a million excuses: he was tired; he had a headache; he was preoccupied with work. She said that she had heard of wives having these kinds of problems, but never husbands. She emphasized that the problem was not hers, but his. In addition to exhibiting sexual disinterest, he seemed reluctant to engage in any affectionate behavior at all. They rarely argued; they just didn't connect emotionally.

When questioned directly, Professor D. admitted that his wife's rendition was essentially correct. He didn't know why, but he had hardly any interest in sex. He had never had a strong sexual desire, even as an adolescent, but now he seemed to have none. He wished it didn't matter so much to his wife—truthfully, he would have been satisfied to live as roommates. But, since it did seem to matter to his wife, he agreed to a series of appointments. The therapist suggested that some of these appointments might include Mrs. D. She seemed willing to participate. The therapist also suggested that Professor D. get a full physical examination, including testosterone level and thyroid functioning evaluation, to which he also agreed.

Professor D. arrived promptly for his second appointment, alone as had been requested. His physical examination had turned up no abnormalities, except mild high blood pressure, for which he was now being treated with medication. He did not speak freely. He seemed not to know what to say. He answered questions directly, though, so the therapist asked a great many.

What emerged is that Professor D. had been deeply disappointed with his marriage. His wife, who had seemed hearty and competent when they married, had experienced a series of health problems, including kidney stones, migraines, back pain, and "fibromyalgia" (the quotes being Professor D.'s, complete with fingered signs of quotation marks). She had quit her job within the first year of their marriage and was barely able to keep up with housework. In fact, Professor D. frequently did laundry, and almost always cooked dinner, as he found her in bed with a headache or back pain more often than not. She professed to be exhausted by the demands of child care, so their son was in day care every afternoon. Professor D. picked him up on his way home from work. Mrs. D. took "boatloads" of medication, including several pain medications, which left her lethargic and sometimes "loopy."

The couple had no real social life. They socialized some with her sisters. When Professor D. had work related social obligations, his wife was generally too ill to attend. He got used to going alone, but was embarrassed by having to do so. At leisure, he spent a chunk of time with his aging parents, mowing their lawn, changing light bulbs, or just visiting. He often took his son, which pleased his parents and gave his wife a break. His parents had never said anything directly, but he knew they disapproved of his wife's indolence. In their view, she was not so much sick as lazy. He didn't agree, he said. She could hardly be blamed for medical problems beyond her control. Still, his marriage had not proved to be the working partnership that he had expected and for which he had hoped.

Professor D. had colleagues at work, but no real friends. He played a little golf, and sometimes rode a bike. He had always been self-sufficient, not needing a great deal of social activity, so he didn't perceive the relatively solitary nature of his life as a burden.

Professor D.'s therapist had a hunch, and he pursued it by inquiring how his client behaved when angry. The question seemed to puzzle the Professor greatly. He professed not to remember the last time he was angry. He felt irritated from time to time, and frustrated, of course, but never what he would call angry.

How did his parents express anger, the therapist inquired. Well, it seems they didn't get angry either. There was no need to be angry, they had often said, when a rational discussion could clear up most problems and compromise could solve most any disagreement. Professor D. could not remember ever having seen either of his parents angry. Nobody in his household raised their voices, threw things, slammed cabinets, or slammed doors. He could tell when one or the other of his parents was "upset" because then they avoided each other for a while, and the household became even quieter than usual. This situation could last for several days and then would gradually return to normal.

How did his wife express anger? She was "more vocal," and often Professor D. felt uncomfortable when she complained in querulous tones or if she yelled at him. Like his parents, he responded by withdrawing, which only seemed to enrage her further. Sometimes, he admitted, she followed him from room to room, shouting out her complaints and insisting he listen to her.

The therapist felt his hunch had been validated. He believed that Professor D.'s sexual feelings for his wife had been submerged and blocked by anger and disappointment that he had no way of expressing. Therapy, then, would have three stages: in the first, Professor D. would become more aware of and able to put into words his feelings; in the second, he would express them to his wife; and in the third the couple would work out some mutually agreeable solutions.

However, sometimes simple plans are decidedly difficult to enact. The first stage of treatment was beset by Professor D.'s resistance to admitting to anger. His value system, his role models, his rational understanding that he "shouldn't" be angry at someone for something that she couldn't control, and his lifelong experience suppressing and alternately labeling his own experience of anger all worked against the first therapeutic goal. His therapist spent months helping him identify anger (tightness in the jaw and stomach, flushed feeling in the face, rapid heartrate, unconscious clutching of the fists). He worked to help him understand that feeling anger wasn't, in itself, a bad thing. It could be a guide to the need for change. Whether it was "bad" or "good" depended upon what he did with it once he was aware of it. It took a long time before Professor D. was able to admit that he was, indeed, angry that his wife was a poor companion and partner to him, and he didn't entirely believe that she had no control whatsoever over her choices. Finally, though, the therapist judged that Professor D. was clear enough about his own feelings that couples' therapy could commence.

But as difficult as handling the first stage of treatment proved to be, the second stage proved even more challenging. The couples' part of therapy did not go smoothly. Not surprisingly, Mrs. D. was not liking the changes that were occurring in her husband. She wasn't happy that he was questioning whether she was doing the best that she could. Despite the therapist's best attempts to control the flow of the sessions, she routinely got furious, yelled at both of them, and stalked out. By the end of the fourth session, she refused to come back, saying that she wasn't going to tolerate being ganged up on by her husband and his therapist.

Since therapy was at an impasse, Professor D. had some decisions to make. Would he stay in this marriage to a woman who would never be the partner for whom he had hoped and with whom he could not communicate? Should he end the marriage and seek a more suitable spouse? Would his own problems with identifying and expressing his feelings follow him into another relationship? What would be the effects of separation on their child? On their finances? These were the questions that occupied the remainder of the time that Professor D. worked with his therapist.

Thinking About The Case

Most people think of lack of sexual desire as a female problem, but it is not. While women have a higher incidence of the disorder, men experience it as well. The disorder is defined as lack of sexual fantasies and desire for sexual activity that causes significant distress and interpersonal difficulty. Further differentiations include general versus situational lack of desire and lifelong versus acquired lack of desire. There are three subtypes: 1. lifelong generalized lack of desire, 2. acquired situational lack of desire, and 3. acquired generalized lack of desire. The case of Professor D. illustrates that these types are not completely distinctive. He had lower than normal desire from early adolescence reflecting the first sub-type, but the strongest component is related to his marriage and reflects the second or even the third subtype.

Causes of the first subtype are unknown but are assumed to be related to imbalances in neurotransmitters between inhibitory and excitatory systems. Others have posited that it is due to a deficit in testosterone or an imbalance between testosterone and other sexual hormones.

This subtype is not without controversy: asexual activists argue that asexuality is no more a disorder than is homosexuality (which used to be included as a disorder in the DSM but was removed in 1973.) DSM-5 handles this problem by precluding the diagnosis if the individual is self-identified as asexual. Indeed, such a person would not meet the criterion of experiencing significant distress, in any case.

The first subtype is generally impervious to treatment. Testosterone treatment has not been shown to be particularly effective, nor have other medical or psychological interventions been successful. Most therapists would probably focus on helping the individual and his partner to accept and make the best of his lack of desire. He might be encouraged to respond to his partner's sexual needs despite his own disinterest, and certainly he would be encouraged not to see himself as damaged, but rather as different.

The second subtype is diagnosed when the man has no desire within the current relationship, but experiences desire for sexual stimulation either alone or outside of the relationship. It is generally caused by intimacy or relationship problems as it appears to be for Professor D. In addition, studies indicate that chronic illness in the man's partner can also precipitate the problem as can addiction to pornography. Psychotherapy, generally including couples' therapy, is the treatment of choice, and has modest success when the underlying problems can be addressed and resolved. Often, behavioral strategies, like pleasuring exercises, play a role in treatment as well.

The third subtype, acquired generalized lack of desire, is often precipitated by physical problems or medications. Some blood pressure medications and some antidepressants can inhibit sexual desire. Diabetes, menopause, hypothyroidism, drug abuse, coronary artery disease, and heart or renal failure can also diminish or even destroy sexual desire. Overwork and stress can suppress sexual desire. Relationship problems can also result in generalized lack of desire, as they appear to have done in the present case.

Hypoactive sexual desire disorder has high comorbidity with other psychological conditions, including schizophrenia, depression, and substance abuse. Obviously, when more than one disorder is present, the clinician must develop a treatment plan that addresses each of the issues, whether simultaneously or sequentially, depending on what approach is most likely to be effective.

Questions to Consider

1. Consider the cultural context in which sexuality is embedded. Homosexuality was once considered a mental illness; now it is not. Hypoactive sexual desire is considered an illness only if the individ-

ual experiences it as such. What does this say to you about the reliability and validity of psychiatric diagnosis?

2. Professor D.'s therapist worked with him first, and then brought his wife in. This worked out poorly, at least insofar as strengthening the marriage is concerned. Could he have anticipated that this would be so? How? What other strategies for working with this couple might you suggest?
3. If the couple breaks up, should therapy be considered a failure? Why or why not?

LANAHAN NOTES
Sexual Dysfunctions

Sexual dysfunctions are a heterogeneous group of disorders that cause significant disturbance in one's ability to respond sexually or to experience sexual pleasure with a partner

Types of sexual dysfunction

Female orgasmic disorder: characterized by excessive delay, infrequency, or absence of orgasm

Female sexual interest/arousal disorder: female experiences a combination of a lack of desire for sex and a lack of physical response when engaged in sexual activity

Male hypoactive sexual desire disorder: male experiences a significant lack of desire for sexual activity

Male erectile dysfunctions

Delayed ejaculation: occurs without desire for delay

Erectile disorder: difficulty in obtaining or maintaining erectile rigidity

Premature ejaculation: ejaculation occurring during partnered sexual activity within approximately 1 minute

Causes

Learning theory: proposes that dysfunctions arise from performance anxiety

Psychodynamic perspective: looks at unresolved childhood conflicts about sexuality; considers the connection between sexuality and one's self-definition

Interpersonal context: sexual problems often reflect problems in the relationship like poor communication, power issues, anger, resentment

Cultural and religious issues: one's group social norms may affect the quality of sexual behavior

Treatment of sexual dysfunctions

Factors to consider: sexual partners' lack of knowledge about effective stimulation; quality of the personal relationship outside of sex; cultural and religious factors; medical issues; substance use

Masters and Johnson: 1960s pioneers in studying and treating dysfunction; focus on a progressive, step-by-step approach to sexual behavior

Cognitive therapy: examines partners' dysfunctional beliefs about sexuality

Multifaceted approach: incorporates behavioral, cognitive, interpersonal, and psychodynamic principles

CHAPTER FOURTEEN

Gender Dysphoria

Now that homosexuality has been largely accepted as no longer a pathological variant of human sexuality, public interest has shifted to the "trans community." Gender dysphoria is diagnosed when there is a marked incongruence between one's experienced gender and the gender of his or her birth. While some transgendered people have only "come out" as adults, most have experienced the dissonance between their assigned gender and their self-identification since early childhood.

The growing acknowledgement of transgendered people is following much the same course, and has generated much the same controversies as did homosexuality several generations ago. Should gender dysphoria be considered an illness or a non-pathological variant of human gender identification? Should children who identify as transgendered be permitted to dress and behave as the gender with which they identify? What sports team should they play on, for example? And should children who identify as transgendered be permitted to get gender reassignment surgery if they strongly desire to do so?

In this section we present a fairly typical case of gender dysphoria in a young child. It illustrates well the challenges faced by parents who have a transgendered child.

CASE 37

GENDER DYSPHORIA IN A YOUNG CHILD: THE CASE OF BILLY B.

BILLY WAS THE MIDDLE of three boys. He looked like his brothers—fair-skinned, blue-eyed, and stocky—but there the resemblance ended. Although an assortment of toys was available to him, Billy, from as early as his parents can remember, ignored the trucks and cars, and guns and hammers in favor of dolls. While his older brother went flying around the house, dressed as an "Indian" and whooping it up, Billy, at two-and-a-half, sat quietly in the corner dressing and feeding one of his "babies." He eschewed rough-and-tumble play, preferring, instead, to follow his mother around while she went about her household routine. She also found him to be especially "sensitive" and in need of more gentle disciplining than her other sons. He would burst into tears at a harsh word from her and rarely need the "time-out" punishments that seemed a part of daily life with his brothers.

By three-and-a-half, Billy had started his collection of Barbie dolls. His only playmate was the child next door, a girl of about the same age as he. Arriving at her house, he would run directly to her bedroom and spend the next several hours trying on all of her clothes. Together they would produce a "fashion show" for whatever parent was around, with Billy wearing his friend's clothes while she wore her mother's. Like most children, Billy and his friend spent a lot of time in fantasy play, but he always insisted on being a girl in their role-playing. Sometimes they would argue about who got to be the "princess." Her suggestions that he could play the part of the "prince" were met with stony resistance.

His friend's mother found the obsessive, driven quality of his behavior disturbing, commenting, "it's as if he were possessed by the desire to try on every dress." His parents didn't know what to think. His mother was worried about his preference for traditionally feminine types of play, but her gentle attempts to redirect him were met with strong resistance or even tantrums. Motivated to raise nonsexist children in an atmosphere that downplayed traditional gender roles, she was hesitant to stifle his natural proclivities or damage his self-esteem by excessive criticism. When Billy asked her, as he often did while parading around in his friend's clothes, "don't I look pretty?" she would tell him, with much misgiving, that he did, indeed.

His father was much more upset by Billy's single-minded interest in things feminine. Following a period of denial, he became increasingly agitated in Billy's presence, alternating between ignoring him and screaming at him to "knock if off and act like a boy." He tried spending more time alone with Billy doing "guy stuff," but these outings were usually disappointing for both father and son. In the toy store, Billy wanted to look at Barbie outfits, while his father wanted to look at the sports section. Billy was bored and distracted playing catch, and when his dad asked what he'd like to do next, he invited his father to a tea party. Mr. B. tried to participate in his son's play, but it made him uncomfortable and frustrated.

A real parenting challenge came when Billy began to refuse to take off his friend's clothes when it was time to come home from her house. He threw such a fit that his mother, to calm his obviously real and palpable distress, finally let him wear the dress home, where he wore it all evening, much to his father's consternation, and insisted on going to bed in it that night. After several months of constant battling and anguish, Mrs. B., over her husband's vociferous objections, bought Billy his own dress. This did not end their struggles, however, since Billy also wanted to wear barrettes in his hair, his friend's shoes (which were too small and hurt his feet), and her underwear.

By the age of five, Billy was voicing the clear wish to be a girl. At his fifth birthday party he told his mother, "I always thought that when I was this many (holding up five fingers) I would like being a boy, but I don't." She had observed him many times standing in front of the mirror, exclaiming that he was ugly, but that when he grew up he was "gonna be a pretty lady." He had no boy friends in nursery school, but the girls liked him just fine. He fit right into their play, and they treated him as if he were one of them.

At the time he entered school, his parents made several changes. First, they set limits on his cross-dressing. He was allowed to wear a girl's nightshirt and tights to bed and to wear girls' slippers, but otherwise had to dress in boys' clothes. His mom and her neighbor agreed that the children would be allowed to dress in adult's clothes for "dress-up," but that

Billy would no longer be allowed to wear his friend's clothes. In fact her bedroom was off-limits.

In addition, the B.'s enrolled Billy in a local ballet class that was run by a husband and wife team. They felt that this might give him a socially appropriate outlet for his feminine interests. They also hoped that the male ballet teacher would offer Billy a model for how to integrate the masculine and feminine sides of himself. Billy loved ballet and didn't seem to mind at all being the only boy in the class. He did throw a bit of a fit when the other students got to wear a tu-tu and he didn't, but he seemed to get past this and settle into the class well.

Finally, at the urging of their neighbor, they agreed to have Billy evaluated by a child psychiatrist. The psychiatrist saw Billy alone for several sessions, took a family and personal history from his parents, and saw the family together once. His pronouncement was that Billy was the worst case of transsexualism that he had ever seen, and that the fault lay in a disturbed mother-child relationship. Mrs. B. was devastated. With a family history of depression and alcoholism, she felt that she herself had been raised "in the original dysfunctional family." She had had problems with depression herself from time to time and was primed and ready to believe that Billy's problems were somehow her fault. Her husband, though, was having none of it. He rose to her defense, stating his belief that Billy had been like this almost since birth, that his wife had remarkable patience and wisdom in handling his "differentness," and that he wanted a second opinion.

The B.'s searched around until they found a program that specialized in gender identity disorders at the local university. Billy was accepted into the program where he had individual psychotherapy on a weekly basis for about a year. Therapy failed to produce any profound changes, although Billy seemed to accept limits on his cross-dressing with a great deal less struggle as time went on. In kindergarten and first grade he did well academically and behaved in a way which did not get him singled out for ridicule by his classmates, although he had no real friends.

Now eight years old, Billy still plays with his Barbies and avoids more typically "boy" activities. He has found the computer, though, which now occupies much of his free time. It is also a conduit to a relationship with his father. Together they explore the Internet and play computer games. Billy's gender cross-identification has become somewhat of a non-issue in the family. "Bill is just Bill," his parents say. They understand from their consultations with the therapists at the university that he is unlikely to change. They assume that he will be homosexual and have prepared themselves to love and accept him regardless. Bill's mom says she finds him easier to manage in some ways than her other two sons. He shares her interests and is content to hang around with her, while his brothers seem to need to be entertained in a more active way. Bill's dad has moved past anger and frustration to sadness and resignation. He sees a tough and possibly lonely road ahead for Billy, but he considers the situation to be "an act of God," and one that must be accepted with grace and forbearance.

Thinking About the Case

Gender identity disorder, also known as transsexualism, is diagnosed in individuals who feel trapped in a body of the wrong gender. It is a rare disorder, occurring in about one in 100,000 people. It is distinguishable from transvestism in which clothing of the opposite sex is worn for erotic or playful reasons, but in which the individual is fully identified with his or her own gender. Nor is it synonymous with homosexuality. While most transsexuals are sexually attracted to members of their own gender, some are not.

Billy's case is quite typical in that the disorder appears startlingly early, with fixed cross-gender identification in place by the age of three or four. It is diagnosed much more often in males than in females, although it should be noted that cross-dressing and other cross-gender behavior is much more available and socially acceptable for women than for men, so perhaps there are many undiagnosed cases. It is a chronic condition, yielding to no psychotherapy or behavioral therapy.

The early onset and immutable nature of gender identity disorder have led investigators to conclude that some hormonal disturbance that occurs some time in the second to fourth month of pregnancy is responsible for this fascinating but heartbreaking condition. In the early fetus, both male and female internal organs are present until, in male fetuses, two masculinizing hormones are secreted from the testes. These hormones affect the subsequent development of sexual organs as well as having psychological effects on the brain—in effect, masculinizing the brain. In transsexuals, it appears that, for as yet unknown reasons, organ development proceeds normally, but the masculinizing of the brain does not. While familial and social factors also play a role in the development of gender identity, these later influences appear to reinforce or disturb a core identity that is established well before birth.

It is difficult to overstate the anguish felt by transsexuals. Many become profoundly depressed and even suicidal. Some mutilate their own genitals. Almost always, disturbances of personality develop as they try to adapt to the demands and the stigma to which they are subject from an early age.

Until recently, despair was the certain future from those afflicted.

However, within the past several decades, advances in medical knowledge and techniques have made the possibility of sex reassignment through hormonal and surgical procedures a viable alternative. Typically, an individual who wishes to have the surgery is required to undergo a careful psychological evaluation to ensure that the apparent gender identity disorder is not secondary to another disorder (like schizophrenia for instance). The psychological health and resilience of the person are also assessed. Then he or she is required to live in the new gender role for a period of several years while hormone therapy is begun. This may entail a change of name, dress, and sometimes even occupation. Finally, genital surgery is undertaken. For male to female sex reassignment, this involves transforming the penis into a vagina. For female to male reassignment, the procedure is more complicated and involves multiple surgeries over several years to remove the breasts and ovaries, and sometimes, to build a penis. Since the penis cannot become erect, a prosthetic device must be used for intercourse.

The outcome of sex reassignment surgery is variable. Probably half or more of patients have a favorable outcome, reporting improvement in their sense of well-being and overall satisfaction with life. However, a substantial minority experience fairly serious surgical complications or feel that their life has been altered in negative ways. Perhaps it will be possible some day to identify and correct the fetal hormonal disturbance so that gender identity disorder can be prevented.

Questions to Consider

1. Close your eyes and imagine, for a few minutes, what it would be like to be forced to wear the clothing of and to act like a member of the opposite sex. If you feel really courageous, try it for a day. What changes occurred in your mood, self-esteem, and ability to engage in everyday tasks and relate to others? What might it be like to have this be your permanent lot in life?
2. As we move from sexual identity, through sexual orientation, sexual interest, and sexual behavior, we appear to move along a continuum from biological to environmental/experiential influences. Can you construct a coherent biopsychosocial model that describes the development of adult sexuality?

LANAHAN NOTES
Gender Dysphoria

Basic terminology in understanding gender

Sex: refers to the biological indicators of male or female such as sex chromosomes, gonads, sex hormones and non-ambiguous internal and external genitalia

Gender: refers to the public lived role as a boy or girl, man or woman that develops from biological factors in interaction with social and psychological factors

Gender Assignment: the initial assignment at birth or prenatally as a male or female

Gender-atypical/non-conforming: somatic features/behaviors that are ambiguous

Gender identity: one's social identity

Transgender: individuals who transiently or persistently identify with a gender different from their gender assignment

Transsexual: transgender individuals who seek to undergo somatic transition

Characteristics of gender dysphoria

A significant distress felt by an individual due to the incongruence between one's experienced or expressed gender and one's assigned gender

Tends to develop after the first 2-3 years of childhood when it begins to interfere with daily social activities

Lack of age-typical same-sex peer relations/skills often leads to isolation from peer groups

Individual is often teased and harassed for not being like "a proper boy or girl" sometimes resulting in anxiety, disruptive impulse-control, depression, and substance abuse

Gender Dysphoria in Children

Affective symptoms: dislike of autonomy

Behavioral symptoms: engagement in cross-gender roles in make-believe play; activities include cross-dressing and choice of playmates; rejection of stereotypically gender appropriate toys

Cognitive symptoms: strong desire or insistence that one is an alternate gender

Gender Dysphoria in Adolescents and Adults

With onset of puberty, the incongruence between one's gender and gender assignment becomes more intense; some individuals desire to rid themselves of their primary and/or secondary sex characteristics

Some individuals perform genital mutilation

Some have suicidal thoughts and attempts

Treatment

Biological: cross-sex hormone treatment; sometimes major surgery

Psychotherapy: a primary focus on coping and acceptance of self with attention to co-morbid diagnoses

CHAPTER FIFTEEN

Disruptive, Impulse-Control, and Conduct Disorders

This category is new to DSM-5, bringing together diagnoses that were distributed through the previous DSM-IV-TR among childhood disorders, personality disorders, and elsewhere. They include disorders in which the individual appears to lack sufficient motivation and/or behavioral control to conform to society's standards of conduct. These disorders are quite disruptive to society as the individuals who have them tend to prey on or harm others. They are often quite difficult to treat. So, it is not surprising that these disorders present a dilemma for society. Are people so diagnosed responsible for their behavior? If they commit a crime, should they be incarcerated or receive treatment? We have not sufficiently answered these questions at the present time.

Oppositional defiant disorder is defined by a pattern of angry/irritable mood and argumentative/defiant behavior. It was previously classified as a disorder of childhood and adolescence. We have included one case for your review. This case is drawn from *The Lanahan Cases in Developmental Psychopathology, Second Edition* (Bernheim, K.F., Rescorla, L., and Rocissano, L.), and includes a discussion of developmental issues. We have also included a case of conduct disorder and one new to this edition of kleptomania.

This category also includes intermittent explosive disorder (failure to control aggressive outbursts), conduct disorder (a youthful precursor to antisocial personality disorder in adults), pyromania (fire-setting), and other or unspecified disorders of impulse control and conduct.

CASE 38

OPPOSITIONAL-DEFIANT DISORDER: THE CASE OF TIMMY G.

TIMMY WAS A SMALL, slightly built nine-year-old boy who had been referred for mental health treatment by his parents, at the suggestion of his pediatrician. An intellectually gifted youngster, in second grade Timmy had been identified as having a reading disability. Despite receiving specialized educational services, Timmy was doing poorly in his third-grade class. The problem, as reported by his teacher, was that he rarely turned in his homework, and when he did it was likely to be sloppy or incomplete. He had also been referred to the principal several times in recent months for refusing to work on an in-class project and for repeatedly interrupting class discussions. He was fine, his teacher reported, as long as not much was asked of him and as long as things went his way. When they didn't, he quickly became sullen and rude.

The therapist chose to interview Timmy's parents before meeting with Timmy. Mrs. G., a teacher's aide in the same school district, confirmed that Timmy tolerated frustration poorly at home as well as at school. He seemed irritable and argumentative much of the time, fighting her over homework, household chores, and bedtime. When asked to describe his positive traits, Mrs. G. hesitated briefly. Then she talked about his creativity and ability to work with his hands. He could also be pleasant at times and had a good sense of humor when he wasn't annoyed at someone or something.

Mr. G. worked night shift as a prison guard in a nearby minimum-security state prison. He reported that he didn't see as much of Timmy's problematic behavior as his wife did because he often slept until after Timmy and his younger brother had eaten dinner. They only had an hour or two together as a family before the children's bedtime on weeknights. On weekends, Mr. G. moonlighted as an emergency medical technician, so his contact with his children was, by necessity, fairly limited.

Generally, when Mr. G. asked Timmy to do something, it was done, although often with a scowl, foot stomping, or rolling eyes. Mr. G. considered it normal for a boy to resist doing what he was asked. He had been like that himself, he reported, and he was not inclined to worry about it much. His wife, he said, just wasn't firm enough with Timmy. She tended to use a disciplinary strategy she had learned about called "time out," a version of sitting in the corner, whereas he himself opted for a more activist approach. He felt that moving Timmy bodily from in front of the television when he resisted, or providing the occasional slap on the backside, was more likely to be successful.

The tension in the consulting room mounted noticeably as Mr. G. offered these opinions in a manner that seemed to imply that any disagreement was patently idiotic. For a few moments, nobody spoke. Finally, the therapist commented that it was natural for parents to have somewhat different perspectives on a child's behavior. Mrs. G. then muttered, "Yeah, his perspective and the wrong perspective."

What emerged in the ensuing conversation was that the marriage had been fairly rocky for some time. Mrs. G. felt generally unsupported by Mr. G. She complained that he never took her out, never complimented her cooking or cleaning, and never bought her little gifts. Recently, he had even forgotten her birthday completely and seemed not to care when she felt wounded by it.

For his part, Mr. G. felt that nothing he did was ever good enough for his wife. He worked long hours to support the family while she worked six hours a day and had summers off. He didn't hang out at bars. He didn't cheat on her. He tried to spend a few hours each week with her and the children. In return, she begrudged his hunting in the fall, nagged him about helping with housework, and fought with him any time he wanted to spend money on anything other than clothes and food.

At the end of the initial interview, the therapist suggested that perhaps they might begin with some sessions with Mr. and Mrs. G. alone. The goal would be to strengthen the parental unit so that Timmy would face a more united front and so that home life would be less tense. While Mrs. G. was willing to agree to this plan, Mr. G. was not. He did not have the time, he said, to come for regular sessions. In his mind, Timmy's behavior was fine when he was around and it was his wife who needed the help. Further, he said, pointedly turning toward his wife, money was short and they could not easily afford extended therapy. Again, silence fell. Finally, the therapist suggested that they go home and think about how they might like to proceed and give him a call. Not surprisingly, he did not hear from them again.

Thinking about the Case

All children are oppositional from time to time. To receive a diagnosis of oppositional disorder, a child (or adolescent) must exhibit a pattern of hostile, defiant, and negativistic behavior that lasts at least six months. These children lose their temper easily and tend to be argumentative and even spiteful. They may behave in purposely annoying ways, refuse to do what is asked of them, and blame others when things go wrong. Unlike youngsters with conduct disorder, they do not consistently violate the rights of others; rather, they seem hypersensitive to making sure that their own rights (as they perceive them) are not violated. Oppositional-defiant disorder may co-occur with other disorders of childhood or adolescence. It is not uncommon for these children to be depressed, to have learning disabilities like Timmy's, or to have attention-deficit hyperactivity disorder.

An oppositional behavior pattern can result from an interaction of many factors: the child's genetically determined temperament, the adequacy of parental limit setting, the level of stress in a child's environment and the child's own strategies for managing stress, parental modeling and reinforcement of oppositional behavior, and peer group influences, among others. We can surmise, in Timmy's case, that his father's tacit acceptance of his behavior, his parents' inability to agree on how to manage his oppositional behavior, the stress imposed by his reading disability, and his own inadequately developed capacity to tolerate frustration are all implicated. The general level of marital discord and tension in the household and the absence of his father in his daily life may also play a role.

The two most common modes of treatment for oppositional-defiant disorder are behavioral treatment and family therapy. In behavioral treatment, parents and teachers are taught to reward cooperative behavior consistently and to ignore or punish oppositional behavior. Sometimes, a token system is used, in which a child can earn tokens with good behavior. The tokens can then be exchanged for a treat, a toy, or time spent alone with a parent in a special activity. For this treatment to work, the target behaviors must be clearly defined, the rewards must be things the child genuinely wants, and the system must be rigorously applied. For example, if a parent ignores most oppositional behavior but responds when the child escalates to the point of having a temper tantrum, the parent may be inadvertently reinforcing the tantrum with attention, thereby increasing the probability of its occurring again. A behavioral plan is virtually impossible to implement if parents undermine each other as Timmy's parents did. In cases like this, family-oriented counseling may be a preferable intervention.

Family therapy is based on the premise that the dysfunctional behaviors play a role in maintaining family homeostasis or that interactional factors are responsible for maintaining the behavior. One might hypothesize, for example, that Timmy's behavior serves a purpose in taking the focus off the marital problems his parents are experiencing. Or one might wonder whether Timmy is acting out (or imitating) Mr. G.'s anger at his wife. Or, more simply, one might surmise that reducing the level of parental dysharmony and increasing their ability to co-parent would help them respond more effectively to Timmy's provocative behavior.

Both forms of treatment can be combined in what is called "behavioral family therapy." In this form of treatment family members come together to develop a behavioral plan in which the target behaviors, the rewards, and the punishments are all spelled out, often in the form of a written contract.

Timmy's case illustrates how the choice and timing of a treatment intervention can make a difference in a case. The therapist's decision to offer marital therapy so early in his relationship with Mr. and Mrs. G. was probably, in hindsight, an error. In doing so, he appears to have scared them off. He might have done better to meet with Timmy first or to try a few sessions with the whole family present, keeping the focus on Timmy rather than on the marriage. In general, it is best to start with what the family defines as the problem, rather than what the therapist thinks is the "real" problem.

The prognosis for untreated oppositional-defiant disorder is extremely variable. In some cases, youngsters progress to more serious rule-breaking behavior as they get older. They may then be rediagnosed with conduct disorder. In other cases, they seem to grow out of it, becoming more tolerant of limit setting with time. Often, these youngsters will continue to have similar problems into adulthood: conflicts with bosses and loved ones, difficulty accepting responsibility, sullen resistance to perceived demands. Generally, the less severe and prolonged the behavior, the better the prognosis.

The outcome of treated cases is also variable, depending on which and how many of the variables are sustaining the behaviors. The higher the parents' level of motivation, intelligence, and ability to cooperate with each other and with the treatment plan, the better the prognosis. The fewer the outside stresses and the stronger the outside supports experienced by the family the better. Prognosis will also be improved to the extent the therapist makes an accurate assessment of the biological, psychological, and environmental factors involved and develops a plan that addresses as many of these as possible.

The Developmental Perspective

Everybody has heard of the "terrible twos." At about this age, children learn the meaning (and power) of the word "no." They begin to assert their own independence and resist attempts by others to control them. Thus, oppositionality is a universal and normal development. At this point, cultural and social determinants begin to exert an impact on the child's development. Some cultures (and some parents) rigorously enforce discipline, teaching children to subordinate their needs and wishes to those of the parents. Others value independence and initiative and will tolerate more defiance from children. In any case, the preschool years are taken up by socializing children to act appropriately in a variety of settings.

Entering school presents another challenge for youngsters. Now they must conform their behavior to the demands of a new set of adults (and increasingly to peers as well). If their previous socialization has prepared them well and their own temperament allows them to tolerate frustration, they will make this transition smoothly, treating their teachers with the same respect and compliance they have learned to apply to their parents. If, on the other hand, they have been inadequately socialized (or socialized to a set of rules that is markedly different from that found in school) or have impaired ability to delay gratification of their own needs, they may have a difficult time accommodating themselves to the level of behavioral self-control required by the school setting.

Even if a child has managed the transition to school well, entering adolescence presents another adaptive challenge. Here the youngster's job is to become an independently functioning adult, gradually relying more on his or her own judgment than on that of others. Therefore, it is common for parents to see another surge of oppositionality from about thirteen through about sixteen or so. Youngsters of this age often think of their parents as dumb, outdated, embarrassing, and overcontrolling. They resist doing what is asked of them, because it seems to them a threat to their ability to choose for themselves what they will do. They argue, pout, and sometimes defy in an attempt to develop confidence in themselves.

Again, cultural and familial values will have an enormous influence on how youngsters travel through this developmental phase. In some cultures (and in some families), overt oppositionality is the exception rather than the rule, whereas in others the opposite is true. The child's own temperament and psychology will also affect this journey. Generally, youngsters who have been relatively mature, successful, and self-confident proceed through adolescence with less defiance, probably because they have less need to prove themselves to themselves. Children who have had difficulties finding a successful niche for themselves during the earlier school years may, at adolescence, identify with a more marginal peer group, in which oppositionality to the dominant culture is the badge of identification. These youngsters are then at greater risk for difficulties as they move through the developmental tasks of the adolescent years. They may, for example, devalue education and drop out of or do poorly in school or they may become involved in self-destructive substance abuse. Again, parents who are able to maintain standards while showing increasing flexibility and willingness to allow their growing children to make and take responsibility for decisions will minimize stimuli for oppositionality.

Questions to Consider

1. What do you think Timmy's prognosis is? Why? If you think his prognosis is poor, what might be done to change it?
2. Everybody knows someone who is oppositional by nature. Whom do you know who is like this? What biological, social, or psychological factors have you assumed were implicated in his or her behavior?
3. How did your own parents handle oppositional behavior in you and your siblings? What were the strengths and weaknesses of their strategies?
4. Consider movies, books, videos, television, celebrities, the news, and so on. Do you think American popular culture encourages or inhibits oppositional-defiant behavior? Give examples to support your opinion. If you wanted to reduce oppositionality in adolescents, would you change the culture in some way? How?

CASE 39

ANTISOCIAL PERSONALITY: THE CASE OF WILLIAM HARDIN

GANGS HAVE BECOME A UBIQUITOUS and frightening feature on the American landscape. In a society in which familial and cultural institutions have broken down, gang norms and relationships can replace those that are no longer available elsewhere. One particularly horrifying gang activity is known as "wilding." This is savage violence without comprehensible motive like robbery or personal antagonism, perpetrated on victims seemingly chosen at random. Wilding crimes, like the widely publicized near fatal attack on a jogger in New York's Central Park which occurred in the spring of 1985, seem to be engaged in for fun and amusement. Most gangs are not organized around violence as a central principle, nor are most incidences of gang violence examples of wilding. Rather, violence occurs more often in the service of economic, turf-protection, or group cohesion reasons. Similarly, many gang members are not primarily antisocial in orientation. They are capable of love, loyalty, and conformity to rules—the rules of the gang rather than the rules of the larger society. However, wilding gangs tend to be loose-knit groups composed of more isolated, disturbed youngsters. Many of these fit the classic profile of the individual with antisocial personality disorder.

William Hardin is a real person. His case history is drawn from *Gangs* written by two sociologists, Scott Cummings and Daniel J. Monti (New York: State University of New York Press, 1993). In April 1983 he was found guilty of capital murder in the beating deaths of three elderly residents of Rosedale Heights, an urban community of about ten thousand people located in the Greater Fort Worth, Texas, metropolitan area. He was also linked to several rapes, street robberies, and residential burglaries. Most of the victims were between seventy and eighty-five years of age. See if you think he meets the criteria for antisocial personality disorder.

William was twenty years old when he was arrested for murder. By that time he had already been involved in many incidents of burglary, petty theft, and car theft. Money from these crimes usually went to buy drugs. He was a fairly heavy alcohol user, and also used marijuana, hashish, and cocaine. He had one child, age three, whom he never saw and whom he did not support. He had no girlfriend, but rather a series of casual, emotionally unattached sexual connections. He happened to be working at the time of his arrest, in a job that paid $4.00 per hour. He had never held a job more than a few months at a time.

William was the fourth of seven siblings. He had never met his father and knew him only by name. He had brothers and sisters by different fathers. His mother had been absent from the home for several years, and William had lived with an older brother, who had tried, unsuccessfully, to parent him, and an older sister with whom he was living at the time of his arrest. He seemed emotionally unconnected to his siblings.

William had a brief and unrewarding school experience. His tested intelligence was lower than average and he had limited verbal skills. By the time he was in fifth or sixth grade, he was out of school more than he was in, often leaving in the middle of the day to go have sex with one or another girl. He was expelled for truancy on at least one occasion, and finally dropped out of school altogether in seventh grade.

From the age of fourteen on, William was on the streets. He was not associated with a formal gang, but rather seemed a marginal character in the neighborhood dramas, joining in when the impulse moved him. He liked getting high and he liked sex. Other than that, he seemed unmoved by anything or anybody.

Thinking About the Case

Criminal behavior, impulsivity, aggressiveness, and lack of remorse—core features of antisocial personality disorder, and core features of William Hardin's personalty. Do all people who are habitual criminals have antisocial personality disorder? The answer is clearly "no." People who steal or deal drugs because they have few legitimate opportunities to make a living may be capable of self-restraint, planfulness, committed relationships, and strict adherence to a code of behavior. These individuals may exhibit antisocial behavior (by the standards of the larger society), but not signs of antisocial personality disorder. Antisocial personality implies that the individual's behavior arises, to at least some extent, out of conditions that are beyond his or her control. The behaviors are thought to be compelled rather than chosen.

People with this disorder are distinguishable from ordinary criminals in three ways. First, their crimes are impulsive and often irrational (although they may be capable of more rational crimes as well). Second, they lack a conscience, guilt, and the ability to care deeply about others. Finally, they seem unable to experience strong, sustained emotions. Rather, they seem possessed of violent, brief feelings that quickly give way to new ones. Only a small percentage of people who are incarcerated are antisocial personalities. Further, many people with features of this disorder are not behind bars.

Clearly, the ability to control one's behavior and connect emotionally with others is a continuous, not a discrete variable. How much lack of control, impulsivity, or self-centeredness is enough to qualify an individual for a diagnosis of antisocial personality disorder? The line is arbitrary. This represents a problem with the diagnostic system in that it introduces a strong element of subjectivity in what should, in principle, be an objective process.

To what extent are antisocial behaviors the result of some individual psychopathology and to what extent can they be attributed to social and economic forces? In *Gangs* the authors suggest that in certain circumstances "crime becomes a rational response to the absence of tangible opportunities" (p. 70), and that wilding gangs "are aberrant and antisocial adaptations to the cycle of poverty and racism prevalent within urban ghettos like Rosedale" (p. 70). Like the other disorders we have studied, a biopsychosocial explanation seems applicable. Studies suggest that there may be inherited dysfunctions in normal arousal mechanisms in people with antisocial personality disorder. However, brutality and extreme conflict in the family have also been implicated. Many antisocial sons have antisocial fathers, leading to the possibility that modeling may also be a contributing factor. In any case, we are likely many decades away from being able to pinpoint the causes or cures of this disorder from which so much misery springs.

Questions to Consider

1. The incidence of antisocial personality disorder is about 4.5 percent in men and less than one percent in women. Why might this be so?
2. Why might the average age of onset of this disorder be earlier in men than in women?

3. Symptoms associated with antisocial personality disorder seem to improve spontaneously as the individual reaches his thirties and forties. What are some reasons why this might be so?
4. Can you design a study to tease out biological from social factors in the development of antisocial personality disorder? After you have done so, play devil's advocate and critique your own study.
5. What aspects of our society might nurture the development of antisocial personality disorder? What steps might be taken to reduce the incidence of this disorder?
6. Some public figures—in sports, entertainment, and politics—appear to have antisocial personality disorder. Pick one and defend your choice.

CASE 40

KLEPTOMANIA: THE CASE OF DONALD S.

DONALD WAS REFERRED FOR THERAPY by his colleague at the office. She could see that he had been pretty depressed since his wife had left him about three months prior. She was worried that he would start drinking again if he didn't get some help. AA meetings alone didn't seem to be cutting it.

Donald arrived promptly for his first visit, looking disheveled and forlorn. He had not shaved and his socks were unmatched. His clothes were clean but wrinkled. His face was gray, and his eyes had no spark of life in them. It was clear that his colleague had made a good call.

Donald offered his history in a toneless monologue. He was the middle of three children in an intact, Catholic family. Both parents were heavy drinkers. He had attended Catholic school, as had his siblings, and had gone to Catholic college. The religious background had not stopped him from becoming an alcoholic like his parents and his brother. He found work as an accountant at a large corporation where he had been continuously employed for eighteen years. In the tenth year of his employment he had almost lost his job due to the effects of his drinking on his work performance. He was given the option of entering substance abuse treatment or being fired. He chose the treatment and had been sober ever since with the ongoing support of Alcoholics Anonymous support groups. His work performance in recent years had been exemplary and had earned him several commendations and bonuses.

His personal life had been somewhat less successful. He had had numerous "addictive relationships" throughout his first and second marriages. His third marriage had seemed to be going well, despite his occasional outside dalliances, until his wife abruptly left him . . . for another woman. She took the furniture but left the cats.

He was alone once again, and he didn't like it one little bit. He also felt humiliated by his inadequacy in that he had made his wife choose a woman for her next companion. He had been a good deal older than she, it was true, and he had not always been one hundred percent faithful, also true, but he felt that, on balance, he had been a good husband. But apparently, she had felt differently.

Early therapy sessions focused on stabilizing Donald's mood. He was prescribed antidepressant medications by his personal physician in consultation with his therapist. Therapy sessions were conducted twice weekly to begin with since Donald was projecting a sense of hopelessness and had voiced a passive wish to die. He wasn't suicidal, he said, but he wouldn't mind if he didn't wake up the next morning. He was working hard to maintain his sobriety, but he wondered aloud why he bothered. With the therapist's help, though, Donald remembered that previous psychic pain had passed with time, and he began to realize that his current suffering would likely pass as well. Discussions about his wife's sexuality helped Donald realize that his sexual performance probably had very little to do with her choice to leave him, though the difference in their stages of life, his self-centered perspective, and her own sexual confusion might well be relevant. These explanations were less painful to him than the thought that he had been sexually deficient.

Gradually, he began to feel better—more hopeful. He began to enjoy his job again and reported that his appetite and sleep had improved. At about the three month point, the question of whether to continue therapy arose. Initial symptoms had been resolved, and Donald was functioning as he had before. Donald insisted that he still felt fragile, and felt ongoing therapy was warranted. He wanted to work on understanding his "addictive" relationships so that he might make better choices in future. He also wanted to feel more peaceful and more authentic. Underneath the bluster, he said, his self-esteem had always been low.

Donald had found himself a woman therapist. It seems he had some idea, perhaps not even conscious, that he could manipulate her as he had manipulated so many other women. He flattered, cajoled, subtly flirted with her. When he coyly asked her why she hadn't sent him a birthday card on his birthday, she had replied "I'm your therapist, not your girlfriend. It would help our work together if you kept that in mind." Donald was stunned . . . and embarrassed . . . and intrigued. This interaction marked the beginning of a more honest relationship between them. They began to discuss how he felt about and related to women. They talked at length about his relationship with his mother whom he had at once loved, feared, and disliked intensely. Her opinion of him had mattered a great deal when he was a youngster, but her drinking had interfered with the consistency and rationality of her behavior towards him and his siblings. He couldn't count on her. He had developed strategies for mollifying her when she was angry and for avoiding her as he grew to adulthood.

For many sessions, Donald worked to understand how his relationship with his mother, his frustrated expectations, and strategies for managing his feelings affected his relationships with women in his adult life. He began to understand that he had treated women as objects to be manipulated, rather than as persons with feelings of their own.

Despite the positive progression of therapy Donald returned time and again to feelings of worthlessness. He began hinting at a secret that he had not told anyone. His therapist commented that hiding from his therapist was like hiding from himself. He had to be honest if he hoped to continue to make gains. Finally, Donald revealed his secret: he had been stealing small items from stores since he was a young teenager. Sometimes he took razor blades, or a paperback book, or a candy bar. The items were never expensive, and sometimes he didn't even want them. He just wanted to succeed in stealing them. While the behavior had waxed and waned, it had never really stopped. He had continued to this day, sometimes more than once a week, sometimes only once every few weeks.

Donald described a cyclical pattern: first he would experience a gradually increasing sense of tension coupled with fantasies of stealing. This preoccupation would grow in intensity until he felt compelled to steal something. The moment this was accomplished he felt a sense of relief and elation. But hours later, at home, he would be overcome with feelings of shame and guilt. After some days, the pattern would begin again. Donald understood that his stealing was compulsive, as his drinking had been, but he had been unable to curb it. There were no Thieves Anonymous groups. There was no one to call when he felt the urge to steal. Besides, he felt vaguely entitled to the small objects he would steal. They were not worth a lot of money, he rationalized, nor had he taken them from an individual person. He would never do that. Often he donated what he had stolen to a homeless shelter. He couldn't really see that his behavior was hurting anyone. Still, in more rational moments, he knew that the stealing was not only wrong, but unhealthy.

Donald's therapist had two choices: explore the psychological roots of the stealing in the hopes that Donald would choose to stop, or take a more behavioral approach to the problem. She chose the latter. Intending to interfere with the denial associated with the stealing, she asked Donald to describe what would likely happen if he got caught. Despite his asssertions that this was unlikely as it had never happened yet, she still insisted that he face the possibility directly. She got him to describe (and experience) the shame and guilt that he would feel when his name appeared in the small town newspaper. She asked him how his colleagues at work and his boss would respond. She asked him to describe how he would feel standing in front of a judge or even having to explain to an attorney what he had done. She asked him what his siblings and his current girlfriend would feel and say when they found out what he had done. While describing these consequences Donald broke out in a sweat. To him it was like the nightmare where you find yourself naked on the street, or at work—embarrassing in the extreme. The therapist asked Donald to engage in an "experiment" in which he would spend a few minutes several times a day imagining himself getting caught and feeling the feelings that this brought. He reluctantly agreed.

When Donald returned for his next session a month later, he reported that he was astonished to find that his urge to steal was almost nonexistent. In fact, when the thought crossed his mind now and again, he almost immediately felt nauseated and anxious. He had had some dreams in which he had gotten caught stealing, and awoke with an acute sense of doom followed by relief that it was only a dream. Donald's therapist cautioned him to continue his "practice" sessions despite his feeling that the problem was solved. He again agreed to do so for another month.

Donald did not return to stealing. Subsequent discussions explored the role of denial in his life, his persistent avoidance of considering the consequences of his self-destructive behaviors. They also covered his need for risk and his penchant for thrill-seeking behavior. Drinking and womanizing both had thrill-seeking aspects for him. He and his therapist also discussed familial and religious roots of his need to "cross the line." Sharing his "crimes" with his therapist, who continued to value him, even as she disapproved of the behaviors, proved a breakthrough for Donald with respect to his deeply held belief in his "badness."

After a time, Donald was able to share his history of stealing in his home AA group. He was surprised to find that he was not the only person who stole or who had hidden certain behaviors from the group. This further helped reduce his sense of shame and increased the trust which group members felt for each other. Gradually, his self-esteem began to heal, and the verbal bluster with which he propped himself up diminished. He remained in therapy and involved in AA for many years.

Thinking About The Case

Kleptomania is diagnosed when there is a recurrent failure to resist the impulse to steal. It differs from simple thievery in that the stolen items are often unwanted or unneeded, and the individual has the intent not to steal. The behavior is associated with a great deal of guilt and shame which also differentiates it from common theft. It is diagnosed, in DSM-5 as an impulse control disorder.

Donald's case is typical in that kleptomania often co-occurs with other psychological or behavioral disorders, particularly addictions, anxiety-disorders, and depression. It also is diagnosed more often in individuals with family members who have addictions, obsessive-compulsive disorder, or other impulse control disorders. While the cause or causes of kleptomania are unknown, it has been hypothesized that compulsive stealing, like other addictive and impulse-control disorders, may be related to low levels of serotonin or dopamine, two of the neurotransmitters most involved with pleasure and reward. In addition, Donald's case lends itself to psychological hypotheses—perhaps his low self-esteem contributed to a need to buoy himself up with repetitive "success," and stealing proved a way to achieve this. Alternatively, maybe the stealing began as a way to violate the rules of, and thus gain independence from, his mother. By stealing he could repudiate her, though guilt and shame derived from failing to meet her expectations. As this conflict remained unresolved throughout his life, the stealing continued.

Treatment for kleptomania is generally of the cognitive-behavioral variety, though outcome studies are scarce. Donald's therapist chose one of these therapies, called "covert sensitization," to treat Donald. In this type of treatment, the individual is asked to imagine (hence the term "covert") painful emotional consequences of stealing. Then, in Pavlovian fashion, the unpleasant feelings thus produced would come to be associated with stealing itself. This appears to have worked particularly well for Donald. The success of this treatment depends, of course, on the ability and willingness of the client to actually engage in the necessary imagery. A related technique is called "aversion therapy." It involves pairing an actual painful consequence with the urge to steal. An example might be having the client hold his breath for as along as possible when he felt the urge to steal. A different cognitive-behavioral treatment would be "systematic desensitization," in which the client is taught to relax in the presence of the urge to steal. This would, in principle, counteract the physiological excitement and reduce the need to steal.

While medications have sometimes been tried, there is little if any research on the effect of medications on kleptomania. Both selective serotonin reuptake inhibitors (SSRI's) and opioid antagonists have been used.

Again, though no studies have been done, it might be that Twelve-Step groups like Alcoholics Anonymous and Overeaters Anonymous would be helpful. It is interesting that Donald, despite a long history of AA involvement, had never shared his stealing with his peers. The shame associated with stealing was, for him, far greater than the shame associated with drinking. He was only able to disclose this behavior in the context of a long and trusted relationship with an individual therapist. But, once having admitted to the behavior aloud, he was able to access the support within AA to help maintain his recovery. There are numerous "Shoplifter's Anonymous" type groups and resources, both live in some larger communities and on-line.

Questions To Consider

1. Kleptomania is diagnosed more often in women than in men. What are some reasons why this might be so?
2. It has been suggested that shoplifting and stealing in general is related to our culture of consumerism. What do you think of this idea?
3. Why do you think that Donald's own shame and guilt was not effective in curbing his stealing, while the "covert desensitization" used by his therapist was successful? What do your ideas about this question tell you about the biopsychosocial roots of this behavior?
4. If it is true that impulse-control disorders like addictions, stealing, gambling, and others have common roots, what might these be? How would you go about answering this question if you had unlimited resources and a scientific frame of mind?

LANAHAN NOTES

Disruptive, Impulse Control and Conduct Disorders

Characteristics of disruptive, impulse control, conduct disorders

Generally becomes apparent in childhood or adolescence

Individual manifests behaviors that violate the rights of others

The behaviors bring the person into significant conflict with societal norms or authority figures

These disorders often take a developmental trajectory, but diagnosis of an early disorder is not a guarantee of later diagnosis of more serious disorders

Types of disruptive, impulse control, conduct disorders

Oppositional defiant disorder (ODD): A repetitive and persistent pattern of behavior encompassing:

Angry and irritable mood: loss of temper; easily annoyed; often angry

Argumentative and defiant behavior: often argues; actively defies or refuses to comply; deliberately annoys; blames others

Vindictiveness

Distinguished from normal developmental behaviors by the frequency of behaviors, e.g., once a week for children under 5 years old

Intermittent explosive disorder (IED):

Verbal or physical aggression toward property, animals, or other individuals causing destruction or injury that is grossly out of proportion to any provocation or precipitating event

Outbursts come on suddenly, not premeditated

Conduct Disorder (CD): A repetitive and persistent pattern of behavior violating the basic rights of others as shown in:

Aggression toward other individuals, e.g., bullying, initiating fights sometimes using a weapon; for older adolescents, mugging, extortion, rape

Hurting animals

Vandalism, including fire setting

Deceitfulness and theft: e.g., breaking and entering, setting up "cons"

Serious violation of rules: truancy and staying out all night before the age of 13

Antisocial personality disorder (also described in Chapter 18, Personality Disorders); includes many of the same behaviors as conduct disorders and the individual is 18 years or older

Pyromania: individual deliberately sets fires for arousal before the act (causing biological and/or affective tension) and for release of tension (causing pleasure, gratification) during or after fire setting

Kleptomania: recurrent failure to resist impulses to steal objects that are not needed for personal use or for their monetary value where arousal is experienced before the act (biological and/or affective tension) and release of said tension (pleasure, gratification) during or after stealing.

Risk factors

Temperamental factors: problems in emotional regulation, e.g., poor frustration tolerance, high levels of emotional reactivity

Runs in families: probably combination of genetics and modeling

Social factors: social class, family chaos, strong or inconsistent discipline

Treatment

Emphasis on early intervention to avoid difficult-to-break patterns of behavior

When working with a child, involve the entire family in treatment

Provide parent training and support services

Involve a team: parents, school counselors, social service agencies

Prognosis for conduct disorders and antisocial personality disorder is poor, regardless of treatment

CHAPTER SIXTEEN

Substance Related and Addictive Disorders

It may seen odd, at first, to find substance use disorders and gambling disorder under the same category. Yet they share several properties that we call "addictive." First, they involve loss of self-control. Second, those afflicted continue the behavior in the face of clearly adverse consequences. Third, these disorders appear to reflect a compulsion or an irresistible need to engage in the behavior in question. Fourth, they show "tolerance," which is the need for increasingly larger amounts of the behavior or substance over time.

Substance abuse is arguably the number one health problem in most Western societies. Alcohol- and cigarette-related morbidity and mortality are enormous. Alcohol, for example, is now the third leading cause of death in the United States trailing only coronary heart disease and cancer, a substantial percentage of which is related to cigarette smoking.

Included in this chapter are two substance abuse disorders. In the first, alcohol abuse shades into dependence and is treated successfully. In the second, mixed-substance-abuse results in a psychotic episode, or "bad trip." Both cases are fairly common.

Gambling Disorder (also known as compulsive gambling) occurs in approximately one percent of the American population. Like substance addictions it takes an enormous physical, financial, social, and emotional toll on its sufferers. We have included a case description of an elderly woman whose gambling is worsened by the loss of her husband. Her gambling problem becomes so severe that she contemplates suicide.

CASE 41

EMERGING ALCOHOLISM: THE CASE OF SIMON S.

SIMON S., A FORTY-TWO-YEAR-OLD attorney was brought, somewhat reluctantly, to therapy by his wife of seventeen years, Carla. The couple were having increasingly painful arguments over the last year or two, and while neither was considering leaving the marriage, they both felt that they needed help in communicating more effectively with each other.

Carla took responsibility for her share of the problem. She thought she might be having a "midlife crisis" in which her lifelong defense of "clamming up" when she was disappointed or angry was breaking down. She found herself nagging and arguing and feeling resentful much of the time. She wondered, too, whether perimenopausal hormonal changes might not be relevant as well. Her complaints about Simon included his not being as "accepting" of her parents as she would have liked, his not spending enough time with the children (two pre-teen daughters), his overcommitment to spending time at a lake property that had been part of his family for several generations, and his lack of help with household chores.

Simon did not dispute these charges. For his part, he wished Carla, a teacher, would not become so preoccupied with school and the children that she neglected to spend time with him. They didn't have as much sex as he would have liked, nor as much "down time." Mostly, though, it seemed as if Simon would have been happy if Carla hadn't been so unhappy. He described her as a "terrific teacher and mother," felt "incredibly lucky to be married to her," and thought that, in general, she was "just great." He was perplexed by her growing dissatisfaction with him and seemed genuinely to want to work on the problem.

Both Carla and Simon had had previous mental health treatment. Carla, three years previously, had purposely lost one hundred pounds. In conjunction with her diet, she underwent regular psychotherapy in which she explored issues related to self-image, subtle societal messages about weight and self-worth, and familial patterns of relating around food. Her parents, farmers, were both alive. She also had two older brothers, one of whom still lived at home and seemed to function at a marginal level. The other was married and, from all appearances, successful. Carla maintained a close relationship with her parents, particularly her father, and she felt that her husband was jealous of that relationship. She also played the mediator between her brothers when they quarrelled.

Simon had a history of clinical depression for which he had been treated with both psychotherapy and antidepressant medications, although he had had neither for several years. Only his mother was still alive, his father having died three years earlier. He had an older brother who had a serious drinking problem. His maternal grandfather and maternal uncle were also alcoholics. Simon, himself, reported "occasionally" drinking to drunkenness. Carla voiced concern that the frequency of these episodes seemed to be increasing lately. Depression also ran in his mother's side of the family.

At the second session, Carla again raised her concerns about Simon's drinking. She reported that their daughters and his mother were also concerned. Simon acknowledged that he might, perhaps, have a "small problem" in that once he began to drink, he couldn't seem to stop. He would decide to have one beer, and it would turn into a six-pack. One glass of wine would turn into a full bottle. He also acknowledged drinking alone sometimes, generally while working in his basement shop. Drinking beer while he worked helped him relax. Carla pointed out that Simon also drank during periods when he was taking antidepressant medication, despite the doctor's admonishment that he should not.

The tone of this conversation was exploratory and respectful rather than confrontative. By the end of the session, Simon had agreed to maintain sobriety for one month to see what this might teach him about the role alcohol played in his life.

In the session one month later, Simon admitted that he had been unable to keep his abstinence pledge. He had had alcohol at a party. In addition, Carla revealed that she had found Valium tablets for which Simon had no prescription. Valium is a medication used to treat anxiety and muscle spasms. It is cross-addictive with alcohol and commonly abused by people who also abuse alcohol.

Carla was angry and disappointed. Both reported that their relationship had gotten bleaker, with a virtual absence of loving behaviors on either of their parts. Simon agreed to consider accepting a referral to the local alcoholism treatment agency. He also agreed to consider attending Alcoholics Anonymous. However, he had serious concerns about both these routes. As a professional in the community, he had a certain reputation to uphold. If word got out that he was receiving treatment for alcohol abuse, his authority and the respect he was granted would certainly diminish. He still felt that he could successfully abstain from drinking without outside help. Carla agreed that he should have the opportunity to try again, and they spent the rest of that session and the next several working on ways to improve their communication and increase the level of trust and affection between them.

At each session, Simon's drinking behaviors and feelings were examined, at least briefly. He began to realize that, even though he had not been drinking recently, he continued to have strong cravings for alcohol. He had "made it" through Thanksgiving without a drink, but felt that he was "not out of the woods." Gradually, it dawned on him that the struggle with alcohol was going to be a protracted, possibly lifelong one.

Carla confessed that she had told their physician, who was also a personal friend, that Simon was working to overcome a drinking problem. Simon was dismayed, and talked movingly about his sense of shame and the stigma he felt. How could he look his friend in the eye, knowing that his friend now knew how "weak" he was? The therapist, with Carla's input, helped Simon to confront the truth—that many of his friends and relatives knew that he drank too much. He was particularly horrified when he learned from his wife that their daughters had been frightened and worried about his drinking. At the end of this session, Simon agreed to do two things: First, he would talk to his daughters about his drinking and assure them that he was going to work hard to stop, and second, he was going to speak with a colleague who had been attending Alcoholics Anonymous regularly since getting caught driving while intoxicated.

Over the next several sessions, held at monthly intervals, Simon remained abstinent, but he procrastinated about talking to his colleague. Carla admitted that one of the reasons she hated his spending time at the lake was because she knew that he and his brother would be drinking virtually the whole time they were there together. The lake property and the presence of his brother were both strong stimuli for drinking. By the next session, Simon had confronted his brother about their mutual drinking problems, but had received virtually no response. The couple continued to work on understanding each other's needs and feelings.

Six months into therapy, Simon had a major slip—he got drunk while home alone with one of his daughters. He was horrified and ashamed. Much to his relief, Carla handled the matter calmly. She told him that she knew how hard maintaining sobriety had been for him, that he had done better than she had expected him to, and that she felt he needed some assistance. He gratefully agreed to seek alcohol counseling. At the end of the session, they both rated the quality of their relationship as a seven or eight on a ten-point scale.

It took four more months, and one more episode of drinking, for Simon to overcome his resistance enough to actually make an appointment for evaluation at the alcohol treatment service. He had been gardening and had found an old, open bottle of wine on the back porch. Impulsively, he drank it.

Simon decided to seek treatment in a neighboring county so he would be less likely to run into friends and associates. At the suggestion of the alcoholism counselor by whom he had been evaluated, and with the support of his marriage therapist and his wife, he elected to attend outpatient group treatment three times a week for six weeks. This experience rapidly expanded his knowledge and ability to talk about his alcoholism. Carla attended several family meetings, in which the role of the spouse and other family members in rehabilitation was discussed.

At the insistence of his substance abuse counselor, Simon agreed to begin attending Alcoholics Anonymous meetings, and finally made contact with his colleague, who brought him to the first meeting. There, he heard about other people's experiences with alcohol and about strategies for preventing relapse. He learned that negative emotional states like "tired, hungry and lonely" were triggers for drinking. He learned that he had to avoid "people, places and things" that he had come to associate with drinking. He confronted the risk that being at the lake with his brother presented to him, and decided he would always take one of his children (or his wife) with him, and that he would promise that child that he would not drink. He felt sad at the loss of private time with his brother, but he knew that he would be unlikely to maintain sobriety in that context. He began to identify the social anxiety that had always plagued him, and that had been relieved so successfully by alcohol. He began to practice using social skills sober, and tolerated the discomfort that accompanied the practice.

Through all of this, Simon relied heavily on Carla's support and respect. For her part, she reported that their relationship had been substantially improved by Simon's abstinence. They continued to work on communicating their appreciation for each other, and on making space for each other's "passions"—Carla's for teaching and Simon's for gardening and the lake. They continue to attend monthly marital therapy sessions and may decide to do so for several years. They think of it as a sort of "insurance policy" against slipping back into old patterns of relating. Simon continues in Alcoholics Anonymous, and in biweekly individual counseling for his alcoholism. He expects to stay connected with AA indefinitely, perhaps for life.

Thinking About the Case

Alcohol is clearly the most serious drug of abuse in the United States and Western Europe. Excessive drinking is responsible for untold misery and cost at both the individual and societal level. Of the possibly ten million problem drinkers in the United States today, only one million are receiving treatment. Further, treatment is far from foolproof. Studies suggest that at age sixty-five, about one-third of problem drinkers are dead or disabled, one-third have successfully abstained or are drinking socially, and one-third are still trying to quit. Alcohol abuse is often accompanied by a number of other psychological disorders, including depression, anxiety, and antisocial personality disorder. Generally, the greater the level of overall psychopathology, the poorer the prognosis.

The case of Simon S. gives the lie to the commonly held belief that an alcoholic must hit bottom before he or she can begin to recover. While Simon's marriage and relationship with his children were beginning to be affected by his alcohol use, his occupational functioning and social relationships were, as yet, relatively unimpaired. Still, he was able to acknowledge that his drinking was becoming problematic and, after some additional evidence was brought to bear, he took steps that helped him to arrest the problem.

It is more common for people who abuse or are dependent on alcohol or other substances to be overwhelmed by "denial," an unconscious psychological defense mechanism that prevents the individual from accurately evaluating the meaning and consequences of his or her behavior. Examples of denial include the following: "I'm not an alcoholic—I only drink beer, never the hard stuff"; "I never drink before five o'clock in the afternoon"; "I could stop whenever I wanted to, but I don't want to"; "I never drive when I'm drinking, so I can't be an alcoholic." While there is some evidence of the presence of denial in Simon's case (for example, he needed several episodes of unwanted drinking to get him into treatment), his therapist and wife were able to break through relatively easily. Alcoholism is thought to be a progressive disorder, with the quantity consumed, tolerance to its effects, and denial increasing over time. Generally then, the earlier the intervention is made, the more likely it will be to work.

The course of Simon's ascent into sobriety is quite typical. Relapses are common, so that Alcoholics Anonymous teaches that one can be a "recovering" alcoholic but never a "recovered" one. Therapy aims to reduce the risk of relapse by identifying the circumstances or feelings that might predispose the individual to drink, and by teaching the person strategies for avoiding or managing those situations without drinking. For example, after Simon drank the open bottle of wine, he and Carla decided to make a sweep of the house, garage, and grounds to make sure that all bottles were gone. His decision to take one of his children to the lake with him, and his working on his social anxiety in therapy, are also relapse prevention strategies.

It is generally thought that working with the family of individuals with drinking problems can be crucial to their recovery prospects. Over time, family members may have accommodated to the drinking by trying to reduce the negative consequences of it. For example, a spouse might call the person's workplace to say he or she was ill, when in fact, drunkenness was the real problem. Or, the spouse might minimize the drinking when talking to friends or family, or nag incessantly about drinking which may raise the level of stress in the household and lead to increased, rather than decreased, alcohol consumption. These behaviors are called "co-dependent," meaning that the spouse has developed drinking-related behaviors just like the alcoholic. Children of alcoholic parents are, of course, also affected. Research suggests that they are at increased risk for a host of psychological problems as adolescents and adults. Therefore, one of the components of treatment aims to minimize the deleterious effects of alcohol abuse on the family system.

To date, no one treatment method has been shown to be obviously superior to another. Simon's case is typical in that a combination of interventions is used: marital therapy, individual psychotherapy, group treatment, and self-help in the form of Alcoholics Anonymous.

There are two serious controversies in the field of alcoholism treatment. First, it has long been held that abstinence is the only sensible therapy goal for an individual with alcoholism. However, recent research suggests that a sub-group of people who have a history of addictive drinking can achieve moderate, controlled social drinking. Many clinicians in the treatment community think such a notion is dangerous in that it may encourage alcoholics to remain in "denial." The second, related, controversy concerns whether alcoholism is even a "disease." If it is, then individuals with alcoholism are entitled to the rights and privileges of the sick role, for example, time off from work with pay when the "illness" makes work impossible. But some people think of alcoholism as a moral rather than a medical problem. This disagreement is unlikely to be resolved any time soon.

Questions to Consider

1. Why did Simon develop a drinking problem? What does your answer say about which model(s) you rely on to explain this disorder?

2. The line between alcoholism and alcohol abuse is a fine one and not all clinicians draw that line in the same place. Consider the criteria for substance abuse versus those for substance dependence. Does Simon's use meet the criteria for alcohol dependence, or might he be better thought of as a substance abuser?
3. Consider the drinking habits of your friends. Which of them might be at risk of developing a drinking problem? Why? Consider your own drinking habits in the same way.
4. When people drink too much, they generally experience dizziness, nausea, vomiting, and a headache. The next day they may suffer from a hangover, not to mention the negative consequences of their drinking-related behavior. How, then, would a behaviorist explain the development of compulsive drinking?
5. Do you think alcoholism and other problems of impulse-control, like pathological gambling, are truly "diseases?" Why or why not? What, if any data, would make you change your view?

CASE 42

MIXED SUBSTANCE ABUSE: THE CASE OF MIGUEL S.

MIGUEL S. WOKE TO FIND himself tied to a bed. Both his wrists and his ankles were lightly but securely bound with fabric straps. His head hurt and at first he was dazed and confused. Looking around, he ascertained that he was in a hospital—faint sounds from a far-off public-address system drifted into the sun-lit, double-bedded room. Before he could respond to the rising panic he was beginning to feel, Miguel noticed that the call button was placed near his right hand, where he could reach it. Soon after pressing it, a nurse came in and began to untie his restraints as she told him what had happened.

Apparently, Miguel had been admitted to the hospital the night before. He had been dropped off at the emergency room by a carful of "friends" who hadn't stayed around long enough to offer any information or to see that he was okay. He was dressed in blue jeans and a t-shirt, but he stood out from the rest of the people waiting for care because he was covered from head to toe with stripes and blobs of what appeared to be oil-based paint.

Alone and clearly very agitated, Miguel couldn't sit still. Instead, he had created quite a stir, pacing and hollering, "they're after us; they're following us." When asked who the "us" referred to, he had responded, "me . . . us, all of us, we're breaking apart and they're after us." Alternately paralyzed with fear and lashing out in a rage, he had been unable to speak coherently or to maintain his attention for more than a minute at a time. Every sound startled him and sometimes he stared fixedly at the emergency room door, as if he were seeing something horrible. Unable to calm him or to figure out initially what was wrong with him, the emergency room physician had ordered that Miguel be restrained, admitted, and tranquilized. It had required one policeman and two orderlies to carry out the physician's directives.

As the nurse spoke to him, Miguel began to remember bits and pieces of the evening, although most of what she told him about the emergency room was news to him. He had been smoking pot and drinking wine with his college housemates and their girlfriends. At some point, several of them had decided to drop some acid. Miguel's trip had begun in a pretty mellow way. An art major, he had been sketching and listening to music, when the urge to paint a wall-sized mural came over him. He went to his room and began to mix paints and spread them on the wall. The paints seemed to shimmer and pulse as he applied them in wide swaths to the large, empty space. He could hear the beat of the music through the floor of his room and he felt that the paint and music were moving in the same rhythm. He began to feel very certain that this painting would be his master work—that it would portray the unity of the universe and that, somehow, when people looked at it, the paints would move and they would hear music as he did while he painted.

As he thought about unity, Miguel realized that he and his painting were one and he felt the need to remove artificial boundaries. So he took off all of his clothes and began to paint himself with the same paint he had been using on the walls.

At some point, one of his housemates wandered by and was, of course, struck by the sight of Miguel, naked and furiously painting. At first he thought it was pretty funny, and called several of the others to come watch the artist at work. However, Miguel's response to his girlfriend's attempts to get him to put on some shorts alarmed everybody. He turned toward her, made the sign of the cross and spoke a few words that weren't English . . . and didn't seem to be Spanish, his first language, either. His emotional tone was angry, even threatening, and when he turned back to his painting with total singlemindedness, his friends didn't know what to do next. One of his housemates tried jokingly to cajole him into stopping for a while. Another brought him a cup of coffee which Miguel threw at the wall, using his hands to mix it into the paint. His friends decided to take definitive action when he urinated on the wall, again using his hands to mix the urine into the paint and coffee mixture. Knowing that calling the police or an ambulance would get them busted for sure, they overpowered their friend, threw some clothes on him, and took him to the emergency room of the nearest hospital.

Miguel was terrified and confused. His friends, he thought, must have been able to see that he was on the verge of making a huge breakthrough—why would they want to stop him? Perhaps they were not really his friends after all, but imposters who meant to see that the world would not be saved by his work. If so, they would certainly want to kill him. They must be taking him someplace to kill him. Screaming for help and lashing out, he nonetheless found himself inside the hospital door and the rest, as they say, was history.

Miguel was the third child in a family of six siblings. His father, a Mexican immigrant had married his mother, a non-Hispanic, when she was just eighteen. She was already pregnant with Miguel's older sister, Maria, at the time of their union. Mr. S. worked construction jobs in the summer and brought in unemployment money in the winter. Mrs. S. worked in a local factory, sewing women's clothing. The S.'s marriage was not an ideal one. They fought frequently and loudly—mostly about Mr. S.'s drinking and womanizing, and about Mrs. S.'s nagging and complaining. Sometimes Mr. S. would stay away for several days on end. Other times, Mrs. S. would take the children to her parents' house, where they spent most of their after-school time anyway, until her husband came to get her, all flowers and sweet talk.

Still, the family unit was strong in certain ways. Both parents were strict disciplinarians. Miguel and his siblings were expected to do well in school, to be respectful and polite to their elders, to do chores without complaining, to attend church each Sunday, and to obey their parents without question. The S.'s believed strongly that their children could do better than they had done in life, and they meant to see that it happened. In addition, Mrs. S.'s parents and siblings provided a ready-made support network for the children, while Mr. S.'s family members were all in Mexico City. Babysitters and playmates were always available, as were adults to listen to Miguel's problems. Mrs. S.'s family didn't exactly approve of Mr. S.'s ethnicity or behavior, though, and sometimes they let the children know it. Miguel always felt uncomfortable when that happened. He didn't know whether to defend his father or keep quiet. After all, he was part Mexican too, and anyway, his father was his father.

Miguel was thought of as pretty normal. His grades were good enough to keep his parents off his back, and he was a talented soccer player throughout junior and senior high school. He was gregarious and likable and had many friends. He was also attractive to the girls in his group. In fact, he began having sex when he was twelve, the same year he began using marijuana. Smoking marijuana and having sex were portals to adulthood among the young men who were his friends. Miguel was proud to have been accepted into the brotherhood of older guys and strove to emulate their fearlessness and machismo. Although he knew that his father would beat him if his drug use and promiscuity were discovered, he felt that secretly, his father would be proud, too.

By the time Miguel went to college, he was a regular marijuana and alcohol user. It wasn't difficult to find other students who had developed the same habits in high school. Naturally, they became his friends. While he seemed to be able to drink and smoke marijuana with little effect on his school performance, he saved cocaine and LSD use for weekends when the workload wasn't too heavy. He also dabbled in amphetamines and barbiturates—mostly to help him stay awake to study and then to sleep. This, then, was Miguel's pattern of substance use at the time of his hospitalization.

Miguel's hospital stay was brief. Showing no further signs of confusion or unrealistic ideas, but having produced a urine sample full of positive indicators for drugs, Miguel was discharged after two days with a referral to an outpatient drug abuse treatment program. The doctor had sort of blackmailed him into going by telling him that if he did not follow through on the referral, his parents would be notified of the true reason for his hospitalization. It seems that Miguel had told them that he had had a bad case of flu.

The drug counselor met with Miguel and took a very careful history of his drug use. Miguel didn't really want to believe that he was addicted to alcohol and marijuana, but he had been pretty frightened by "going off the wall." While he told the counselor that he would stop using all mind-altering substances, in his own mind he only resolved to stop using acid. He began to attend the campus group of Alcoholics Anonymous, which was filled with other multidrug users like himself, and learned to spout the party line—abstinence "one day at a time." And he did, indeed, remain abstinent—for about three weeks.

Miguel hadn't changed who his friends were, nor had his friends changed their drug-use behavior. They agreed with Miguel that maybe he shouldn't use LSD, but he had seemed to handle drinking and marijuana just fine. They felt uncomfortable being stoned while he looked on, sober, and they encouraged him to join in. It didn't take much encouragement to convince him. He didn't use much the first night, or even the next. But by the next weekend, he felt safe in getting high for real. Only this time, he had a mini-version of the "breakdown" that had originally led to his hospitalization. He began to feel that his friends had malevolent intentions towards him, that perhaps they had laced the pot with LSD or cocaine. Maybe they were even plotting with the police to get him busted. Their laughter seemed to him forced—even false. They appeared to be staring at him in an odd way. Miguel went to his room, locked himself in, and stayed there until morning.

When he awoke, he called his drug counselor and made an appointment. This latest episode had made it clear to him that drugs were "messing with my head," as he put it. Now he had some questions: would smoking marijuana always result in a "bad trip?" Had he done some permanent damage to his brain? What if he just drank alcohol and stayed off the other drugs? Could he smoke marijuana again if he waited longer before trying it the next time? The counselor suggested that Miguel engage in an experiment in which he would cease to use all drugs, including alcohol, for one month. They would then discuss the results of the experiment together. Miguel agreed.

A month later Miguel was back in the counselor's office. He had stuck to his word and had made a number of discoveries. First, he felt better about himself. His mind was clearer and studying was easier. He had also begun to play on the intercollegiate volleyball team. He loved the exertion, and he was beginning to make friends with the other young men and women on the team. The downside, though, was that his relationship with his old friends had become strained. He still hung out with them, but being straight for a whole evening in the company of people who were stoned was pretty boring. Their silly laughter annoyed him, and their single-minded pursuit of getting "wasted" seemed senseless. As he spoke, Miguel had an insight: talking in this way about his friends had made him feel oddly guilty, and he stumbled upon the feeling that somehow he was betraying his father by doing so. This led to a fairly extended discussion (the first, as it would turn out, of many) about his father's drinking and its effect on Miguel's family.

Miguel continued to experiment with using alcohol and marijuana over the next year or so, but, at the same time, he continued in counseling and in AA. His substance use dwindled to very occasional use and finally stopped after eighteen months. His circle of friends had changed, too. He now hung out with a "dry" crowd—some were his friends from AA, and some from volleyball. On follow-up, at his graduation from college, Miguel was still abstinent and now identified himself as a "recovering" substance abuser.

Thinking About the Case

Miguel would have qualified for a number of diagnoses: hallucinogen-induced psychosis with delusions, cannabis-induced psychosis, alcohol abuse, cannabis abuse, hallucinogen abuse, and possibly cocaine abuse. Miguel's two psychotic episodes are fairly typical of those experienced by some drug users. Symptoms include paranoia, hallucinations, delusions, and sometimes delirium. These problems typically resolve on their own as the level of psychoactive chemical in the body diminishes. Therefore, treatment involves simply keeping the person comfortable and safe. While substance-induced psychoses can mimic schizophrenia and mania symptomatically, their brief duration sets them apart. The diagnostic picture is cloudier for a small group of individuals who develop psychoses in response to drug use but do not appear to get thoroughly better on their own. Many of these people probably have an underlying psychotic process that was precipitated, rather than caused, by substance use. For these patients, treatment with antipsychotic medications and re-evaluation of expectations may be in order.

Polysubstance abuse like Miguel's is common among young people in today's society. While alcohol and marijuana are staples in the drug culture, amphetamines, cocaine, hallucinogens, barbiturates, ectasy, heroin, and more recently, opioids tend to come and go as fads and supply change over time.

This case illuminates the various factors that are relevant in the etiology of problematic substance use. The family history of alcoholism may indicate the presence of a genetic predisposition to substance use problems. Parental modeling may also be at work, as Miguel grew up in an environment in which the adult male was a heavy drug (alcohol) user. The "macho" culture which was exemplified in his father's behavior, and which was emulated by young males as he grew up, supported heavy substance use as an indication of manhood. This was probably supported by images presented in the larger culture in which some of the more visible sports heroes and movie stars are known to use a variety of drugs with little, if any, negative effect on their popularity or income-producing potential.

The case also indicates a fairly typical course of treatment, although of course, not all people who abuse drugs improve. Miguel, at first, denied that he had a problem, even in the face of the frightening psychosis he experienced. His first attempt at getting straight and sober was not a very serious one. Once his motivation level increased, because of another "bad trip," he still had to make numerous social changes to support his new lifestyle. Alcoholics Anonymous calls this process changing "people, places, and things." Miguel made new friends and went to AA meetings and volleyball practices rather than bars and off-campus apartments, and he spent his time in different activities than he had before. He also had to explore the ideas he had had about substance use and about what it took to be a man. He was forced to embark on a journey of self-discovery that went far beyond his use of drugs and alcohol. As you can see, this is a fairly extensive process that requires commitment of time and energy, as well as motivation to change.

We should note that insight-oriented psychotherapy, in the absence of sufficient sobriety, is generally ineffective. Most psychotherapists, once they identify a substance-abuse problem in a patient, require that the person be active in substance abuse treatment and be generally abstemious in order for psychotherapy to proceed. If relapse occurs, therapy may be suspended for a time so that energy can be focused on regaining sobriety, or the psychotherapy may continue but be focused exclusively on regaining sobriety for some period of time.

Alcoholics Anonymous has another motto: "One day at a time." Substance abuse often has a chronic course, with periods of abstinence punctuated by periods of renewed use—sometimes referred to as "falling off the wagon," or having "slipped" or "relapsed." Twelve-step programs like AA teach participants never to take their sobriety for granted since relapse can occur in the blink of an eye. Miguel's sobriety at the end of college is a good prognostic sign, but by no means a guarantee of future sobriety. While there is considerable debate about whether lifelong participation in some sort of "treatment" is required for the maintenance of sobriety, it is generally agreed that ongoing vigilance about emotional and environmental risk factors for renewed substance use is necessary.

Questions to Consider

1. Do you think that polysubstance use like Miguel's would be easier or harder to treat than use of only one drug, like alcohol? Why or why not?
2. Twelve-step programs like Alcoholics Anonymous teach that "a drug is a drug is a drug." By this they mean that if you have a problem with any substance, you must quit using all other mind-altering substances (except, apparently, for nicotine and caffeine) as well. Do you agree with this? Why or why not? Are you basing your answers on scientific data, your own experience, or that of your friends?
3. While there are things in Miguel's background that might have predisposed him to substance abuse problems, there are also things that would suggest that he has a fairly good prognosis. What are they?
4. Family involvement is often helpful in the treatment of substance abuse. What do you think might be the effects of involving Miguel's family in his treatment? What might be the benefits? Are there any possible drawbacks? How would you decide how to proceed?
5. Do you think that Miguel's parents deserve to know about his substance abuse problem? Does he have rights to privacy? When, if ever, should these be breached?

CASE 43

GAMBLING DISORDER: THE CASE OF VERONICA A.

VERONICA, A SEVENTY-SIX-YEAR-OLD woman, sat in her minister's office. She was wringing a handkerchief in her hand and tears leaked from her eyes. Her sweater was stained with what looked like coffee, but she was otherwise neatly attired. She had just confided in Pastor L that she felt so frightened and her future seemed so bleak that she was not sure she wanted to go on living. She had even had difficulty keeping herself from veering off the road and smashing into a tree on her way to his office.

Pastor L. was shocked. Normally, Veronica was vivacious and upbeat. She attended the Church's bingo on Friday evenings without fail and knew everyone there. She helped out with the food pantry, and got along terrifically with her co-volunteers. The pastor knew that Veronica's second husband had died a little over a year prior (she had been divorced from the first one), but she had seemed to be bouncing back from a mild period of mourning. He also knew that she had lost her son to pancreatic cancer about a decade earlier, but she had seemed to recover from that great loss without complication as well. Her despair seemed totally out of character.

When Pastor L. inquired gently what had brought Veronica to feel so hopeless she whispered "gambling, pastor." It seems that Veronica had gone through her own savings, as well as the $20,000 inheritance from her husband, in the fourteen months since his death. Her small social security income and a very small pension were not enough to pay for her regular expenses. School taxes were coming due, and she had not saved the money to pay them. She had not paid them the prior year either, but that was because her husband had just died and she had been overwhelmed by the paperwork that fell to her. Now it was autumn and heating bills would begin. She didn't know where she would find the money to pay them.

Veronica hadn't told anybody about her rising anxiety, or about her gambling. She didn't want to burden anybody with her problems, and besides, she was deeply embarrassed by her behavior. Her daughter-in-law, who loved and helped her, was very strict and judgmental. Veronica knew she would be deeply disappointed and angry that Veronica had spent all the money left by Mr. A. on "such stupidity." And all along, Veronica had believed that she could make the money back with a streak of good luck. After all, she had won $10,000 TWICE over the last thirty years. So she knew it could be done again. She hadn't really paid much attention to the dwindling bank balance until it sank under $500.00 about a month ago. Then the panic broke through and suicidal thoughts began to run through her mind. They had gotten so strong in the last week that she had been propelled into her minister's office. He was the only one would would not, perhaps, judge her.

Veronica's gambling had been going on for many, many years. In her home town she went to bingo at her church on Fridays, and at other churches on Tuesdays and Wednesdays. These were small games. You couldn't lose more than about $20.00 even if you played ten cards at a time. When she could convince her neighbor to drive her, she went to a bigger game in a nearby city. Once, on the anniversary of her son's death, she had won the $1,500.00 grand prize and had felt elated, as if her son were sending her a gift from heaven.

She also played scratch-off games. Her family and friends knew she loved them so she would receive tons of scratch-offs for her birthdays and Christmas. She also bought them, as did her friends while they were sitting around waiting for the bingo game to start. They would pass the time scratching off and cheering whenever anyone won a couple of bucks. In the days since her husband's death, Veronica found that she enjoyed the scratch-offs even more. Even a small win would lift her mood. Losses made her feel bad so she would buy a few more until she could end on a high note. By the time she saw her pastor, Veronica was spending up to $50.00 at a time on scratch-off tickets.

But the real downfall for Veronica was the casino. During her marriage, she and her husband had gone, on occasion, on bus trips with other seniors to casinos. They enjoyed these trips immensely. They always set a $20.00 limit on their spending, and when the allotment was gone they went to the buffet and had a great dinner. They had made many friends on these trips. After Mr. A. died, Veronica kept up the habit by herself. It helped with her loneliness and with not knowing what to do with herself when she was home alone. At first she had set a limit on her losings as she and her husband had done when they were together, but after a while, she found that she became anxious and depressed at the thought of leaving the slot machines. It wasn't much fun being at the buffet without him, and anyway, she didn't have much of an appetite these days. So she used her credit card and discovered that her bad feelings were relieved so long as she stayed at the machines. Had she not been constrained by having to be on the bus by 4:00, she didn't know how she would be able to break away.

Virginia knew that her gambling was becoming a problem. Each time that she got home from the casino she felt frightened by how much she had lost and vowed that that would be her last trip. However, as the date of the next available trip approached, she decided that she would go, but would strictly adhere to a spending limit. Despite promising herself, she was never able to stick to the limit. She gambled until it was time to leave. Finally, frequenting the casino twice most months for the last several months, she had reached the credit limit of her credit card the week before, and this was the immediate precipitant for her seeking help. The thought of not going to the casino filled her with despair. She knew that she could not go on this way.

Pastor L. was at a loss for words. He was deeply shocked by Veronica's story. He had had no inkling that she was in trouble. After some thought, he decided that the most immediate problem was housing. Veronica would not be able to keep her house as she couldn't pay the taxes or heating bill. Following a great deal of quiet reasoning on his part and tearful resistance on hers, Veronica finally agreed to let the pastor call her daughter-in-law Barbara who agreed to come right down. She took Veronica home with her for the night and agreed that they would meet again the next day.

Together, over the course of the next several days, the three agreed on the following plan: Veronica would move in with Barbara who would arrange for the sale of Veronica's home. Additionally, Veronica would not be able to make any more casino trips. Barbara did not want Veronica to pay any rent, but she did insist that she be the one to manage Veronica's money for now. Barbara would give her an allowance each week and bank the rest against medical co-pays or any other expenses she might have. Veronica would have a full physical exam, and would discuss the gambling problem with her physician. She would also attend at least three meetings of "gambler's anonymous." Barbara would go with her for moral support. Barbara was willing to do anything she could to help Veronica, but she insisted that Veronica must be willing to help herself.

Meeting with Pastor L. alone for the last time, Veronica voiced misgivings about living with her daughter-in-law, but could really see no alternatives. She doubted she would be able to "have any fun," and mourned the loss of her friends in town. Barbara lived almost sixty miles away, and Veronica knew that she would rarely, if ever, be able to visit.

Pastor L. didn't hear from Veronica for the next two years. Then, he had a surprise. Sitting at his desk one day, he heard a knock on his study door. Upon opening it he saw Veronica, a big smile on her face, and arms open wide for a hug. Beside her stood a small, merry-faced man dressed in a suit coat and a string tie. This was her "boyfriend." They had met at the assisted living center where Veronica now lived.

Apparently, Veronica had been pretty lonely living at Barbara's. She didn't know the area and didn't have friends of her own. Despite Barbara's kindness and attempts to include Veronica in her activities, Veronica mostly watched television and tended the garden. She missed gambling a lot, but had no access to scratch-offs or bingo games. She had attended the "gambler's anonymous" meetings as she had promised, but they hadn't really seemed helpful to her. Most of the people there were younger than she, and their issues didn't seem similar to hers. After about a year, she and her daughter-in-law decided mutually that Veronica might be happier in a setting where she could socialize more and have activities available to keep herself occupied. She was able, with the proceeds from the sale of her home along with funds that Barbara had saved for her and her own money to enter an "assisted living" facility. She had been living there for about a year now, and was much happier than she had been at Barbara's.

Veronica seemed to Pastor L. to be her old self, smiling and joking and teasing her "boyfriend." Apparently, he was a real catch because he was still driving his own car. And, he could dance. In fact, this was their joyous pastime once a week on Friday afternoons at the local senior center. Veronica admitted that she sometimes was tempted to buy scratch-offs now that she could get to places where they were sold, but she hadn't done so. Wisely, she had shared with her boyfriend that she had had a gambling problem so he helped to distract her when she "got the urge." He steadfastly refused to take her to buy "even one" scratch-off ticket. But she didn't feel the need to gamble very often. She wasn't lonely or bored any more. She had friends and plenty to occupy herself. She had her life back and was enjoying every minute.

Thinking About The Case

Gambling, like drinking, is not harmful in moderation. But when a person is unable to resist the urge to gamble despite the desire to stop and despite worsening negative consequences of the behavior, then gambling disorder is diagnosed. DSM-5 includes gambling disorder with other addictions and like other addictions it can ruin not only the gambler's life, but the lives of his or her family and even friends. It is thought that the prevalence of gambling disorder is increasing as the availability of casinos, on-line gaming, and state sponsored lotteries has increased. Prevalence estimates vary, but most suggest the disorder occurs in about one percent of the population in our culture.

Gambling disorder frequently co-occurs with substance abuse, mood and anxiety disorders, and personality disorders. It is not uncommon for the problem to worsen during periods of stress or sadness, as it did for Veronica, nor for it to cause additional emotional problems as it did for her. This is true for other addictions as well. As the addiction proceeds, it causes life problems, like divorce, financial problems, even illegal behavior. These, in turn, qualify as reasons to indulge the addiction.

Veronica's case is somewhat atypical in that she was quite old to develop a new gambling problem; most gambling disorders begin in early to late middle age. In addition, more men than women develop gambling disorder. Women tend to develop the disorder later, and are more apt to have a pre-existing or co-occuring mood disorder as Veronica did. Interestingly, women tend to become addicted more quickly once they begin to slide into problematic gambling behavior. For Veronica, gambling appeared to ameliorate grief, loneliness, and boredom, a one-two-three punch that she had not encountered before, and therefore had had no experience in managing. It is also interesting to note that the problem subsided when she found a boyfriend and became engaged in social activities. This is also not particularly typical. More often, problem gamblers become associated with other gamblers, and their lives narrow rather than expand. Veronica got lucky that intervention occurred when it did, that she was prevented from gambling for a time, and that she found a boyfriend who discouraged her gambling.

There is some evidence for a biochemical underpinning to gambling disorder, as well as other addictions. Gambling stimulates the body's reward system like opiates. Some people with the disorder have been shown to have low levels of the neurotransmitter serotonin (associated with depression) and/or norepinephrine (associated with stress and arousal). Family history of addiction predisposes to gambling disorder as well as other addictions. Still, even with a biological predisposition, the individual must still have access to gambling and perhaps a precipitating emotional condition as well.

Treatment is similar to that for other addictions. Counseling may take a number of forms. Motivational interviewing is designed to help the individual combat denial and become more aware of the reasons to address the problematic behavior. Indeed, he or she might not have even accepted that the behavior is problematic. Sometimes a scripted family or friend intervention is used. Here, family members and friends specifically address the harmful effects of the addiction within a context of love and support.

Cognitive-behavioral therapy aims to counteract irrational beliefs that fuel the addiction. Step programs, like Gamblers' Anonymous provide peer support and strategies for avoiding relapse. Skill building therapy works on assertiveness, practicing gambling refusal, problem solving, and the development of gambling-inconsistent behaviors (like Veronica's spending time with her non-gambling boyfriend).

Questions to Consider

1. Gambling has recently been re-classified as an addiction. It used to be called an "impulse control disorder." Do you agree that it is an addiction? Why or why not?
2. What is the evidence that Veronica suffered from a true addiction? Is there any evidence presented in the case that would lead you to question the diagnosis?
3. What are the social consequences of labeling a behavior an "addiction?" Do you think these consequences represent appropriate societal approaches to the behavior in question? For example, if a person steals from another person because of a gambling or substance abuse addiction, is this an "extenuating circumstance?"

LANAHAN NOTES
Substance-Related & Addictive Disorders

Effects of drugs

Direct activation of the reward system in the brain

Reward system central to the reinforcement of behaviors and production of memories

Ten classes of disorders

Alcohol, caffeine, cannabis, hallucinogens, inhalants, opioids, sedatives, hynotics & anxiolytics, stimulants, tobacco

These disorders are divided into two groups: substance use disorders and substance-induced disorders

Other addictive disorders, like gambling, are so similar as to be included here as well

Characteristics of substance use disorder

Drug use typically creates a pathological pattern of behaviors relating to:

Impaired control: individual desires to cut down on drug intake but is unable; spends time obtaining, using, or recovering from the drug; suffers cravings for the drug

Social impairment: individual fails to perform basic everyday tasks at work/school/home; recreational activities given up because of the time involved in substance use

Risky behaviors: operating a motor vehicle; trying to take care of children, showing up at work under the influence, etc.

Pharmacological criteria: the development of tolerance and symptoms of withdrawal.

Characteristics of substance-induced disorders

Intoxication, withdrawal, and other substance/medication-induced mental disorders, e.g., psychotic disorders, bipolar and related disorders, depressive disorders, anxiety disorders, obsessive-compulsive disorders, sleep disorders, sexual dysfunctions, delirium and neurocognitive disorders.

Substance abuse can speed the onset or be a contributing factor in these mental disorders

Risk Factors

Individuals with lower levels of self-control which may reflect impairments of brain inhibitory mechanisms

Sociocultural factors: peers, family, ethnic group, and religious orientation all affect norms and expectations about substance use

Treatment

Detoxification: gets the person off the substance and treats subsequent withdrawal symptoms

Education: explains the addictive processes; helps break down psychological mechanism of denial; engages the person in treatment

Cognitive-behavioral methods: skill-training, cognitive restructuring, lifestyle intervention—help prevent relapses

Twelve-step programs (based on Alcoholics Anonymous): provides group support, enhancement of self-esteem, mutual learning, and additional cognitive-behavioral techniques

Psychotherapy: helps repair self-esteem, develop awareness of conflicts and emotions that precipitate substance use

Note: Psychodynamic psychotherapy generally not used until the person has achieved stable sobriety

Medications:

Anti-depressants, anti-anxiety drugs: used to treat co-existing disorders; though beware of substituting one drug addiction for another

Antabuse: inhibits alcohol use by making the person sick (typically nauseous) when he or she drinks

Naltrexone: reduces cravings for drugs by blocking opioid transmission in the reward centers in the brain

CHAPTER SEVENTEEN

Neurocognitive Disorders

Neurocognitive disorders are defined as impairments of memory and/or other cognitive functions resulting from physiological causes. These causes include various forms of dementia, traumatic brain injury, Parkinson's Disease, HIV infection, Huntington's Disease, prion diseases (those in which prion, a protein normally found on the surface of many cells becomes abnormal and clumps in the brain), and neurocognitive disorder from other or multiple sources.

New to DSM-5 is the inclusion of diagnoses for "mild neurocognitive disorder." This is to facilitate the early detection and early treatment of neurocognitive disorders before symptoms become severely debilitating.

We have included here two cases of neurocognitive disorder. The first describes a case of dementia arising from acquired immunodeficiency syndrome (AIDS). The second is a first person account written by a man whose wife had Alzheimer's disease. We have chosen it to highlight the effect on families of living with and caring for a person with neurocognitive impairments.

CASE 44

MAJOR COGNITIVE DISORDER RELATED TO HIV INFECTION: THE CASE OF SAMUEL G.

LIEUTENANT JUNIOR GRADE SAMUEL G. was a twenty-seven-year-old African American man on the threshold of a successful Navy career. A bright young man, the oldest of three sons in a middle-class family, Samuel made up for his smallish stature with aggressive, tenacious competitiveness. As a youngster, he did well in school, ran track, and practiced martial arts. He also was an accomplished pianist who took satisfaction in besting his father by learning all of the Bach *Inventions* by heart. At his summer job in the county youth department, he was known for being an efficient, no-nonsense guy who also had a quick wit and an ability to get along with almost everybody.

Samuel went to Catholic school and then on to a private college from which he graduated in 1978. Jobs were scarce so Samuel joined his younger brother, who had just graduated from high school, in enlisting in the United States Navy. He easily passed the examination for officer's candidate school and, as an ensign, was assigned to the personnel office on an aircraft carrier. Again, his job performance was exemplary, and he was reassigned to surface warfare school, where he was to be trained for service on a destroyer as a full lieutenant. It was then that his problems began.

Samuel appeared not to be responding well to the stress of his new academic responsibilities. He began to have a series of viral infections that left him weak and tired. Several times he fell asleep during class. His mood began to change. This once aggressive officer became listless and apathetic. He suffered from insomnia, anxiety, and depression. His self-esteem seemed to wane, as did his weight. He was unable to concentrate, and his grades slipped drastically.

At around the same time, his parents, living on the opposite coast, began to be concerned about him. They noted, in retrospect, that he seemed to be confused. He kept getting digits of phone numbers scrambled, so that they had trouble reaching him. His voice had become harsh from a seemingly never ending sore throat, and he seemed depressed and unwell. He complained to his parents that he was being harassed by the Navy. His inability to concentrate or even to stay awake, had prompted them to suspect him of drug use, and he had undergone a series of drug tests. Of course, the tests were negative, but his feelings of "harassment" continued. In January of 1984, his commanding officer wrote a report that reads, in part, as follows: " . . . low motivation, inadequate study habits, and the poor example this 'fleet JG' set for many Ensigns in the class. . . . He repeatedly fell asleep at his desk or in class and had to be often told not to read unofficial material at his desk. The few satisfactory tasks he did perform came only when PXO gave him highly structured and elaborate guidance. . . . Shows no initiative and appears content to simply sit at his desk until asked to do something. . . . In sum, LTJG G. is more of a liability to this unit than an asset. Because of his documented performance alone, I feel his selection for SWOS Department Head School should be reappraised." At the same time, his promotion to full lieutenant was put on hold.

Finally, in February of 1984 Samuel was admitted to the psychiatric unit of the Naval hospital for evaluation and treatment. Embarrassed and ashamed, he told his parents that he was being admitted because of concerns that he might have cancer of the liver. Once in the hospital, he was diagnosed as having an adjustment disorder with depressed mood. He seemed to improve while on the unit, and was discharged with the recommendation that he continue counseling on an outpatient basis.

Shortly thereafter, his condition seemed to worsen. His parents were informed by a physician who had been involved in his care that Samuel might have a condition called Acquired Immunodeficiency Syndrome, a rare but serious autoimmune disease. At the time, fewer than five thousand cases had been diagnosed in the United States, so knowledge was scarce. If Samuel had AIDS, he would likely also have a rare tuberculosis of the bone with which it seemed to be associated. Testing for this tuberculosis would take three months.

In the meantime, Samuel's behavior became more and more erratic. He got married—briefly. The marriage only lasted two weeks. He bought four buildings in the inner city and hired a manager to collect rents. But, he never made a mortgage payment, despite having the money to do so. Apparently, he thought the money that his manager sent him represented his net profits after the mortgage had been paid. In April, he wrote an articulate and heartbreaking letter to President Ronald Reagan, which ended as follows: "Mr. President, I am a very patriotic man. I have always wanted to be a naval officer, and now because of one man's insensitivity towards a person suffering of mental duress, my career is all but over. I implore you to intervene on my behalf."

In June, the diagnosis of tuberculosis of the bone was confirmed. The physician sent Samuel's parents a copy of an article recently published in the *New England Journal of Medicine* about AIDS. Confused and frightened, his parents sent him a ticket to come home for a visit. What they saw horrified them. His clothes hung on his gaunt frame. In the oversized fedora which came down over his ears he looked unkempt and bizarre. His color had darkened and his eyes were deep-set. Within minutes he was talking about having a cosmic relationship with Michael Jackson. But worst of all were his rantings about women. He called them, among other things, "nasty, greasy bitches." He was vile and hateful, and completely uncontrollable.

After two harrowing weeks, Samuel returned to the naval base where, in July he was readmitted to the psychiatric unit, this time with the diagnosis of narcissistic personality disorder. By this time he had virtually no sense of anybody else's needs. He was demanding, hostile, and completely self-centered. His attention span was continuing to decrease and his confusion was continuing to increase. On the day of his discharge, while driving back to his apartment from the base hospital, he got into four automobile accidents—the last of which totalled his car.

His parents hurriedly flew out to California, again having trouble finding him because of his inability to get numbers or directions straight. When they got to his apartment, they found it empty. Three hours later, Samuel returned. He had taken a neighbor to the hospital and gotten lost on his way home. He looked awful, having lost more weight in the short time since his parents had last seen him. They took him to a restaurant where he ordered fifty dollars worth of lunch . . . but ate none of it. He was so weak he could not walk to the car, but had to lie down on a couch in the restaurant's lobby for a while. His parents say that this was the first time they realized that their son was going to die. They made arrangements to have him discharged by mail from the Navy and took him home.

For three months his parents cared for Samuel. In his lucid moments, he told his father that he was gay, that his marriage (to a gay woman) had been "for show." He expressed sadness about his illness and about the stress he was creating for his family. He seemed particularly pained by his inability to read music or play the piano any more.

But he was not always lucid. Often he was quite demented. His recent memory deteriorated, and he made things up to cover the gaps. He wanted to become an astronaut, to buy a Mercedes. He ordered thousands of dollars worth of merchandise from the television, ultimately maxing-out his credit card. His social skills continued to deteriorate—in restaurants (until his parents stopped taking him), he would wander around, telling all of the patrons about his having AIDS, or about there being ice in the urinals in the men's room. Most heartrending for his parents was watching him stare into the mirror, talking about how handsome he was.

In November, Samuel developed a blood infection and his kidneys failed. He suffered a series of violent seizures and died before Christmas. His bereaved and angry father decided that his son had deserved his promotion, so he decided to promote him, himself. In his obituary and at his funeral, full Lieutenant Samuel G. was properly memorialized.

Thinking About the Case

When Samuel G. was alive, neurological complications of Human Immunodeficiency Virus (HIV), the virus that causes AIDS, had not yet been identified. It is now known that approximately 40 percent of AIDS patients have observable neurological disorders. Upwards of 80 percent have neuropathological findings at autopsy.

Many patients, like Samuel G., exhibit symptoms that are particularly suggestive of frontal lobe damage. These include marked personality change, loss of social judgment accompanied by disinhibition resulting in socially inappropriate behavior, decreased volition and motivation, and difficulty placing events in temporal sequence. The earliest symptoms of AIDS-related dementia are typically depression, forgetfulness, and poor concentration, with the more serious cognitive deficits showing up somewhat later.

There is no treatment for AIDS-related dementia, although medications can sometimes be helpful to treat specific symptoms like depression or anxiety. Supportive psychotherapy to help with the reactive components of the problem—including the individual's reaction to the stigma associated with AIDS—family, social, or financial problems that may arise, and coping with impending death, may also be useful. Professional support for family members to help them anticipate, understand, and manage cognitive and emotional changes associated with AIDS is invaluable. Here, the focus is on assisting caregivers to support the patient, as well as on bolstering their own resistance to the often devastating emotional effects of the caregiving burden.

The question of whether or not individuals with AIDS-related complex (ARC), who have not yet developed AIDS, show cognitive deficits cannot yet be answered with certainty. Gross impairment is not observed, but studies indicate that subtle disturbances in memory and fine motor coordination may exist.

Questions to Consider

1. Do you think that neurological disorders like AIDS-related dementia and Alzheimer's disease should be included in the DSM categories? Why or why not?
2. Which of the symptoms exhibited by Samuel G. are similar to those of Alzheimer's patients? Which are different? Do these patterns tell you anything about the localization of certain functions in the brain?
3. The (mis)diagnosis of adjustment disorder with depressed mood in this case is easy to understand. However, there were clues that the diagnosis of narcissistic personality disorder was incorrect. What were they?

CASE 45

ALZHEIMER'S DISORDER: THE CASE OF GINNY

No chapter on neurocognitive disorders would be complete without a selection on Alzheimer's disease, a progressive deterioration in cognitive functions that tends to afflict elderly people. Alzheimer's has drawn more and more attention lately, as the baby boomer generation ages. Since the incidence of Alzheimer's increases with age—approximately 5 percent of people age sixty-five are afflicted, while five times that many have Alzheimer's by age eighty—an aging population means that treatment and care of Alzheimer's patients will be a major public health concern for the foreseeable future.

We have chosen an excerpt from the book, Ginny: A Love Remembered, *written by G. Robert Artley whose wife died of Alzheimer's. The excerpts record her progressive loss of function as well as how her condition affected those who loved her.*

IT IS HARD TO PUT A DATE ON WHEN the insidious disease that stole the mind and vibrant spirit away from Ginny first began to show itself. As we look back, we can now detect, from the perspective of what has transpired over time, different isolated episodes or incidents of peculiar behavior that were manifested perhaps as far back as 1978.

In 1980 Jeannie first noticed something being wrong when we were visiting her in Washington, D.C., when little Jennifer wanted to play the game of "Clue" with her grandmother and Ginny could not manage it. But those of us who had been around her more back home had been noticing other disturbing things about her behavior before then.

When the children, all gone from home, would come back for a visit, they would take me aside and ask, "What's the matter with Mom?" I, trying to deny my own fears, would be almost angry in replying, "What do you mean, what's wrong with Mom?" It was almost as if I considered them disrespectful of their mother. However, deep inside, I knew that their questions were legitimate, that there *was* something wrong. . . .

. . . [T]he last year the Print Shop was in business, an increasing number of printing jobs had to be done over because of some unexplainable errors that showed up in the finished work. This could prove quite costly, an expense that, of course, had to be borne by the Print Shop. Ginny felt terrible about these "goofs" for which she was responsible, and in my blindness I became impatient with her.

"Why in thunder did you do that?" I'd ask in exasperation. "I don't know *why* I did it!" she would reply, nearly in tears.

Little by little, the Print Shop seemed to be getting to be too much for her. The work was making her nervous and tired her more than before. Finally, we decided that, if we couldn't sell the shop as a going business, we would simply close it up, sell off the equipment, and put the building up for sale.

It was a relief, once we'd made up our minds, to finally deliver our last printing job. Yet with a feeling of sadness, too, we closed another chapter on our life together.

Unfortunately, we could not enjoy Ginny's retirement as we'd hoped. Her mental problems gradually became more evident. She would forget things that I, in my chronic forgetfulness, had depended on her to remember for me. She became easily confused, whereas she had been the one of us who knew what the score was. Ginny had been the one to take care of the monthly bills, write the checks, keep track of appointments and, in general, keep her home, husband, and business running on track.

Sometimes she did inexplicable things that were foreign to her usual way. On one occasion, putting on a new pair of pants for the first time, I discovered the button missing that would have fastened the little tab and held the front closed before pulling up the zipper. I asked Ginny to sew on the button when she had time, and I wore another pair that day. To my chagrin, when next I put on the new pair of pants, I discovered that, instead of the button being sewed on, the tab had been cut off, thus eliminating the need for the button.

This discovery was quite a shock. It bothered me to the extent that I never mentioned it to Ginny. Knowing that such behavior was not akin to Ginny's nature, I didn't want to confront her with it. I simply wore the new pants sans tab, with no one being the wiser. But every time I put them on, I saw Ginny's handiwork and was reminded that something *was* wrong . . . not only with the pants.

Other aberrations began to appear more and more often. When Ginny and I were visiting with friends, she would suddenly interject a thought that was entirely foreign to the topic of our conversation. This broke the thread of our intercourse and caused puzzled embarrassment to all of us, especially to Ginny, who realized she'd said something wrong.

Through the years, even though she was naturally shy and had a tendency to hold back, Ginny had always made worthwhile and even witty contributions to a discussion, so this verbal misstep was but further evidence that something was not right with her mental process. Sometimes she would use wrong words in a sentence. This could be humorous, and we all, including Ginny, would laugh at it. At first we poked good-natured fun by calling her Mrs. Malaprop, a character in a play who makes ludicrous blunders in her use of words. But, after a while, instead of laughing at these malapropisms of Ginny's, we'd try to overlook them, realizing that she was not *trying* to be funny.

One evening Ginny had invited friends for supper. As the time for their arrival drew near, Ginny, who loved to have people in for meals, seemed ill at ease and reluctant. As I helped her with the last-minute details, when it was necessary to rearrange some of the table settings, it seemed almost too much for her.

The meal was fine and our guests seemed to enjoy it, but Ginny seemed to not be really with us—to be somewhat in a fog. Years later, after Ginny's condition had been diagnosed, our friend, referring to that supper, confessed she had thought maybe Ginny was a closet alcoholic.

During the early stages of Ginny's mental problem, before a name had been put on it, these strange behavior patterns were stressful for all of us—certainly Ginny, because, as yet, she was still aware that she was apt to say or do something "stupid," and this only compounded her sense of insecurity and her suffering. . . .

The rest of that autumn and into December, Ginny was functioning about as she had been in Adrian. But there was increasing evidence that she had a health problem. She still drove the car occasionally but began to show signs of confusion and even got lost once or twice in our small town. Without making an issue of it, I gradually took over all the driving, until her Minnesota driver's license was no longer valid. However, she did ask me to pick up an Iowa driving test booklet for her to study in preparation for taking the test. She tried valiantly, for she had every intention of passing the test to get her Iowa driver's license. She spent hours going over all the driving rules and regulations and traffic sign recognition. Then she asked me to quiz her. However, those sessions were not successful at all and only caused her further frustration.

It was sad to see one who had always been so diligent in her studies and able to absorb facts, who had put me to shame with her ability to memorize, now not able to remember the simplest things in the book. When she would miss a question, she'd ask to take the book and study it again, but to no avail. Finally, she would put the book aside, determined to go at it again when "my mind is clearer."

This went on for quite a while. Ginny had always liked to read in bed; now, if she retired before I did, I'd come in later to find her asleep with the Iowa driver's license booklet propped up on her chest. As I'd always done, I would carefully remove her glasses and book and lay them aside. And, as always, if she was not in a deep sleep, a faint smile would flicker across her face.

So the weeks went by, with Ginny always preparing for the test that was given at the courthouse every Saturday morning. But, as Saturday arrived each week, I helped her forget the appointed time. I felt guilty in this subterfuge, but I had no intention of letting her suffer through the humiliation of trying to take a written test she was bound to fail miserably. Nor, for that matter, did I want her to attempt to drive again with her obvious state of confusion and erratic behavior. After a while, she forgot about taking the test, and I sadly put the little booklet away, realizing this to be but another part of Ginny that was in the past. . . .

As time went on, social exposures became more difficult, and we withdrew more and more into our shell. One time when I realized that Ginny's condition had brought us to this stage was at a function to which we had been invited at the Methodist church. It was a buffet supper with the food laid out on tables before the call to start the line. As we waited, Ginny and I were visiting with someone when I suddenly realized she was not beside me. Instead, she was at the food table, going from dish to dish, picking up and sampling morsels of food. As discreetly and quickly as possible, I went to her side and gently moved her away to where, hopefully, we could melt into the background. . . .

As time went on and Ginny's condition deteriorated perceptibly, people made allowances for her strange behavior or her inappropriate or incomprehensible speech. Even the Hampton police were aware of our problem and kept an unobtrusive watch over her. They were actively involved a couple of times.

Usually, when working at my drawing board, I would hear her moving around on the floor above me, going from room to room in a restless state. Sometimes, if I didn't hear her, I'd go up to find her lying on the couch or sitting quietly in a chair. At other times, she might have gone outside. This, of course, was my constant concern.

One time, as I was working in my basement studio, the phone rang, and a woman, whose voice and whose name I did not recognize, said that Ginny had come into her house and seemed confused, not knowing where she was or how to get home. I was shocked, for I had not even been aware that she was out of the house.

Just as I arrived at the home of the woman who had made the call, about three blocks from our place, a police car pulled up. The officer said that he had received a call, too. I assured him that I would take care of the situation and thanked him for his concern. When the woman of the house let me in, she said that Ginny was in the kitchen. I went there to find her standing in the middle of the room, quietly crying. Taking her in my arms, I kissed her, thanked the lady for her kindness, and we went home—Ginny in confusion and humiliation and I in sadness for my dear wife. I realized anew how vulnerable we were.

Some months later, Ginny again slipped out without my knowledge. Again I was alerted by a phone call. This time she was at a convenience store and gas station at the intersection of highways 3 and 65, about two blocks from our home. I took the car, and as I drove up to the store, I saw Ginny standing by a police car, talking to the officer inside. My nephew, George, was standing beside her.

It seemed that when Ginny had appeared in the store, quite confused and not able to make much sense to the clerks, someone called the police. When they had realized that she was Mrs. Artley, they had phoned my brother Dan's house. George, being the only one at home, had jumped in his car and come to see what help he could be to his Aunt Ginny.

Ginny's tendency to slip out of the house and wander away kept us all on the alert and on edge. . . .

Although all of this wandering about and suddenly appearing unannounced could in itself be disruptive and disturbing to those being visited, Ginny never did anything that was in any way antisocial or unfriendly. She was, as she had always been, soft-spoken and kindly disposed toward people. Thus, rather than antagonizing her surprised hosts, she elicited from them sympathy and concern for her well-being. . . .

There were countless stressful, embarrassing situations brought about by Ginny's growing confusion and memory loss, which, had it not been for the kindness and understanding of those around us, could have become even more painfully complicated. One such time was when the minister of our church surreptitiously handed me a check Ginny had given her—written for an amount much larger than we had been giving. I don't recall how I handled that situation, but I appreciated the minister's understanding, and the incident served as a flag, alerting me to keep track of the checkbook . . .

If Ginny's mental deterioration had happened all at once, as with a stroke, I think it might have been easier for us. Of course, there would have been the initial devastating shock, but later, faced with the reality of the thing that had happened, we would have resigned ourselves to the fact that all we could do was adjust to it.

But such is not the case with the insidious nature of Alzheimer's disease. Instead, especially in the early stages, one is not quite sure whether there is something wrong or not. It teases, and even, at times, dangles false hope before one. There were times when I would tell myself that Ginny was seeming better and that she was going to beat this thing that was destroying her while we who loved her stood by helplessly. Then there would be a cruel relapse and I knew the nightmare was real. . . .

I will not soon forget the first time I experienced Ginny's not knowing me. She had gone to bed, and after my usual nighttime rounds, locking the front and back doors, checking to see that the fire was okay in the fireplace and that Simon and Kelly (our cat and dog) were in the basement, and turning off the lights, I went into our bedroom to get ready for bed. As I entered, Ginny, with an expression of alarm on her face, said, "What are *you* doing here?"

Perplexed, I told her I was going to bed.

"Not in *here*, you aren't!" she said, and drew the bed clothes up tight around her. . . .

Never in all our married life, up until that fateful night, had I been denied entrance to our marriage bed. Thus, this harsh order from the lips of my loving Ginny struck me to the heart in total disbelief. Even though I knew that "this was not Ginny," still I felt profoundly betrayed and hurt.

After getting an extra blanket from the closet, under the stern, watchful eye of a Ginny I did not know, I retreated to my recliner in the darkened living room, wallowing in self-pity and with a sense of great loss of the closeness we had always shared.

At a very late hour, after Ginny had finally gone to sleep, I crept quietly back to our room and very carefully, so as not to jiggle it, lay down on my side of the bed. When morning came, at long last, Ginny had apparently forgotten about the "strange man" who had tried to invade her privacy and seemed to accept my presence for whomever she might think I was.

Another time when the chagrin of being perceived as a stranger by my loving wife was brought home to me, I was working in my studio, thinking Ginny was upstairs, when the phone rang. It was Rob, saying that his mother was there and for me not to worry, that she was fine but maybe, after a while, I should come for her. Then he went on to explain: Ginny had appeared at their door, about two blocks from our house (across busy Highway 65) to say that there was a strange man at her house and that she wanted her children to know that she was "not *that* kind of woman." . . .

In 1984 she began to have hallucinations. This didn't get to be a real problem in Ginny's case, but she would occasionally indicate that she saw something or someone in our house that none of the rest of us could see. But what she "saw" did not frighten her or cause her any concern. Here, too, we did not tell her she was "only seeing things" or try in any way to dissuade her. Instead, we either ignored her remark or acted as if we too saw what she saw. This could make for some fun in which Ginny seemed to enter.

Ginny and I usually walked about a mile every day—sometimes more. We most often took the same circuitous route, going south from our house and returning from the north. (I had calculated this way to be about a mile.) It took us through residential areas, past some homes of people we knew, past two school yards and the old Waterworks Park. It was a pleasant walk and we sometimes, if I felt up to it, took Kelly, our rambunctious Irish setter, along on a leash. But most of the time, it was just Ginny and I, walking briskly.

We walked mostly in silence, as Ginny's speech was increasingly becoming incoherent muttering. But sometimes, as we approached a fire hydrant, she would say to me in confidence, "Isn't he cute!" and then say "Hi" to it as we walked by. Eventually, if there was no one else nearby, I, too, not wanting to be left out of the camaraderie, would also greet the little iron fellows. We even stopped, sometimes, to briefly visit with these friendly fire hydrants that we were getting to know on our daily walks.

This all seemed to please Ginny. Now I look back, with a mixture of humor and longing, on those walks as another phase of our togetherness.

Accompanying Ginny's restless wandering was her inclination to pick things up and put them elsewhere. During this period, she was constantly rearranging and stashing items about the house. Maybe one shoe would be missing, or something from the kitchen would show up in the bedroom. I opened the refrigerator door one day to find the electric iron sitting on a shelf next to the butter dish.

Her diamond ring came up missing and we both searched throughout the house without success. I kicked myself for not being on top of the situation and not having put it away for safekeeping. Months later, when we moved from our house in town to the farm, one of the women helping us found it while wiping a cleaning cloth along the top shelf of the kitchen cupboard. Evidently, Ginny had *herself* put it away "for safekeeping." . . .

The strange behaviors of some people suffering from dementia include disrobing—sometimes in public. Thankfully, Ginny was spared that humiliation. Instead of taking *off* her clothes, she *added* to what she already had on, layer upon layer.

At such times, when she would slip out of the house for one of her wanderings, she was literally overdressed. This gave her a ludicrous appearance, like a circus clown before he takes layer upon layer off in his comic act. I felt embarrassed for her to be seen this way before I could get her back into the house, but I was thankful I didn't have to rush out with a blanket to cover her nudity. However, one time I *did* rescue her before she went out the front door with an extra bra over her blouse.

One night during this period of overdressing, I went to help her get ready for bed and found her to have on three or four blouses and a like number of skirts, as well as underwear and stockings, one over the other. After peeling off her things, a layer at a time (similar to what the circus clowns did) until I got down to the real Ginny, I helped her get into her nightgown and into bed. Then I went into the bathroom to prepare myself for bed. I couldn't have been gone for more than three or four minutes, but when I returned I found Ginny out of bed and almost completely dressed again . . . with all her layers. In exasperation I blurted out, "Ginny, what are you doing?" and set about to get her ready for bed again.

Apparently, Ginny saw the humor in this situation (not far different from what she might have pulled on me as a trick in former years) for she burst out laughing, her familiar joyful laugh. We ended up by falling across the bed in one another's arms, in a paroxysm of laughter—the kind of deep, joyful laughter we had shared many times in our years together, but something we had not enjoyed for a long time. . . .

Another time, when some unexpected guests dropped in for a short time on their way through town, Ginny startled the man by suddenly bringing in from the kitchen and presenting to him a tray on which was a spatula, a serving spoon, and some other kitchen utensils. This, too, was her attempt to be the gracious hostess she had always been. The incident, like many situations brought about by the disease, was not without humor, yet not without pathos for the sensitive victim. . . .

[T]he family had finally persuaded me that, in view of Ginny's steady decline, I should begin planning for her to enter a care facility. For economic reasons, as well as the need for specialized care for Alzheimer's victims, we decided to check out the Iowa Veterans Home in Marshalltown, which we had heard was an excellent care facility and also included a new Alzheimer's unit. . . .

As we drove toward home in the gathering darkness late that afternoon, I was glad to be in the back seat among the shadows. Rob and Kris tried valiantly to bolster my spirits by recounting the attractive features of the place and "how good it will be for Mom"; how it was designed to give the residents freedom to do their restless wandering without being in danger; how it was made so as to minimize those things in their environment that might aggravate their confusion; how the decorator had used calming, harmonious colors that were nevertheless cheerful; how the television was fixed so that only the staff would be able to operate it so that they could select programs that would not agitate.

They reminded me how, mounted on the walls along the hallway between the rooms, were knobs that could be turned or moved to various positions through slots by the Alzheimer's patients in their constant need to be doing something; and how, for their safety, the doors in and out of the unit were secured by making passage possible only by a key carried by staff members at all times; and how sensitivity to the patients' needs had been shown by the planners, in providing that one door opened onto a porch from which patients could walk along walkways through an attractive, fenced-in garden area that included a gazebo, where on mild days they could sit on benches and listen to piped-in music; how even the flowers, shrubs, and trees of this garden were selected for their nontoxicity, in case they would be ingested.

By reminding me of all these features designed for the welfare and comfort of the residents who would be living there once it was open, Rob and Kris were trying to make me glad for the action we had taken that day. But I could not be glad. My heart was heavy and full of dread.

Such had been my mood as we came home that winter evening, as it would be for much of the time from then on until Ginny was actually admitted. And now, with the disturbing (to me) message from Marshalltown giving a specific date, March 2, 1987, when they would be ready for Ginny, the timer had been set. Each day ticked off, relentlessly bringing closer that fateful day when Ginny would no longer be at home. There was a conspiracy, I felt, that Ginny, in her trusting, loving, nature, would never have suspected—and I, of all people, was a part of it!

I don't recall any two months passing as quickly as January and February. Our time was active and full, with family and friends doing their utmost to help us in our helpless situation, but even though Ginny's condition continued to decline, she, as always, seemed pleased when folks came calling.

One time, when some friends were leaving after a pleasant afternoon visit, Ginny, who had sat quietly in our midst (a welcome change from her restless pacing) apparently enjoying the sound of voices around her, unexpectedly said with a warm smile as they were leaving, "You must come again." Even though this warm, gracious gesture, sincerely spoken directly from the heart and appropriately timed, was typical of Ginny, we were all startled, because for a long time most of her utterances, if there were any, had been unintelligible.

With the exception of a rare moment, now and then, the Ginny-that-had-been became further buried in the debris of a deteriorating mind. As the fateful day of her entrance into the Iowa Veterans Home drew ever closer, in spite of my dread, I was coming to realize (in my more rational moments) that she would no doubt be ready. Along with increasing confusion and other evidence of mental decline, there were beginning to be instances of incontinence. She was increasingly requiring constant supervision and more vigilance on the part of her caregivers, including me when those I'd hired were off duty. . . .

There were times when I thought I would collapse under the burden, and I longed to be able to share it with her, the one who had been my strength and comfort in times past—in all the crises we had gone through together. But *this* one, our greatest ever, she would not even be able to comprehend. I thanked God for a loving, supportive family.

Thinking About The Case

A diagnosis of Alzheimer's Disease invokes despair and hopelessness. The most common form of dementia, Alzheimer's Disease affects five and a half million Americans. It is progressive, incurable, and always fatal. Prior to death it gradually robs sufferers of their memory as well as their ability to care for themselves.

Alzheimer's is not a normal part of aging. It can affect younger people as well, though in far fewer numbers. When it occurs in people younger than sixty-five, it is called "early onset Alzheimer's." Nor is Alzheimer's the only cause of memory loss in the elderly. Other forms of dementia, like vascular dementia, Lewy's Bodies dementia, Parkinson's and Huntington's Disease also cause cognitive deterioration. In addition, depression and medications can also cause memory problems.

Age is, however, the greatest risk factor for Alzheimer's as the risk rises with each decade of life. Other risk factors include family history and the presence of certain genes that can predispose or even cause Alzheimer's in susceptible individuals. Head injury and heart and/or blood vessel disease are also risk factors. The risk is higher in Latinos and African Americans than it is in Caucasians.

Alzheimer's begins insidiously. It may take many months or even years before the disease is diagnosed. At its start, the individual begins to have difficulty retaining newly learned material but distant memories remain intact. Misplacing objects, getting confused while driving somewhere relatively unfamiliar, and forgetting an appointment are examples of problems that may occur early on. Gradually, skills are lost. The person can no longer follow a recipe, or perhaps, even remember to turn off the stove. He or she may forget how to dress properly and may wear too many or outlandish clothes. Well-rehearsed routes and routines are forgotten. Car keys wind up in the refrigerator. The person goes out for a walk and can't find the way back home. At the end, loved ones' faces and even their existence may be forgotten. Or the person may remember them, but think that they are still children.

Emotional reactions to having the symptoms of Alzheimer's vary widely. Some sufferers have little to no insight and therefore no emotional changes. Others who are more aware of the changes in their functioning may experience depression, paranoia (thinking that someone has been stealing your money when in fact you have misplaced it), anxiety, and hopelessness. Some severely demented people are cheerful while others are angry or frightened most of the time.

Caring for a person with Alzheimer's is a great challenge. While many families do so at home, some with help from professional caregivers and others without; other families find that they can not manage their relative at home and institutional care is required. As the baby boomer generation enters the period of high risk for Alzheimer's, the need for facilities appropriate for residents with memory problems is increasing. And, where once Alzheimer's patients were warehoused in nursing homes with little attention and scant services, it is now thought important to maximize the quality of life for these people through providing a more homelike environment and through attempts to stimulate whatever cognitive skills each person retains. Therefore, art, music, cooking, and crafts are often available in good memory-care facilities.

As Ginny's husband makes clear, Alzheimer's takes its toll on caregivers and other family members. They gradually lose the person they love, bit by bit, while roles shift from partner (in the case of spouses) or cared for (in the case of adult children) to caregiver. Often social networks are strained as the patient's behavior changes over time and family members find themselves isolated and stressed. Financial stresses can mount as the patient's needs for professional services increases. Depression, anxiety, and despair are common sequelae in relatives, especially caregivers. Support groups for caregivers, often sponsored by local churches, hospitals, or the Alzheimer's Association can be invaluable tools for those who have family members or even friends who suffer from Alzheimer's.

Alzheimer's has no cure at present but research is ongoing. There are now a few medications that may slow the progression of the disease in some sufferers. Abnormalities in brain structure and chemistry associated with Alzheimer's in at least some sufferers have been identified. If any of these are found to be causal, then reversing these abnormalities may be possible in future. A great deal of publicity and money has been dedicated to this cause, and we can be hopeful that progress will be made in the foreseeable future.

Questions To Consider

1. Do you have a family member with Alzheimer's? Do any of your friends? How has the illness affected the family?
2. `Alzheimer's is clearly a neurological disorder. Should it be listed in the DSM-5? Why or why not?
3. If you were designing a facility for Alzheimer's sufferers what would it look like? What aspects of its design would be most important? What services would you offer? Why?

LANAHAN NOTES
Neurocognitive Disorders (NCD)

Types of Neurocognitive Disorders

Delirium: generally a short-term (hours, a day or so) disturbance in one's attention and awareness; confusion, disorientation; affects executive function, learning and memory, language, perceptual-motor, or social cognition; typically seen in older individuals, though high fevers in children might cause delirium

Major neurocognitive disorder: a significant cognitive decline in one or more cognitive domains including: complex attention, executive function, learning and memory, language, perceptual-motor or social cognition; so profound a deficit that it severely interferes with one's everyday activities

Mild neurocognitive disorder: a more modest cognitive decline in one or more cognitive domains including: complex attention, executive function, learning and memory, language, perceptual-motor, or social cognition; tends not to interfere greatly with one's everyday activities

Causes of neurocognitive disorders

Pathological processes associated with aging

Alcohol and drugs, including some prescription drugs (or combinations thereof)

Traumatic brain injury (blows to the head; also, tumors)

Physical disease

The following specific diseases can also bring about NCDs

- Alzheimer's disease
- Frontotemporal lobar degeneration
- Lewy body disease
- Vascular disease
- HIV infection
- Prion disease
- Parkinson's disease
- Huntington's disease

Treatment

Medical approach: remove (if possible) medical source of problem, e.g., treat the disease causing NCD

Medications: some may slow the progression of symptoms

Psychotherapy: retrain and rehabilitate the individual's cognitive skills (sometimes possible depending on physical injury to the brain); supportive psychotherapy may help the individual (and family) cope with cognitive deficits

CHAPTER EIGHTEEN

Personality Disorders

Some people seem to make the same mistakes over and over and over again. One person seems to distrust everybody he meets, leading people to behave towards him in distant, distrustful ways in return. Thus, he creates a self-fulfilling prophecy that only strengthens his views of others. Another seems to overreact emotionally—he falls hopelessly in love, demands absolute devotion and attentiveness, only to become suicidally depressed when his lovers inevitably run from his smothering affection. His life seems to be a screenplay for a grade-B movie. Yet another seems stubborn and unmotivated, sabotaging her chances for career improvement by never seeming to get things done on time, forgetting important meetings, and resisting suggestions. She lacks assertiveness in personal relationships as well, frustrating those who might become her friends by finding ways to get out of taking her share of responsibility for the relationship. These people, and many others like them are said to have personality disorders—longstanding, pervasive, and entrenched patterns of perceiving, thinking about, and relating to the world that result in impaired functioning and/or subjective distress.

Personality disorders are grouped into clusters based on similarities in the symptom picture. Cluster A includes disorders marked by odd or eccentric behavior. Cluster B disorders are characterized by dramatic, impulsive, and erratic behavior. The Cluster B disorder is particularly vivid and can result in enormous difficulty for those who come in contact with people who have them. These disorders raise fascinating and important questions about distinctions between "bad" and "mad," and when people are or are not responsible for their behavior. Cluster C is marked by anxiety and fearfulness. Many individuals fit the criteria for more than one personality disorder, and many people with personality disorders also have other disorders, like addictions or depression. For this chapter, we have chosen one disorder from Cluster A, one from Cluster B, and one from Cluster C.

CASE 46

PARANOID–SCHIZOTYPAL PERSONALITY DISORDER: THE CASE OF PETER N.

PETER N. IS A FORTY-FOUR-YEAR-OLD MAN who lives alone in a rundown trailer several miles outside of a small New England town. His appearance is decidedly odd. He is a small, emaciated man who has a full beard and wears old, often torn, clothing. He smells awful, as if he hadn't bathed in months. Townspeople give him a wide berth, not only because of his odor, but because he has flown off the handle at shopkeepers and bank tellers, yelling and cursing at what seem to be imaginary insults and slights. Everyone recognizes him, and while some people feel sorry for him, most are afraid of him. The sheriff's deputies are also familiar with Peter. Most of them have been on duty when he has created a scene in the community, or they have been to his trailer in response to neighbors' complaints that he threatened them or frightened them.

The appearance of Peter's trailer is also decidedly odd. His bedroom is covered with scraps of newspaper articles dabbed with blue paint. The articles are about the mental health system at which he is currently quite angry. Blue is his special color, reflecting, he says "the deepest parts of my personality." Blue paint is everywhere, on furniture, cooking utensils, even his shoes.

Also everywhere are the strange objects that he collects for his "projects." These projects always have to do with shielding himself or his possessions from harm. One of these projects, for example, involved using lime to clean lead which he then intended to melt down and coat other metal objects to protect them. He spent the better part of his welfare check to purchase huge bags of lime which sat around until his attachment to this particular project was supplanted by another project, as it always was. Then he returned the lime. Often, he was unable to return supplies, even when he berated the shopkeeper, so his stock kept gradually increasing. The trailer, both inside and out, exudes chaos. Weeds choke out grass. Clutter overwhelms order.

Peter doesn't work. Over the years, he has tried one job or another, but he has never been able to tolerate being involved with others for more than a few days. Invariably, he would become convinced that people were plotting to ensure that he would never have a relationship with a woman, that he didn't deserve such a relationship. He believed that other people thought that he was homosexual. He was enraged to think they believed this of him. On occasion, he would confront someone about this plot and get escorted off the premises. He hasn't tried to work in years now, and seems offended if anyone suggests that he should earn a living. This strong sense that he is entitled to be supported and to get what he wants when he wants it is a consistent thread in his view of himself in the world. Rather than work, Peter's habit is to spend intensive time on one of his projects for weeks or months, then impulsively go on a trip. While away, he lives in cheap, dingy single rooms. Nobody really knows how he spends his days while he's gone.

Sometimes he house sits for his parents. Generally, he arrives a day or so before they leave, and he leaves shortly after they return. He looks forward to seeing them, but can't stay in their presence for more than a few hours without getting into a noisy argument. Mrs. N. often gives him small gifts of money so that he can keep his truck going or buy a pair of shoes. Her husband objects because he feels that Peter should be supporting himself, but to no avail.

Peter is the second son, born to first-generation Jewish immigrants. His father is an accountant and his mother is a homemaker. Little information about his childhood is actually available, since his distrust makes communication with others, particularly about personal matters, difficult. Apparently, his older brother had an uneventful childhood and is now married, a father, and employed. Peter, on the other hand, seemed to have difficulties from the start. What seems clear is that he exhibited school refusal and other oppositional behaviors from an early age. His parents found him more and more difficult to manage and placed him in a residential treatment setting when he was ten or eleven. He hated it there because most of the children had severe behavioral problems and he was often targeted for batterings by more aggressive youngsters. He blamed his parents, especially his mother for "dumping" him there.

Although quite intelligent, Peter was in and out of school over the next several years, often running away for weeks at a time. It is unclear whether he actually graduated from high school—sometimes he talks about dropping out, while in other conversations he mentions having attended some community college classes.

Peter has been involved with the mental health system since he was a child and, at one time or another, has been on the receiving end of nearly every kind of service available—residential treatment, outpatient treatment, rehabilitation training programs, psychotherapy, and pharmacotherapy. None of these has seemed to have much impact, although, to be fair, it is hard to assess what his life would have been like without these interventions. His mental health connections seem to afford him his only safe human contact (outside of his parents, to whom he remains ambivalently attached), a tenuous but sufficient connection with the real world. He has lived like this for over twenty years, and may well do so for forty more.

Thinking About the Case

Psychiatric diagnosis is an inexact science. Nowhere is this more apparent than in the area of personality disorder where an indivdiual's symptoms may range across diagnostic categories within one of the clusters, and even between clusters. The case of Peter N. is a good example of this kind of diagnostic overlap. He certainly exhibits the pervasive distrust and suspiciousness that is the hallmark of paranoid personality disorder, and would probably be classified as such by many clinicians. He also meets the diagnostic criteria for schizotypal personality disorder: ideas of reference (thinking that others are talking about or laughing at him), odd beliefs inconsistent with cultural norms (the idea that painting things blue will protect him in some way), odd thinking and speech, suspiciousness, paranoid ideas, inappropriate emotions, behavior and appearance that is peculiar, a lack of close friends, and excessive social anxiety associated with paranoid fears.

To complicate matters, an argument could be made that Peter's symptoms almost meet the criteria for the Cluster B disorder, antisocial personality disorder. He fails to conform to social norms, is irritable and aggressive, and is irresponsible in terms of working for a living—three rather than the four necessary symptoms. Clearly he exhibits the sense of entitlement that invariably accompanies this disorder. Finally, his behaviors are also indicative of avoidant personality disorder, a Cluster C diagnosis. He shows the characteristic pattern of feelings of social inadequacy, avoidance of social interactions and hypersensitivity to negative evaluation at a level that would clearly be sufficient to meet the criteria for this diagnostic category. However, his thinking and behavior are so bizarre, and his social avoidance so clearly related to paranoid ideas that this diagnosis seems inadequate to capture the flavor of the case. According to the DSM-5, multiple diagnoses can and should be given if appropriate, so Peter would probably receive the diagnoses paranoid personality disorder and schizotypal personality disorder, with avoidant and antisocial features.

Many clinicians would entertain the possibility that Peter actually has schizophrenia. However, while he has fleeting delusional ideas (although not really a well-formed delusional system), he does not report hallucinations nor has he ever exhibited the gross disorganization of speech and behavior that characterize the acute phase of schizophrenia. Rather, the syndrome he exhibits has the characteristic childhood onset and unchanging course that is typical of personality disorders.

Questions to Consider

1. Do Peter's symptoms meet the criteria for any of the disorders discussed earlier in the book? Consider specifically social phobia and depression. If not, what criteria are not met?
2. What do you make of the fact that Peter's brother appears to have developed normally both as a child and as an adult? What factors could explain the differences in how the brothers turned out?
3. What are the implications of the fact that an individual like Peter can meet the criteria for several personality disorders at once? What does this say about our present diagnostic system?

CASE 47

BORDERLINE PERSONALITY DISORDER: THE CASE OF ROBERTA F.

"I'd like to make an appointment, please," she murmured softly into the telephone.

"Certainly. May I have your name, please?"

"No, I'd rather not . . . "

"I'm sorry, but we need your name in order to schedule you with a therapist."

"I don't see why that's necessary. Don't you people have some kind of thing about confidentiality?"

"Yes, we don't give out information about our clients without their written permission. Still, we need to have your name in order to set up an appointment."

"I suppose if I had the money to pay for a private therapist, I wouldn't have to go through all of this. My name is Roberta."

Roberta arrived fifteen minutes late for her first appointment. Her therapist, Dr. T., was impressed with how thin and gaunt the young woman appeared. When he inquired as to why she had requested counseling, she said that her boyfriend had told her to come—the choice was his, not hers. She didn't feel she needed any help. Dr. T. asked her why she thought her boyfriend had decided she needed counseling. She replied, "because of these," and rolling up the right sleeve of her white blouse, she revealed a line of small circular burn marks that started about three inches above her wrist and meandered up her inner arm with an inch or two space between each burn.

"Are those cigarette burns?" Dr. T. asked.

"Yes," she whispered.

"Where else do you have them?"

Silently, she touched her chest and her belly and then drew her fingers lightly up the inside of her left arm.

Dr. T. paused and then said, "Your boyfriend thinks you should get help to stop burning yourself, but you're not at all sure that you agree. Is that right?"

"Very perceptive, doctor."

Noting the sarcasm in Roberta's voice, Dr. T. knew that his next comment would have to be chosen carefully. In an instant, he decided against commenting upon her apparent anger and said instead, "perhaps we could explore together the meaning and value that the burning has for you so that you can become clearer in your own mind about whether you'd like to give it up. Would that be okay?"

Roberta considered before replying, "maybe. We'll see."

Over the next seven months, Dr. T. met with Roberta twice a week. Their sessions were unpredictable and stressful for the therapist. Sometimes Roberta was almost mute, seemingly too depressed (or sometimes too angry) to speak. At other times she was sarcastic and demeaning towards everybody and everything, including Dr. T. Occasionally she seemed lively and energized, quite normal in fact. Her warm, engaging behavior in these sessions bordered on the seductive. Even then, she could turn in an instant, becoming angry or hurt. Through the storms and the silences, Dr. T. learned some of Roberta's history.

Roberta was the third child, and only girl, in her family of four children. Her father ran an automobile scrap business in the small midwestern town in which they lived. Her mother kept the business's financial books but otherwise did not work outside the home. While the family was not exactly poor, neither were they financially comfortable. They had ample food and warm clothing (often passed down within the family) but little in the way of luxuries.

Roberta's father worked long hours, spending his free time hunting and fishing with his friends and sons. Her mother worked hard as well and often seemed tired and edgy. While Roberta's parents didn't argue much, she discovered when she was about eleven that her father had been having a long-term affair with a woman from a neighboring town. Apparently, her mother had decided for reasons of her own not to confront or leave him, but rather to suffer his separateness in silence. Roberta remembers that dinnertimes were eerie, with conversations that kept to "please pass the potatoes," and "this meatloaf isn't as good as the last one you made." She sometimes felt that she lived in a household of strangers.

"Roberta was a shy, clingy child from the start," her mother would later say. She had been easily upset by loud noises and changes of routine. The tumult and disorder created by her two older brothers seemed to overwhelm her. Mrs. F. often felt smothered by Roberta, whose needs for soothing and reassurance seemed endless. What Roberta remembers is that "my mother was never there for me. My father spent time with my brothers. Nobody spent time with me."

Mrs. F. has heard these complaints from Roberta many times over the past ten years. Her reaction is mixed, composed of equal parts astonishment, resentment, and guilt. Looking back, she doesn't see how she could have done more, as busy as she was and as isolated as she felt, but Roberta's blaming seems always to hit home anyway.

Roberta's early school years were uneventful from her parents' perspective. She attended regularly and got acceptable grades, unlike her brothers whose academic performances were marginal and whose social behavior at school left much to be desired. Mr. F., himself a bit of a "hell-raiser" in his own youth was tolerant of his sons' misbehaviors, despite his wife's silent disapproval. Still he and his wife were both grateful that Roberta seemed to be achieving some measure of success without the constant surveillance their sons seemed to require.

Roberta's own recollections of these years belied the surface calm. "I always got picked on," she told Dr. T. bitterly. "The kids didn't like me because I wore my brothers' clothes. At lunch I sat by myself. That's when I learned the difference between the 'haves' and the 'have-nots.' Even the teachers pushed me away, despite my doing everything they asked me to do."

In fourth grade, something even worse happened. Roberta's oldest brother, Sam, turned fifteen and began babysitting his younger siblings two evenings a week while his mother went to Bingo and his father was out with "the boys." On one of these evenings, a few weeks after he'd started babysitting, Sam decided to "help" Roberta with her bath. Overriding her protests with the statement that he was in charge while their parents were gone, he demanded that she stand naked in front of him so that he could "make sure I was clean." Gradually, over the next several months, Sam's demands escalated. He watched her undress. He watched her urinate. By spring he had begun to masturbate as he watched her.

Roberta hated Sam for what he was doing. His behavior embarrassed, shamed, and sickened her. But she was also afraid of him. She knew from her own experience that he would slap or even punch her if she were uncooperative. Sam said, and she agreed, that her parents would blame her if she told them what he had been doing. So she cooperated, and in doing so came to feel even more worthless, dirty, and unlovable than she had felt before.

Not until the next winter did the situation gradually change. Sam got a girlfriend who often kept him company while he babysat. On these evenings he left Roberta alone. More and more often, Sam himself went out, leaving Roberta and her younger brother in the care of Steve, the second oldest brother, who basically ignored her. By summer, when Sam was almost eighteen and Roberta was fourteen, the abuse had virtually stopped.

Still, the prolonged trauma had taken its toll. Roberta, feeling desperate for attention and acceptance, and having been taught how finally to get it, became sexually active at age fifteen. She had believed her boyfriend really loved her, and she was emotionally devastated when he dropped her after going to bed with her twice. It was then that Roberta first burned herself—in response to overpowering feelings of self-loathing and fury.

Thus began an addictive pattern in which Roberta responded to painful feelings with self-destructive behavior that produced immediate relief but, in the long run, contributed to her self-hatred. She burned herself whenever she felt mistreated, isolated, or depressed. She told Dr. T. that she usually felt a lot better after she did it, but that the peaceful feeling gradually eroded over the course of a few weeks, giving way to increasing emotional discomfort as she absorbed innumerable slights, insults, annoyances, hostilities, smirks, sneers, and snubs from her co-workers at the supermarket, where she now worked as a checkout clerk, and from her brothers.

Externally, Roberta was living a fairly normal life as others saw her. She still lived at home—an attempt to share an apartment with an acquaintance right after high school hadn't worked out. She had a social life of sorts—an ever-changing assortment of people to do things with, but she declined to call any of them friends.

She even had a boyfriend. Richard, a twenty-five-year-old high school drop-out, was both possessive and abusive. He and Roberta went to bars on weekends and both invariably drank to the point of drunkenness. Typically, under the influence of alcohol, he'd get angry at Roberta for some real or imagined flirtation and was not above slapping or shoving her against the wall. Roberta felt that Richard both loved and needed her. Abuse was far preferable to neglect.

Lately, Roberta had become increasingly concerned about her weight. She'd seen Richard staring at other women, and she was convinced that he thought she was fat. When she looked in the mirror, her thighs looked huge and her waist appeared thickened. She reported to Dr. T. that she had recently lost twenty-three pounds by exercising and severely restricting her food intake, but still she felt fat. Whenever she got on the scale and discovered that she had lost another pound or two, she experienced the exhilaration and relief that burning herself produced, but the feeling never lasted very long. Lately, she often felt dizzy and weak from lack of food, but she found this strangely comforting. "At last," she thought, "I'm really doing it."

Aside from getting some sense of her history, Dr. T. made little progress during the therapy. Roberta seemed unable to maintain a comfortable distance from him, vacillating between feeling uncomfortably dependent and completely unconnected and untrusting. She confided once that frequently she spent hours prior to a therapy session thinking about what she would tell him and how he would react. Often she made up things just to see what he would say. She continued to express a great deal of self-loathing and the frequency of burning remained essentially the same. Dr. T.'s suggestions that Roberta try a medication that might help with her depression and her impulsively self-destructive behavior were met with complete resistance. She seemed to take these as attempts to get rid of her—"you just want to give me pills, because you can't stand to talk to me."

After a while Roberta's boyfriend tired of her alternating moods and her ceaseless demands for attention. Upon discovering that he had been seeing another woman behind her back, she became enraged and impulsively swallowed all the pills in her medicine cabinet—a combination of aspirin, cold medicine, and muscle relaxants. A few minutes later, she called and left Richard a message on his answering machine, telling him what she had done. Luckily, he came home shortly thereafter and called 911. Later that day, after getting her stomach pumped, Roberta was admitted to the psychiatric unit of her local hospital.

During the two weeks she was in the hospital, Roberta was seen daily by a psychiatrist. She also attended a therapy group where she was angrily mute. Attempts to get her to participate in occupational therapy or other ward activities were unsuccessful. Shortly before her release, Dr. T. visited Roberta to help prepare her for the transition back to outpatient therapy. During that visit, she confided that she was still suicidal, and, in fact, intended to kill herself as soon as she was released. This placed Dr. T. on the horns of a difficult ethical dilemma. On the one hand, his duty was to protect Roberta from harm. On the other, he was bound by the obligation to keep Roberta's communications confidential. Further, he knew that Roberta had set him a test, but he was unable to figure out what decision would constitute the right one. He suspected that he had been put in a lose-lose situation.

Dr. T. decided to notify the ward staff of Roberta's intentions. His decision enraged Roberta, who berated him for violating her confidentiality and for trying to interfere with her right to make an independent decision whether to live or die. Dr. T. spoke with the nurse in charge of the unit, and left with the sounds of Roberta yelling and cursing at him reverberating in his ears. The next day, the hospital psychiatrist called Dr. T. and suggested that he not visit again, since his visit the preceding day had obviously upset Roberta. The following morning Dr. T. received a letter from Roberta, firing him as her therapist. Despite his attempts to follow-up, he did not hear from her again.

Thinking About the Case

What is "borderline" about borderline personality disorder? It was originally conceived of as a disorder that had elements of both neurotic (in touch with reality) and psychotic (out to touch with reality) functioning, and was therefore on the hypothetical "borderline" between the two states. Our current classification system characterizes it as an enduring behavioral predisposition that increases the likelihood of and exacerbates a host of conditions like depression, anxiety disorders, somatization disorders, dissociative disorders, substance abuse disorders, and eating disorders.

Roberta's behavior patterns fit the criteria for borderline personality disorder. She is impulsive, self-destructive and moody. Her relationship with Dr. T. mirrors other significant relationships in her life in its intensity and instability. Roberta alternates between idealizing those she cares about and devaluing them. She is intensely frightened of losing them, yet she pushes them away. She can't seem to maintain a comfortable emotional distance from others. Her primary emotion seems to be anger, although she is prone to feelings of emptiness and depression.

Conducting therapy with people with this disorder is challenging in the extreme. Because of their difficulty maintaining a consistent level of attachment, individuals with borderline disorder have enormous trouble establishing a truly therapeutic relationship—one in which they feel valued and safe. It is not uncommon for them to behave in ways which provoke inappropriate behavior from people trying to help them. Therapists may find themselves uncharacteristically uncertain about boundary issues, tolerating gradually increasing demands for time and attention, or becoming unduly rigid. They may struggle with strong feelings of fury, attraction, or loathing for their client. Genuine violations of the therapist-client relationship, like sexual contact between client and therapist, while rare in general, are more likely to happen when the client has borderline personality disorder than when he or she has most other disorders.

Borderline disorder has become highly controversial on at least three counts. First, it is diagnosed much more often in women than in men.

This might reflect a genuine difference in prevalence, or it might reflect gender-based bias in diagnostic practices. Second, the diagnosis tends to carry a strongly pejorative charge. Clients with this diagnosis are avoided by many mental health professionals because their care is so often unrewarding. They are unlikely to be grateful and they often fail to improve. Third, studies indicate that a large percentage of women diagnosed with borderline personality disorder have a history of prolonged childhood trauma—often in the form of physical or sexual abuse.

Dr. Judith Herman, an expert in traumatology, suggests that borderline personality disorder is really a stigmatizing way of describing a kind of chronic post-traumatic stress syndrome. One of her patients, quoted in her book, *Trauma and Recovery* (Basic Books, 1992, p. 128), describes her own experience this way:

> Having that diagnosis resulted in my getting treated exactly the way I was treated at home. The minute I got that diagnosis people stopped treating me as though what I was doing had a reason. All that psychiatric treatment was just as destructive as what happened before.
>
> Denying the reality of my experience—that was the most harmful. Not being able to trust anyone was the most serious effect. . . . I know I acted in ways that were despicable. But I wasn't crazy. Some people go around acting that way because they feel hopeless. Finally I found a few people along the way who have been able to feel OK about me even though I had severe problems. Good therapists were those who really validated my experience.

Dr. Herman points out that adult abuse survivors show symptoms similar to those shown by other survivors of chronic trauma, namely Vietnam veterans who engaged in prolonged combat or were prisoners of war. She feels that the common component is psychological or physical captivity. Borderline personality disorder will likely remain among the most controversial and challenging disorders to understand and to treat for some time.

Questions to Consider

1. Speculate about biological factors that might be relevant to the development of Roberta's disorder. How might these interact with environmental factors to produce her symptoms?
2. What do you think of Dr. Herman's hypothesis that prolonged captivity and abuse lead to the development of borderline personality disorder? How might you explain the presence of the disorder in a person with no apparent history of that sort?
3. Why do you think borderline personality disorder co-exists so often

with other psychiatric disorders? How would you expect its presence to affect the outcome of treating the other co-existing disorders?

4. Design a study (or series of studies) to decide whether borderline personality disorder truly occurs more often in women or whether there is some sort of diagnostic bias operating.

CASE 48

AVOIDANT PERSONALITY DISORDER: THE CASE OF CARL S.

Carl S., an eighteen-year-old college freshman, had been in psychotherapy off and on since he was nine. He was first referred by his mother, a psychologically-minded public school teacher, who felt he was overly shy, socially isolated, and unhappy compared to his peers. Carl's father, a successful attorney, was less convinced that Carl had a problem warranting outside intervention. He, too, had been shy as a youngster (still was, although he hid it better now) and had done alright in the world. He and Carl's mother had been divorced for two years by the time Carl was first seen, and disagreement seemed to be their primary mode of interaction.

At nine, Carl was a short and chubby child who only reluctantly agreed to accompany the therapist to her office. Once there, he hopped up onto the seat she pointed to, each hand clutching an armrest, and looked anxiously around the room. His formidable intelligence was immediately apparent. His vocabulary and sentence organization was advanced, and his capacity to talk about computers, his singular passion, was astonishing.

Carl described himself as "somewhat" lonely at present, because his best (and only) friend had moved out of town a year ago. He didn't seem to have much in common with other boys, he felt. They were into sports and he was the least athletic kid he had ever known. "I can't throw or catch a ball, and if I try to kick it, I fall on my face," he related wistfully. Gym class was a torment for him. He felt himself to be a huge liability to any team he was assigned to, and he was embarrassed by his weight and his lack of skills. Kids did tease him some, but even when they didn't he felt awful. Often, he had stomachaches before gym class, and twice he had even vomited while suiting up and had spent the period in the nurse's office.

Carl did play in the marching band, a fairly popular activity, but no one spoke to him very much, and when they did, he didn't know what to say. His social awkwardness seemed to put other children off and for the most part, he was left alone. In the school lunchroom he ate alone. He walked to and from school alone. He wanted friends, he told the therapist, but he didn't think he was "made to have friends." He had long since given up trying. For several years now, he hadn't spoken to people outside of his family unless he was spoken to first.

Carl's life was not altogether unhappy, though. His teachers loved him. He was bright, diligent, and eager to please. He worked well on an independent basis and never participated in class shenanigans. His home life was pretty peaceful (except for the verbal wars between his parents which mostly went on outside of his earshot). When he was at his father's, he played chess with his dad or computer games most of the weekend. At his mom's house (his primary residence), he felt "sometimes good and sometimes bad." While he loved spending time with his older sister and his mom, he was acutely uncomfortable with his new stepfather who had sons of his own with whom he engaged in the kind of rough-and-tumble relationship that Carl couldn't seem to do right. He felt awkward and inadequate around his stepfather. He didn't know what to say to him at the dinner table. When his stepbrothers came to visit, Carl generally went to his dad's. This was fine with him because sharing a room with them made him really anxious. He knew they thought he was a wimp, and for some reason, he always acted "even stupider" when they were around.

Carl's therapist did not think that he was clinically depressed. While he did seem sad, he was eating and sleeping okay, his concentration was fine, and he seemed able to have a good time when not in a socially stressful situation. Carl said that he was interested in feeling better, but he vehemently denied wanting to make friends. He was fine, he said, with his family and his computer. The idea of trying to talk to children he didn't know was just too painful to entertain.

His therapist decided to try cognitive therapy to help Carl think about his social interactions in a new way. She had two major goals. The first was to help Carl stop "mindreading" other people—assuming that he knew what they were thinking about him. The second was to help him "decatastrophize," so that he wouldn't feel awful every time he perceived himself to have made a social blunder. Since Carl was verbal and loved academic tasks, she decided to use a chalkboard as a therapy tool. Together, she and Carl embarked on examining what he told himself about various situations. First, he identified a thought like "all the kids think I'm a total geek and I can't stand it." Then, writing it on the chalkboard, he learned to identify the "illogical" components of the thought with his therapist's help. "How do you know that 'all' the kids think you're a geek," she asked. "Do you mean that they're thinking about you all the time, and they think you're a geek all the time?" "Isn't it possible that you only act in a geeky way some of the time?" "What do you mean by 'I can't stand it?'" "Haven't you 'stood it' up until now?" "Don't you really mean that you don't like it?" Finally, he constructed more "logical" sentences: "It's possible that some kids think I act in a geeky way some of the time. It's also possible that some kids admire my brains or want to get to know me better. Even if some kids think I'm a geek, it doesn't make me one. And even if some people think I'm geeky, I can still be happy and successful."

Carl enjoyed the verbal sparring with his therapist. He enjoyed writing on the chalkboard and modifying the sentences to his therapist's satisfaction. She gave him an assignment to identify irrational sentences he found himself thinking while at school, and he enjoyed reporting back to her about what he had discovered. Over the course of twelve sessions, his mood improved substantially. By that time, school had come to a close and Carl's mother and the therapist agreed to terminate his treatment, at least for the summer.

Carl returned to the therapist's office two years later. He had asked his mother to set up a visit, because his father had remarried and he was having difficulty feeling comfortable around his stepmother. Now eleven, Carl was still a social isolate. Academically, he continued to perform in the superior range. He had quit the marching band because watching the other kids interact with each other at practices had been too painful for him. He continued with private trumpet lessons, which he enjoyed. He had found the Internet and had developed a number of long-distance relationships. When people couldn't see him and when he had time to construct his responses, he worried somewhat less about what they might think of him. The Internet brought him a great deal of pleasure, but also further distanced him from face-to-face interpersonal contact.

Carl's father and stepmother were willing to participate in therapy, so the therapist conducted several family therapy sessions in which she attempted to find some common ground between Carl and his stepmother, Mary. Mary appeared to be a shy and awkward person herself. She had been an only child and didn't have any experience living with a pre-teen boy. She wanted to be a good stepmother to Carl and seemed willing to work at it. When Carl heard his stepmother describe her own adolescence, he realized that her behavior towards him did not reflect her evaluation of him, but rather her own shyness. Using the "sentence-modifying" skills he had learned in his previous therapy experience, he was able to reduce his fear that Mary didn't like him and wished he weren't there.

Together he and Mary practiced asking each other questions about how their respective weeks had gone until they were able to have brief conversations together. This gave them both more confidence, and therapy was once again terminated by mutual consent.

When he was fourteen, Carl and his parents returned for a consultation. Over time, their post-divorce relationship had mellowed so that they were increasingly able to cooperate when it came to Carl's and his sister's well-being. Now, they were thinking seriously about sending Carl to a Catholic school about fifteen miles away from the town in which he lived. Not unexpectedly, he was strenuously resisting this effort, as the thought of being with all new people terrified him. His parents felt that if he were in a school in which students valued intellectual strengths and talents as well as athletic prowess, he might have a more successful high school experience. They also wanted him to have the best possible education, and they felt that the rural school in which he was currently enrolled could not offer that. The therapist saw Carl's parents alone for the first session, Carl for the second, and all three of them for the third. The family was able to reach an agreement that Carl would attend the Catholic school for one year, at the end of which he would decide whether to continue there. While Carl wanted to be able to transfer back after one semester, his therapist convinced him that since it took him a long time to get comfortable in new social situations, three months would not give the Catholic school a fair chance. Reluctantly, he agreed.

A year-and-a-half later, Carl returned, this time self-referred. As expected, he did feel better at the Catholic school. The work was much more demanding, and he found the teasing much diminished. In fact, an atmosphere of mutual caring existed. Still, he felt completely on the margins of the school's society. As an adolescent, his isolation was becoming ever more painful. He now felt he wanted to work on making friends, even if the idea was very frightening. He still felt like a "geek" and couldn't imagine that anyone would want to be friends with him, but he was now willing to try.

He saw his therapist every few weeks for about a year. Continuing to use the cognitive techniques they had worked with years before, they now added specific behavioral assignments. The first was to make eye contact and smile at two people in the hallway each time he changed classes. When he was able to do this successfully, he took on the task of saying "hi" to at least one of these people each time. Gradually, the tasks increased both the duration and intensity of interaction. By the end of this course of treatment, he was eating lunch with a regular group of acquaintances each day, was able to call other students to discuss assignments, and engaged in casual conversation before and after classes. His final triumph before terminating was going on a school trip in which he had to room with three guys he didn't know for two nights. Choosing to go on the trip was itself an act of courage, and while he didn't actually make friends, he was able to interact with the other students, and he found to his surprise that he "wasn't miserable all the time." Even though he had not yet reached his goal of having friends with whom he felt comfortable doing things outside of school, he felt able to progress on his own from this point on.

The summer before college, he returned to his therapist's office once again, this time to discuss the transition ahead of him. He was worried about how he would fare with a roommate, whether he would be miserably lonely, how he would survive his father's directive that he should not return home to visit until Christmas, so he wouldn't be tempted to "retreat" into the comfort of his family. He still hadn't developed any personal friends. Virtually all of his socializing, what little of it there was, was done with his sister and her friends. He had had, however, a very successful experience working part-time at a computer supplies store. After some months, he had finally become reasonably comfortable with his coworkers and had felt valued, although "not for myself, but for what I know." The store had a branch near the university he was planning to attend, and his boss had offered to make sure he would be hired there.

At this point, therapy was mostly supportive, reminding Carl that he had developed a set of skills designed to help him meet and interact with new people and reinforcing his self-esteem. He went off to college with some trepidation, but also with some hope that he might not be "a complete and total isolate like I was before."

Thinking About the Case

Carl's problems fit the criteria of avoidant personality disorder quite well. He is socially inhibited, feels inadequate, and is exquisitely sensitive to criticism or negative evaluation by others. Notice that the criteria for social phobia are also met. These include marked fear of one or more social or performance situations related to concerns that the individual will be embarrassed or humiliated. Social phobia is diagnosed alone when the number of situations that stimulate the symptoms is relatively circumscribed or when the problem began sometime later than early adolescence. Avoidant personality disorder is more pervasive, earlier to develop, and generally carries with it a more extreme deficit in self-esteem.

Notice also that many of Carl's symptoms can occur in a normal condition that we call "shyness." Like the other personality disorders, this one appears to be an extreme variant of a normal personality dimension—in this case, extraversion-introversion. In order to qualify as a personality disorder, the condition must cause clinically significant distress or impairment in social, occupational, or other important aspects of functioning. Clearly, the cutoff point is a matter of subjective judgment.

This case is also noteworthy in that several kinds of therapy are employed: cognitive, behavioral, and supportive techniques, parent consultation, and family therapy. This eclectic approach is more common in day-to-day clinical practice than is dogmatic adherence to a single type of intervention. In fact, studies indicate that therapists with different theoretical orientations become more similar to each other in their actual behavior as they gain experience.

Finally, while Carl had a lot of therapy—off and on for nine years—his gains were modest. This is also not uncommon, particularly with respect to the personality disorders that are considered difficult to treat. In general, the more specific and limited (both in duration and pervasiveness) the disorder, the greater the chances of significant change with one or more psychotherapeutic approaches. More longstanding, generalized problems are more difficult to modify.

Questions to Consider

1. Do you favor nature, nurture, or a mixed model to explain this case? What evidence are you relying on?
2. What do you think of the therapist's decisions about choice of techniques and duration of treatment? Might you have made different choices at some point or another? Why or why not?
3. Do you consider Carl's therapy a success? Why or why not?
4. Why might experience change therapists such that they behave more alike over time, despite differences in theoretical orientation?
5. What other disorders (besides social phobia) might commonly co-occur with avoidant personality disorder? Why?

LANAHAN NOTES
Personality Disorders

Characteristics of personality disorders

Individual displays patterns of maladaptive behavior

Often appear early in life (late childhood to early adolescence)

Typically longstanding (possibly lifelong)

Pervasive (show up in lots of different situations)

Greatly affect one's social, intimate, and work life

May co-occur with other clinical disorders, among them, anxiety, depression, obsessive compulsive disorder; attention deficit disorder makes these co-occurring disorders more difficult to treat

Types of personality disorders: three groupings, or clusters

Cluster A: characterized by odd, bizarre, or eccentric behavior

Paranoid: individual is unusually distrustful and suspicious of people or surroundings

Schizoid: individual is socially detached; fails to connect with others; often emotionally blank

Schizotypal: marked by extreme social isolation and cognitive oddities; person may display behavioral eccentricities

Cluster B: characterized by dramatic, overly emotional, and/or erratic behavior

Antisocial: individual continually violates societal rules and expectations from being highly disruptive to actual criminal behavior (are they "bad" of "mad"—the courtroom conundrum)

Borderline: marked by instability in mood and personal relationships; individual often displays impulsive and emotionally destructive behavior toward self and others

Histrionic: individual seems overly dependent; has an excessive need to receive attention

Narcissistic: marked by grandiosity; excessive need for admiration; individual needs to be held high above others; often lacks empathy

Cluster C characterized by anxious or fearful behavior

Avoidant: individual is greatly inhibited socially; shows hypersensitivity to criticism; has feelings of inadequacy

Dependent: excessive need to be taken care of
Obsessive-compulsive: overly orderly, rigid, perfectionist

Personality disorders present challenges to researchers and clinicians

Despite their grouping into clear discrete "Clusters," there can be much overlap among them

Many people exhibit some of these behaviors: at what point are they considered disordered?

Causes of personality disorders

Much uncertainty as to what causes these disorders; probably some combination of the following:

Neuropsychological factors

Antisocial: may have impaired brain function compromising their ability to concentrate, plan, or inhibit behavior; or, they may be deficient in anxiety—unable to learn through the results of negative behavioral consequences

Cluster C individuals may have an inherited tendency toward heightened autonomic nervous system reactivity that is experienced as anxiety or timidity

Schizotypal (and maybe schizoid): possibly genetically related to the schizophrenia

Psychological Factors

Borderline: such behavior, psychodynamic theorists speculate, arises because of a failure of mother–infant bonding

Obsessive-compulsive: traits reflect an individual's attempt to control shameful or upsetting thoughts

Environmental or Social Factors

Borderline: important role of trauma; prolonged and severe physical, particularly sexual, abuse can produce lasting changes in an individual, esp., prevailing mood, ability to modulate emotions, self-concept

Modeling effects

Antisocial: an individual's behavior arises out of a chaotic and abusive background

Histrionic (esp. women): social role expectations encourage dependency behavior in women and their need for attention

Treatment of personality disorders

Generally thought to have a low to moderate probability of success: improvement rather than "cure."

Psychotherapy: emphasizes interpersonal relationships, particularly the therapy relationship (transference and countertransference)

Cognitive/behavioral therapy: some success with borderline individuals with controlling self-destructive behavior; helps reduce anxiety; helps some Cluster C individuals with their avoidance behavior

Medications: sometimes used as adjunct to psychotherapy, (antidepressants, anti-anxiety medications, anticonvulsants) to help with impulse control; antipsychotics help some Cluster A individuals).

CHAPTER NINETEEN

Paraphilic Disorders

Paraphilia is a condition in which a person's sexual arousal and gratification depend on fantasizing about and engaging in sexual behavior that is atypical and extreme. It can revolve around a particular inappropriate object (children, animals, underwear, shoes) or around a particular act (causing pain, exposing oneself). The focus of a paraphilia is usually very specific and unchanging and necessary for sexual gratification.

The most common paraphilias are pedophilia (sexual activity with a child), exhibitionism (exposure of one's genitals to strangers), voyeurism (observing private activities of unaware victims), frotteurism (touching or rubbing against a nonconsenting person), and sexual masochism and/or sadism.

Treatment of paraphilia is difficult as the urges tend to be intense and recurrent. Since some of the behaviors are illegal, some people in treatment may have legal situations surrounding their behavior, and some may resist seeking treatment because of the fear of becoming involved in those situations. Of course, these disorders, like the substance addiction disorders, raise once again the issue of whether treatment or punishment is a more appropriate societal response.

We have included two representative cases for your review. In the first, a man describes wanting to be spanked during sex. In the second, a person has gone to prison for repetitively involving children in sexual activity.

CASE 49

SEXUAL MASOCHISM DISORDER: THE CASE OF THE ANONYMOUS CALLER

AT MANY COMMUNITY MENTAL health centers where several clinicians might be working together, each clinician takes turns being "on call" for telephone calls and for people who walk in off the street without an appointment. On one such day, a receptionist at one of these centers buzzed the therapist on call about a caller who wanted to speak with "one of the doctors." The following is that therapist's own report of the telephone conversation.

"This is Dr. Frank. How can I help you?" I began.

"What I want to know is, is it abnormal to want to be . . . well . . . you know, spanked?" asked the male caller.

"Well, I need a little more information before I can answer your question. Can you tell me a bit more about it?"

"It's kind of embarrassing to talk about. . . . I like to be, like, spanked, during sex and I want to know if it's crazy or anything."

"Why has it become a problem for you right at this time?" I asked.

"Because my wife won't do it anymore. She says it's crazy and I should get help. I figure it's not hurting anybody, so it's O.K., you know? Still, I guess it is kind of weird. I want to know if she's right. Am I crazy?"

Carefully, I began, "What you're describing is called 'sexual masochism.' Statistically, it's abnormal, but so is being six-foot-four. Humans engage in a wide range of sexual behaviors. Some are more common than others. Odd sexual behaviors are only considered disorders when they cause significant problems for the person or those around him. What's normal or abnormal is less important than what works for you and your partner. How long have you been married?"

"Just about seven years. We get along pretty well, except for arguing about this." The caller must have been feeling more comfortable, because he went on. "You know, I know just how this started. I must have been about ten or eleven. I went to Catholic school. When you misbehaved, they were allowed to punish you . . . you know, physically. They had one nun there, Sister Catherine, who used to take you into the broom closet, take your pants down, put you across her lap, and hit you on the butt with a switch a couple of times. I don't know, I guess it was kind of a turn-on, you know? Lying on her lap, with my butt hanging out. I remember I'd get, you know . . . erections. Boy, I sure got into a lot of trouble the year she was my teacher!"

"Yes," I said, "that's often how these attractions develop. Some behavior or object, in your case, being spanked, is linked with sexual pleasure in childhood or early adolescence, and the association remains strong right into adulthood."

"Can you change it or is it permanent?" he asked.

"That's a good question. In general, old habits are hard to change, and habits associated with sexual pleasure seem particularly hard to change. The method that seems to work best is called "behavior therapy,' and it would involve pairing the spanking with something unpleasant like electric shocks or nausea or masturbating to the point of discomfort so that the spanking-pleasure link would be broken. Tell me, are you capable of becoming sexually aroused and enjoying sex without getting spanked?"

"Oh, yeah. I don't need it, really. I just like it, is all . . . although sometimes I imagine myself getting spanked when my wife won't do it."

"Well, then, since it's uncomfortable for your wife, maybe you could just choose to do without the actual behavior. You could keep the fantasy part if you like. Not many of us get absolutely everything we'd like in a real-life sexual relationship. Or, perhaps with some marital counseling, she might decide she could do it once in a while, just as a gift to you. If you do decide to do without, you could try some 'at home' behavioral techniques that might help to reduce your craving for getting spanked."

"What would that be like?"

"Well, it would involve using your imagination in a somewhat different way from the way you are using it now. It works like this: You find a quiet spot, develop a picture in your mind of getting spanked, just the way you like it, and then, when you begin to get aroused, you would substitute a picture of something you really dislike or are frightened of."

"What, you mean like getting punched in the face or put down in front of a whole bunch of people?"

"Exactly! See how that feels when you say it?"

"Yeah, creepy."

"Right," I said. "Creepy and pleasurable don't go together very well, do they?"

"I'll say they don't," he said emphatically.

"After you get good at developing the images, you'd begin to practice them when you find yourself thinking about getting spanked when you're with your wife. You'd also want to practice developing a wider range of erotic thoughts and images to use when you're making love so you'll have something to substitute for your spanking fantasies."

"So," I concluded, "what can we do for you? Would you like to come in for some behavioral therapy? Would you like to bring your wife in for some marital counseling so we could all talk about this together and maybe bring a little more harmony into your sexual relationship? Would you like to come in by yourself, just to talk it all over?"

"Nope," he said after a pause. "I don't think I need to do any of those things right now. I'm going to talk to my wife about what you said and see what she thinks. I'm glad to know I'm not crazy—that's all I really wanted to know. Thanks for your time."

The conversation ended here—the caller was never heard from again.

Thinking About the Case

Sexual masochism is one of the paraphilias—disorders in which sexual arousal is attached to unusual and/or inappropriate objects or behaviors. Note that strong urges or fantasies are enough to qualify for the disorder, even without the actual behavior, as long as the urges or fantasies have lasted at least six months, are intense and recurrent, and cause significant distress or dysfunction. This leaves a great deal of room for subjective judgment in the diagnostic process. An individual with intense masochistic fantasies who never acted them out but was greatly distressed by them would qualify for a diagnosis, while the caller in this case would probably not have been diagnosable as long as his wife was a willing partner, because the criterion of distress or dysfunction would not have been met. Still most of us would consider the caller to be the more "maladjusted" of the two.

Most research supports a learning theory explanation of the development of paraphilias as follows:

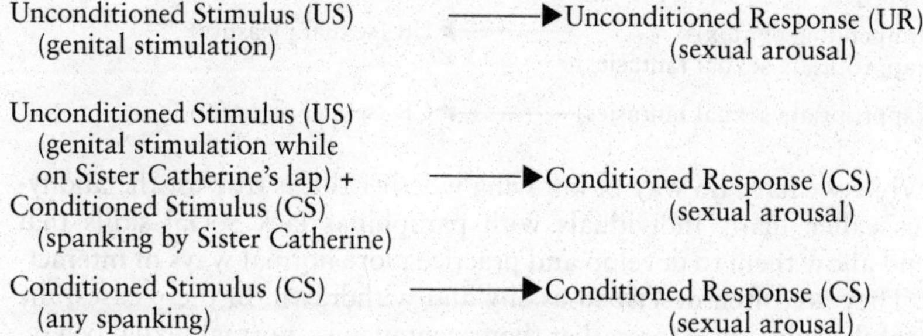

The same principles suggest how the disorder might be treated. Aversion therapy, including the imaginal kind suggested to the anonymous caller, is generally the treatment of choice. In actual treatment, the caller might be subjected to electric shock or chemical nauseants as he becomes aroused in response to masochistic stimuli, either supplied by the therapist in the form of tapes, movies, or readings, or self-produced in the form of fantasy. This procedure, in which sexual arousal in response to deviant stimuli is paired with aversive unconditioned stimuli is called "covert sensitization." A related technique, called "masturbatory satiation" might also be used. In this procedure, the caller would be asked to masturbate for a period of time, perhaps a half hour, following orgasm while continuing to fantasize about being spanked. Since masturbation after orgasm is unpleasant and uncomfortable, this would effectively pair an aversive US with the behavior to be extinguished. We diagram the treatment as follows:

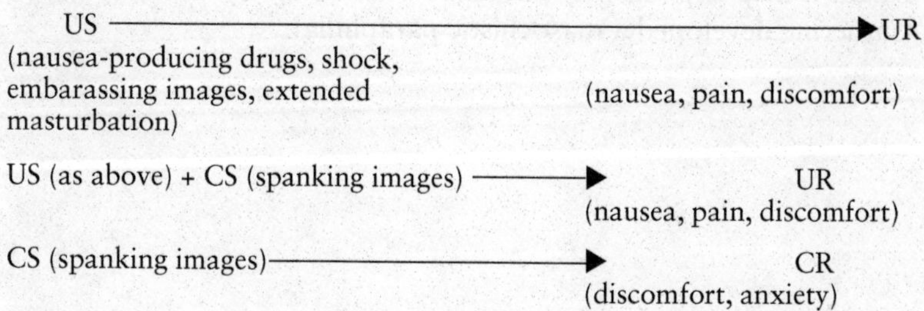

In order to strengthen the bond between non-spanking fantasies and sexual arousal, "orgasmic reconditioning" might be employed. The caller would be asked to masturbate, while narrating his fantasies aloud. As he reached climax he would substitute a more acceptable scene for the masochistic fantasy. Note that this was also suggested in the telephone call. We can diagram this as follow:

US (impending climax) ⟶ UR (sexual pleasure)

US (impending climax)+ ⟶ UR (sexual pleasure)
CS (appropriate sexual fantasies)

CS (appropriate sexual fantasies) ⟶ CR (sexual pleasure)

While we have no way of knowing whether this is true for the anonymous caller, many individuals with paraphilias lack social skills that would allow them to develop and practice more normal ways of interacting. They are often described as shy and withdrawn. In these cases, the paraphilia substitutes for, rather than accompanies, normal sexual behavior. Therefore, behavioral treatment directed specifically at the paraphilia might be accompanied by social skills training and therapy designed to increase self-esteem and self-confidence. In any case, treatment success is generally modest with many individuals dropping out of treatment or reverting to old ways once treatment has been completed.

Questions to Consider

1. Except for sadomasochism, the paraphilias occur almost exclusively in men. Why might this be so?
2. What does learning theory have to say about why the paraphilias are so persistent and resistant to change?
3. Does psychodynamic theory have anything useful to say about the paraphilias? Can it be applied to the case of the anonymous caller? Might it help explain why not all of the children spanked by Sister Catherine developed a masochistic paraphilia?

CASE 50

PEDOPHILIA: THE CASE OF JAMES Q.

James Q. is a forty-two-year-old single man who is presently incarcerated in state prison, having been sentenced to seven-to-twenty years for sexual abuse of children. He is known to have sexually fondled and pornographically photographed at least six children, but it is possible that he abused up to a hundred or more others. Until his arrest, he lived quietly in a small New England town, where he worked as a university groundskeeper. As a prisoner, he still lives quietly, keeping to himself and tending to the two decorative flower beds just inside the prison's gates.

James, the younger of two children, was raised in a middle-class household. His father, a plumber, was a heavy weekend drinker who was emotionally removed from the family. His mother stayed at home until all of the children were in school. Later, she worked as a clerk in a local shop. She was a quiet woman whose pasttimes were mostly crafts activities which she did in the company of her two sisters. She was especially proud of the handmade quilts she had made for each of her children and for each of her nieces and nephews.

While James' older sister was a good student, he was not. He had trouble learning to read and write and, in second grade, he was classified as intellectually "slow" and provided with special services that continued through his school career. He was not particularly athletic, so fitting in with other youngsters was somewhat difficult. In fifth grade, he learned to play the drum, which allowed him to participate in the marching band and afforded him some sense of acceptance at school.

James always seemed more comfortable with younger children, and his primary playmates were his two younger cousins. His first sexual experience was also with these cousins. When he was eleven, and they were five and seven, he convinced them to take off their clothes and let him fondle their penises. Within a few more contacts, he had taught them to stroke his penis to ejaculation. Shortly thereafter, his mother caught him and his cousins in the process of disrobing. She was horrified and strongly reprimanded him. Later that evening his father delivered a brief lecture on sexuality. Its primary message was that sex was to be saved for marriage. While it was normal for young men to have "urges," his father said, these had to be suppressed. In the meantime, vigorous physical exercise and occasional cold showers were the treatment advocated by Mr. Q., as they had been advocated to him (albeit unsuccessfully) by his own father a generation before.

Mr. and Mrs. Q. argued for several days over whether any additional intervention was warranted. Mrs. Q. wanted to seek a mental health evaluation for James, but Mr. Q. was adamantly opposed, saying that his son's behavior had been nothing more than childhood curiosity about sexuality. After several discussions in which Mrs. Q. was tearful and distraught, and Mr. Q. was angry and defensive, a compromise was reached—James was taken to the parish priest for a frank conversation.

Apparently, eternal life in hell was not an adequate deterrent for James. Despite his attempts to control himself, he found himself masturbating several times a week, always with fantasies of sexual acts with children in his mind. While he did not actually touch a child for the next ten years, he was never free of the wish to do so.

During that decade, James moved through and out of high school. He had graduated in a special program that spent half the day on academic subjects and the other half on a vocational skill. There he learned enough about landscaping and gardening to be taken on as an assistant groundskeeper at the local college. He started working there part-time when he was a junior in high school and accepted a full-time job upon graduation.

James had not developed much of a peer support network in school and had few friends when he graduated. Being shy and socially insecure, he had never really dated, although he had managed to get a date for the senior prom. During that date, he made an awkward attempt at sexual contact but was firmly rebuffed. Three months later, however, he had intercourse with a young woman he met at a bar. He saw her sporadically for the next fourteen months, had intercourse with her several more times, but each time he found himself thinking about watching and touching nude children. The relationship ended when the young woman began to complain about James' apparent lack of real devotion to her, evident in the inconsistency of his contact and his unwillingness to engage in social activities with her. Her increasing demands, in concert with his feelings of guilt about engaging in intercourse before marriage, resulted in his ceasing to call her.

Meanwhile, James was fairly happy in his work. His one additional source of pride, success, and social contact was through church, where he had remained active in youth bible study and community service. At age twenty-one he volunteered to teach a Sunday School class of second and third graders. This proved to be his undoing because, before long, he was unable to resist the lure of being surrounded by young children.

James' pedophilic fantasies increased in frequency and intensity until, one day, he fondled a little boy while helping him on with his snowsuit. The boy's lack of objection seemed to James a sign that what he was doing was not really harmful. He rationalized that the children seemed to like him very much and the his sexual attentions caused them pleasure, not pain. Besides, he was introducing them to sexuality in a low-key, low-anxiety way. He remembered how anxious and guilt-ridden his one age-appropriate heterosexual relationship had been, and felt that he was doing the children a genuine service through his attentions.

Despite these rationalizations, James knew that if he were caught, his life would be effectively over. Therefore, he tried hard to resist his urges to fondle children. He took to visiting prostitutes from time to time, but found their attentions unsatisfying. They were too seductive, too worldly, too aggressive. In truth, they made him uncomfortable. Occasionally, he tried to date someone from the college, but was rarely successful. Students ignored him and staff members tended to have their own boyfriends or husbands. Besides, his awkwardness seemed to put women off. During his twenties, James' encounters with children were rare, but not entirely nonexistent.

When he was thirty-two, his mother died. James was surprised by the pain and loneliness he felt. While he had not thought himself close to his mother, she had been closely woven into the fabric of his life. He now felt bereft and adrift without her. His needs for companionship and emotional succor increased, and again, he turned to children from his church-related activities to meet these needs. Over time, he developed a little "club" in which he would invite youngsters over to his apartment for pizza and videos. Needless to say, the videos he showed the children had gradually increasing sexual content. He organized "games" that followed the videos—games in which mutual touching and exploring of genitalia were the primary activities. Photographs of the games were used to determine the "winners" at each session. The club was very elite—and secrecy was emphasized at all of the meetings. Still, it is astonishing that James' games went on for eight years before one of the children told his parents what was happening. That parent went to the police, and the house of cards quickly collapsed. While only a few of the parents allowed their children to participate in the court process, James' conviction was easily obtained.

While in prison, James participates in a sexual offenders' treatment group that meets weekly in the office of the prison psychologist. Attending the group is voluntary, although it is widely known that participation is virtually mandatory for prisoners who wish to be paroled. The group is strongly confrontational in orientation. Members are encouraged to point out rationalizations and other distortions in thinking when they hear them from other members. The men are encouraged to take responsibility for their behavior and to develop some understanding of the effect of their behavior on their victims. Several of the men were themselves victimized as children. They are encouraged to share their experiences with other group members, both to increase members' empathy for victims of sexual abuse and to help these men identify how the abuse they suffered predisposed them to abusing others. James participates actively in the group, but there is no way of telling whether the treatment is effective, so long as James is still in jail. His prospects for release any time soon are not good.

Thinking About the Case

Between one-quarter and one-third of adults report having been sexually approached by an adult when they were children. While the number of pedophiles is probably fairly small, each can have dozens, even hundreds of victims. James' case is fairly typical of one type of pedophile—those whose behavior represents a deviant sexual arousal pattern. Another type seems to engage in pedophilic behavior as a regressive response to some life stressor or loss. These individuals may prefer adult sexual objects most of the time but turn to a child object when the adult is emotionally or physically absent. Incestuous behavior is often of this latter type, although some people who sexually abuse their own children have a primarily pedophilic orientation and also abuse children outside the family as well.

In order for pedophilia to be diagnosed, the sexual object must be prepubescent (generally younger than thirteen). Sexual abuse of older teenagers is also common, both within and outside of the family, but is not diagnosed as pedophilia. Generally, perpetrators are known to the victims as family members or friends. Many, like James, are drawn to situations in which they can develop a relationship of trust with children.

Pedophiles are much more likely to be seductive, like James, than violent. They tend to rationalize their behavior as being instructive or valued by the children they abuse. In addition, actual penetration is rare, occurring in less than ten percent of the cases. Manual or oral sexual contact is much more the norm. While some pedophiles prefer either girls or boys, many abuse children of both sexes.

Pedophilia is now known to have longstanding and often quite serious repercussions for the children involved. Among the adult disorders associated with childhood sexual abuse are depression, anxiety, eating disorders, substance abuse disorders, somatization disorders, dissociative disorders, and personality disorders. As you have probably already noted, many of the cases reported in this book have sexual abuse as one of the precursors of emotional disorder. Therefore, the successful treatment (and, ultimately, prevention) of sexual abuse constitutes an urgent public health goal.

Unfortunately, treatment is still rare and even more rarely an unqualified success. Pedophiles, like others with paraphilias, generally do not submit to treatment voluntarily, and most prisons do not have a pedophilia treatment program. Further, as we have seen, the treatment of paraphilias is only modestly successful at best. Still, some model programs do exist. They generally use a combination of behavioral techniques like aversion therapy, experiential methods aimed at increasing empathy—for example, role-playing and writing letters of apology to victims—and psychotherapy aimed at increasing self-esteem, social efficacy, and self-understanding. Experts in the area are unanimous in suggesting that long-term, possibly life-long, supervision and follow-up is essential if recidivism is to be prevented.

Questions to Consider

1. Do you think that a man who sexually abuses his thirteen-year-old stepdaughter, but no other children, might have a different prognosis than James? Why?
2. Sexually-abusing adults have often been sexually abused themselves as children. Why might this be so? What theoretical model best encompasses your explanation?
3. What do you think of the use of drugs that suppress the production of the male hormone, testosterone (thereby diminishing sexual arousal and the ability to get an erection) as a treatment for pedophilia? What are the ethical issues involved? What are the legal (civil rights) issues involved? Under what circumstances, if any, would you approve of its use?
4. Mandatory reporting of child abuse to social service authorities by clinicians to whom it is revealed is now the norm in virtually all jurisdictions. What are the pros and cons of this mandate, in your opinion? Do you think the requirement should be the same if the abuse is disclosed by the abuser or by the victim? Why, or why not?

5. Do you think a child would be affected differently by sexual abuse if the perpetrator is a neighborhood acquaintance rather than a family member? Why or why not? What other factors might affect how severe the consequences of the abuse are for the victim?
6. Would you endorse a behavioral or a psychodynamic explanation for the development of James' pedophilia? What aspects of the case description lend themselves to your hypothesis? Do you need additional information? If so, what do you wish had been included?

LANAHAN NOTES
Paraphilias

General definition

Sexual desire/behavior directed at inappropriate objects or people that cause distress /harm to the individual or to the object of such desire and behavior

Classification of paraphilias

Voyeuristic disorder: individual gets sexual arousal from observing others who are naked or engaging in a sexual act; the classic "peeping-Tom"

Exhibitionistic disorder: one gets sexual arousal from the exposure of one's genitals to a non-consenting person; the classic "flasher"

Frotteuristic disorder: individual seeks sexual arousal by touching or rubbing against a non-consenting person

Sexual masochism disorder: individual gets sexually aroused through receiving pain or physical/sexual humiliation; also, sexual enhancement brought on by reducing oxygen to the brain (asphyxiophilia)

Sexual sadism disorder: one receives sexual arousal through inflicting pain or sexual humiliation on another

Pedophilic disorder: adolescents or adults who get sexual arousal from viewing, fantasizing, or engaging in sex with prepubescent children

Fetishistic disorder: individual gets sexually aroused from inanimate objects or a highly specific non-genital body part(s); e.g., the classic "foot fetish"

Transvestic disorder: sexual arousal to through cross-dressing

Note: Actual behavior is not required for diagnosis—strong urges or fantasies meet the criteria if they cause significant distress or dysfunction. Question: Many people have paraphiliac fantasies. What is normal? How strong do the fantasies have to be to qualify as abnormal? Who does the judging? (Homosexuality was once listed as a paraphilia, but is now not considered a disorder—is this "medical" or "societal" judgment?)

Causes of paraphilias

Generally, little is understood about the causes; some possible directions

Biological: neurological abnormalities in limbic system and temporal lobes

Learning theory: classical conditioning, vicarious conditioning

Psychodynamic theories: focus on the individual's early psychological development and family dynamics

Environmental: growing up with a lack of normative sexual boundaries/environment; history of sexual abuse

Treatment of paraphilias

Behavioral: attempt to replace inappropriate object with more appropriate one through re-training procedures or punishment (aversion therapy) which is controversial

Medical: hormone inhibitors; hampered by a lack of double-blind, placebo-controlled studies; antidepressants/anti-anxiety medicine may treat underlying social anxiety that could give rise to a paraphilia; chemical castration has been used with pedophiles

Prognosis is generally poor; recidivism is common

Question: How should society manage sexual offenders since treatment results are so poor yet offenders are typically given court-ordered therapy? Lengthy incarceration? Life-long supervision? Chemical castration?